Introduction

"It is not possible for this history to be truthful"
(Sir Alfred Cope's 1951 letter to the Irish Bureau of Military History)

Carl Sagan, the astronomer and science communicator, said 'To find the truth we need both imagination and scepticism.' When being interviewed about writing fiction and storytelling, novelist Edna O'Brien said, 'What matters is the imaginative truth.'

Despite or perhaps because of, the huge number of witness statements and numerous texts, we will never know the true details of important events that happened in Ireland during the 1916 Uprising, its War of Independence, the 1921 Treaty talks, and the Civil War. Some events have been either ignored or given minimal prominence whilst basic facts have been stated as gospel truth even though they are contradictory.

Some texts seem to be slanted to paint certain people in the best (or worst) possible light. Some witness statements were produced 30 years after the event by people who may have read or heard the memories of other witnesses.

An example is the 'attack' on Dublin Castle at the start of the Uprising. Major Ivon Price, British Intelligence Officer, stated (in a report to MI5's Colonel Kell, 30 April 1916[*]) that he rushed to the Castle gate and fired at the attackers, hitting 'only one'. However, there is no corroborating evidence of this, nor any record of any Irish or British being killed or wounded inside the Castle.

Major Price states, in a Falstaffian way, that 'we were practically at the mercy of 50 armed men' but gives no details of

---

[*] *https://www.bloodysunday.co.uk/castle-intelligence/price-ih/price-ih.html*

how the situation resolved itself. Helena Moloney (Irish Bureau of Military History Witness Statement 391) describes marching towards the Castle. She says that there were about 20 men and nine women in her group of Irish Citizen Army Volunteers and 'I thought no one had succeeded in getting in'.

Curiously, almost all Irish Bureau of Military History Witness Statements cover only 1913-1921. For the Civil War years (1922-23), which would include Michael Collins' assassination and the brutal killings and reprisals by the pro- and anti-Treaty forces, there are very few statements.

The specifics of the attempt by Casement to bring weapons from Germany, the 'attack' on Dublin Castle, the arrest of Kevin Barry, and the death of Collins, are all open to debate.

In view of the difficulty in assessing which facts are exaggeration, true, accurate, or misleading, this book of historical fiction speculates on some of the main characters – their beliefs and personal strengths and frailties. It ranges from complete imagination, such as James Connolly's younger days and politicians' conversations where they discuss events known to have happened. The descriptions of Kevin Barry's capture and Michael Collins' death are obviously imaginative; but balanced against this is the truth that young men died in tragic circumstances.

Sir Alfred Cope[1] was an Assistant Under Secretary of State in Dublin, 1920-22. He could have been a forerunner of 'Harry Palmer' and 'George Smiley'* in that he was not an 'establishment' man and he liaised with leaders of Sinn Féin, exchanging confidential information. The Irish Bureau of Military History invited him to provide a 'Witness Statement' concerning

---

*Harry Palmer: character in the film Ipress File, based on Len Deighton's novel ; George Smiley: character in John Le Carre's spy novels.

his part in the events which brought about Irish independence. He responded by stating,

'*I regard the period ... to be the most discreditable of your country's history – it is preferable to forget it; to let sleeping dogs lie. It is not possible for this history to be truthful ... the job is beyond human skill.*' He predicted that the I.R.A. would be '*shown as national heroes and the British Forces as brutal oppressors. Accordingly, the Truce and Treaty will have been brought about by the defeat of the British by the valour of small and ill-equipped groups of irregulars. And so on. What a travesty it will be and must be. Read by future generations of Irish children, it will simply perpetuate the long-standing hatred of England and continue the miserable work of self-seeking politicians who, for their own aggrandisement, have not permitted the Christian virtues of Forgiveness and Brotherhood to take its place. Ireland has too many histories; she deserves a rest. Her present need is a missioner (*sic) *to teach her that Love, not Hate, is still the only password both to Earthly Happiness and the Heavenly Kingdom.*'[*]

A cynic might suggest that if Sir Alfred had produced a 'Witness Statement' his inborn honesty would have required him to document uncomfortable facts concerning British strategies and conduct, especially those of Lloyd George. Hence, perhaps, his decision not to provide a Statement.

Ireland certainly deserves a rest, but Irish (and British) children have the right to consider all aspects and opinions of their history. This book is an attempt to address Sir Alfred Cope's concerns.

---

[*] Letter, 1951, to Private Secretary, Irish Embassy, explaining why he did not wish to contribute to the records of the Bureau of Military History 1913-1921.

https://bmh.militaryarchives.ie/reels/bmh/BMH.WS0469.pdf

'And we shall in the end be shamed or, if not shamed, coerced, into releasing Ireland from the connexion; or we shall avert the necessity only by conceding with the worst grace, and when it will not prevent some generations of ill blood, that which if done at present may still be in time permanently to reconcile the two countries.'

'England and Ireland', John Stuart Mill (1868)

Contents

Chapter 1 – Dublin, November 1919 9

Chapter 2 – A Chip Off The Old Block 20

Chapter 3 – Time's Up, Mr. Bell 32

Chapter 4 – James Connolly, The Early Years 37

Chapter 5 – A civilized people 43

Chapter 6 – A high-minded, courteous man 46

Chapter 7 – A Good Life 52

Chapter 8 – British Justice 57

Chapter 9 – Anything's legal if you're a Protestant 65

Chapter 10 – Three of a Kind 71

Chapter 11 – Self Respect for Ireland 80

Chapter 12 – March 1914 88

Chapter 13 – Rifles Go Leor 105

Chapter 14 – *What a Piece of Luck!* 113

Chapter 15 – Three Little Maids from School 118

Chapter 16 – A Little Help From Some Friends 125

Chapter 17 – Travellers in Germany 136

Chapter 18 – I need a job 145

Chapter 19 – D'yer Want a Rebellion or Not? 151

Chapter 20 – Powerful Friends 159

Chapter 21 – Going Back Home 163

Chapter 22 – 'Throttling and Neck Breaking, Sir?' 167

Chapter 23 – Getting Things Together 176

Chapter 24 – 'Yes-No-Yes!' 182

Chapter 25 – Charge! 186

Chapter 26 – A Republic at Last 190

Chapter 27 – Lions and Donkeys 194

Chapter 28 – Cup'la Murders 198

Chapter 29 – The End of the Beginning 206

Chapter 30 – Surrender? God Save Ireland! 209

Chapter 31 – *"Tears fall from the Skies"* 217

Chapter 32 – 'Well, that's something!' 223

Chapter 33 – A Reprieve? Yes, No 229

Chapter 34 – *Let's Eat Grandma! Let's Eat, Grandma!* 235

Chapter 35 – August 1916 247

Chapter 36 – Outlived the failure of all her hopes 251

Chapter 37 – Autumn 1917 259

Chapter 38 – A German "Plot" 262

Chapter 39 – Saint Enda's: The Sequel 272

Chapter 40 – Just Stop 278

Chapter 41 – Three Events, November 1920 282

Chapter 42 – You Go and Talk to Them 292

Chapter 43 – Get Together In London 299

Chapter 44 – Well, I'm Happy 310

Chapter 45 – The Split 319

Chapter 46 – We Did the Right Thing 323

Chapter 47 – Trip Back Home 328

Biographical and Nomenclature Appendix 339

Bibliography and Reference List 398

Acknowledgements 415

INDEX 417

End Notes 429

"Come all ye young rebels, and list while I sing,
For the love of one's country is a terrible thing.
It banishes fear with the speed of a flame,
And it makes us all part of the patriot game."

The Patriot Game, Dominic Behan 1958

Chapter 1 – Dublin, November 1919

"How's poor ould Ireland, and how does she stand?" [*]

'This tea's cold!' There was no reaction. Mrs Bull glared at the elderly waiter. He had his back to her and, with a none too clean cloth, was dusting a large clock with numerals that showed slight traces of green enamel paint; in the centre of the clock-face was a small rusty wire something that might have once represented a shrivelled shamrock ... or a harp. The clock's hands were at twenty-five minutes past three – as they had been when she entered the breakfast area more than an hour ago. Every so often, the minute-hand tottered forward, quivered feebly, and then fell back.

Mrs Bull prided herself on always thinking the best of anybody, whatever their station in life. However, she had to admit that it was difficult to maintain this admirable trait in Dublin's Granville Hotel. It was owned by people whom she had met in a respectable part of Belfast[2] so she thought it unlikely to be frequented by Sinn Féiners.

She clicked a thumb and finger, then pointed to the ceiling, rather like an umpire at Lord's adjudicating a dismissal, and called, 'I say!' enunciating the words imperiously and following up with another declaration of 'This tea's cold!!'

The waiter, untidily grey-haired and tottering, had begun poking a small and innocent but slow-burning log amongst a few red coals in the huge fireplace. He stopped and turned, as if wondering whether he was imagining that somebody had spoken to him, 'I beg your pardon?' – this was accompanied by a slight tilt of the head, reminiscent of a child asking forgiveness whilst

---

[*] "Wearin' o' the Green," folk song of the Irish Rebellion 1798

uncertain as to the misdemeanour that might have been committed.

Smiling without humour and eyebrows raised, Mrs Bull lifted her cup and wiggled a tiny chubby finger in his direction, 'It's cold.'

His chin and forehead went up and down as he grinned, 'Yes, madam. T'is fierce weather we're havin' for da time o' year. I'm thinkin' it's startin' ter rain as well. Terr'bull weather. Terr'bull.'

She waited. There was nobody else in the room or she would have thought he was mocking her. The only other guest had rushed out after bolting his breakfast so fast that she'd felt quite ill. A nasty type. Probably a salesman of some kind. Church candles, something like that. Common as muck.

She had always thought the Irish working class to be congenitally slow-witted but the Granville staff gave every appearance of living in a world of their own[3]. Her husband often had confidential meetings here. He shouldn't, really, have told her about them of course and she'd always wondered what it would be like to spend a night in one of the rooms. Now she knew. The same as all the other Dublin hotels. Worn-out carpets. The suspicion that kidneys were being fried somewhere. Ingrained smell of cigarette smoke and beer, an atmosphere of waiting for something that everybody knew had been indefinitely postponed, and staff that would prefer you to be anywhere else.

Her breakfast had included a peculiar black, inedible, substance that the waiter called drisheen*, accompanied by a small fried egg with one bacon rasher that was burnt and another that was underdone. One of her compulsive habits was to wriggle when annoyed. Frustratingly, it was impossible at the moment due to her overly-endowed buttocks having sunk into the worn-out cushion of a too-

---

* Drisheen=blood pudding or blood sausage

small dining chair. 'I'd like another cup, please.'

He tottered towards her table and looked first at the apparently full cup and then at the good lady. 'You'd like another? ... another cuppa tay?' His mouth remained open so that it was obvious he had few front teeth.

'Yes.'

'In-sted'er dis won?'

'Yes.'

'Right you are ... Oh and er ... I should be careful'a d'at chair, if I woz you ... got bockety* legs. Prob'ly been sat on be Major Sirr!' The waiter apparently thought this was quite funny, 'Major Sirr? Yer know? The wan that was so cruel to Anne Devlin?'

She stared in total incomprehension then, as he shuffled towards the kitchen with the cup and saucer, saw him taking a sip of the tea and shake his head as if acknowledging an inability to understand the English.

She hated to admit it, but he was right. It was going to be a wet, slow day; rain was already spattering on the grimy-greasy windows and it was at least 20 minutes past the appointed time for her meeting with Mrs Houlihan. No doubt the dear woman would be waiting in the street – coming into the hotel would have been unthinkably embarrassing for her, partly because she'd be sure to wear that very strange black-blue coat that she'd had for years but mainly because she certainly would never in her life have stepped foot into a residential hotel. Yes, she'd be alright. The rain wasn't too hard. Yet. Anyway ... sighing and deciding not to wait for the tea, Mrs Bull squeezed up and out of the unstable chair and transposed herself majestically upstairs to the rather small rooms she'd been allocated. After dressing for the morning's outing, she

---

Bockety=physically unsteady

parted the curtains as if they were contagious. Perhaps a few minutes staring out the rather smeared window would be pleasant.

Dublin seemed to be the same as it was when she and her husband had left. The British field guns had shattered many of the buildings in the commercial district and after three years some of the rubble remained, albeit pushed aside into neat piles. Rich and poor, businessmen and street urchins, horses and trams, bicycles and carts, all moved quickly and efficiently through the wide Dublin streets, ignoring the memories of that bloody Easter week. The deafeningly unintelligible noises and overwhelmingly malodorous smells were still the same. Laughter and arguing, dogs barking and horses neighing, screams and curses. Rotting vegetables, odd-smelling fish and horse manure. Gentility and poverty. Thank goodness she was going back home to Oxford and civilization tomorrow.

The sale of their Dublin house in Palmerstown Road had been completed quite satisfactorily. She'd even been able to squeeze an extra £50 out of Mr and Mrs Murphy by strongly suggesting that there'd been a counter offer. And they had failed to notice the cracks in the chimney. So, all she had to do now was meet with dear little-old Mrs Houlihan, her housekeeper from back then. It would have been rude not to at least meet briefly and there might be some interesting gossip about the erstwhile neighbours.

She enjoyed that word, erstwhile, and rolled it around idly in her brain whilst daydreaming about the street where she'd resided for three years. Those at Number 26 took in British Army officers as boarders who always appeared so nervously alert. Some of them had been born in Ireland, of course. Fine upstanding young men.

Most of the Irish race though, broadly speaking anyway, were like ungrateful children who thought themselves adult and cultured. Some of the worst had joined, she recalled, with the Boers fighting against our Empire and a few had even wanted to help the Germans in the Great War. Thank goodness for Sir

Edward Carson and the Unionists. Dear Sir Edward! Dublin born and Dublin educated, so handsome and loyal to His Majesty. And those wonderful Ulster Unionists ... hundreds of thousands of Protestants who signed oaths in blood to never surrender their country to Papists.

As she came majestically down the stairs, wearing her expensive new coat from Fortnum and Mason and humming 'Rule Britannia', the eyes-weary waiter was coming slowly and very laboriously up.

'Ter'day's de day.'

She paused. 'Pardon?'

'Robert Emmet being murdered.'

She had to admit it. She was unnerved.

The old man was shaking his head. 'Not d'at long ago either. 1803. They got the executioner's block down at Saint Enda's, yer know, ... if yer in-ter-rested in seein' it.'

Then she remembered. 'Oh. Yes. Emmet. No, not murdered. British justice. Tried for treason, found guilty, and sentence duly carried out.' She nodded as if approving the butcher's promise to deliver a pound of sausages. While her husband had been working in Dublin Castle and she had been keeping an eye on the neighbours, she'd learnt all the Irish history that decent people needed to know.

The old man ignored the interruption. 'Not much more than a boy, madam. 25 years old. Sentence: Hung, drawn, and quartered. Public execution. 45,000 people. D'ere in front 'er Sent Cat'-er-ine's, in Thomas Street. A hundred an ... a few years, ago ... ter'day. A Protestant. But, even so, a good and great man, never-der-less. God rest his soul.'

'Well, I'm sure you know more about it than I.' (Public execution? You were no doubt in the crowd watching ... she smiled at her little joke.)

'Indeed, madam ... Well ... Of course ... Yer know', he cleared his throat.

(*Oh dear, he's going to talk for Ages…*)

' ... if only he hadn't gone to see his sweetheart, Sarah ... he could'a got clean away. He was scared they'd use der love letters he'd written her and charge her with treason. Fer his trial he could'a been defended by John Curran, the greatest people's advocate of his time, instead of which his own lawyer was bribed by der British Government ... an' according to ...'

(*... for Ages! Yes, he is going to keep on talking!. Dear God, the Irish can talk.*) She tried to interrupt, 'Really? Well, I must ...' but failed.

'... Could'a saved him, but Curran was Sarah's father and he hated Emmet, yer'know ... and Lord Norbury the Hangin' Judge sat 'dere an' interruptin' poor Emmet's gallous[4] speech, and ... his friend Byron once said, Freedom ... and Uncle Tom's Cabin ... and as someone once said, is loyalty held to be a crime[*] ... '

She'd stopped listening to the cascading history-literary lesson. Emmet, she thought, was another romantic Fenian who could talk the talk of freedom but failed when real action was needed. More than a hundred years ago his pathetic so-called rebellion had fizzled out. But then the Irish, unlike the English, prefer to celebrate rather than forget their failures. The more disastrous and bloodier, the happier the Irish were. That Easter comedic business a few years back, for example.

She sniffed loudly, 'Yes, indeed. Goodness, look at the time. Must rush, bye!' and pushed the front door. It slammed after her, so she failed to hear the old man's echoing sniff.

Mrs Kathleen Houlihan was Kitty to her friends. She stood, slightly soaked, almost under shelter and tried to smile at Mrs Bull

---

[*] Roger Casement: 'In Ireland alone, in this twentieth century, is loyalty held to be a crime?'

who had not yet noticed her.

Kitty was the epitome of Ireland. Small, under-nourished, and elderly. Time had not been kind with that which had been beautiful. Long black and lustrous hair was now faded, sparse, and thin. She still had a few teeth, but her eyes were watery and she seemed to shiver, wrapped inside what might once have been a man's overcoat, with a shawl covering her head. Kitty had thought about ignoring the invitation but decided it might be interesting to meet someone, even if nowhere near her equal, who had once been her employer.

'Kathleen! Ah, there you are!! ... ', the loud and overly-Home Counties voice accused Kitty of deliberately hiding from public sight, 'I hope you haven't been waiting long? How are you, m'dear? You're looking very ... er ... ? Keepin' well, I hope?'

(*'Bout feckin' time, yer ole bitch. Are yer blind or what? An' here's me stood waitin' for yer like a drown-ded rat on a dustbin lid. Sha, I mus be doo-lally, wait'n on the loikes a' you. Have I been waitin' long? Oh no ... jus a cup'la centuries or so. Yer feckin' ole bitch.*) 'As a matter of fact ... I've ...'

'Oh good. Shall we catch this tram? I thought we'd see if the little tea shop that I used to free-quent is still open. The West End Café. It'll be my treat. For all your years of devoted service. Of course, since I'm no longer your employer ...' she laughed winningly, '... feel free to address me as Joan ... if you wish.' There was a smile, but nothing else.

Mrs Bull found public transport rather, well, daunting at the best of times. The thought of having to share the same air as so many Dubliners of doubtful cleanliness was something she would simply have to cope with for a short while. Luckily, the tram was nearly empty. She chuckled to herself. There was no likelihood of anybody from Oxford seeing her with Mrs Houlihan.

'So ... you've been well, Kathleen?' The question clearly assumed that there was just one correct answer.

'Sha, I've been grand, t'anks. Although last year I did have the new-moan-ee-ya and d'en d'int I go 'an break me leg when I …'

'Oh, my! Yes, well, I know … I know, it's so annoying, isn't it? Being ill. I've had a terrible time with catarrh. And five … no, six … no, five … weeks ago one of my elbows was causing such pain … then it stopped … still, we British must bear up, eh?'

They each paid for their fares and the trip was enlivened by Mrs Bull's description of the almost life-threatening ailments that had inconveniently chosen to inflict themselves on her during the previous half century.

'And you, Kathleen? Where's home now? Still living in … where was it?'

'No, no. I'm after movin' from Mount Pleasant Bil'dings. I'm in Henrietta Street now.'

'Oh, yes? I don't think I know it … Is it naice?' The word was pronounced in a very deliberate way through a condescendingly pretend smile.

(*'My home? Is it nice? It is if yer loike bein' in a rat-infested hovel with more than a hundred other people. In the one house! and only 2 filthy outside toilets, you stupid feckin' cow. If a nation is the same people living in the same place like some young fella said then I s'pose Henrietta Street must be a big feckin' nation … Useless! Useless tryin' to get yer to understand.'*)

Kitty relented, 'Oh, well, it's better than Monto and, yer know, friendly enough like.'

'Ah? Oh! Oh, we're here! That big school over there … Wasn't it set up by one of the Easter people? One of the leaders that was shot? Oh! What was his name?'

'Pearse. Pad-ricg Pearse. He read the prock'la-mation on the Easter Monday. In front'a da Post Office.'

'Ah yes. I recall John telling me about him and the school he ran. School for boys. Apparently … this is confidential of course

... there was a lot of Intelligence collected at the Castle ... but Pearse preferred boys ... If you know what I mean.' She managed to raise both eyebrows and nod her head.

Kitty stared at her and said, 'But he opened a school for girls as well? Saint Ita's.'

Mrs Bull was confused, 'Saint .... ?'

'Ita. She was a Holy nun in Killeedy ... died when a beetle ate her side ... it swelled up into the size of a pig. The beetle, I mean.' She spoke as though she were describing something perfectly normal, such as the process for boiling potatoes, to an idiot.

'Really? Yes, well ... Anyway, this Pearse chap. He was especially keen on teaching the boys Irish dancing ... with kilts. Nothing worn underneath, of course.' Her tongue was lodged in a cheek as she winked. Kitty managed not to respond out loud, '*And your own fella? He woz one for da ladies, eh? And the girls. And the boys, too. Most of d'em fellas up in Dub'lin Castle woz doin' the Oscar Wilde biz'ness. That's why d'ay had to hush up the shenan-neeguns with da Crown Jewels – stolen by yer man Shackleton[*] an' his boyfriend ... wonder how much they got for dem diamonds and whatnot? Sha, all Dub'lin knows about that malarkey.*[5]'

Mrs Bull's accent broke into her thoughts, 'Ah, look! We've arrived. And it's stopped raining. I wonder if they still have cream cakes.' The café was crowded with people all in dripping and steaming coats but Mrs Bull edge-nudged her way to a table that was being vacated in a corner close to the window. 'So ...

---

[*] Francis (younger brother of Sir Ernest Shackleton, Antarctic explorer) was a friend of Captain Richard Gorges in Dublin.

Kathleen, how is dear ole Oy'land getting along ... since the ... Uprising nastiness ... everything better now?'

'I'm sorry ... what did yer say? Dear ...old ... ?' (*If you say 'Begorrah' or 'To be sure, To be sure' ... I'll slap yer stupid fat feckin' face.*)

Mrs Bull laughed. 'Oy'land! ... Ire-a-land, my dear ... how are things? ... oh! Wait! Look-look!'

She pointed at a woman walking along the street, towards Saint Enda's School, with two small children. 'That! That's ... that woman with the children ... Her! Wearing the peculiar fur gloves. More like hand boots, ha! I never forget a face. It's ... Grace ... Oh, dear ... what is her surname ... well, well!'

Kitty, eyebrows up and mouth open, had no intention of providing any assistance.

There was a cultured, celebratory, gasp. 'I remember now ... she was friendly with that young chap who lived a few houses down from us. Catholics, he was in and out of it – his family home. It's all coming back to me, now. She and he were very friendly, if you know what I mean. But ... his parents, were not at all ... keen on her. But what was her name?'

(Kitty gritted her teeth.)

'I'll remember it in a moment ... she and her sisters being Protestant ... although their father was Catholic and quite well-off but he never knew his own father. And the mother, she was the boss! Yes, she was fiercely Protestant ... Someone told me the mother was one of 23 children, for goodness sake!' She peered at the young woman as she walked past the window. 'Yes, I remember you. Gifford! Grace Gifford! Her young chap ... Joseph Plunkett? Now, his father was very very wealthy and had connections with Rome, I think. So, what with the Plunketts being both snobbish and Catholic ... they didn't want a Protestant for him … and the Giffords certainly didn't want anything to do with a Catholic family of Irish Nationalists. Plunkett never looked well. Didn't he have something wrong with him? It was all very odd. Fancy seeing her again! Grace Gifford! Yes, I remember now. I did read in the newspaper about young Plunkett's involvement in that Easter business.'

Chapter 2 – A Chip Off The Old Block

Grace, 31 years of age, looked at the executioner's block in front of Saint Enda's School – a huge, terrifyingly huge, chunk of wood. 'Now, children. Listen. I'll be called away in a moment ... and I'll need to go over ... there ... just for a minute and then ... Well, yer don't have to ... watch, but ... anyway ... you'll be good? Yeah? Stay here. OK?'

Hopefully the trek on the tram to Rathfarnham had tired them out. There was quite a crowd; the usual people that gathered whenever something was happening, even if they didn't know what it was. Children gaping, idle men with hands in their pockets and women looking sideways at other women. But there were also some very well-dressed people who were gathered around the wooden block at the bottom of the school steps politely chatting as if they were old friends, even if they weren't. The type of friends who felt only a little guilty because they thought that they knew each other's secrets. At the top of the steps the school's huge double doors were framed between two Doric columns. And standing next to the one on the left were three men with something, probably guns, almost hidden under their raincoats, conspicuously trying to appear like bored onlookers.

It was all a bit weird but at the same time typically Irish. Royal Irish Constables and British detectives were being killed by Michael Collins' hit squad; IRA volunteers were stealing rifles and escaping from prison; the Lord Lieutenant of Ireland had been lucky not to be assassinated. And yet standing here, in the middle of Dublin, was the 29-year-old Director of Intelligence of the IRA, Collins himself, being publicly filmed. At any moment a Crossley machine-gun carrier packed with British soldiers could scream to a halt and he'd be arrested for murder along with everyone else for being members of the, recently proclaimed illegal, Sinn Féin movement.

Grace felt a hand on her arm – she jumped and turned, 'Oh! Nora! It's been a long time. How's it all goin'? I've brought those little ones, Don and Babilly. Behaving them'sels over there on the bench. I hope! Sha, they're both rascals, right enough. The boy's a real kinat* ... always trying to whistle. Jus' like his ... Da.' She looked over at the little boy and wiped her nose with a handkerchief.

Nora, 26-years-old and waif-like, put an arm round Grace. 'Yeah. Didn't his Da like to whistle? ... I heard about your mither kickin' yer out for marrying a Catholic Shinner of all things ... and then your sister ... poor Muriel ... God rest her soul. Holy Mary Mother of God, you've had your troubles.'

'Haven't we all? But, yeah, true enough ... it's not been easy fer me ... Anyway, I get by. Sell a few pictures, so. God helps those that help themselves, eh? Katie, me eldest sister, you remember her? She's helping Big Mick† with the paperwork or some such for dis loan^6 business ... that's how come I got instructions to get me'sel down here. I couldn't very well refuse, what wit' Muriel's brother-in-law over there behind the camera. Trust John MacDonagh to take advantage of makin' a picture house fill'um^7 ... an' using any'ting spare for a bit a' free rebel work‡.'

'Yeah? Won't he get into trouble when the investors find out?'

Grace shook her head. 'Apparently, the producer is Jim

---

* Kinat = cheeky youngster

† Michael Collins

‡ 'Dáil Bonds Film' is a 1919 short propaganda film to promote the sale of Dáil Loan bonds. Accessible on YouTube.

Sullivan. A Yank that got arrested in 1916 and knows Mick … Ah well … But …. You got an invite, too?'

Nora Connelly gave a little laugh. 'Invite? It was more like an order. Anyway … I'm glad to help. Dunno why they wanted me, though. Looks like there's lots of bigwigs. Arthur Griffith is here. So is Erskine Childers. I doubt those two will be giving each other the time a' day. And there's Joe MacDonagh … Isn't that the Plunketts, as well?'

Grace frowned. A well-dressed elderly couple were standing at the top of the steps, looking down on everyone else. They were wealthy supporters of the fight for Ireland's independence and Count Plunkett had tried to get German assistance in WW1. He'd been given his title years ago by the Pope after making large donations to the Catholic Church.

Grace couldn't help sneering, 'Count Plunkett! … doesn't he look well-fed … standing there with herself. Would yer look at 'er, though. Mutton dressed as lamb. Doing all right with the rents from her slum tenements, no doubt.'

Nora didn't fail to note the bitterness. She tried to lighten the moment by nudging Grace and whispering, 'I met a fella in America, Seamus, he works for Mick Collins and ... Would yer look at the Big Fella over there. … what d'yer think … He's a pure feen*, isn't he? See the way he pushes that lock of hair across his forehead? Enough to make a dead woman tremble and quiver, eh? Almost ev'ry woman in Dublin, yeah and not a few men, gets excited when he looks their way. What 'boat you, Grace? You'd give Kitty-wots-er-name … Kiernan … a run for her money. Will I let Mick know yer inter-rested?'

'Whisht! G'wan wit' yer! No … I'll always be married to Joe.

Pure feen = A very sexy man

There's no man can take his place ... But what a'boat yerself? What've you been up to? Apart from Seamus, I mean. I'd heard you were making a nuisance of yersel' in America.'

'Yeah. Da told us we should go there 'coz we'd be on the Brits blacklist once they were finished with him. I couldn't get a passport ... still, there's ways and means, eh? I wrote a book telling the truth 'boat the Brits but President Wilson banned it. But, hey! I know yer were lookin' after our Ma fer a while. T'anks for that ... Did yer hear what happened when she went to the Castle to get our Da's things that he'd had in his pockets? The few bits and bobs? They gi 'em to her, and 'den General Maxwell stuck his hand out to shake her's. Can yer b'lieve it? Ma turned her back on the bas'tard ... Wait-wait! The Plunketts are tryin' not to look over here, Grace. Are they speakin' to you yet, at all?'

'Speakin'? Only t'rue their solicitor. I can't afford one. There's a will but they're refusing to acknowledge any'ting that wasn't properly witnessed, so.' Grace sneered. 'Ah well, maybe we'll earn a cup'la bob here.' Nora stared at her, 'Why? What's happening?'

'Sha, we gonna be fill'um stars! Look, they're settin' up the camera. Mick's the Finance Minister[*] ... they need money, so they're after takin' the people's. Isn't that what all governments do? These big wigs are going to be filmed buying bonds ... to encourage others to do the same.'

Nora's mouth dropped and waited for more.

'... they'll be takin' the fill'um[8] round to picture houses and asking the fella in the room upstairs to show it before the big picture.'

'Asking?'

---

[*] January 1919; an Irish parliament, the First Dáil, was formed.

'Yeah ... Well, I doubt if the projector fella will refuse if there's a Webley shuved in 'is ear.'

Nora shrugged. 'So, what are they wantin' from you an' me? Dunno 'boat yousel, but I've no money to be buyin' bloody bonds. And I feel a bit out of place 'mongst 'dis lot.' Nora had no time to discuss it further because a small and insignificant man, Joe O'Reilly, had come from nowhere – he ducked between them and dramatically whispered, 'Grace? Nora?' His eyes were never still, as if desperate to avoid meeting their's. They both hesitated before agreeing. 'This is just between der t'ree a' us, so? Here's a quid each. Go over to Mick when you'se gets the call. Hand over the money and buy a bond from him ... ... And, don't be fer'gettin to look at the camera after yer get the bond certificate. Then ... a bit later, when yer hand them over to me, I'll be behind that column, I'll give yer five bob each for der tram fare an' a drink, so.'

When he'd gone Grace looked at Nora and said, 'That was weird. I had the feelin' it was the first time that fella'd ever spoken to a woman. What'd you t'ink?'

'I t'ink we should leg it and enjoy our'sels with the two quid ... before day catch up wit'us ... or ... we could ...'

'... be fill'um stars for Ireland and make der best we can of ten bob?'

'... AND live longer than a Black 'n Tan caught with his trousers down in a Monto knocking shop? Yeah, good idea.'

Their whisperings were interrupted by someone urging the dignitaries to move up the steps in front of the school doors. 'Yes ... A group picture before yer buy the bonds, t'anks. An' you two young ladies as well, please ... towards the centre ... in front a' Mr Griffith. Now ... wait for me to say Action.'

Grace felt self-conscious with her big fur gloves and knowing that Nora was giggling behind her somewhere. It got worse when the Director or whoever he was said, 'Could that young lady be sq-eeez'n a little more ba'hind Mr Collins? Squeeze up tight, now. Oooh! 'dats luv'ly ... yeah, keep 'dat.'

Grace heard, even if everybody else pretended not to, a stifled giggle from the rear and she read Nora's thoughts, 'Oh, I wish! I wish!'

'Smile!' There was a flash ... The moment was frozen for eternity and the internet. 'Now, Mr Collins. I t'ink you're doing a speech, yeah?'

Collins, in a rather crumpled and baggy tweed suit, was doing his best to appear relaxed and like a Minister responsible for Finance. The short silent film, which would be available for posterity on *Youtube*, begins with him opening and reading a letter aloud but apparently to himself. It was from the Bishop of Killaloe concerning the purchase of £100 of loan certificates and ends with '*it should be the pride of every Irishman to hold one*'. Irishman? Apparently gender equality was not at the forefront of the cleric's mind at the time of writing, perhaps due to him being focused on arranging low-level peace talks with Australia's Archbishop of Perth[*], a friend of the British Prime Minister.

In the film, Collins is now sitting on an ornate, heavy-looking, wooden chair behind the huge hexagonal lump of wood. It was on this block that Emmet's head had been separated from his body after he'd been hanged for 30 minutes until almost, but not quite, dead. Someone must have now had the bright idea that using it as a writing desk would add some historical significance to Collins presence. The goriness and parallel with current times, of murders and executions, were obviously not considered. Apart from all else, the 'desk' made it extremely difficult for the Big Fella to sit comfortably.

---

[*] *Archbishop Patrick Clune tried to negotiate a temporary truce during the British-Irish confrontation, 1920*

He was not much taller than many men. Above age height, yes. Robust build, certainly. But not a giant. It was more his decisiveness, confidence and charisma, which emphasised his sheer presence. Some said that he could be overbearing and even arrogant. But nobody doubted his courage. Despite a £10,000 reward for his capture, he walked and cycled Dublin streets seemingly without a care. One Friday he was almost caught by the Black and Tans[9] when they blockaded a street in Portobello, also known as 'Little Jerusalem'[10], and started a search of every home in Longwood Avenue.

Pursued, Collins moved from house to house by climbing walls into back gardens until, borrowing a black overcoat and wide-brimmed hat, he walked down the street with Rabbi Abraham Gudansky. Behaving like an elderly man and mumbling what he thought might be considered Yiddish, he had leaned on the Rabbi as they joined a large crowd of Jews moving towards the synagogue. A cordon of gun-wielding Black and Tans was totally confused by the mass of Russian, Lithuanian, and Polish speakers so they waved them onwards. Gudansky later arranged for the Lucania bicycle that had been left behind to be delivered to an office in Harcourt Street[11].

That was weeks ago, in his role as Director of Intelligence (IRA). Now, here in front of St. Enda's school, he was the Minister for Finance.

Action! Collins stands and turns his head awkwardly to make a rather formal speech to, what the film's subtitles would later call, the 'Interesting Group of Sinn Féin Notabilities' standing on the steps behind him. Collins turns to the camera and sits down ... he places, or rather throws, a piece of paper on the table ... and then decides to stand again and talk a little more to the Group. Unfortunately, this means that the back of his head is to the camera. He seems to realise this, so he speaks to people out of camera shot to his left. And then sits once more. And seemingly waits, his long legs wrapped awkwardly around the 'desk'.

The 'Notabilities' having vanished out of camera shot, Diarmuid O'Hegarty is now seen sitting alongside Collins, undertaking the role of some sort of auditor/accountant. Margaret Pearse, mother of Patrick and Willie, is the first to buy a bond. Patrick was executed because he was the leader of the 1916 rebellion. Willie, the dreamy thespian who had not fired a shot and only ran a few messages, was taken to see his older brother at dawn on May 3rd 1916, … only to be told that Patrick was already dead. At his own trial, for some reason Willie had pleaded guilty to treason. It didn't make any difference because the 'trial' lasted a mere 15 minutes and the next day, as dawn was breaking, he also faced a firing squad. Why? Well, he was Patrick's brother.

All the Notabilities, including Nora and Grace, were filmed as they took turns trooping to Collins, handing over money in exchange for a signed bond certificate, some dropping it and then picking it up, and most of them remembering to look at the camera.

Eventually filming stopped and Collins spent some time meticulously checking and cross-checking figures and documents. The group behind him had dispersed and he looked over at O'Hegarty,

'You ok with all that now, Diarmuid? Good. I'll leave the rest to you. Oh … Now, I know you wouldn't do it but yesterday I noticed one of our people signing documents in pencil. A pencil! Make sure they all know that's not on. Yeah? … I'm getting' sick an' tired of chasin' after people to make sure internal controls are followed. Such as properly certified receipts for expense claims. We paid a fortune for people to attend the Allies Peace Conference at Versailles. And we got nothing. They didn't get 'ter speak ter President Wilson or the French or the Italians or …'

O'Hegarty couldn't resist thinking, '*Well, sha, I s'pose the Allies weren't too happy with us for shooting at British soldiers when the Jer'mins woz also shootin' at British soldiers ... and at French and Yanks*'.

Collins was still complaining, ' ... and our people at Versailles only managed to have meetings with tin-pot people from the tiny nations pressing their cases for independence and recognition ... like ... French Indochina. What was the point a' meeting that communist kitchen-fella*? ... Waste a' feckin' time an' money. Musha! ... But, right now, I need to call in somewhere. Thanks, for all the hard work, Diarmuid.'

Instead of the usual Vaughan's Hotel, Collins and Paddy O'Daly met in a small room in Crow Street, above Fowler's Printers, close to Dublin Castle.

'You still smokin', Paddy? Not a good idea, jer'no that? Bad for your health, altogether. I gave it up ... you could, if you try. OK, now ... what's happening?' He poured two large whiskies. Paddy took a long drag from his soggy, tailor-made, fag. He was enjoying the drama, 'They're being a bit more careful at the Castle, Mick. The wastepaper baskets are only filled with lunch remains and genuine shite like that. Nuttin' secret or worth grabb'in ...'

'Ah well. It was worth it for a while. But? You got summat more to tell me, Bai†?'

'Yeah. Lily's Gran'Da, Timmy, works at the Granville hotel ... she was helpin' out in the hotel kitchen las' night... and she checks out the guest register to see who's stayin' there ... D'ere's just

---

* *Nguyễn Ái Quốc = 'Nguyen the Patriot', Ho Chi Minh ('He Who Enlightens'), Vietnamese communist*

† *Bai = Boy, Cork usage, for a man of any age*

two. One's in der most expensive set 'a rooms. English biddy for a few days. The other's in the cheapest, long term. Top rear.'

Collins looked at Paddy, 'Lily's Gran'Da? Is it Timmy O'Mahoney yer talkin' a'boat? Sha, I know him! Nice fella. Lives at Clontarf. He's not really that old. From Cark, too. He found a pocketbook in the street belonging to young Plunkett and returned it to the rightful owner. Just as well he did, otherwise the Castle Document might not'er seen the light a' day.'

'Yeah, well, dis fella's tol' Timmy that he's a salesman. Registered in the name of Jameson. Timmy had a sly look round his room and sees an envelope addressed to a Mr. John Byrnes.' Collins was not impressed, 'And? Jameson, Byrnes! Sha, there's plenty runnin' aboat with those monikers!'

'Yeah. But Lily says she managed to catch sight a' him in the hotel ... and she's seen him before ... wait fer it! Talking to me! ... in Devlin's, midday on Sun'dy. And the only fella I was talking to then was ... Have a guess?' Paddy tapped the bottle of whiskey.

Collins looked at the label. 'Janey Mac*! Jameson? Jack Jameson?'

'The very same. The hard chaw† Cockney that's been sayin' he's a communist and wants to help us smash the British capitalist empire. He's only booked himself into the Granville, would yer b'lieve. Wait. 'Der's more. Old Timmy saw a fella going up to this wan's room. Well-dressed type. Came down after twenty minutes, in a hurry. Prob'bly didn't wanna get caught by the curfew. But before leavin' doesn't he rush into the lounge an' throw some writing paper into der fire, then dash out.'

---

*Janey Mac = Jesus!

† Chaw = Tough nut, another Dublin term

Collins stroked the stubbly hair above his top lip, 'And here's me thinkin' our Jameson was more kosher than a synagogue on a Sat'er'dee[12]. The snakey bastard.'

Paddy handed him a piece of paper. Crumpled and brown in places. A few lines typewritten. 'Timmy managed to get 'dis out of der fire before it got burnt altogether.'

The Big Fella held it delicately as if it were his mother's birth certificate. *Hibernian Bank Branch Managers* was one heading with Henry Campbell, Christopher Tierney, Thomas Read, under it. Then *Munster & Leinster Bank* with James Davidson and a big cross, alongside this there was a question mark against the name Daithi O'Donoghue and Drumcondra. The handwriting was distinctive.

'Well, have a sconce of this! I'd recognise that scribble anywhere. It's BT's,' said Collins, 'BT! ... Basil Thomson. British Director of Intelligence? Thomson! That's the fella who's apparently found out, somehow, I'm after growing a moustache. And now he's given some information here to Jameson's pal ... and we know who Jameson's evening visitor pal is, don't we? The wan that chucked this in the fire? The well-dressed fella?'

Paddy looked blank.

Collins let loose. 'I'll tell yer who he is! The wan that's after takin' our money. That's who. The bastard. The feckin' pure bastard! ... it's gotta stop! OK, now. Lissen. Liam Tobin tells me that d'eres officials from d'ese banks that's been ordered to attend the Police Courts, Monday ... to answer questions about dummy accounts and our money. The names here must be the Bank Managers. I'm certain dis paper-burning fella'll be the Accountant or Magistrate whatever asking the questions. Get yer'sel down there before it starts ... take ole Timmy to point him out, so's yer know what yer man looks like.' Paddy still looked vacant even though now he knew what was coming.

'Don't make it obvious but find out where he lives. Find out every-feckin'-t'ing 'boat him. And then … I don't care how… jus' make sure he's not aroun' dis time next week.'

'OK, Mick… what about Jameson?'

'He'll keep, Bai … I'll get Tom Cullen to have a look round his room though. Yer' a good man, Paddy, well done. And me? I'll be shaving off 'dis feckin' 'stache.'

Chapter 3 – Time's Up, Mr. Bell

19 Belgrave Square, Monkstown, near Seapoint Beach, Dublin.
Friday March 26th 1920

'Alan?'

'Yes, dear?' Mr Bell was trying to eat his breakfast. It was twenty past nine. Running late again, but like any Irishman he did like a bit a' bacon for breakfast. His wife enjoyed showing her knowledge of government business, even if it was sometimes wrong, confused, or both. 'Der there woz sum'ting in der evening paper about yer man Parnell … the politician troublemaker what was wantin' to stop the Land Evictions and to get the Home Rule t'ing a few years back.'

'Hmmm.' He paused for half a second, pretending not to be discomforted, then continued eating.

'Well, yer remember some Shinners … Fenians, I mean, had killed two English fellas in Phoenix Park and people woz saying Parnell was involved? Because he'd written letters about the murders … before they'd happened … if you know what I mean. Only he hadn't, because they were forgeries.'[13]

'Hmmm.' Despite the convoluted words, he knew exactly what she was talking about.

'I t'ought you'd be inter-rested … witch you workin' in that office … Land Evictions[14] or something … '

'Working there? No, not really. Not for long, dear.' He wiped some egg off his chin.

'Well, the fella responsible for the forged letters committed suicide in Spain … it was a few years back … Someone was telling me …'

'It's almost half past nine! … I've gotta go. That tram is sometimes early of a Friday.' Mr Bell gathered up a briefcase and umbrella, kissed his wife abruptly, and set off down the garden path. He had a revolver nestling in his armpit and there was a two-man escort from his gate to the tram stop. There'd be another escort waiting for him when he got off near Dublin Castle.

He just had time to buy the morning newspaper before the Number 8 tram pulled up; crowded as usual, and it would get worse nearer the City, so he grabbed a vacant seat near the door and began reading the business page, whilst surreptitiously poking his tongue in a gap between two teeth and managing to dislodge a tiny piece of bacon. Behind the tram, two men on bicycles strived to keep pace. They almost caught up at Blackrock village when pedestrians and carts slowed the tram's progress. Seagulls screamed and bickered overhead. The cold Spring sea air blew refreshingly as the vehicle swayed and dinged through the suburban streets to Williamstown, past Booterstown, and then on to Merrion, jolting to a stop and picking up passengers, and bump-starting again. The conductor's monotonous and hypnotic calls of the street names and 'Fares, please… thank you … Fares, please … hold tight, please … Fares, please' lulled the passengers. One cyclist was managing to keep up, but the other, Paddy O'Daly, was falling further behind.

At the Anglesea-Ailesbury Road stop there was a crowd of people. Six men stood smoking, obviously with no idea which tram they wanted, and straining their eyes at the on-coming traffic. But they were looking for bicycles, not trams. Finally, a Number 8 stopped; a long-legged bicycle rider, Tom Kehoe, went past, his knees jutting out and bouncing up and down. He waved to them and pointed at the tram. Several passengers got off and the six pushed their way on board, two went upstairs and the rest squeezed inside. Paddy on his bike almost caught up again, wheezing and puffing, and continued pedalling as the tram moved away.

Mr Bell was half-reading the paper, half-dozing. Then his eyelids fluttered, mouth slightly opened, and his head drooped forward. He didn't hear the muted conversation behind him, apparently about the Punchestown horse racing.

'Is that the one?'

'Yeah. The favourite.'

'He's the one? Yer sure, now?' The man thrust a torn section of the March 13th edition of the *Freeman's Journal* [15] under his companion's gaze and pointed at a photograph.

'Yep, that's him. Dead set certainty.'

The tram slowed as it approached the busy junction of Simmonscourt Road, Sandymount Avenue, and Merrion Road, near the Show Grounds. Businessmen in their bowlers, street urchins, and women with shawls wrapped around themselves and carrying babies ambled and skipped between trams, horse drawn carts and bicycles.

'Mr Bell?'

He jerked awake. Huge hands reached across and pinned his arms.

'Come on Mr Bell, your time's come.'

Realisation arrived with a shudder. This was it. Death. As sure as the foul breath in his face. Unless he could break away. He struggled to be free of the piercing grip of fingers squeezing his arms, but someone else was grabbing him around the chest from behind, yanking his whole body upwards. His revolver was useless, entombed under his raincoat. He was being lifted, pulled violently aloft, feet jigging at fresh air like a condemned man dancing after the lever's been pulled. Other passengers were turning their heads and then just as quickly turning away. He managed to lurch for a handle near the exit and squeezed tightly … but his fingers were ripped from it. One of the men upstairs cut the rope connecting the tram's power pole; passengers and bags were flung forwards and everything shuddered to a stop. The clutching arms that were pinning him held even tighter.

One of the men whispered loudly enough for the whole tram to hear, 'Careful, he's got a gun in his oxter*!'

'Nah. S'okay. I got him tight.'

Mr Bell was outside now and he again felt the fresh sea air smack his face as they pulled him away from the tram, falling almost to his knees, scrabbling to get upright. He possibly heard the click as a gun misfired close to his ear. But he wouldn't have heard the shot from Mick McDonnell's gun, nor the next, nor another. Bone splattered and blood streamed over the pavement, women screamed, and a man shouted, 'Lookout! They've kill't him. Lookout, now!' People couldn't resist the urge to stretch their necks and peer around each other.

Bell's body slumped and fell flat. One of the murderers had picked up the newspaper that Bell had continued to grasp and threw it over the shattered head, 'Should I take his gun?'

'Nah, nah. Leave it! C'mon. Go! Go!' They ran down the tree-lined street, turned a corner, separated, and were away in the confusion. The cyclists had disappeared.

'They've kill't him!'

'Killed? Sha, t'was murder.'

'Ah, der poor man.'

'How many were there? T'ree … four?'

'No idea. Didn't get a good look at any of 'em. If yer know what's good fer yer, you'll say the same.'

'Me? I seen nutt'in. All happened too quick.'

'Sha, der's never a priest a-rown' when yer wantin' wan.'

'Well … Hersel' 'll be havin' dinna on her own tonight, so.'

'Ahhhh, c'mon … der might be children at home?'

'Enny'way, she'll be' cookin' fer one less tomorra.'

---

* *Oxter:* Armpit

'Hey, it's nutt'in to be laughin' at!'

'Did yer say laffin'? Who'se laffin'? I amn't laffin'! … Wait, now. I heard 'em talkin' a'boat a race … What was the name of the horse? All Sorts, was it? Poethlyn's the favourite for the Grand National, Ernest Piggott is on him. But I heard a whisper for Troytown… if it's wet.[16]'

'No matter what, nobody has the right to do that, so. Exer'cuted, jus' like dat. At least Emmet got a trial … sort of, … poor bugger.'

'Who's Emmet? Is it this fella?'

Chapter 4 – James Connolly, The Early Years

"Think of the children who swarm and die
In loathsome dens where despair is king.[17]*"*

Cowgate, Edinburgh 1878

John Connolly, father of James, was 44 and worked with shit. He emptied buckets of it from homes, pubs and slums, and carted it away. There were tons of it. Thousands upon thousands of unemployed Irish had relocated from the hovels of Dublin, Londonderry and Belfast to less worse hovels in Edinburgh. 'Cowgate', the main area to which they went, was one huge mass of unhealthy, sweetly-odorous, animal detritus. The smell seemed to increase every second so that it overcame every other sensation. Every day the shit from dogs, horses and humans, had to be removed. And every day it was back again. The smell was always with John, seeping into the small room in the slum that was home for him, his wife, and the three children … along with the other poor souls that resided at number 107, Cowgate. The census of 1871 shows 126 humans, so it could well have been 140 or more by 1878.

John's youngest son, Jimmy, was 11 years of age and could read now. But the good intentions of the Elementary Education Act[18], which was extended to Scotland in 1872, didn't persist for children who had survived past the age of 10. Time for him to find work. He knew it and didn't really need the push from his Da. Unfortunately, there was no work for an 11-year-old in Cowgate.

There were bridges here even though there were no rivers. Bridges which enabled Edinburgh people who preferred to ignore the existence of 'Little Ireland' to pass from one side of the city to the other without getting their noses, let alone their feelings, soiled too much. So, Jimmy had to climb up out of the Cowgate hell and walk miles to the streets where people with money lived; people who had no real problem paying the rent. There were offices with clean windows and shops where the owners could employ assistants. There were even factories where children could work until they became too big and wanted more pay – or were injured and had to disappear before the Government Inspector arrived.

Jimmy, small for his age and bandy-legged, wandered down a quiet, comfortable-looking street. A butcher. A shoe shop. A greengrocer. Boxes of fruit neatly stacked on wooden trestles. A piece of cardboard in the window.

'*Boy wanted. Deliverees. Able to read and ride bike.*'

The doorbell dinged and he shuffled inside, head down and hands in his pockets. There was a musty, dry smell of apples and wood shavings – the shelves were sparsely filled with tins and paper packets of varying shapes and sizes.

'Aye?' A man, in a grubby apron, who had been stooping behind the counter stood straight and looked down at Jimmy. He was about 50 years of age, overweight and expressionless.

'C'n I have the job, Mister?'

'Delivery boy, eh?'

'Yeah. I c'n read. An' ride a bike. Well enuff, ennyway.'

'Aye? What's yer name?'

'Jimmy ... '

'Jimmy what?'

'Jimmy ... McDonald'

'Oh, aye? And where'd yer live, Jimmy McDonald?'

'... Er ... up there, awa.'

'Awa where?'

'T'wards the Castle. Edinburgh Castle.'

'Where?'

'Near Cowgate.'

'Oh, aye? Little Ireland? And what school d'ye go to?'

'Dinnae go to school. Not noo. Lef' last month.'

'What school did ye go to?'

'… Saint Patrick's.'

The man came round from behind the counter and opened the door. With a speedy, strong hand he'd caught Jimmy by the scruff of the neck and dragged him outside.

'Lissen … yer wee, Papist Bastard. The Irish are always after takin' the wages o' goo' Scots. Always chorin*'. I'm no gi'ing a job to a Cath'lic shite … go on, wid'jer! Wastin' ma time. Fuck off!'

The smack behind Jimmy's head was more like a very solid punch. He was concussed, blood trickled from his stinging ear and, staggering, he almost fell. The man looked around, clapped his hands, spat into the gutter and ambled back into the shop.

Jimmy wobbled in the quiet street, dazed and humiliated, tears trickling down his cheeks. Touching the slippery blood on his tingling ear made him wince with the pain. He staggered away. Then he stopped, paused, and turned.

He was again at the shop door, pulling it open. Two smartly-dressed, chattering women went in. They shoved past him as if he wasn't there.

'Yer bastard! Yer big fat, feckin' bastard!'

The women glowered at Jimmy; the shop-keeper was coming round the counter but he was large and slow and the women were in his way. Jimmy backed up to the door, wiping away tears and pointing a bloody hand at his swollen ear.

'Look wha' he did! Jus 'cos ah would'nae tak his shillin' an let

---

* *Choring* = stealing

'im play wi' ma will'ee.'

The shopkeeper made a grab, too late, and Jimmy was away down the street – but not before pulling a tray of fruit onto the pavement. The man was scrabbling amongst rolling apples and pears and the women were walking away quickly, red-faced and whispering.

The next few years dragged on with Jimmy finding occasional work at a printer's, a baker's, and in a factory. Nothing lasted and the wages were no more than pennies. As with most young people in those years, his work experiences included sexual and physical abuse, long hours and dangerous work. If he left a job for whatever reason, getting another became harder because employers wanted younger children that would take lower wages.

His brother John had joined the British Army when he was 15; so, why shouldn't Jimmy do the same, even though he was small and still only 14. The British Army had never been too officious regarding size and birth dates and he'd soon be eating regularly and putting on weight. They weren't overly bothered with names either, because he enlisted using the surname Reid.[19]

So it was that he was standing on the parade ground with other recruits in their stiff ill-fitting uniforms. A kilted Sergeant appeared from nowhere, swinging his arms, marching quickly, and crunching to a boot-slamming halt.

'A-ten-SHUN!!! Move yer 'orrible lot! MOVE! Get yer'sels to-gevVAH!!!'

They shuffled into a rough line which they hoped looked fairly military.

'Stan' still! Stan' STILL! ... 'Ats betta! Yer lookin' ver-ver nice.... NO ! I'm lyin a'cors!!! You're 'orree-bull ... ORR-EE-BULL!' He marched along the line, staring for long awkward seconds into each terrified face. 'N'er min'. I'll get yer right. You'll learn to luv me better'n yer do yer own Ma! .... Now! ...

cup-la things to remember … I'm Sergeant MacCafferty and you will address me as Sarnt! SARNT! Yer sol-jers in the greatest regiment in the greatest army in the greates' feckin' m'pire in the world! … That means … yer do as yer tol' … You obey every feckin' order that you are given! EVER-ree … one. Unnerstan'? UNDER-STAN?'

'Yes, Sarnt!!'

'Good. Dis'nae matt-er wevv'ar it's a lance corporal or a General … Or … or the Duke of feckin' Wellington…' He paused.

Someone in the ranks, Scots humour being what it was, couldn't help himself, whispered loudly, 'He's ded.' Silence. The Sergeant froze. Then, 'Oh-ho! We got a Moo-sick 'all co-median 'ere ! … I wont arsk the wee man to step forward … yer pals ken 'oo it woz. They'll discuss it wiv yer … AFTER … after I've finished wiv all of you'se!'

'Right. Where woz Ah? Oh aye. Ye'll obey orders. Dis'nae matt-a whevv'ar it's daf't, or dangerous, or yer don't like it, or yer dinna unner-stand why yer're doing it … or meb'be ye'd like to think a'boot it fust… NO! …. Ye'll jus' … feckin' … DO it!! Even if you're tol'a shoot at a mob of strikers in yer own home toon. Yer DO it.'

James Connolly was one of the few that passed through the British Army's world-perfect sausage factory, processing human beings into obedient trained killers, without having all his humanity crushed. Eventually, he was stationed in Ireland. This was the time of evictions. Not like those during the Famine years of 1845-1852 and 1879 when half a million were thrown out of their homes. The 1880s' evictions were fewer in number, but no less heartless. Prices for crops had crashed but rents on farms of 20 or so acres were still due. Only a few of the Lords and Dukes that leased out their thousands of acres reduced the rents. Evictions took place – civil servants went out with their legal documents, accompanied by crowbar brigades, police constables and soldiers.

Sympathetic crowds gathered, wondering if it would be their turn next, and shouted abuse at the loyal officers of the Crown.

One of the officials was Edward Carson. Tall, arrogant and sneering, he carried a blackthorn club as he pushed his way amongst the angry Irish mob, unafraid and almost daring them to touch him. Battering rams were used to smash cottage walls. The tiny homes that once sheltered loving families for decades, sometimes surviving illnesses – sometimes not, enduring births and coping with deaths, were quickly and efficiently demolished. Often, homes were barricaded using logs and thornbushes as men, women, children and grandparents tried to fight and retain their property. But sheer weight of numbers meant the authorities overcame them. Sticks of furniture and pathetic belongings like a few cracked cups and pots, were thrown out whilst the shivering families cowered. They were left with nothing and nowhere to go. Soldiers like Connolly were there to preserve the peace, for what it was worth, and to ensure that British justice, so called, was actioned by men like Edward Carson.

Chapter 5 – A civilized people

Neither of the two Royal Irish Regiment soldiers that left the Dublin pub was Irish. One was from Stepney, East London, the other from Tonypandy in Wales. They'd been given a day's leave and spent the best part of it drinking beer. 'Gorn then, Taffy, ... you ain't tol' us yet ... why'd yer join the Paddy's?'

'I was pissed, like. Thought they was the Royal Welsh, see.'

'Royal 'ooo? No such regiment[20] yer stupid berk! ... me? I got red 'air, ain't I ... An' wiv a name like O'Brien ... Ah fought I'd join the Royal Irish and not git sent 'er India. Looks like I might'er got that wrong... Ph'oar ... reckon that beer we 'ad woz off.' He belched. Followed by a loud fart. 'Ahh. Th'as bett'a ... needed that... you ain't been 'ere long 'ave yer?'

'Nah. Missing me Myfanwy, though.'

'Yeah? Well, absence makes the 'art ... go fash-ter ... Or sum'ink like that ... 'ere! Wotch-cher fink of the Paddy sch'vill'yunns?'

'Civilians? Ah dunno, man ... haven't had anything to with 'em. They're British though ... like you and me ... Britons. We're here to stop 'em killing each other. I think.'

'Nah, nah! Lem'me 'ed-juch-kate yer. First, they're all Fore'n Aft ...'

'What?'

'Yer know! Fore 'n Aft ... Daft. No! No. Ish mor'n that. They're un ... civil ... un-shivyl-lished. They ain't as ... developed as wot you 'an me ... Ah mean look at 'im over there!'

'Who? Where?'

'Ole Micksy ... 'im over there ... that! Car'nt yer smell 'im? ForWoar! 'king 'ell! Ee's always there. Dirt-ee-Ole fucker,' pointing at a large pile of rubbish heaped in a shop doorway. Rags of some kind, filthy remnants of what might once have been clothes, old torn curtains or blankets no longer wanted even by homes for the destitute.

A voice emanated from its depths, 'Good evening to yer, sor ... I'm after giv'n up the chat*, yer know! Truly. Would you'se be havin' a spare copper or two for a poor ole fella? Sha, wasn't I a sol-jjer like your-sels' ... the 2nd Battalion Royal Irish in Shue-dan ... 'an then fightin' Boooers ... 'Ave yer got a shillin' fer an ole fella? or jus' a copper?' The voice wasn't just croaky; it was full-bodied matured meths with an aftertaste of fag-ends.

'Nah, Micksey! Fuck'orf, yer silly ole ... er ... no! No ... 'old on ... fink I got som'ink 'ere.' He checked that there was nobody else around. 'Yeah ... Shtick yer 'and out.' A supplicatory arm appeared from within the pile. The soldier turned away again and then spun back urinating into the old man's filthy, withered hand. 'Ha-Ha-Ha!... ', the Londoner's hysterical laughter continued while the stinking stream poured over the rubbish heap. There was a startled scream, 'Argh! Yer filt'y little bowsey bugger!!'

The Welsh soldier gasped, 'Wotch yer doing, man! Pack it in!'

'Ah! Jush 'aving a larf. S'all right ... got warm 'ands now ain't eee? ... lucky I didn't want a pony an' trap†! ... lesh go ... c'mon, quick.' They carefully weaved their way over the cobblestones. 'I'm telling ya. They're not much bett'a than an-nee-mals ... Paddies! They dunno they need a shit until issh too late. An' the wimmen! 'Tween you an' me ... Irish wimmen 'ave gotta 'ave a fuck ev'ry day, else they go funny in the 'ead. Issh true! ... why'd

---

* *Chat = (Irish) methylated spirits. B. Behan Quare Fellow (1960) Act I*

† Cockney slang for 'crap'

yer fink they're always 'aving kids? Eh?'

A young woman, with her head down, passed them, walking quicker and quicker along the poorly lit street. They turned to watch her.

'I mean it! Look at 'er. Stuck up Paddy bitch ... pretending she's in 'urry to get a tram ... She's garsh-pin' fer a fuck! Did yer shee the look wot she gi' me? She's want'in it, orl'right! Now ... if I woz on me own, I reck'on I'd give 'er sum'ink ter gasp for.' Unsteady and mouth open, he gawked at the back of the woman's body as she moved rapidly towards the tram stop. 'Maybe you 'an me, we both could ... Nah. Besh not ... C'mon, I'll take yer up Monto an' we'll get us a cup'la May Oblong's* tarts.' A tram clanged past with a small tubby soldier running behind as if his life depended on catching it.

---

* May Oblong (May Roberts) was a brothel keeper in Montgomery St

Chapter 6 – A high-minded, courteous man

There were a few, not many, places in the world which were worse than Dublin. In 1890 the Congo Free State, ten times the size of Britain, was the personal property of Belgian King Leopold II*. Immense wealth from great quantities of ivory, rubber, and minerals flowed to him whilst millions died from beriberi, forced labour and torture. Józef Korzeniowski had been employed by Albert Thys, on behalf of the King, to take a steamer up the Congo River. He arrived at the Matadia trading station, basically just a small collection of huts. It was the last navigable point before the rapids that made the river impassable for miles and miles upriver. Steep, steep hills stretched above the poor devils that sweated and struggled carrying massive loads up the narrow, rocky paths.

There he met a very tall, bearded Irishman wearing, despite the heat, a white tropical suit and a perfectly knotted worsted tie. Roger Casement, 26, was recruiting and supervising the 2,000 labourers on the new Matadi–Kinshasa railroad which would enable an unnavigable part of the Congo River to be bypassed. Recruitment was a major task because upwards of 10 workers died every day from disease or exhaustion.

The two white men shared one of the huts for several weeks. Casement was gay. And Korzeniowski? If anybody had asked him whether he'd had any homoerotic thoughts, he would have vehemently denied them. But Józef's later writings focused on male-male relationships. Regardless of what the two men did or didn't do, they became very close and shared their concerns for the people of Africa. 'So, Roger ... how did you come to be here? Me, I was expecting to go on an expedition for Albert Thys with

---

* Queen Victoria's first cousin once removed

Alexandre Delcommune, but for some reason he took against me. Did Mr Thys recruit you, as well?'

'No, no. It was Henry Morton Stanley. The man who found Mr. Livingstone.'

'Oh, yes? English wasn't he? I know very little about him.'

'Welsh, I think. Apparently, he had quite a … difficult childhood. He was abused in a home for boys. Made quite a name for himself out here of course for Leopold, as an explorer. He had a young native boy, you know? … I heard that he was always … very protective of the lad … took him to England.' Korzeniowski lit another cigarette and waited for Casement to continue.

'Actually, Józef, you're only the second man that I've met here with whom I've felt … comfortable. The other was a chap named Herbert Ward. He was picked up, like me, by Stanley. Herbert went with him to rescue Emin Pasha. They saw some dreadful things being done to the natives by an Englishman named Barttelot[21]. Now? The black-hearted devil's dead and Herbert's back in England. A sculptor, would you believe? I suppose we shared some ambivalence here … this … in-between colonial space, perhaps it could be called. He once told me that if he ever had a son he'd name him after me. And, yes, we keep in touch … and, yes, I miss him.'[22]

Korzeniowski was mystified by Casement. An adventurer, a romantic, and so full of sympathy for others that it almost tore at one's soul. A man much like himself, or rather … a man that he would like to be. His voice had a softly musical, enthralling, quality. Almost 2 metres tall. Curly dark hair, blue eyes, lean but muscular. He was honourable, noble-minded and unfailingly polite. Korzeniowski didn't want to appear intrusive but couldn't help himself and said, 'Tell me about yourself.'

'Well … I was born in Dublin. Parents both Protestant. At least initially. My mother became a Catholic and had me secretly baptised. She had eleven babies – four survived. My father was an army officer though we were by no means wealthy. His father went bankrupt and disappeared off to Australia. We lived in the East End of London for a while. Didn't have much, but better off than most. Mother found it especially tough. I was nine when she died at 39 years of age, and we went to live with father's family in Ulster. An uncle helped me get a job when I was 16 with a big Liverpool shipping company. The owner Alfred Lewis Jones, a single man, was known as The Uncrowned King of West Africa. Ha! Uncrowned King! How many of those have we had? ... Anyway, Mr Jones liked ... well ... the look of me, I suppose, and took me under his ... He does consular work for the Belgian King ... I think Jones recommended me to Henry Stanley when I was 19.'

'Why though, Roger? Why did you come to Africa? And especially ... why here? This place of darkness?'

Casement paused, 'But I could ask you the same question ... and I think we'd both give much the same answer. Needed a job and it looked like an adventure ...' They both sighed.

'You and I now realise that King Leopold lied to the other European nations by telling them he wanted to undertake humanitarian and philanthropic work and that he wouldn't tax trade. You and I thought we'd be bringing white civilization to improve the lives of impoverished unfortunates ... we were told we had to prove our superiority over the savages by controlling them. We weren't told about the atrocities and exploitation; no, nor about the forced labour, murder, and cruel whippings; no, not told about the soldiers of the Force Publique private army[23] and how they slice a child's arm off to force the parents into working harder.'

'But Roger... I'm Polish ... I admire the British empire and its tradition of doing the honourable thing ... Surely modern empires can use their knowledge, experience, and traditional justice, to empower the less evolved ... less civilized ... nations to learn and improve themselves? I don't know ... blend together different cultures so that the world benefits from ... cross-fusion.'

'Hybrid? Not quite the correct word? Hmm ... No, all I see is torture and killing human beings so that Leopold can get rubber and ivory. The poorest savage in a hut here has more morality and decency and civilization than that creature in Europe.'

They stopped gazing at each other and went back to their notebooks. Each of them had an obsessive desire to write and write and write.

Korzeniowski wanted to be a novelist. His English was extremely good but he had a tendency to flaunt his knowledge. If he could write using two long words when a single short one would have been sufficient, then why not? Better still, why not three. That didn't mean he was careless in choosing a word. Each was tested and analysed, so that it conveyed the exact sentiment and sensitivity that he wanted the reader to feel. Just at that moment though he was struggling and the half-written novel about a Dutch trader in Borneo was not flowing.

'Józef?'

Korzeniowski put his pen down and lit yet another cigarette. He was grateful for the interruption and waited for Casement to continue.

'Sorry, old chap. I just wanted to say that ... when I get back to England, I intend doing my very best to ensure that the world is informed about this horrible, horrible darkest of all hells.'

Korzeniowski held out his hand, 'I'd always had a ... hankering ... to become a British citizen. I'm glad that I did, four years ago, and meeting you has confirmed that I made the correct decision ... Roger ... I'm sure that you will always do what you think is right ... because you're the most incorrigible Irishman that a man could ever hope to meet. And when you do inform the world ... I will provide you with all the support that I can.' They shook hands.

'Thank you, Józef. Incorrigible Irishman? I like that. I might use that myself.[24]'

Korzeniowski did a lot of writing in the years to come. So did Casement. Others had tried to publicise the corrupt behaviour by King Leopold but the exploitation continued until the British government was at last goaded into action by the Stokes issue.

Charles Stokes[25] was Irish and had been a missionary in the Congo until he found it more lucrative to deal in ivory. But he made the mistake of selling guns to the slave traders who were fighting against the Congo Free State. When he was captured, the Belgian troops didn't bother with a trial; they simply hanged him from a tree. News got back to Europe, but King Leopold trivialised the matter. But this was not the death of an unknown black savage – this was a British subject. The Press and Government became involved. Casement was now the diplomatic consul in the Congo and Leopold must have been pleased, mistakenly, on hearing that he'd be the one to undertake an investigation. Casement's official report on exploitation and abuse of human rights was shocking[26]. However, Leopold used Alfred Jones' influential friends in England and the US to emasculate and discredit it.

The Irishman didn't give up. His long-time friend Herbert Ward introduced him to Edmund Morel who had been one of Leopold's accountants. Morel had also learnt the truth of the inhumanity in the Congo and he and Casement together created the Congo Reform Association. Then they encouraged publicity from high-profile people, like Mark Twain and Joseph Conrad* (Józef Teodor Konrad Korzeniowski), and eventually they succeeded in using global pressure on the Belgian Government to cancel Leopold's responsibility for the Congo.

Casement stayed in the diplomatic service, supporting the British Empire in the Boer War. Then he was sent to Brazil. In 1910 the Foreign Secretary, Sir Edward Grey, instructed him to investigate reports of British subjects being abused in Peru. The investigation was widened by Casement to include Putumayo Indians who were being subjected to murder, rape, and forced labour by the rubber company Peruvian Amazon. His writing was regarded as journalism of a very high quality, helped by his detailed diaries. Of special interest was the fact that his report included first-person comments from the local population, people that would once have been regarded as savages. In recognition of his work and his determination to expose atrocities he was given a knighthood in 1911. He could have refused it – but then he would have had to resign and been unable to furnish significant help to the Putumayo Indians[27]. His health had suffered – he may have always been bipolar and was now suffering from arthritis, malaria, eye infections, and traumatic stress disorder; he retired with a pension in June 1913 aged 49.

---

* **Twain** wrote *Leopold's Soliloquy* and Joseph Conrad wrote *Heart of Darkness*.

Chapter 7 – A Good Life

If Lillie Reynolds, a young governess for the Wilson family in Merrion Square, ever thought about Love she would have considered it something for rich people or silly, weak girls. Then late one evening she realised that she was going to miss her tram. She quickened her pace and avoided looking at the two drunken soldiers that were stumble-wandering down the street towards her. There was nobody else at the stop more than fifty yards away. She looked behind and saw the tram trundling down the hill, then flying past her. It wasn't going to stop. A short, rather tubby, soldier was running after it with a desperation that she could almost feel. Being bow-legged probably didn't help but he would have made it – if he'd accelerated and jumped on. But he slowed and stopped; that slight smile of her's caught his eye, and she seemed to be saying, 'Well, I'm not running for it anyway.' He could have caught it. But now he didn't want to.

'I'm noo bothered,' he managed to gasp. (*'Wha'd I say that fer? Wha' a glaikit* thing to say.'*)

She wasn't sure how to respond. 'Are you not, now?' (*'Why'd I say that? I don't speak to strangers, least of all soldiers.'*)

'Ay-weel-there'll-be another, ye-ken? ... tram-ah-mean.' (*'Noooo!?! D'ya think she's waiting here fer a train? C'n yer no say summat sensible to the lass?'*)

'Yeeesss ... (*'Sha, I wish I knew what he was saying.'*) ... Yes. Indeed.' (*'At least he hasn't been drinking. I can't smell anything on his breath.'*)

Connolly cleared his throat. Twice. 'Sorry ... Ah should'na spoke. Rude'a me. Strangers.'

---

* *Glaikit* = Stupid

'That's quite alright.' (*I wish I could take a real look at his face. I think his eyes are grey-blue.*')

'Would-a ... Ah mean ... '. (*'Ah wish ah could look at her face properly ... Her hair is ... Say summat quick! You've noo got much time!*') 'Sorry, Ah'm being rude ... Ma name's James. James Connolly ... Er ... Well ...'

'... *(Oh, Dear God ... quick, he'll think that I think he's being rude.)* 'How do you do ... I'm Lillie Reynolds.'

She was 23 and he was 22 when they married in 1890. That was after he ceased to be an employee of Her Majesty – not that he went through any of the formalities like telling the British Army about the cessation. Lillie learnt that James had been a decidedly uncommitted soldier of the Queen. He learnt that Lillie was as politically determined as he was; they both wanted to make the world a better place for those living in poverty, especially women. He believed that workers were slaves and women were slaves of slaves.

They struggled together in the slums of Dublin and, for a time, Scotland. He worked in many jobs including emptying shit like his Da, anything to feed and clothe a family. But he never stopped reading and learning, principally about politics, even in the darkest evenings when the last of the coal was twinkling in the grate.

The years passed, children were born, and Connolly developed a unique philosophy about the need for improved workers' rights and greater fairness for the distribution of wealth. It was based on communism, but it recognised that religion, for some people, met special needs which communism never could. He knew that there were urgent issues which had to be addressed before a Communist Utopia happened; workers, with their families in desperate poverty, needed to unite and go on strike for better wages. He wrote articles, gave speeches, and fought on the picket lines. The special quality of his ideas became known. He, and the family, were persuaded to go to America where he gave lectures and helped inspire others. But these were the days when leaders competed for control. It was fine to be a follower, but if you argued then there'd be trouble. If you had ideas of your own and tried to voice them ... well, anybody that had been around longer was likely to put you in your place – hard. So, America was good for a while until Connolly and Lillie realised that they needed Ireland and Ireland needed them. They went back.

'Sha, Jim, you'll be ruining your eyesight in this gloom. We've no more wood or coal for the fire. Did you do that Government thing? The ... Census* whatnot?'

'Aye ... but it doesn't have to be done by me ... you could'a done it.'

'Jim, it has to be done by the head of the household.'

'Aye ... And who says I'm the heid?'

'You're the man ...so it's you that must do it. That's what the government fella said.'

'I dinna see why being a man makes me the Heid of the Household. Women work as hard as men ... harder. You know what I've always said ... women are the slaves of slaves.'

'James Connolly, you're just a troublemaker... anyway, what did you write down for my Place of Birth?'

'County Wicklow. Religion, Church of Ireland.'

'Good. What about yours?'

'Never you mind ...'

'C'mon ... let me see that ... What's this! Roman Catholic? Well, yes, in your own way ... Occupation ... National Organiser Socialist Party ... Oh, doesn't that sound grand. Does it pay well?

---

* 1911 Census

Ahhh, I'm only coddin' yer. Place of Birth ... Oh! Jim! That should be Edinburgh, Scotland. You've put County Monaghan!'

'Aye ... well ... how they gunna ken? Ah could'a put Timbuck-too and they'd never question it ... dis'nae do any harm to keep 'em in the dark.'

'Hey ... You've put here that yer can speak the Irish ... I thought you always said People can't teach starvin' men Gaelic ... but you put me as not speakin' Irish? And what's this infirmity that you have? Deaf and dumb? They're not gonna believe that! How can you be National Organiser for the Socialist Party if you're deaf and dumb? And speaking Irish! Deaf and Dumb! Sha, I can't read it in this light.'[28] She was holding her sides laughing.

'Well ... I'm no bad at yer Irish language ... Esperanto's better, anyway. Seriously, Lillie, I like confusing them and the less everybody knows about me past the better. Tommy Simpson'll certify it.'

The fire was almost out. Lillie shivered. Connolly put the pen down and rubbed his eyes. 'I'm sorry, Lillie.'

'What? What's that yer sayin'?'

He said, barely above a whisper, 'I've made a hard life for you, haven't I? One stinking room here for all of us, scrabbling for pennies to feed the bairns. Moving from job to job. Failed as a cobbler. Could'nae even keep me job emptying the shit. My own Da was nae much but at least he kept workin'. Meb'be ... it would been better if ye'd ...'

'Wisht! James Connolly! I bless the day I met you! When I see the men that some women have ended up with! Yer don't touch the drink or swear and you've never raised yer hand to me ... And when we lost Mona, God rest her ... I know it near broke your heart ... like it did mine ... but you never blamed me. Yer helped me in ma time of need.'

'I ken it was naebody's fault, hen. Och, Mona was 13 and didn't she love to look after the weans? God bless her memory ... She was that excited by the thought of us moving to America ... and she wanted to help your sister in the steamie* by washing the clothes in the big old pot at the fire ... there was no betty† aroon it ... it was naebody's fault.'

They stared at the dwindling flames; the smoke and crackling had almost ceased. They were both thinking of Mona and wondering what she would be like now if she were with them at that very moment.

Lillie stretched her shoulders and began to think of Connolly '... And I know, Jim, that you don't just ... pretend to care about people ... you really really want to make things better. All this studying communist books and articles, in the original German, and writing your own ideas!'

'Aye, well ... you've helped with the writing ... I was never able to keep ma mouth shut when I disagreed with something.'

'Isn't that the trut'. And yer can't stop yersel when yer see others being bullied or hurt or treated unfairly. Doesn't matter whether it's one or a t'ousand ... Yer ideas about women's rights and independence for Ireland, socialism and religion ... they scare people. Scare them because they know that those ideas are different ... and make more sense ... than anybody else's. And the way you can voice those ideas, be it in German or Esperanto ... or ... Scots ... or .... Yes, Irish ... makes me proud of yer .... Never, never, ever, say sorry to me. We've had a good life together.'

---

* *steamie* = communal wash-house

† *betty* = fireguard

Chapter 8 – British Justice
"The truth is rarely pure and never simple."*

One of the sycophants, who would later find it convenient to deny knowing his companion, said what nobody wanted to hear. 'You'll be up against Carson.'

'I trust he will conduct his cross-examination with all the added bitterness of an old friend'[29]. Oscar Wilde spoke spontaneously, as if he hadn't been savouring them for the last half hour – silently selecting a word, testing how it would sound, discarding it, then trying another. He knew that many of his comments were regurgitated by others and was certain, with his honest immodesty, that they would be quoted in years to come.

He sighed and stroked the fur collar, short shiny hair from newborn sheep, of the coat to which he was devoted. Was he concerned about the forthcoming court case? Nobody could tell. Outwardly, he was supremely confident even if his first impulse had been to ignore the ungrammatical insult. It was a calling card from the Marquess of Queensberry, delivered to the Albemarle Club and labelling him a 'sodomite' – the result was that Oscar had been persuaded to take court action for libel.

Edward Carson was legal counsel for the Marquess of Queensbury. The accusation being accurate, Wilde was always going to have to tell lies convincingly in the witness box or lose the case. When it came to it, he couldn't even tell the truth about his age. He lost and, various young men having sworn that he had paid them to have sex, there was an inevitable prosecution for gross indecency[30].

---

* Algernon in *The Importance of Being Earnest* (opened Feb.14, 1895). Wilde's defamation case started on April 3.

Oscar Wilde had grown up in a wealthy Dublin home which was about twenty minutes' walk from the slightly less affluent, but equally Protestant, residence of Edward Carson. Born in the same year, they both went to Trinity University, and both were Freemasons. Nevertheless, their lives could hardly have been more different. Wilde liked to wear green carnations; Carson most certainly did not.

Carson was the Member of Parliament for Dublin University, leader of the Ulster Unionists, and could speak Gaelic – Wilde couldn't and had an English accent. Carson was more Irish than a shedload of shamrock, a pint of Guinness, and the smell of burning peat. But he was also British to the tips of the shiny boots lurking under his spats. He would argue, with all his strength, against the possibility that Ireland, or any part of it, should ever cease to be part of Her Majesty's realm. He was horrified by the thought that Catholics might be able to usurp power from a British Parliament and take Ireland out of, what he was certain was, the greatest Empire the world had ever known.

If Carson ever smiled it would be the only time in his life. He had a high forehead, strong nose and heavy lips which curled downwards into what could become a sneer were he to ever feel a person worthy of it. He was clean-shaven, but if he'd had a moustache he could have been typecast for the villain who chains a heroine to a train track.

His best friend was F.E. ('Freddie') Smith, who was to become Lord Birkenhead. As a barrister, Smith was even more talented than Carson despite being a very heavy drinker. But then if he had drunk less, his surgically incisive wit and very snide remarks would not have been so well known. Apart from being cleverer, he was 6 ft 4 inches tall so he could look further down his nose than Carson who was two inches shorter.

Smith had no doubts about his superiority over other mortals. During his early days in court, he often clashed with those more senior. A judge once told him that he was being extremely offensive. He responded that, 'As a matter of fact, we both are – the only difference between us is that I'm trying to be, and you can't help it.'

The two towering men, striding through the dark and foggy streets near Parliament, were well-matched. Carson spoke in a deceptively polite, except when pretending to be enraged, well-bred Dublin accent. Smith's time at Oxford, plus his accelerated progress in the bewigged London legal chambers, and years as a Member of Parliament, had almost, but not quite, resulted in his Lancashire accent becoming a suitably contemptuous drawl. He was wearing a shiny, cheerfully balanced top hat while Carson had a serious Homburg. They walked proudly down Whitehall warmly wrapped in overcoats with Astrakhan collars. Dinner, and plenty of alcohol for Smith, at their club beckoned. They blithely crossed the road as the London Bobby stopped the traffic for them. He saluted; they ignored him.

A doorman invisibly bowed them through into a narrow hallway that was both understated and opulent. A portrait of Disraeli peered down at them as if he had full confidence in their ability to defend the Conservative heritage which they were convinced was deservedly their birthright. Handing their hats, umbrellas, and coats to a silent and faceless attendant they went into the apparently empty dining room and chose a secluded table.

Smith had a whisky and soda in his hand just after he sat down. They both chose mock turtle soup to start. Carson had steak, very rare with the blood oozing; Smith chose coq au vin – and champagne. The vegetables were plentiful but rather, as required by club tradition, over-cooked. While they waited for the cheese platter, Smith managed to drink two glasses of champagne and smoke three cigarettes. Their smalltalk thus far had been about Winston Churchill's family.

Smith said, 'His cousin ... Clare Sheridan. D'you know her? Bit of a Bohemian? Radical?'

Carson sensed why Smith was asking, aware that the lady was very good-looking and responded, 'The family has some property at Innishannon in Cork. 3,000 acres. Near Bandon[31]. Her father's Moreton Frewen ... the Member for Northeast Cork ... Sha, he tried to support your stance on keeping the House of Lords veto! ... Remember him now? Known to some, rather unkindly, as Mortal Ruin! Got some interesting ideas about Federalism ... But he's willing to fight to keep Ireland in the King's Empire. Solid man ... brother-in-law's Lord Randolph Churchill. And his brother, Stephen, has a daughter named Ruby, I believe ... Yes, Ruby Frewen ... she's ... very pleasant ... But Clare? I heard Clare was getting married ... have you met her fiancé?'

'No, no ... Winston introduced me to her yesterday ...' Smith lit a cigar – the wispy blue smoke wafted around his large, well-oiled head – and, eyes closed, he leered dreamily.

Carson needed to know whether what he'd already been told was correct ... 'Anyway, what's happening with the King ... what's his view on Home Rule and Ulster?'

'The King? Put it this way ... he, of course, has a mind of his own ... but he relies upon information and advice. And we have to make sure that he's provided with the, er, correct information. As to advice? Well, there are sources of advice ... and then there are, let's call them 'other' sources. As far as we're concerned ... we must make sure that he has ... and relies upon ... the source which provides the advice that we want him to have.'

Carson could see they were of like mind, 'And what about His Majesty's Liberal Government? Is the Prime Minister going to stab Ulster in the back and give full independence ... Home Rule to all of Ireland? I don't trust Asquith. All he ever tells the nation is Wait-And-See.' Smith giggled, 'I don't think Asquith tells anybody his real plans, not even his wife. Perhaps he keeps Venetia Stanley[*] informed, though ... in the adulterous bed? I'm told he writes to her every day and gives more consideration to her ideas than he does to those of the Cabinet.'

Carson finally let loose. 'Everything to do with the Liberals is hypocrisy! ... very, very, damned annoying ... Asquith and Lloyd George both hate and detest Catholics but they're so desperate to stay in Government that they're happy to negotiate with the Nationalists on independence for Ireland. If they have their way, make no mistake, this will destroy the Empire. First Ireland, India next.'

Smith was obviously annoyed too, 'They won the election by running a mile whenever Home Rule was mentioned. The electorate had no idea that Irish independence would result from Asquith winning. They've altered the Constitution to suit themselves ... well, if that's the way they want to play it ... the Empire must be defended. And we'll do it by all means necessary. History may call it treason but sometimes, for the greater good, bad laws must be opposed. Democracy is the ideal. But if legislation has been passed in bad faith ... Well, the process has been corrupted. It must be opposed. By a counter-revolution.'

Carson's chin jutted in that determined way he had, 'I've always believed in the rule of law. Pogroms and attacks on homes by Orangemen against Catholics are indefensible; the

---

[*] British aristocrat and socialite

Presbyterians' hysteria about Catholic education is ridiculous ... but Protestants in the South are so apathetic. Thank goodness those in Ulster are patriotic. That's why we need people willing to, literally, take up arms and fight. Loyal Britons in Ulster, Glasgow, Liverpool, and Manchester ... willing to swear they'll go to war for the well-being of Ulster ... for the welfare of the whole of Ireland ... and the unity of the Empire.'

Smith and Carson had no doubt about what was required. Rifles and ammunition. People to be trained in warfare. Officers, the right ones of course, in the British Army must be contacted and advised as to what was expected of them. Money, of course, was needed. There were plenty of wealthy Protestants.

Carson leaned towards Smith. 'What about your pal? What's he up to?'

'Winston? He might be a Liberal now, but he's as much an Empire Loyalist as we are. We can use him as a go-between with Lloyd George. It's obvious that he and Winston are ... well, realistic. They've no intention of forcing Ulster Protestants into the arms of Rome. But they can't let the Irish Nationalists know that .... Not yet. The Prime Minister though? Asquith's a cunning Devil. He'll keep the Irish thinking, for as long as possible, that they'll get Home Rule for the whole of Ireland ... '

Smith leaned back and blew a great cloud of cigar smoke, ' ... but the whole of Ireland? No. You'll get to keep six counties in Northern Ireland ... maybe nine ... if you want ... although some in Ulster prefer, don't they, not to have the three that have a large majority of Catholics. Anyway, it'll mean giving up on the Protestants in the South. They'll need to ... sorry, simply do their best under an Irish Dublin Parliament. One that will, of course, stay within the Empire under the King. Asquith and Lloyd George are happy to accept that there'll be ... hardships for Protestants in the South.'

Carson's fury was increasing. 'I know ... I know ... I've many friends in the South, especially in Cork around Bandon[32*]. And I hate to think of Churchill getting away unscathed when he speaks in Parliament.'

Smith laughed. 'I may be able to help you there... I thought about this the other day .... When I needed to go for a pee. I get caught short sometimes when I'm walking to Parliament. So I often pop into that club of Winston's ... the Athenaeum and use the facilities. Well, yesterday, damned if the doorman doesn't stop me and have the nerve to ask me if I was a member! So I said, 'Good God, d'you mean to say this place is a club?' Smith rolled with his own laughter. He chuckled and continued, 'Anyway ... You used to be a member of the Liberal National Club, didn't you? But you're a Conservative! A Liberal club? And Winston's always teasing you about it, eh?'

Carson's face reddened, 'Hrmph ... Me! A Liberal! That was 30 years ago ... I'm a Conservative Unionist ... and I was elected as a Unionist.'

'Well, if he brings up your past Liberal membership ... remind the little chap that he was once a member of the Conservatives ... before he became a Liberal and ratted on us.'

Their quiet conversation was interrupted by a vigorous discussion at a table on the far side of the room. Two judges that Smith vaguely knew from his experiences practising Law, looked across at him. They'd obviously recognised him – one nervously approached. 'Excuse me, Freddie old boy ... sorry to intrude upon your dinner ... I wonder if I might ask for some advice?'

Smith frowned. 'Yes-yes! What is it?'

'Well, we've been wondering ... what does one give a young man

---

* Bandon was initially populated by English and Scottish settlers. Ireland's first Protestant church was built there.

willing to allow himself to be buggered?' Smith puffed out his cheeks, 'I dunno! A pound. Thirty shillings. Whatever you have on you.'

Chapter 9 – Anything's legal if you're a Protestant

He signed the Covenant* on 28th September 1912 with his own blood. That was what Fred Crawford, proud 51-year-old Ulsterman, later claimed. Whether he really did boggles the imagination because of the logistics required. Perhaps he took out a razor or sharp knife and sliced into a finger before dripping enough blood into a dish, dabbing a nib into the rich Protestant blood and signing ... and then wrapping a handy cloth over the oozing wound. There would have been, literally, thousands of men standing in line behind him in Belfast City Hall waiting their turn to sign at one of the 540 desks lining the walls. So, perhaps the blood was wishful thinking.

Outside, 2000 volunteers from the various Orange lodges† marshalled people and kept order. By the end of the day, more than 200,000 men had signed and an even greater number of women had put their name to a Covenant specially modified for them. Normally, Saturday was a workday in Belfast. But the city had closed down – businesses, factories and shipyards were silent because everybody, apart from Catholics of course, had participated in an almost religious bonding which culminated in signing the Covenant. Carson, unsurprisingly, had been the first to do so. Later that afternoon, he walked to Ulster's Reform Club for

---

* A formal promise to help defeat the 'conspiracy' to create a Home Rule Parliament in Ireland.

† Orange lodges: support and defend the Protestant faith. Name is derived from William of Orange (King William III of Great Britain) who defeated Irish Catholics in 1690.

lunch. It should have only taken ten minutes, but the cheering crowd was so large and so eager to shake his hand that it had taken over an hour. Reaching the Club, he was exhausted and ravenous; lunch was perfect. Now though, a quiet visit with a small group to Lord and Lady Londonderry's Mount Stewart 1000-acre estate was perfect.

James Craig was feeling justifiably proud. He was an influential businessman and had been responsible for the massive increase in Ulster Unionist Council membership. 'The day went rather well, I think, Edward. Oh, here's Fred. D'you know Fred Crawford? Major in the Boer War. Fred! Come here and meet Sir Edward Carson.' Carson shook Crawford's hand, 'You've done a great job in organising today's events! Well done!'

'Thank you, but your Frank Hall was the main organiser. Anyway, the people of Northern Ireland are desperate to continue to be British citizens.'

'Yes, indeed I ...'

'If something's not done, Asquith will ram Home Rule for Ireland through Parliament and we'll have Rome ordering us around. Well, I'm not having my children and grandchildren indoctrinated by priests and nuns ...'. As he got into his stride, Crawford's Ulster accent strengthened and boomed through the gracious dining room '... bow-in an' scrape'ing an' kneelin' an' cross'un thum'sels in front of their plash-ter graven images ... Home Rool? Home Rool? An' what'll happen to everythin' we've done in Ulsh-ter? All our God-given prosh-pair-ee-tea 'an ... homes and ... indush-tree ?! Handed down by our Fore-fathers ... Bel-Fasht'll end up like LUN-don-derry an Dub-lin! Schlums and HOV-vels!' He was getting red-faced but wanted desperately to continue with his sermon.

If Carson was a lookalike for an aristocratic cinema villain,

Craig could have played the part of the corrupt Sheriff. He had a dour and podgy face, a disciplined moustache, and eyes that appeared to be arguing with each other. Thinking that Crawford needed to slow down, Craig interrupted. 'Fred here, he tried to smuggle in firearms for us but it all fell through. Eh, Fred?'

'True, but that experience was worthwhile …' Fred had thankfully calmed down.

Carson's eyebrows shot up, 'Really?' Crawford looked at Craig who nodded and urged him to continue, '… Yes, my dealer* in Hamburg can supply a large shipment of rifles. He's offered a selection of cheap but not very good ones. But he's also got much better German and Italian … Frank Hall can organise it all. Just like he coordinated the Covenant signing. I know that you don't like him, Mr Craig. He might not be an Orangeman, but he's a passionate Unionist … Sir Edward knows him well.'

'How much? For the shipping … and the better rifles … the whole exercise?' The speaker was a tall, elegant woman – Theresa Susey Helen Vane-Tempest-Stewart, Marchioness of Londonderry, also known as Lady Londonderry by people in a hurry. She was very persuasive, hence the nickname Queen of the Tories. Parties at her various stately homes in London and Ulster were attended by gossiping royalty, military officers, and socialites. Popular (to put it politely), with men she managed to get not only considerable funds for the Council but also information. She, with her husband, had now joined the select group of Craig, Carson, and Crawford in the corner of the ballroom. 'Come on! Come on! How much?'

Crawford took a deep breath before saying, 'How much? £70,000'.

---

* Benny Spiro

Lord Londonderry*whistled. 'Are you sure you can trust this fellow in Hamburg? He's a Jew, isn't he? You know what they're like. Not sure if this is ...'

Lady Londonderry said, 'Be quiet, Charlie dear ... £70,000? That can be ... I'll talk to the other ladies on the Ulster Unionist Council and I have a few other people I can lean on ... Yes. Shouldn't be a problem. Come on, Charlie – I can see Lady Whatever-her-name-is over there. She's always good for £100.'

Craig turned to Carson, 'Er ... If it does happen that we're forced to accept partition and Northern Ireland forms a Provisional Government ... we think that you ought to be Leader ... my skills are in networking, administration, and organising. Not public speaking. Unlike yourself.'

Carson said, 'Fine by me ... Northern Ireland?' Craig was adamant, 'Aye but without Donegal, Cavan and Monaghan – they've too many Catholics ... '

'But the Covenant?'

'Yes, I know. It'll upset many Protestants. Can't be helped. ... Ah, Look! Here's another ex-Army chap! Robert Wallace ... Robert, how are you? What have you been up to?' Wallace was not just wealthy, he was also a very senior member of the Freemasons and the Grand Master of the Orange Order.

'Fighting fit, thanks, James. Hello, Sir Edward. I need to talk with you two.' Wallace took them both to a small room, 'I suppose you know that the military training being done by thousands of members of the Ulster Unionist Council has been illegal? Well, I've been advised that any two Justices of the Peace could authorise it, and I know plenty of the right type of JPs.'

---

* Lord Londonderry, when Secretary of State for Air, tried to reach an 'understanding' with Nazi Germany

Next day, 70,000 people were massed at Belfast dock to sing the hymn 'Oh God, Our Help In Ages Past' and cheer Carson's departure – an adoring crowd of 150,000 met him in Liverpool. Many people in England had signed the Covenant. Rich and poor, workers and employers, business owners and homeless, clergy and congregations ... anybody who had been born in Ulster could sign. And most of them did.

*

Protestant Field Marshal Sir George White was one that didn't. The 'Hero of Ladysmith' and winner of a Victoria Cross was born in Ulster, but he didn't sign the Covenant – he had died 3 months earlier. Nor did his English-born son James 'Jack' White, DSO. Jack was educated at Winchester College[33] and later went to the Royal Military College. Like his father, he fought in South Africa. Like his father, at 6 foot 3 inches, he was a dominating figure. There the similarity ends. Jack was still a Presbyterian but also considered himself a Christian Communist. He had abruptly resigned his commission, worked as a teacher in Bohemia, then became a vegetarian and worked as a lumberjack in Canada. When his father died he went back to Ulster and spoke at meetings to persuade Protestants that they had nothing to fear from Home Rule for Ireland. He wasn't the only speaker in Antrim.

'Sir Roger Casement? How d'you do? I'm Jack White. We've both got family here in Antrim, I think. I'm pleased to meet you ... The Irish people have suffered too long, Home Rule for Ireland is desperately needed, isn't it?'

Casement was tall but, even so, he found himself looking up into White's eyes, 'Yes, certainly. Imperialism has had its day. Far too cruel. We need to convince these people that a Dublin Government doesn't mean rule from Rome.'

'Sir Roger, I've heard about the great things you've done for oppressed people in Africa and South America ...'

'I've heard about you, too. Went to Winchester College with Edward Grigg, didn't you? He's now a journalist with The Times, head of the colonial department. So I know him quite well. He told me that Warren Fisher, high up in the Civil Service, was at Winchester too. And the Prime Minister's son, Raymond. And Wilfred Spender ... he's one of the main organisers of the Ulster Volunteer Force. Isn't that strange? All of you at the same school pretty much at the same time.'

White shook his head, 'Can't say I remember them.'

Casement knew many senior people in the Civil Service, 'What about Robert Seton-Watson? Recall the name? Now, he's an activist ... friends with Tomas Masaryk ... the Czechoslovak philosopher chap who's keen on fighting for independence of small nations.'[34]

White laughed, 'Seton? Nope. I've forgotten my time at Winchester. Expelled, yer know. I do recall though giving a speech in the Debating Society about how great Cromwell was ... I hope you're not going to publicise any of this?'[35]

Casement laughed, 'No, no. I don't think Connolly or Larkin would be too impressed. It'll be our secret.'

'Thanks. I'm going to Dublin in a few weeks ... another bloody speech. But I'll also be seeing Connolly. I want to raise the possibility of a Citizen Army. The idea is that the strikers locked out by employers and unemployed men would be trained and drilled, just like being in an Army. Marching as a single entity in perfect formation gives a feeling of pride and confidence. Connolly is temporarily head of the Irish Transport and General Workers Union, whilst Larkin's in jail, so I'll see what he thinks of the Citizen Army idea.'

Chapter 10 – Three of a Kind

*"The rich man in his castle, The poor man at his gate"**

Connolly was sitting on an armchair in the well-furnished living room of 49B Leinster Road, Dublin, talking to two visitors. 'It's nae much but it's home,' he laughed. The owner[†] of the plush house, who made it available for Connolly, was absent. He lapsed into guilty silence as he thought of Lillie in their bleak Belfast lodgings, before rousing himself, 'Aye, there's plenty that'd think this was Paradise.'

At first glance, the trio were as awkward as a bad joke; a Scotsman, an Irish woman, and an Englishman. Connolly, a 45-year-old lapsed Catholic, was small and chubby; Nellie Gifford, 33 years of age and a determined Protestant, was sitting straight up; James Larkin, 39, with a strong Liverpool accent, towered over the other two. The common denominator was their pursuit of social justice and a determination to think for themselves.

Nellie shrugged, 'I grew up in affluent areas but, sha, yer never far from poverty in Dublin ... then, when I went to work in the country ... well, I've seen people literally scrabbling to survive. Here, there's the sheer filthiness of Dublin with families starving from day to day. And then in the countryside there's the rural genteel hunger and malnutrition that's become so accepted in Ireland that it's regarded as traditional and the National culture.'

In Larkin's imagination he could see and smell the deprivation

---

* *'All Things Bright and Beautiful', written by Cecil Frances Alexander (born in Dublin. She also wrote 'Once in royal David's city' and 'There is a green hill far away').*

† Countess Constance Markievicz

and misery. He asked, 'You were teaching, weren't you? For how long?'

'Seven years. My father's a solicitor. A Catholic. But Mother insisted that we six daughters would be Church of Ireland Protestants like her. I still am. My six brothers? They're rock-solid Unionists, loyal to the King and can't be bothered with religion.'

Connolly was intrigued, 'Aye, but Constance Markievicz has convinced you and your sisters to be Irish nationalists and suffragettes. Seven years teaching? And yer've done some acting with Constance Markievicz in the theatre. Have yer no met any nice young men? ... Sorry! It's alright ...I ken! None of my business.'

She blushed, 'Matter of fact, there is a chap ... Joseph Donnelly of County Tyrone. But I don't know if ...' She shrugged. 'What about you, Jim Larkin? Yer not Irish-born?'

'Yer c'n prob'ly tell by me accent ... Scouser, me. Born in a Liver-poool schlum but me Mam and Da were Paddies. I started sch-kule when I was seven; went in der mornings and then work in dee afternoon. Doch-ker when I was sixteen, 'til I got the suck fer joinin' a union. Seems loi-kkke I'm never 'appier than mac-kkking any-mes. For example? That Irish Parliamen-ta-ree Par-tea, yer know ...the fellas still t'ink-king d'ey'll get Home Roo-le? Their leaders say I'm a t'ret to England's glace-cial movement to'ards Irish independence. Den d'ere's little Art-hur Griffith, the fella wot started Sinn Féin*. He hates me 'coz I'm a socialist. Who else hates me? Well, d'eres the Cat-a-lic higher-Rarchy what hate me for toleratin' Prod-testants ... An' der Trades Union Congress wot expelled me 'cos of me en-too-see-asm fer boycotts and sympathy stroykes; craa-ft unions hate me fer supportin' unskilled

---

* Sinn Fein was of little importance ... in 1913.

weer-kers. For me, there's no con-flict between Cath-olicism and Mar-ckk-sism. Ooo else 'ates me? The coppers a'course 'an Oi don't really like meself much either!' His great frame shook with laughter.

'Seriously though,' said Connolly, 'Catholicism and Marxism should be able to co-exist.[36] Jim here is much like me … neither of us smoke, swear, or drink alcohol. Yer know, Nellie, the union of Liverpool Dockworkers suspended him. So, he formed the Irish Transport and General Workers' Union and started a newspaper that named corrupt officials. He's alright is Mr Larkin! Which is why we started the Irish Labour Party together.'

Gifford pulled her Protestant shoulders back and looked at them both, 'Wonderful! So? So, what happens now? Dublin's unskilled workers have no job security. Dock workers are employed by the hour; unloading a cargo and paid a few pence; then made unemployed; then taken on again … if they've managed to push their way to the front at the gate … for another hour. Children ten years of age work 12 hours a day, seven days a week. Working conditions are notoriously unsafe.' She stared at them in turn, her voice growing quieter but more passionate, 'The Dublin community is the poorest, worst housed, and least healthy of any European city. Streets run with filth and TB is endemic. Irish children don't get free school dinners because the Archbishop of Dublin has warned against undeserving children being provided with food; the rest of Britain has had them for seven years!' She was determined to tell the two men what they already knew.

'Every Dubliner knows that young girls made pregnant by priests, or siblings, or their own fathers, are imprisoned in 'Magdalen Laundries' run by nuns[37]. They stay there, literally imprisoned forever, their babies having been taken from them, physically and psychologically abused as they wash the sheets of hospitals and prisons. It's as if nobody cares about them at all.'

Larkin looked at Connolly.

Gifford said, 'Well? Look ... We have to break William Murphy. The richest and most influential businessman in Dublin, he's got the England-Ireland ferry, the trams, three newspapers, a major retail store, and the Imperial, that posh and exclusive hotel in the centre of Dublin. His newspapers constantly say he prides himself on providing employment and having good relations with his workforce. And that he has a strong social conscience. If he has, then he's pathetically feeble in making use of it.'

Connolly agreed, 'We'll get 20,000 Dublin workers out on strike. Shut the city down.[38]'

Gifford tapped the table, 'He'll get his business pals to lock out the unskilled workers, sha yer know that as well as I do. It'll be a hell of a fight.'

Larkin stood up and said,'Yep. And it might take 6 months or more to make William Mair-feey see sense. So, we best get started.'

*

In the summer of 1913, 400 of Dublin's richest employers answered the call of Murphy, former politician and now international businessman, to lockout any worker that was a member of the Irish Transport and General Workers Union.

On Saturday 30th August, a woman phoned the Imperial Hotel and booked two rooms in the name of Donnelly, saying that her elderly uncle was going into hospital. Around 12:45pm next day she arrived at the hotel in a taxi with a very smartly dressed, bearded, elderly clergyman who said nothing but seemed to be deaf and very ill. A short time later he walked gently past the politicians and business-people enjoying their meals in the dining room, went into the smokeroom, holding an unlit cigar, and sat down. After a few minutes he jumped up, pulled off a false beard, and strode towards the balcony overlooking Sackville St. The floor to ceiling windows were open; he stepped out and waved vigorously to the crowd, mainly Sunday strollers, before roaring from a barrel-sized chest, 'Comrades and friends, the police have forbidden a meeting to take place in Sackville Street to-day but I, James Larkin, am here to speak and will remain till I'm arrested.' He didn't stay long. A huge number of police quickly arrived and dragged him away under arrest. More and more Dubliners, eager to find out what was happening, rushed to the hotel. Miss 'Donnelly', who was apparently an actress and expert in make-up, had disappeared.

The authorities were aware of Larkin's plan to give a speech. Riots had been occurring all over the city. There was a massive number of police on the streets eager to maintain, if not the peace, then their definition of law and order. In retrospect, probably too many police. Most of them had rushed to the Imperial Hotel, along with sightseers and locked-out workers. The inevitable happened; the crowd surged; the police pushed back; the crowd surged again. People fell over, got up and punched those that had knocked them down. Heavy wooden truncheons were used. And used. Again and again. Two workers died and many hundreds injured. The lockout went on for the rest of 1913[39].

On a Tuesday evening in September three children and four adults died when two Church Street tenements, filthy hovels packed with hundreds of human beings, collapsed. Jewish suffragette Dora Montefiore sent Larkin a note after hearing one of his speeches describing the horrors that Dublin children were suffering. Larkin had been considered anti-Semitic, but he met her and they devised the 'Kiddies Scheme' to send 300 starving children to families in England – the plan failed. The Catholic hierarchy claimed that the children would be misled and corrupted in comfortable Protestant homes and, on returning to Dublin, would be discontented with living conditions. Some apparent supporters of the strike, such as Arthur Griffith the head of a tiny Sinn Féin movement, derided the scheme and said it was an insult to Ireland. Priests and police attended railway stations to fiercely prevent parents and children, their tickets bought by suffragettes, from boarding trains. Montefiore was arrested and charged with kidnapping. Despite the opinions of many rank and file members, British union officials refused to approve a strike in support of the Dublin workers.

Wealthy Dubliners and many trade unionists had no sympathy for the unskilled strikers. Police used batons to break up meetings and many strikers were injured or killed. Women in the Jacob's Biscuit Factory were sacked for refusing to handle flour supplied by a company whose workers were on strike.

One of the biscuit workers was Alice Brady, member of the Irish Women Workers' Union.[40]

'Alice!'

'Yes, Ma?'

'We've no food, at all … get yersel off to wherever 'der handin' out the food parcels.'

'I was jus goin!' Alice was 16 years old and lived with her mother and father, two sisters and brother in one room in Asylum Yard, Trinity Ward, Dublin. In fact, there were another 76 people in Asylum Yard*. The slum 'cottages' had been built on what had once been the garden of a Magdalen Laundry in Townsend Street. One stinking, filthy outside toilet and a few unhygienic water fountains were the only facilities.[41]

She queued for a parcel of food supplied by union welfare workers and was going home when she passed a cordon of strikers trying to stop a coal delivery in Marks Street. She couldn't resist

---

* Now called Luke St

peering at the commotion and having a chat with some friends.

Patrick Traynor was one of the strike-breaking scabs. He was protected by police but, when the screaming cordon swayed towards him, he panicked and waved a gun. The sounds of screaming and shouting and cursing were silenced by the shooting.

'Arggh!' Alice screamed. She was hit in the hand. Somebody tried to bind the wound with a filthy rag and she was helped back to the Asylum Yard tenement. At first, after the bullet was extracted, there were signs of a recovery.

It would be more than seven days before Alice began having seizures and problems swallowing. Her facial muscles began clenching and her back arching. She had agonising pains throughout her body that became worse and worse. Tetanus. Her breathing became more and more laborious until after two weeks of agony, in Sir Patrick Dun's hospital, it stopped on January 1st, 1914.

Both Larkin and Connelly were in the huge crowd which attended her funeral. They each gave speeches. Connelly, perhaps recalling his own 13-year-old daughter's death, said that Alice had died as a result of the poverty in which they all lived and she was a martyr for freedom.

The starving Irish workers were eventually forced to admit defeat and compelled to swear not to join a union; only then were the gates re-opened. Workers at the Jacob's Biscuit Factory were the last to go back.

Larkin and Connolly realised that they needed to improve their tactics so that in future striking workers were physically protected. Connolly said to him, 'Mate … this fella, Jack White, is no fool. The Citizen Army idea makes sense…'

Larkin wasn't so sure, 'Yeah? … True, an Irish Citizen Army would be able to protect weer-kers from strike breakers and out of control police. But this Jack White? I know a bit about him. A British Arr-me officer, for goodness sake! Son of a Fee-ld Marshal, the Here-ro of Ladysmith!'

Connolly looked him in the eyes – it wasn't easy, him being so short and Larkin so tall. 'Well, he's a solid socialist noo, and no mistake. He's put up £50 to buy shoes for our union members, 'cos half of them have none. Yer can't march without ...'

Larkin's Liverpool accent became progressively stronger, 'Socialist iss'ee? 'ee'd have as much idea of what it's loike to stare-ve an' do wid-out as Winston Chair-chill ... fifty quid? ... that's all well 'n good ... Very noice of 'im ... Mind you, wid all der money that his ole man left 'im ... he c'n a-fford it ... I dunno. Yeah ... might be 'an-dy if he'd buy a caar ... ' Larkin was almost coming around to the idea of an army for protection.

'Och ... C'mon! ... if you listen to the man speakin', yer'll change yer mind about him ... disnae mind gettin' intae a shindy ... tall 'an handy with fists ... he reminds me of you ... apart from the accent!'

Larkin was almost convinced, 'Socialist? OK ... I'll give 'im a go ... and yeah, the Irish Citizen Arr-mee? The ICA? I do like that. What about The Looney? Countess Constance[*]? Mrs La-Dee-Dah English Ladyship.'

Connolly grinned. 'Yeah ... she's all for it too. But, hey, yer ken her husband's not really a Count? She's more communist than you. And ... she likes the idea of women being able to join the Citizen Army ... I'm all in favour o' that, too ... women c'n aim an' squeeze a trigger as well as a man ... Mind, I doot the men would be keen on drillin' an' marchin' wi'wimmen ... Aye, Constance is OK ... hates the Brits ... jus' that she smokes like a

---

[*] Constance Markievicz

volcano, ne'er min' a chimbley! I'm no keen on 'er arty-farty pals though. I'm strong for a republic too, like them ... but that lot? Too busy talkin' history and Gaelic ... dressin' up in flowery costumes ... 'an that's the men!'

Nellie Gifford had allowed the two of them to chatter on, 'What about me? What about the women? There'll be women wanting to be in this Army, so.'

Larkin laughed. 'If I was ... havin' a rifle pointed at me I couldn't care less whether it's a Jessy or a John what's squeezing the trigger ... I jus want 'em to miss ... What about the little journalist fella? Sheehy-Skeffington[*]?'

'Frank? He's all in favour of our Army idea as long as it disnae mean killin' people! ... I'm serious. A pacifist, would yer believe! ... Ah, well ... he's got his heart in the right place. Hates capitalists ... I think. No, he'd probably say he disnae hate anybody[42].'

---

[*] Mr and Mrs Sheehy Skeffington preferred the unhyphenated name, but many sources have Sheehy-Skeffington.

Chapter 11 – Self Respect for Ireland
"Children of misery and misfortune are not all illegitimate"

'Augustine, I've got ... the ... most awful headache. I feel terrible.'

'Yes, well. I've got Ireland ... had it for years ... how'd you think I feel?' Augustine Birrell*, Chief Secretary for Ireland and renowned for his wit, couldn't stop himself from thinking of a humorous response. He knew it was unkind and cruel so he resisted the temptation to actually say it.

His wife closed her eyes and asked, 'Will you ... will you be going back to Dublin next week?'

He put his hand on her forehead, even though he knew that she didn't have a temperature, 'Yes, I'm sorry, darling. I need to check some things at Dublin Castle ... I won't be leaving here though until Tuesday. The King wants to see me ... I could ask Doctor Grandage to call and give you some medication?' They were both aware that the doctor had already suggested the headaches could be a sign of something very serious. She wanted to smile, 'No, no. I'll be fine once it wears itself out. Are things progressing in Ireland?'

Birrell sat on the edge of the bed. 'Yes. I really think that independence is coming very soon. I just wish that I still had the Education portfolio instead of Ireland. I was happy writing my books and occasionally answering questions in Parliament about a school in, I don't know, Hampshire or teachers' wages. Ireland is just such an ... awful, awful ... shame.'

---

* St Augustine (died 430 AD) was a philosopher. People pray to him for better eyesight.

'Shame? That word has double meanings.'

'Yes. I've always argued for Home Rule. I'm not alone, of course. Others think that it's the logical and honourable thing ... but getting it legislated, especially when the Ulster Protestants are completely opposed, has been impossible until now'. He smiled wistfully, 'An independent Ireland. I really do think that it is achievable. Except ...'

'Except what?'

'Partition. It's the only way. Ulster, or parts of it anyway, will have to stay linked to England. The rest of Ireland will govern itself – but only on domestic issues. Not Defence, of course.'

'Well. That sounds fine. It is, isn't it?'

'Yes. Everybody knows it's the best way ... except the Irish Nationalists who want the whole of Ireland to be a single independent entity.'

'Well ... Why doesn't Prime Minister Asquith just tell the Nationalists they can have Independence within the Empire, but for only part of Ireland, not Ulster ... ?'

'Because Richmond's Nationalists would withdraw support for the Asquith Government. So, we must put up with threats from the Protestants and pretend that the whole of Ireland will be independent ... until we arrange partition and break off a portion, as the Protestants demand.'

'Isn't that ... hypocritical?'

'Yes, Eleanor. It is. But it's the only way. In years to come, if anybody remembers my part in all this, no doubt I'll be regarded as a hypocrite for not being completely open about everything[43]. But, of course, they won't ask themselves what they would have done if they were in my position.'

*

Buckingham Palace was an overbearing and unfriendly

bureaucracy. Superficially, everything was spotless and in the correct place, but a smell of stifled mustiness was hiding everywhere with a silence that seemed so enforced and so threatening that anyone rash enough to challenge it would be forever blighted as a traitor.

The uniformed butler stood motionless, staring at nothing. Birrell, seated on a very uncomfortable chair, was waiting outside a heavy, highly polished door. For the last 15 years he'd known that Ireland would have to be given some sort of independence sooner or later. The poverty and inequity there offended his sense of decency; he had no great liking for its people, but the British Government had always treated their country with disdain and failed to ensure the same level of concern as for the Welsh or Scots, let alone the English. Obviously, that was unfair to Ireland and Birrell being a decent man, knew it.[44]

A tinny-little bell rang not far away; the butler quickly turned and opened the door. Birrell entered nervously, took the required number of paces, and bowed his head.

'Ah, Birrell,' the 48-year-old King didn't look up from his desk, 'sit yer-self down.'

'Thank you, Your Majesty.'

'How's your wife? I believe she's unwell?'

Birrell stared at the balding head. 'Yes, Your Majesty ... it's ... apparently ... her brain ... incurable.' The King looked up and Birrell saw the heavy bags under world-weary eyes, 'Ah ... not good ... I am sorry. A heavy burden for you, of course?'

'Indeed ... with me needing to spend so much time in Parliament ... she finds it very hard. Apart from the pain, being left alone. Actually, we both do. Find it hard, I mean.'

'Yes ... yes ... Well ... Ireland ... what's your latest view? Tell me about the Irish Nationalists ... and Redmond ... Is he really still expecting to get total independence?'

Birrell pursed his lips. 'Redmond is ... a good and honourable man ... I think that even he ... now realises that Ulster will have to be excluded and ...'

'Really? That's not what he's saying. I read in the newspapers he's still wanting total independence.'

'What he says, Your Majesty, is one thing. He's juggling many demands from supporters and enemies ... it's impossible for all those demands to be satisfied ... I'm sure that he has become aware of the realities.'

'Hmmm ... so when is he going to ... come to his senses and publicly acknowledge that Ulster will have to be excluded?'

'I think, Your Majesty, he's waiting to see if Protestant people in Ulster are as ... determined ... and willing to fight a British Government ... as Edward Carson says they are. Redmond though still thinks they are just bluffing and that they won't oppose Asquith's mandate to govern.'

'A mandate to govern ... govern, yes ... but does Asquith have the electorate's support to make Ireland independent? He kept it quiet during the last election, eh? Does he have the public's support? Edward Carson and many many Ulstermen think not? Only an election would decide the matter ... but that's not for me to propose ... unless ... well, heaven forbid that I would ever need to formally make that suggestion.'

'Your Majesty, my opinion is that Carson is a rabble-rouser. As to whether he'd really be able to induce many in Ulster to go to war against the British Government, I very much doubt.'

'Hmm. He does though have a lot of support, and not just in Ulster. Plenty in England ... Scotland ... in the colonies, even the Army. Support from people ... some people ... who don't like to see Protestants being coerced into living within a Catholic country. And, yer know, I can ... Anyway ... what do you think?'

'I can certainly understand their concerns, Your Majesty.

Nevertheless, the British Government would retain numerous significant powers. Ireland would stay in the Empire. We should also remember that the Irish people, with their ancient and unique traditions, have had their freedoms trampled upon by, what can only be described as, a foreign nation.' Birrell was aware that he was probably at risk of poking an old and irritable lion.

The King looked enquiringly at Birrell. 'Some people might say so. I recall reading something that you'd written … long ago …some article or essay … on Nationalism* … you mentioned Niobe … the goddess whose children were slain and then, turned to stone, she weeps unceasingly … like Ireland?'

'I also wrote that the children of misery and misfortune are not all illegitimate …'

'Indeed,' the King looked at Birrell as if wondering what to make of him. 'Well, thank you for your time, Birrell … Perhaps we should end this session with the conclusion you wrote in that essay.' He looked at a book open at his elbow, '*The luxury of self-respect is a wise phrase. To make Ireland and Irishmen self-respectful is the task of statesmen.*' Thank you, Birrell.'

'Your Majesty.' He stood, bowed and waited for the King to end the session – 'I hope to God that there are amongst us … some true statesmen ... with integrity and decency … Goodbye, Birrell.'

The door closed silently. King George lit another cigarette and sucked deeply, savouring the smoke as it flooded into his lungs … and then coughed. And coughed. 'Poor old Birrell. Wife probably going to a lunatic asylum. Backwards and forwards to Ireland. People constantly asking him why he doesn't do this, do that. Nobody volunteering to take his place though.' Cigarettes never seemed to last long enough these days.

---

* Essay on 'Nationality' in *Res Judicatae* by Birrell, 1892

He put his hands to his head and sighed. Four years on the throne but it was more like a century. How can it be that thousands and thousands of Ulstermen could claim loyalty to Britain whilst also pledging to fight against their monarch's legally elected government? Was it really true that, as he'd been informally told by senior politicians and military staff, that some of his own Army officers would refuse to obey an order if it meant opposing Carson's Volunteers? An officer refusing to obey an order? Do they not understand the word 'treason'?

He walked to the window, hands behind his back. 'Damn, damn, damn! I wish Asquith would drink less ... He once said ... It's in this book somewhere ... here ... here, I've found it ... Asquith said, *'The interests of the community as a whole ought to be paramount over the interests of any class, any interest, or any section which that community contains. That is the root and spring of Liberalism'*. Why is it that Liberals have such wonderful ideals but can never follow them? There ought to be an election. But nothing will make me pressure him to call one. That's not my role nor duty ...'

He fumbled for another cigarette. So perfect; so reliably predictable and comforting. 'Didn't that queer chap, Wilde, say something much the same?[45]' He relaxed as the yellow flame of a match, with its acrid smell, touched the sweet tobacco. He sucked and immediately coughed long and hard.

' ... Do they not understand that I'm a servant of the Empire? A servant. The black fella sitting in the dust fifty miles from Alice Springs is not 'my' subject, nor is the Amritsar child in the Punjab, nor any of the poor buggers dying of hunger in a Dublin tenement. No. I'm 'their' subject, here to serve them all ... Muslims, Protestants and Catholics, Black fellas and Irish. Men. Women and children ... as best I can ... I must, I must, do whatever I can to keep all people within the Empire safe ... and secure. I swore to rule with justice and mercy and uphold the law. That was my oath. The one I swore on the Bible. It's me that will have to answer to God if I break that oath.'

He sat at his desk and began writing a memorandum to the Prime Minister. It is clear, he wrote, 'many people in Ulster are prepared to go to war in order to prevent them being made answerable to an Irish Government in Dublin. That being the case, and Home Rule occurring, Ulster must be excluded since, to prevent bloodshed, its Protestant peoples must not be forced' ... and yet, he was still unsure whether it was the correct course to take.

It would be several weeks before Asquith formally replied, basically agreeing. But the Prime Minister's secretly preferred policy, summarised by David Lloyd George, was the same as it was for most issues – to allow matters to take their course and do nothing.

Meanwhile, Carson and Craig were preparing for the legislation leading to Ireland's independence. As soon as that happened a government, consisting of their Protestant supporters, would take control in Ulster. The administrative details of the various departments, finance, law, education and so on, were all worked out. There was no intention to leave the monarchy or Empire. Business supporters agreed to create a £1,000,000 fund to compensate families of Ulster volunteers killed or injured if there was any opposition. 12,000 Protestants had registered to fight if need be. Meanwhile, Churchill and F.E. Smith ate and drank together – and intrigued.

In Downing Street, Asquith grinned at Lloyd George, his deputy, 'I think our secret discussions with the Irish parliamentarians went rather well, David.'

The great leonine head of Lloyd George was totally untroubled with niceties such as trust and honesty, 'Yes. It was only a slight blurring of the truth for you to tell them that the King, fearing Civil War, was demanding a general election.'

Asquith swallowed some whisky and immediately wanted another mouthful. He mused, 'Well, His Majesty did refer to Civil War and I'm sure that he raised the issue of an election ... anyway, it was important for us to remind them that an election would result in us losing Government and the Tories taking over...'

Lloyd George continued Asquith's comment,' ... and the Tories would squash any chance of Home Rule, which would mean all John Redmond's hopes were trashed. He must agree to our conditions for Home Rule or he gets the Tories and no Home Rule at all. I've had Birrell make it all very clear to them.'

Prime Minister Asquith smiled. Good old Birrell. It was handy to have him doing the dirty work ... but he did have a tendency to lack ... subterfuge. He was useful for the time being. 'Yes, David, Birrell's told them. Most of Ireland would be given a level of independence but some Ulster counties are to be excluded and stay under British administration. After six years the exclusion will cease and the whole of Ireland will be governed from Dublin, remain within the monarchy and still be in the Empire.'

'Would Ulster agree to that after six years, Prime Minister?'

'We'll have to wait and see.' He laughed, knowing that it was a favourite response for which he was often criticised.

'And Redmond agreed?'

'He had no choice.'

'And Carson?'

'He'll pretend to be furious. But the Ulster Protestants have won the fact that exclusion is acceptable. They'll think they can fiddle with that to make it permanent. Maybe they can, but this agreement will delay the whole thing whilst we continue to govern.'

'Beware the horns of a bull, the heels of the horse, and the smile of an Englishman.' James Joyce

Chapter 12 – March 1914

Clementine found it difficult to understand. She shook her head, put down her cup of tea and looked at Churchill.

'Winston, this is … madness. The Irish business, I mean. Tell me if I have this wrong. The intention is for a temporarily partitioned Ireland … the bulk of it governed from Dublin. The "Protestant North East" would … be excluded and stay under Westminster administration, the boundaries to be decided, somehow or other but nobody is saying how. The actual number of counties hasn't been decided – some counties in the North East have more Catholics than Protestants. And there's going to be a border running through some villages. Is that correct, Winston?'

'Clemmie, Clemmie, we've done the best we could. We will never force Ulster Protestants against their wishes to be under a Dublin administration. But the Irish Nationalists will never give up their demands for self-government; they're demanding the whole of Ireland. And that's simply not going to happen. This exclusion will be legislated to last for just six years. After which time the Ulster people can decide …'

She took the risk of interrupting him, 'If Ulster didn't want to break from Britain now, why would it change its mind in six years' time? Ulster will never agree to being ruled from Dublin, you know that … Never. You said it yourself.'

'Yes. But six years is a long time. Anything can happen. The Government can focus on things other than Ireland. Perhaps the Nationalists will become less … obsessive about wanting the whole of Ireland.'

'Winston. We both know the truth. The benefit for the Liberal Government is that it's a solution … for them and them alone because the problem can be forgotten for six years.'

Churchill laughed, 'My dear, it's a win all round. The Ulster Protestants have won acknowledgement that exclusion is a policy.

The Irish Nationalists, like the leader of the Irish Parliamentary Party John Redmond, can pretend that they've won Home Rule. True, they'll still be within the Empire with allegiance to the King, who is of course the Head of the Church of England, and London will hold most of the significant powers ... but a Dublin government could take responsibility for some administration and a few important issues – and they can call it Home Rule.' He rubbed his chubby fingers happily.

The problem was that some Conservatives, such as Carson, didn't see it the same way. They opposed any possibility whatsoever, even one postponed for six years, of being forced to live under a Catholic government.

Carson gave a mock-angry speech in Parliament saying that it was like being sentenced to die but with the execution delayed for six years; hearing Carson, Churchill told F.E. Smith that the Asquith Government wasn't going to back down. A short time later Birrell told the Cabinet that Ulster was accumulating weapons – Lloyd George wanted the situation to be brought to a head.

March 14th, 1914

Churchill, having told Asquith what he intended to do and, with very strong encouragement from Lloyd George, gave a fiery speech in Bradford to the effect that any revolutionary action by Ulster Protestants would be dealt with quickly and firmly. His repetitive, florid, and inspiring phrases were similar to those that he would later use in defiance of Hitler. In the morning, he luxuriated in the praise flowing from fellow Liberals who'd read the speech in the newspapers.

March 17th, St. Patrick's Day, 1914

Churchill was deliriously happy. He was as much in his element as the biggest, busiest, boar in the piggery. Birrell reported to the Cabinet that there were more than 80,000 Ulster Volunteers with 17,000 rifles. Asquith's Government was led to understand that the Protestants in the north were clearly ready to attack police stations and barracks. Churchill, First Lord of the Admiralty, was energised and eager for action. Troops in England were made ready to be transported to protect government property in Ulster. But he was concerned with far more than defending arms depots. Naval reservists were called up. Ulster police were to be quickly re-organised under a single command, patrol boats increased surveillance, and a huge Royal Naval fleet of destroyers and cruisers was instructed to take on board troops and sail to Ulster.

Asquith gave an almost honest, and fairly complete, summary of the Cabinet's intentions to the King. Lloyd George was content – everything was proceeding according to plan. His plan.

March 18th, 1914

John Seely, Secretary of War, chaired a sub-committee meeting to discuss the preparations to deal with Ireland, and especially Ulster, in detail. Was it all a ruse by him and Churchill to goad the Ulster Unionists? Possibly, but probably not – that would suggest a capability for strategic genius which Seely notoriously lacked.

He was a Captain during the Boer War when Churchill was a lieutenant – they both therefore, of course, regarded themselves as military experts. Others at the Cabinet sub-committee meeting thought differently. For example, General Sir Arthur Henry Fitzroy Paget, commanding the Army in Ireland, and Field Marshal John Denton Pinkstone French, Chief of the Imperial General Staff.

Major-General Henry Wilson, Director of Military Operations (basically military intelligence), was not at the meeting and had no reason to be involved with its decision-making. He'd been born in central Ireland; in England he spoke with an Irish accent but in Ireland he spoke with an English one. Perhaps it was an example of colonial mimicry*. He was certainly regarded by many as being one of the most two-faced British soldiers ever to wear a military uniform. Others argued that this couldn't be true, because if he had two faces why would he appear in public with that one.

When the meeting ended, French rushed off to tell the obnoxious Wilson what was discussed. Wilson then breached the Official Secrets Act by passing the details on to the leader of the Tory Opposition, Andrew Bonar Law, and to Edward Carson. This was treason, Carson being the head of the organisation that the British Army was expecting to fight. Senior military officers and politicians were breaking the law just as surely Doctor Crippen and Oscar Wilde had broken the law; but unlike those two they were never brought to trial. The other difference was that many of those who had sworn to defend the Crown, but defied it, were to be awarded medals, honorary doctorates, and state funerals.

Thursday 19th March 1914

Lady Londonderry made an early morning call on Carson and gave him news confirming the information about army and naval movements that he had already received from Wilson. A contact in Dublin had told her that the Asquith government planned to give Ulster a fright in the coming week. That afternoon, Carson gave a speech to Parliament where he boasted about his newly acquired knowledge and then returned, in much haste, to Ulster. Some people thought that he was in danger of being arrested for proposing war with His Majesty's Forces. Seely let it be known that he was expecting Carson to form a provisional government and that the Protestant Ulster Volunteers were being raised to readiness. Intelligence reports gave a strong indication that they were verging on rebellion and military action.

---

* Bhabha, Homi. "Of Mimicry and Man: The Ambivalence of Colonial Discourse."

The next few days were possibly the most tumultuous in British Army peacetime history.

Friday, 20th March 1914

At 11.30 a.m., Asquith called a meeting of the Cabinet Defence Committee. They authorised the deployment of troops from the Copeland Islands, County Down, in Northern Ireland. At the same time, 10,000 troops were to embark from Liverpool and the naval base at Larne, in County Antrim, was to be fortified. It's said that Carson joked that when Churchill and the troops arrived at Larne he would have a welcoming party waiting for them.

Sunday, 22nd March 1914

'The King is furious.'

'What did you say, darling?' Venetia Stanley, 26 years old, was in bed and suddenly alert. She levered herself up, elbow on the pillow, and stared across at 61-year-old Herbert Asquith, stretched out in his striped pyjamas, 'The King wants General Paget gone. Sacked.'

She chuckled. 'Oooo ... Come on ... I've heard a little about the goings on ... tell me the lovely details. Just between us.'

He laid back, hands behind his head, and ogled her. 'Alright. I'll tell you ... but only because you've got the most wonderful breasts I've ever seen ... Er ... Oh, yes ... General Paget has been doing nothing much in Ireland ... probably thinking it better not to disturb sleeping Irishmen. But we'd been getting information that some of Carson's crowd were planning to march on Dublin. So, we dragged Paget back here to a high-level meeting. Myself, French ... Seely and Churchill[*] ... we told him that Ireland could blow up in flames due to Carson and Craig's crazy Orangemen.

---

[*] Field Marshal Sir John French; John Seely, Secretary of State for War; Winston Churchill (First Lord of the Admiralty)

Well, Churchill and Seely instructed him to ensure the military barracks are protected. They said there's a high risk of a Protestant uprising and promised to give him all the naval and military support he needed ... '

'Really! And you, darling? You were involved?'

'Of course. Birrell was there, too. We had to make sure Field Marshal French didn't ... try to downplay the urgency. Anyway, fortunately Paget wasn't given any written instructions.'

'Ah-ha. Clever.'

'And Paget? What did he do wrong?'

'Well, he dashes off to Dublin and has a conference with the Generals and Colonels.'

'Yes?'

'First, he tells them not to take any notes. And then says there's a danger of Civil War and British troops must prepare for action ... but they won't be shooting anybody unless the Ulster people shoot first. Tells them that everybody must be very soldierly and obey orders. Basically ... officers and men cannot pick and choose between lawful and reasonable orders – they can't announce that they will obey in one case and not in another.'

'Well? That's all good. Isn't it?'

'Yeeesss. And it's what Seely, Secretary of War, told them last December – when there was gossip about military people refusing to confront Ulstermen ... It would have been perfectly fine if Paget had stopped there. He went on to say that any officer, even if they had friends at the War Office, who refused to obey orders would be kicked out of the army. Seely then looked at Brigadier General Hubert Gough and told him that Sir John French wouldn't be able to save him ... Argh! Sometimes, I think soldiers are worse than politicians ... always holding grievances, never forgetting slights, taking revenge ...'

'Well ... '

'Hang on. I'm not finished. He then said that any officer whose home was in Ulster could ... simply disappear for a few weeks ... and come back when it was all over. Said that it was a concession won with the support of Field Marshal French.'

'Disappear? Oh ... good gracious me. No wonder the King's upset.'

'... especially because Paget stressed several times to those officers that the King had sanctioned what he was telling them ... Whether it was Paget's own idea or if Seely agreed with it ... who knows. It meant the officers wouldn't be ordered to do something ... that they didn't want to do. For other officers, it was ... do as you're told or you'll be sacked. Hubert Gough has Ulster friends and relatives, but his home is in the South. He wouldn't be allowed to resign ... he'd be dismissed from the Army ... sacked.'

'Gosh! ... Darling ... that's ... well, ridiculous.'

'Yes. You know that and I know that ... Paget ended up by telling them to go and talk to their subordinates and get a list of names of officers who would refuse to obey an order to fight the Ulster people ... So, off they went to the Curragh ...'

'That's the big Army Camp outside Dublin?'

'Yes ... and they returned with a whole swag of names; most of them in Gough's brigade. Gough telephoned his brother John, a Brigadier-General at Aldershot, told him what had happened and that he was sending in his resignation even if Paget refused to accept it.'

'Oh dear, I must say I sympathise with Gough ... from my viewpoint, as a member of the public. An officer gets special treatment but only if his home is in Ulster ... he can go absent. An officer from the South is required to obey orders. Of course, if he's an ordinary Private or Sergeant whatever ... regardless of coming from Ulster ... if he refuses to obey orders, then he'll be charged and punished, possibly shot. I mean, it's as if the Army and the Government are condoning mutiny by certain people whilst threatening to punish others such as Gough.'

Asquith sighed with frustration at Venetia's refusal to understand, 'Look ... it's not mutiny ... no officer has disobeyed an order ... because they haven't actually been given one.'

'Oh? Riiiiight ... No, not right! Not really ... Is that the best way to run an Army? Allowing officers to do what they want according to their political feelings? Especially if we could be at war with Germany in a few years ... ?'

'Before I tell you any more ... I want to know what you've been doing. I hear gossip that you've been getting up to mischief with your smart set of young ones? In that night club ... The Cave of the Golden Calf*? Alcohol? Decadence? Goodness knows what sort of improper behaviour. Was my daughter Violet involved?'

Venetia giggled. 'No, Violet's too proper. Anyway ... without her, you and I wouldn't have met. She's ... very dear to me, you know.'

'Hmm. Yes ... You're both very ... attached, I know. What about Edwin Montague? He's a clever chap ... is he still pursuing you? Never mind, don't answer that. But what about the decadent get together, who was there?'

'Well ... lots of people that you wouldn't know ... but others ... maybe you do know. Diana Cooper of course. And her sister Majorie ... who's married to Charles Paget! There's obviously some link there to your Arthur Paget, the poor Army chap that's made a mess in Ireland. And Edward Horner, gasping after Diana ... he's training to be a barrister and wants Churchill's Tory pal Freddie Smith to help him. I suppose you know that Raymond was there?'

'My son, Raymond? Was he? Not surprised. He's getting a bit old for that sort of thing though. He 'd better be careful if he wants

---

* Avant garde nightclub in a basement close to Regent St

to know what's good for him ...'

'Old? He's barely ... what, ten years older than me? Actually, he was very well-behaved ... almost kept us under control! Gosh, I must tell you this. Before we got too tiddly, people were talking about schools. Who knew who and so on. And someone said something about all your sons going to Winchester College ... Apparently Raymond was there at the same time as Edward Grigg, who used to be a writer on colonial things at the Times. And ... what was his name ... oh, yes, smarty-pants chap named Warren Fisher ... making a nuisance of himself in ... Treasury, I think. See, I try to remember this stuff because I know you like the gossip.'

'You are wonderful, Venetia. Winchester College schoolboys? ... Did ... Raymond ... or anybody mention a person named ... White? James or Jack White?'

'No. No ... why?'

'Mr White's name has appeared in ... some confidential reports ... in connection with Ireland. He's been involved in the Dublin lockout strike and given speeches to support Home Rule. Raymond saw a newspaper report of his father being a VC winner and guessed it was the same White with whom he'd been at school ... he recalled a Debating Society speech by White about Cromwell and Ireland.

'How very odd ...'

'Yes, but Venetia ... and I stressed this to Raymond ... the Winchester link with White is not publicised. Especially if Raymond is to be the Liberal candidate in Derby ... So ...'

'Oh, absolutely. Mum's the word. ... now tell me all about War-Office-Paget and the Army.'

'Well. Let's see. After Paget's ultimatum to the officers ... it looked like most of them in Ireland were going to resign. Alright, I'm exaggerating. But all of Gough's people ... Paget sent names and details by telegram at 7pm on Friday to the War Office.

Apparently, the Ulster Unionists and officers in Aldershot had already been told everything by telephone before 6pm. But me? Prime Minister? I wasn't told until midnight. And yesterday, as you know, the Times had something about the officers' resignations. The King gave Seely a rare old roasting today.'

'Did the King say anything to you, darling?'

'Hmm. Never mind about that ... confidential. Anyway ... Today, I told Seely and Churchill to cancel all the military and naval operations affecting Northern Ireland. Information was passed to *The Times* explaining that there was never going to be a confrontation with Ulster, simply a reorganisation of troops. No orders were disobeyed, so certainly not a mutiny ... more of a ... oh ... an *incident*, due to a misunderstanding. I'll make it known that in future officers will not be given options based upon hypothetical situations.'

'And Gough?'

'He's been told to appear in front of Seely and Field Marshal French at the War Office first thing tomorrow. They'll order him to take back his resignation and to get his Brigade officers to do the same. Depending upon how the situation flows, comments in the Press, Question Time and so on ... I may need to accept Seely's resignation. And then I'll take over as Minister of War in addition to my current role.'

'Oh?'

'If I do, I'll need to resign from Parliament and seek re-election by my constituents.'

'What?!'

'It's a requirement ... anybody taking a new Cabinet post, Prime Minister or not, must resign and stand for re-election. There's nothing to worry about ... I doubt that anybody will run against me. Even if they do, I'll be re-elected.'

'But ... '

'The benefit is that, for three weeks at least, the Opposition won't be able to ask about this business in Question Time. I will promise the House of Commons that 'The army will hear nothing of politics from me and in return I expect to hear nothing of politics from the army'. When I come back, things will have moved on.'

'Oh, darling. You are clever. Weaving such a web ... '

Unfortunately, events did not flow quite as planned and the web was not only tangled but also slightly torn.

Monday, 23rd March, 1914

General Sir Hubert de la Poer Gough had been in the army for 25 years. His family home was in the southern county of Waterford; his grandfather was a Catholic and had been a Liberal Member of Parliament. Although born in London and educated in England, he considered himself to be Irish and avoided politics. His quick temper, intelligence, and tendency to independence made him plenty of friends but also many enemies.

In accordance with the orders from General Paget, he'd taken the ferry from Dublin and was on his way to the War Office. Nervous? Yes, he was. But only in a way that heightened his awareness of danger and strengthened the determination not to be cowed by those who were in a weaker position than he was. He had always known and accepted that officers had no right to question an order to support civilian powers. If he had been ordered to take his brigade to Ulster, then he would have done so. But he had never been given that order. He'd been offered two alternatives, and he had taken one. It was a stupid offer but it was made by a senior officer in the form of an ultimatum. Gough was in the right and he was not going to back down.

He stepped out of the taxi, paid the fare, and walked through the heavy doors of the War Office. Britain's Establishment – if you didn't fit in with them, then you weren't one of them. You were on your own. In the numerous offices, scarlet-faced Majors and hyphenated Colonels had been watching out of windows and seen him arrive. They scurried to close their doors – the corridors oddly empty. Identifying himself when he eventually found, knocked upon and opened the nominated door, he was shown into a small room with a bare desk and three chairs. He sat and waited.

Field Marshal French entered as if expecting to be attacked by Zulu warriors. The Adjutant-General, Ewart, was slightly behind him. Gough stood and saluted.

French, somewhat relieved, almost smiled. 'Morning, Hubert … please sit down. Look … this is bit of a pickle, eh? Obviously complete balls-up. Total misunderstanding, eh? What?'

'Not a misunderstanding, sir. Not on my part.'

French stopped smiling. 'Very well … now … You, listen to me. This is what you're going to do. You will return to Ireland and resume your duties as if nothing had happened … understood?'

'Yes Sir, I will. But, under the circumstances as they are, I and my officers must be confident that we will not be ordered to enforce on Ulster the present Home Rule Bill.'

'Certainly. I now give that assurance.' French stood up.

'Sorry, sir. In writing. I must insist … that I have it in writing.'

French's face coloured. His teeth glittered, 'What did you say?'

'Sorry, sir. But it must be in writing.'

'My word … as a British officer … not good enough?'

'Sorry sir … that's how it must be. In writing.'

Almost a minute passed. Gough stared at French, French stared at Gough and said, 'Very well, then. Perhaps the Secretary of War can make you see sense. Wait here. I'll see if he's available.' Ewart stood up and then sat back down and fidgeted in his chair.

10 minutes later French returned and quietly said, 'Come with us.'

They walked down the corridor. Up a short flight of stairs and then down another corridor. Ewart tapped on a door. They waited.

A fresh-faced young man with delicate skin, in a charcoal-grey suit, white shirt and winged collars, opened the door. He smiled as if he were meeting his in-laws for the first time.

'We'd like to see Mr. Seely.'

'Certainly, gentlemen ... he's with General Paget but I'm sure he'll see you immediately ... this way.'

When they trooped in Seely sighed and glared at each of them, one by one. 'Sit down, gentlemen.' They all obeyed.

French ran his hands down his trousers. Ewart cleared his throat. The minute hand on the clock clicked down.

Seely started quietly. 'I must say ... I'm disappointed. That officers ... in His Majesty's Army ... should behave in this fashion ... I mean ... Really?' He looked at Gough. Gough looked back at him, expressionless, mouth gently clenched.

'For God's sake man! Do you know what you're doing? We must be able to give orders to the Army and know that those orders will be carried out. Did they not teach you these things at Sandhurst? Sometimes the maintenance of law and order will require the use of a degree of force. Don't you agree?' He didn't wait for a reply. 'You can withdraw your resignation and tell the others to do the same. The Prime Minister has made it crystal clear ... the Government will not be coercing the people of Ulster to do anything against their will. Will you now accept that assurance?'

'I will, Sir ... if it's in writing.'

Seely stared. A slight red glow appeared on his cheeks.

'Listen to me, Gough. Whilst I'm Secretary of War, no soldier ... I don't care who they are ... whatever their rank, or family ... no soldier will dictate to the Government what it can and cannot do. D'you understand?'

'Yes, Sir ...'

Seely began a half smile. But he was too soon.

'... nevertheless ... I must have it in writing.'

Seely's fingers drummed on the table, 'You want the assurance in writing? You don't trust Field Marshal French? General Paget? The Prime Minister? Me? You don't trust any of us here?'

'It's not that, Sir, ... '

'Then why? Tell us why you want it in writing! But please don't just say Current Circumstances or the ... past Grave Misunderstandings.'

The government-issue clock on the mantelpiece, slowly and noisily, tick-tocked.

Seely sighed. 'I must say I find this astonishing ... Yer went to Eton, for goodness sake! I'd heard such good things of you ... but here you are ... with your family's honourable background! ... willing to trash the reputation and traditions of the British Army. And for what? Your own selfish glorification! Extraordinary!'

Tick. Tock. Tick. Tock.

French coughed nervously and whispered, 'May I suggest ... Gough has taken a stand ... for something that he believes is right ... and it is going to be very difficult for him to make a recommendation, to his officers, in line with what we're asking. In order to retain the respect of his subordinates ... I can see that ... he feels something in writing is needed?'

Gough moved his head sideways, 'That does rather sum up the situation. Thank you, Sir.'

Seely was silent for a moment. 'Well ... why didn't you ... I really will not have it said that we bowed to intimidation ... but ... Arthur ... I think that a suitable form of words could be prepared?'

General Arthur Paget quickly agreed, 'Yes, yes. I ... we ... can ...'

'Very well, Ewart ... French will help you ... draft a memorandum for Cabinet consideration. Gough? You'll return here at 4pm and you'll get your ... memo ... from Cabinet ... which, I'm sure, will meet the current needs of everyone. Close the door on your way out.'

Ewart and French came up with a three-paragraph memorandum for consideration by Cabinet. It was nondescript, referring to misunderstandings and the need to obey all lawful orders. It also included a conciliatory sentence to the effect that the Cabinet was pleased to have learnt from Gough that there never was, and never will be, any intention to disobey lawful orders. But it made no reference to the Home Rule Bill or the need to enforce it. Perhaps the intention was to focus on the military aspect and omit anything to do with politics.

During the following Cabinet discussion Seely left the room because the King wanted an appraisal of what was happening. By the time he returned, the Cabinet had finalised the document and ended the meeting. Unfortunately, Seely then decided that the memorandum wasn't quite to his own liking. With some assistance from Lord Morley, he added another 2 paragraphs. One was bland, almost repeating previous phrases. The final paragraph attempted to describe, in one poorly-worded sentence, Seely's own interpretation of, Government policy. It said that the Government had 'no intention whatever of taking advantage of the right to crush political opposition to the policy or principles of the Home Rule Bill.' Seely's thinking as he made the amendments can only be guessed. Perhaps he thought Gough would refuse to accept something without a reference to Home Rule and a Government promise to not coerce Ulster. Presumably he didn't even consider whether Asquith and other Cabinet members would mind his independent addition.

There was to be yet more blundering. Field Marshal French was in a hurry to tell the King everything was settled. But Gough, his colonels, and his brother and Henry Wilson, understandably wanted to read the memorandum before formally accepting it. The final paragraph, with its awkward wording, stood out like a drunken Sergeant-Major inspecting the guard at Sandhurst Military College. Gough wrote a note and attached it to the document saying that the final paragraph was understood as meaning that 'troops under our command will not be called upon to enforce the present Home Rule Bill on Ulster'. Field Marshal French added his agreement to this interpretation.

Gough returned to Dublin and Sir Henry Wilson went back to his own military staff. They both leaked details of everything to the Press and to the Tory Opposition.

As to be expected, Asquith faced ridicule. He said that the final two paragraphs were not approved and that Gough's interpretation was not correct. French, Seely, and Ewart resigned and Asquith took over responsibility for the Secretary of War role. Churchill, unsurprisingly, conducted a glorious tactical rearguard action in Parliament. His speech was one of his best. He attacked the Tories for supposedly being the Party of correctness and Law and Order, whilst they were also conniving with enemies of the British Government and planning to fight against His Majesty's forces in a Civil War. If one did occur, then it would be due to them, and it would be put down with all the vigour that the Government could bring to play.

Enormous damage had been done to the Army's reputation. The relationship of the Military with politicians would take decades to heal. Squabbles and distrust between senior staff would persist. The impact on the Armed Forces ability to operate effectively can only be guessed. And much of it was due to the machinations of one man – Major-General Sir Henry Wilson, later to be a Field Marshal and Chief of the Imperial General Staff. He received honorary degrees from Oxford, Cambridge, Trinity College Dublin and Queen's University Belfast.

None of that helped when he stepped out of a taxi and walked to the front door of his home in Eaton Place, Belgravia, on 22nd

June 1922. Reginald Dunn (spelt without an 'e' in the 1911 Census) and Joseph O'Sullivan were Londoners. Dunn had been in the Irish Guards. O'Sullivan had been injured at Ypres and a leg was amputated. They were both now members of the IRA and they shot Wilson as if he were a rabid dog. Dunn escaped but he returned to help O'Sullivan who was being beaten unconscious by the crowd that gathered around the gasping Wilson. The Field Marshal was given a massive state funeral and mourned by many in the British Government, though not by all. Dunn and O'Sullivan were given a day's trial, hanged, and a quicklime burial.

Chapter 13 – Rifles Go Leor*

'This rifle of yours is feck'n filthy.' Michael Mallin, Chief Training Officer of the Irish Citizen Army, was obviously not happy. Dublin-born, he had been in the British Army for almost 14 years but never rose above the rank of drummer. One reason was insubordination, the other was a clear tendency to express socialist ideals. That was a while back, ten years or more. As a former soldier, he'd been welcomed by James Connolly.

A young lad, taking back the rifle, looked as though he might burst into tears. It had been his father's and his grandfather's before that. Connolly took Mallin to one side and whispered, 'C'mon, Mick. Dinna be sae hard on the wee fella. He's doing his best. We need more like him. We've barely got 200.'

Mallin thought for a few seconds and turned, 'Here ... have a look down there, son ... Go on! Good long look. Have yer ever used a pull-through to clean it? ... look at it down there! The only place you'd see more feck'n shit than that ... is if yer'd lifted up Queen Victoria's skirt and looked at her feck'n arse. '

The young fella giggled.

Mallin held up a long cord. 'Here, I'll show yer how to use this ... but first, I want you all of youse to listen to what I have to say.' The other men gathered round.

'You must treat a rifle with respect. OK? Keep it clean. It's a rifle ... for firing. Firing at Woodbines†; not yer mates. Don't laugh – Cupla weeks ago Tom Clarke got a bullet in his arm thanks

---

* Go Leor = A'plenty

† 'Woodbines'=British Troops (their cigarette issue was Woodbines)

to someone playing silly buggers wid' a gun. A rifle's not for poking at things. And never ... NEVER ... use the butt to smash a glass window. Use something else like the leg of a chair or a broomstick or ... a spade. If yer use the rifle butt ... what's maybe gonna happen? Safety switch is off, yer finger's close to the trigger and ... BANG ... yer've just done the Tommies' job for 'em ... shot yer pal in the guts. Or else the bullet's gone through a window behind yer and into a 5-year-old child's head. So? Do not use the butt to smash on a door or break win-ders! ... Unless ordered to ...'

Later, he was drinking tea with Connolly. 'Jim, what's going on with that Pearse fella? The one that runs Saint Enda's school. That's a queer how's-yer-father, so it is.'

Connolly put his mug down carefully. 'Patrick Pearse? Aye, he's got some funny ideas. No chance of Lillie and me sending our Roddy to Saint Enda's, although Larkin's boys are there. But Pearse ... well, he's very strong on Ireland's culture and Gaelic traditions ... and there's nobody more passionate for Ireland's Independence. He's one of the leaders of the Irish Volunteers.'

Mallin frowned. 'That bunch? A lot of people that otherwise would be joining us, are going with them.'

'Och, well. Some people with influence, mostly academics and literary types, started the Irish Volunteers. They think if Carson and Craig can have a private army of 300,000 ... well, there needs to be an opposing one to fight for Irish independence. There's a young Belfast fella named Bulmer Hobson, bit like Pearse ... soft hands ... if you know what I mean. And ... Eoin MacNeill, university man, Belfast again, he was the one who kicked it off. Oh, of course, they've all got a fair bit of money behind them ... especially Michael O'Rahilly, businessman ... he likes to be called 'The O'Rahilly.' Mallin was still confused. 'So ... are they wanting the same as us? A republic? Socialism?'

'Well ... most of them, not O'Rahilly though, are in the Irish Republican Brotherhood. So, aye, they all want independence ... a complete break from Britain. Some of them see themselves as being defensive – not taking anything by force ... they think Home Rule is coming through Westminster and that they'll be needed for the handover. Maybe Carson's Ulster Volunteers will fight the British Army, so these Irish Volunteers would help the Brits and fight Carson. There's a few ... like Pearse and Tom Clarke ... that are thinking ... Ireland's never going to be free and a real nation ... not until Irishmen take the initiative. As for socialism? They're not too interested. And I tell you what, there's a few gombeen* men that see a change of government from London to Dublin as just as a way of getting their hands on money and power.'

Mallin drank his tea, 'So ... Poets, playwrights, shopkeepers and teachers? Not too much military experience in the Irish Volunteers?'

'Aye, you're correct there up to a point. But old Tom Clarke's a Fenian that's done 15 years in jail for dynamiting in England. Him and his pal Seán MacDiarmada helped us in the Dublin lockout strike. So those two and Pearse would be straining at the bit for an uprising.'

'And, Jim, what about that Member of Parliament fella ... John Redmond? Doing deals with Asquith. He'd be wantin' to keep things calm so that nothing gets in the way of Home Rule laws being passed?'

'Aye. Tom Clarke hates Redmond with a vengeance. Yer ken that song from a few years ago?

'*They say that Johnny Redmond's got a head of solid brass,*

---

* Gombeen = A shady character, particularly a suspect businessperson

He says that Queen Victoria's a Lovely Looking Lass,
He must've been attracted by her big fat ... let it pass.'
Connolly couldn't bring himself to use the swear word.

'Yeah, Jim, Redmond's a shoneen*, no mistake. And they say he's trying to get control of the Nationalist Irish Volunteers? ... Tom Clarke won't be having any of that.'

'Well, they're recruiting Irish Volunteers all over the country. Only men though, the Irish Republican Brotherhood don't take women; they're not too interested in women's equality like we are. The Ancient Order of Hibernians are happy with that – Jim Larkin never liked that lot. He calls them Catholic Orangemen. The Volunteers will take them as members, but not women! Some women that don't want to join us have started their own League, Cumann naBan. Tom Clarke's wife Kathleen is one'er them what started it.'

Mallin was worried, 'I see them Irish Volunteer fellas doing plenty of marching and war games out in the fields ... I'm none too sure though whether they've done much training in house-to-house fighting ... and as for real military manoeuvres! ... I mean, the ones giving orders are teachers an' poets!'

In fact, there was very little military experience in Connolly's Irish Citizen Army. Mallin had been a drummer in the Royal Scots Fusiliers; Connolly kept quiet about his time as a Private; Jack White had been a Captain and fought in the Boer War but he left the Irish Citizen Army early in 1913.

On the other hand, many of Carson's Ulster Volunteers had been soldiers, some of them senior officers, with experience of fighting against different types of adversaries. The leader of the

---

* Shoneen = Anglophile

Ulster 'army' was Lieutenant General Sir George Richardson; he was elderly but had over 40 years Army experience, fought in Afghanistan and had led the attack on Peking in the Boxer Rebellion. 'Mind you,' Connolly sighed, 'it does nae matter how many experienced soldiers we have, if we canna give them rifles. Yer can be sure that Carson will make certain his people are fully armed. Hopefully, the Irish Volunteers will be doing the same.'

Connolly was correct. The Ulster Unionists' Major Crawford paid £70,000 for 9,000 German Mausers, 11,000 7.9 mm Mannlicher rifles, 4,600 Italian rifles, and 5 million rounds of ammunition. He paid for three ships; two carrying the munitions and a third that was empty and a hoax to distract the Royal Navy. Everything was carried out with military precision at night-time. Hundreds of volunteers in trucks and private cars unloaded the cargo at Larne harbour whilst the town was closed down and only those that knew the password* could enter.

Once the operation was completed, the Larne gun-running was reported in newspapers. The impact was one of admiration by almost every Irish person, North and South, for the operational efficiency; Irish Nationalists in the South were determined to do the same. But they struggled to get £4,000 (and there would later be suspicions some of that disappeared) for a weapons delivery to Howth harbour, near Dublin[†]. The funding disparity for Larne compared to Howth was mirrored by the organising personnel. The equivalent to Ulster's Lieutenant General Sir George

---

* 'Gough'

† This was 3 months after the Unionists' Larne gun-running and two days before Austria-Hungary declared war on Serbia, in 1914.

Richardson was the Volunteer's Erskine Childers, a parliamentary official and author, who had eight months experience fighting in the Boer War. The Ulster organisers included Major Fred Crawford and Captain Spender; the Howth operation had Alice Stopford Green, a historian, Roger Casement the diplomat, and Mary Spring Rice (daughter of Lord Monteagle and related to Sir Cecil Spring Rice, author of '*I Vow to Thee My Country*') – the only military person was Childers's friend Gordon Shephard[46], a British Army Captain*. Steering the yacht into Howth harbour was Childers' wife Molly who had broken both hips as a child and needed 2 canes to walk. Nine hundred rifles had been purchased, but three cases were ditched when the sea became too rough. Ulster's Larne operation involved 500 cars; the Howth rifles were unloaded by men who had marched or ridden bicycles nine miles from Dublin, and was in daylight, openly, as a propaganda exercise. At Larne there was no attempt by authorities to stop the activity. In Howth, police tried to disarm the marchers. The only casualty at Larne was a coastguard with a heart attack. In Dublin, three people died and over 30 were injured when King's Own Scottish Borderers fixed bayonets and fired into a crowd of heckling onlookers[47].

'Aye, compare the Ulster Protestants to us down here', Connolly put both hands down on the table and looked at Mallin, 'Mick ... on paper anyway, the Ulster Unionists are far stronger than us. If Partition happens, we're going to be in a real battle ...

---

* Shephard was a Brigadier-General in the RFC. He was killed in France, aged 32. (Highest-ranking British airman killed during WWI.) He has been forgotten by most British people perhaps due to his part in the struggle for Irish independence. And ignored by the Irish because he was English.

the best we can hope for is to light the spark of another revolution.'

'Is it really that …?'

'Mick, the big-big difference, between the Protestant Ulster Loyalists and the Irish Independence activists is that the Loyalists are united and clear on what they want – which is to prevent Ireland breaking away from Britain. Whereas we and all those opposing the British … are neither clear on objectives nor united as to tactics.'

'Jim, that sounds a bit …'

'Listen. Membership of the Irish Volunteers is increasing rapidly. They support the ideals of independence and want to defend Home Rule legislation. But not all of them want a republic. Certainly not a socialist republic. Arthur Griffith and his Sinn Féin for example only want independence. For some of them, Irish culture and tradition are fundamental drivers in the leaders' passion.'

'Like that MP fella, John Redmond?'

'Exactly. He negotiated the Home Rule law for all Ireland to come into effect in 6 years and thinks militant action would risk an election that the Tories would win; the Tories would cancel Home Rule and that's why he and his supporters joined the Irish Volunteers – to get control and stop any militancy. But there's some like Tom Clarke who place no trust in Asquith's promises. Clarke wants an uprising, but not yet.'

'And then there's us, Jim?'

'Aye. We fight for socialist beliefs, workers' rights, and equality for women. Amidst us all is the curse of poverty. We desperately want a rebellion right noo to overturn the Establishment and to create a republic which would provide a more equitable distribution of wealth.'

Connolly had a swig of black tea before continuing, 'We should nae forget the Irish Republican Brotherhood, the IRB – God bless 'em, with a secret oath and open only to men, wanting to fight for an Irish republic ; most of the Irish Volunteers are in the IRB. Och, it beats me how devout Catholics, who are forbidden to swear an oath, can join the IRB ... but there you go.'

Mick Mallin, as devout as they come, fidgeted and said, 'Well, some of the priests reckon it's OK to take the fight up to the British in order to challenge an immoral law.' Connolly laughed, 'Some priests will say whatever's convenient ... which reminds me. There's another faction, isn't there, Mick? The Ancient Order of Hibernians, a sort of Catholic version of the Protestants' thugs. They've got secret oaths and passwords – defending Irish nationalism with violence when considered necessary and even if it isn't; lots of them joining the Irish Volunteers. The Hibernians? Jim Larkin reckons they're anti-socialist. Probably correct, too.' Connolly shook his head, 'Aye, there's that many factions all with their own ideas of what they want for Ireland, it's a wonder we dinna all fight 'mongst ourselves ... oh, aye ... we should nae ignore Sinn Féin – Arthur Griffith's gang of merry men. Dreaming of an independent Ireland based on conservative, not socialist, ideals ... a dual monarchy with Britain. I suppose he thinks that'd keep Ulster Protestants happy. There aren't many members of Sinn Féin of course and some are in the Irish Volunteers. The women? They've got the Cumann na mBan[*] campaigning for Irish independence and women's rights. At least they know what they want.' Connolly finished his tea, 'Anyway ... we'll do our best. Eh?[48]'

---

[*] Cumann na mBan = 'Irish Women's Council', paramilitary organization

Chapter 14 – *What a Piece of Luck!*
War in Europe!

'Happy Birthday, Henry, darling.' Venetia Stanley was stroking Asquith's hand, 'How are things on the Irish Front?'

'Birthday? Oh ... the 12th *? ... of course. Yes ... yes ... things look as though they're sorting themselves out. I've been trying to persuade Raymond to be the Liberal candidate in Derby ... '

'Really? Surely, he'll romp in ... being the Prime Minister's son. Especially now that this Ireland business is being resolved ... it is, isn't it?'

'Didn't look like it at the start of the year. I had to have a few highly secret meetings, remember? With Carson and Bonar Law?'

'Bonar Law? I've never liked him. His Tories have spent three years blocking you on Ireland ...'

'Yes, indeed. I don't like Catholics, but he hates them more than Lloyd George does and he's always conspiring with that evil, treacherous, General Wilson. Bonar Law? Moderation isn't a word he understands. He claims to be a loyalist but he'll cause revolution and mayhem to get his own way ... Lloyd George manages to get on well with him ... but ... well, I find Carson to be less unreasonable.'

'So, did you tell the Cabinet about the Bonar Law meetings? And that you've been negotiating with that Irish MP, Redmond?'

'Yes ... well, I told the Cabinet about Bonar Law ... eventually ... as much as they needed to know ... I may have made a few cosmetic changes during my report. As for Redmond? I had to get Birrell to soften him up before he'd agree to a Partition in which Ulster wasn't ruled from Dublin ... but he insisted on it being

---

* September

temporary, would you believe! He wanted Ulster excluded for only three years. Heaven knows how he thought that was going to work, even if Carson and Bonar Law agreed to it. I told him I'd get the Cabinet to consider it ...' Asquith struggled to stop laughing, 'Of course, I knew that Carson insists exclusion would have to be permanent. So I had to lay it on thick with Redmond; reminded him that we could be forced to call an election which we'd lose and as a result Home Rule would be out the window. That woke him up ... he said he'd accept a five-year temporary exclusion. I told him it'd have to be six, take it or leave it. He took it!'

'Six-year exclusion? But Carson and Bonar Law want it to be permanent?'

'Yes ... I told them that I'd agree to that ... I had no choice ... but, well, Redmond will have to find out about it later.'

'Umm ... what about the number of counties?'

'Ah ... yes. Well, those two Unionist gentlemen had decided that they'd prefer not to have too many Catholics ... potential for problems. They don't want all Northern Ireland ... they just want six counties including Tyrone. And Tyrone is the one that Redmond wanted!'

'Oh, goodness. But I thought you said that everything's sorted out, darling?'

'Hm. Don't you remember, Venetia, when we talked about the war in Europe? I said it was a horrible business but it'd have the good effect of throwing the Irish troubles into the background ... and you said it was like cutting one's head off to get rid of a headache?'

'Yes ... and now we've declared war!'

'Well, it does look like ... wonderful luck for me as far as Ireland is concerned. Bonar Law and Carson called me over for a meeting. They said that, since we're at war, we really need to all pull together and present a united front.'

'Bonar Law and Carson? They want you to go and see them?! I thought that you were the leader of this country. They've changed their minds! Weren't they saying in Parliament, a few weeks back, that they'd be happy to be governed by Germany if it meant they didn't come under a Dublin Government? I'd heard that the German Minister Baron von Kuhlmann had lunch with Carson … and the Germans must surely have been aware of, if not involved in, that huge amount of weaponry bought and transported to Ulster …'

'Yes, yes … that was a while back. Events have occurred … Anyway, they … and I … we decided the Home Rule issue needed to be suspended until the war's end. So, I've suggested it to Redmond, and he agreed. I'll be putting the legislation to Parliament next week. It'll be clear that Ulster will never be forced to do anything it doesn't want to do; as far as Ireland is concerned – nothing more needs to be done. Not by England, anyway.'

'What about Redmond? At first, he said Irish troops would only be used for defending the Irish coast … but now he wants them to fight in France as well … and he wants them to have Irish officers, like the Ulster Protestant troops.'

'Well, they'll get English officers. Like it or lump it.'

'Anyway, you sound relieved, darling.'

'Yes … Home Rule is postponed … a great weight off my chest. I can focus on Europe and forget about being threatened with a General Election.'

'Oh, but that means your Raymond won't be campaigning in Derby?'

'Ha-ha! No, not in Derby. He wants to campaign in Belgium! He's talking about enlisting.'

'Raymond? Joining up? But he's married with two children ... and another on the way ... I don't think he's especially enthusiastic about the war, either.'

'I know, Venetia, ... but his three younger brothers have joined, so I suppose he thinks it the right thing to do ... '

'Perhaps ... it's the same as for thousands of others. They love their country, want to fight for independence, and will put their lives at risk for it.' Venetia might have been trying to make a point about young Irishmen fighting for Irish independence but Asquith was too busy thinking of Europe.

Raymond Asquith was indeed like many other young men. He wanted to wear a uniform and defend his country. Many other men of course wanted the opportunity to eat regularly, hold a rifle, and have the legal right to kill human beings that didn't speak their language.

Irishmen in Dublin and Belfast and everywhere in between, encouraged by John Redmond and Edward Carson, joined the British Army in their thousands. The war would be over in three months, and few wanted to miss the opportunity of legally shooting at other human beings. Politicians competed with each other to show who was the most patriotic by persuading young men to queue up as fodder for German machine guns. The membership of the Ulster Volunteers fell as Protestants joined the Army, and the number of Irish Volunteers similarly decreased thanks to John Redmond's rousing speeches. He had inveigled himself a senior position in the Volunteer movement and now wanted to prove that the promise of Home Rule was appreciated by Irishmen, like himself.

It was ironic that Redmond refused Asquith's invitation to be a member of the Coalition War Cabinet. Here was somebody urging his own countrymen to enlist and fight the Germans but unwilling to participate in the decision-making to win the war. His reasons, 'principles and the history of his Irish Party', resembled excuses. A more defensible reason would have been his reluctance to be in a coalition with, and to sit in the same room as, men like Carson and Bonar Law. But he could have swallowed his pride and risked a, somewhat already damaged, reputation; he could have influenced the Coalition, caused it some discomfort, and affected decisions relating to Irish troops. The future of Ireland would have been very different.

Chapter 15 – Three Little Maids from School

Saint Enda's school was having an Open Day. This meant that various friends of the headmaster, Patrick Pearse, had the chance to chat privately about their favourite topic: the English.

Tom Clarke, the old Fenian with a face that bore the legacy of a hundred prison beatings, glared at Eoin MacNeill, 'Stupid? If Redmond's refusal to be in the Coalition Cabinet was stupid, then what was Asquith's decision to make Carson Attorney-General? ... that bastard should have been arrested and tried for treason. He creates his own personal army and threatens to kill British soldiers ... and now he's the Head of the British judicial system. Chief legal advisor! ... guardian of the public interest ... advising the Monarch ... Carson!'

MacNeill, a university lecturer born in Northern Ireland, felt uncomfortable. He had once supported Redmond and praised Carson for raising his army to fight the British. Yes, it was to oppose Home Rule, but Carson started the ball rolling by enlisting Ulster Protestants. MacNeill at one stage envisaged Carson's army joining with his own Irish Volunteers and together fighting Britain[49]. But MacNeill's political nous was never realistic or cynical enough. And now Redmond was urging Irishmen to join Britain's fight against Germany – as a result, many Irish Volunteers had done so and the movement was split.

Patrick Pearse agreed with Clarke, 'And what about Bonar Law! Doing deals with Carson and Craig and stirring up that Curragh mutiny so that British officers refused to obey orders ... Bonar Law! He'll be called in to the War Cabinet, mark my words.'

Pearse, a school headmaster, and Joseph Plunkett, a seriously thin 28-year-old poet with a pince-nez and a terrifying cough, both wanted desperately to see an independent Ireland. They would do anything, anything, to achieve that. MacNeill may have been an academic but he was no less a patriot – it was just that he wanted to move slowly and surely. Looking at Plunkett he asked, 'How are you going, old chap? Have you been to the quack about that cough?'

'Yes ... I've another appointment for next month ... need to carry on ... Rory O'Connor and the lads at Larkfield are busy with dynamite and grenades ... lots to be done. I'm making my way there now, so I'll say goodbye and God bless.' His father and mother, devout Catholics, were landlords and wealthy property owners in Dublin. They allowed the Irish Volunteers to make use of their large estate at Larkfield near an old mill in the suburbs. Young enthusiasts met there, made friends, slept in tents, and discussed the coming rebellion.

Pearse, Clarke and MacNeill followed Plunkett out of the school gates. St. Enda's hall was almost empty now except for one corner where four women, one middle-aged and three younger, stood awkwardly around a table. A well-dressed man approached.

'Now, Muriel; Grace; Sydney! This fine young man is Thomas MacDonagh. He's Deputy Headmaster here at St. Enda's.' Nora Dryhurst was a suffragette and a journalist – in other words, she was a trouble-maker. Grace had met her in London when she was studying at the Slade Art School and Nora was working at an international school.

'Thomas, these three red-haired women are not the daughters of Zeus, they are the Gifford sisters ... you will fall in love with one of them and marry her.[50]' This was stated as if it were a simple matter of fact. The young chap blushed to the roots of his curly brown hair and grinned. 'That would be easy – the difficult bit would be deciding which one. And that's if she'd have me.'

Somehow his grey-hazel eyes sought to look into the souls of each of the sisters at the same time.

Usually the quietest of the three, Muriel took charge, 'Yes, Nora. I thought you were a suffragette. Equality and stuff? Sha, d'yer not think we might like to have a say in the matter?'

Tom added, '… Anyway, I think there are another t'ree sisters?' Muriel obviously had his attention and wasn't about to let it go. She said, 'Yes, there are … and I believe you have two brothers? So perhaps we could view and select one of the t'ree MacDonaghs?'

Nora laughed, 'Even if you've never met before, you've obviously done your research. Looks like I'm not the only one that's been match-making? Trying to get something started … But then I'm an anarchist as well. So, if a bomb needs to be lit then I'll be the one to do it.'

Tom noticed that Muriel was standing awkwardly and favouring one leg as if it ached. He said, 'Shall we all sit for a moment? There's almost room on this bench.'

Grace said, 'You two sit and chat for a while. We can all meet up at the Larkfield estate, eh? Nora, come along with me now. How's things at the International School in London … tell me again about you meeting Louise Michel.' Grace turned and waved as she, Sydney, and Nora left Tom and Muriel.

Muriel sighed as she sat, 'Ah … yes, that's better. My veins play up a bit. Probably me smoking doesn't help.' Tom was genuinely concerned and, unusually for him, lost for words. Muriel was a stunning woman. Tall, with red hair that framed her face, and a serious smile which challenged you to stop looking into her eyes.

She half shook her head. 'Ah. It's not too bad. There's others worse off than me. Poor young Joe Plunkett for one. He has a terrible cough ... I hope it's not the consumption ... His parents own that Larkfield place, don't they? ...'

There was a long, long, pause.

Muriel cleared her throat. 'I hope you weren't ... Nora was just being silly. I heard that you're engaged to be married, as I am. So, ... '

Tom was embarrassed. 'Engaged? Well, yes ... but ... no, no, Nora was just pulling our legs ... Anyway ... er, Joe? I've been teaching him Irish in the evenings. He's a clever young man[51] but ... You know him?'

'No, no. Not really ... it's just that some people that Grace knows ... told her about him ... and she's ... noticed him at poetry meetings. Grace mentioned him ... sort of ... in passing.'

'Is that so? I know he writes poetry; Bill Yeats told me some of it has a quare sort of beauty. But yer sayin' Grace and Joe haven't actually spoken to each other? I'll have to do something about that!'

'Well, don't be embarrassing the poor chap ... when you're supposed to be teaching him the Irish.'

'No, no. I wouldn't ... but ... Anyway, it's a great and unique language, isn't it? Irish culture has to be encouraged and nurtured. Mind you, he's of the same mind as me ... doesn't matter how many poems or plays we write or literary meetings that we attend, the Ireland we love will die in the slums of Dublin and Belfast unless real action is taken ... by people like us if need be ... Come on, let's go over to Larkfield and catch up with your sisters.'

By the time they arrived, they'd decided that Grace was made for Joseph. 'Hang on, there's the very man himself.'

Plunkett was walking slowly, head down, towards them across the stubbly grass. He was carrying some sort of contraption with protruding wires. From around the far corner of a windowless barn came Grace. She paused when she saw Joe and was on the point of turning back.

'Hey, Grace! Could I have a word?' Tom yelled with enough volume that Joe couldn't fail to hear; he looked up and his previously rather grey face took on a glow.

As they all proceeded towards each other, Joe and Grace walking hesitantly, Tom whispered, 'C'mon Muriel ... help me out, now ... what do we say to them both?' She shook her beautiful head, 'Sha, I don't know ... you're the literary giant ...'

Tom smiled, 'Ah ... Joe ... I was wanting to ... Oh, have you met Muriel Gifford? And this is one of her many sisters, Grace.'

Joe put the contraption down and shook hands with both of them. Then he fiddled with his pince-nez, put it in a pocket, 'Pleased to meet you both,' grinned and took out the pince-nez and put it back on.

Muriel pointed to the wired contraption, 'That's a quare yoke yer got there! What on earth is it?'

'Ah ... well ... it would be a radio ... if I could get it to work.' Joe sighed.

'Does it have valves, at all?' Grace whispered.

'Yeah, yeah ... though I haven't ... D'yer have an interest in them, yourself ... Grace?'

'Yes, a little ... I've read about them ... marvellous invention ... but I'm more into painting and drawing ... of people usually ... but sometimes ... Oh, look at that rose bush! Let's see if the sun shines on the raindrops covering the blooms.' Joseph left his wires and connectors and they both walked across the field, as Tom and Muriel, forgotten, watched them go.

Joseph gently, awkwardly, broke off a white rose. 'There you go, Grace. A present. Ah! It'll look lovely pinned on your blue dress.'

She held it. 'Oooh! ... Oww!'

The smile on Joseph's face quickly fell away, 'Argh! Sorry! sorry, Grace ... the thorn ... oh! ... What an eejit I am! You're bleeding!'

'No! It's alright, Joe. No, really ... see ... it's stopped.'

She gently held the flower in her hand from which some tiny spots of very dark red had fallen on a petal.

Joseph stared at it. 'D'yer mind me askin' ... Are you a Catholic, Grace?'

'Er ... no. Pa is, but not Mother. My brothers were baptised as Catholics. But Mother wanted all us girls to be Protestants ... '

'Truly? Sha, that's very ... Very ... ecumenical ... must make for an interesting Sunday... sorry, it's none of me business.'

'No, no. I don't mind you askin'. In fact, I'm pleased you wanted to know. Your faith is very important to yer, isn't it?'

'It is ... but ... Sha, doesn't Our Lord love all people ... Jews, Hindus, non-believers ... ha! Yes, even Protestants ... your parents must be very ... unusual though.'

'Unusual? Actually ... I'd say they're odd ... very, very odd.'

'Well. It takes all sorts. Our Lord's parents would have been regarded as very odd, I'm sure ... very unusual. And there are some very strange people around these days ... but there's also some ... very ... nice people, too.'

They looked at each other, wondering what to say next. Then Grace said, 'My turn to be nosy ... Don't you find it difficult ... I mean, your Catholic faith says Love your enemies. And Thou shalt not kill ...?'

He took up her thought, '... And wanting to fight the British? Well, Pope Leo XIII said that Catholic citizens are not obliged to obey any law which is contrary to divine or natural laws nor obliged to obey an illegitimate authority ... But I agree, it's sometimes too easy to find an excuse for breaking a

Commandment ... even our Lord's very own one*.'

Grace looked into Joe's eyes as he continued, 'Even so ... My love for Ireland means more to me than anything else. Saint Augustine described the just-war theory, yer know. He said that it can be reasonable and defensible for a war, if justice is the objective of the conflict. If I have to kill the enemies of Ireland by fighting an illegitimate authority, then I will ... if I can.'

'Would you ...,' Grace asked, '... give your soul for Ireland?'

'Barter my soul? I would – if it belonged only to me. But my soul, I believe, isn't mine to give or barter. I could lose it, I suppose, if I were to, say, renounce my religion or fail to ask forgiveness. But even then, I believe the Lord would wait for me to turn again to Him.'

'Will you talk to me some more about being a Catholic?'

---

* "A new commandment I give to you, that you love one another; as I have loved you, that you also love one another" (John 13:34)

Chapter 16 – A Little Help From Some Friends

The Great War was about to start and Roger Casement turned his back on Ireland. The waves smacked rhythmically as the ship left Queenstown Harbour in Cork and pushed its way across the Atlantic. He wept. Strange that he hadn't felt like this before; all those times leaving and he'd never been emotional. He yearned to turn and look back but that would be a sign of weakness. This time was different because he knew his mission could result in Ireland winning its freedom. Patriotic men in Europe were signing up to fight for their country. Casement was no different except he hadn't formally enlisted. He wasn't a British traitor; how could he be? He was Irish – an Irish patriot.

And now here he was, following in the footsteps of Patrick Pearse who had been in the US earlier that year, seeking funds from Irish migrants for his Saint Enda's school; Pearse had met John Devoy, owner and editor of the *Gaelic American* weekly newspaper and a passionate Fenian.

Casement wanted to discuss with Devoy how Irish-Americans could help the fight for independence by funding assistance from Germany. Devoy was 74 and had never married. Born in Kildare during the Great Hunger, he'd been in the business of fighting Britain for 50 years. Now though, his journalism skills had made him an important fund-raiser in the USA. This was why he was suspicious of anybody claiming to be an Irish patriot.

'I was jailed with hard labour, for my activities when I was in Ireland. This was when I was 24 and had just got engaged to marry. Imprisonment and transportation put a stop to that.' Devoy took off his spectacles, his eyes were always hurting these days, and he stroked his beard. 'I hate the English. How about you, Sir Roger?

You worked for them! I know you're Irish, but you look like the type of Englishman that I hate. Are you proud of your knighthood?'

'Me, Mr Devoy? I love Ireland ... I don't hate the English. I hate what they've done to Ireland. I'll do everything I can to force them out of my country. That includes helping their enemies in wartime. As for the knighthood? I really had no choice but to accept it if my advice on atrocities in the Congo and South America was to be effective.'

Devoy frowned. 'So ... I can trust you? ... a Protestant?' he leaned forwards with a hand to his ear.

'My father brought me up as a Protestant but my mother had me secretly baptised as a Catholic. Mr Devoy, look! Patrick Pearse and ... and ... Tom Clarke ... they trust me. They know that I'd give my life for Ireland.'

'Tom? Did you know he's a US citizen? ... Yes, Tom's told me what he thinks of you ... You know that we funded his dynamiting campaign in England? Tom is the greatest patriot that I have the honour to know. Like me, he wants an Irish war with England ... as soon as possible. But he isn't too sure what you want. So, tell me ... why are you going to Germany? Have you got the support of Pearse and Clarke? After all, you're not a member of the Irish Republican Brotherhood, are you?'

'Membership requires swearing an oath ... no, I'm not a member. That doesn't stop me from wanting to go to war with England. But we need money, and guns, troops and experienced officers.'

'OK ... accepting for the moment that I can trust you ... what about this fella sat beside you ... your Mr Christensen? Wanted by the police, is he?' He pointed at the 6-foot tall, well-built person that Casement had brought with him; it was a nervous Nordic-looking young man with a large gap in his front teeth, fair-haired and twiddling a soft dark hat. This was July 1914 and New Yorkers were sweltering, but the temperature in the room seemed to fall a few degrees.

How and when Casement met Eivind Adler Christensen is a mystery. There's no doubt though that they were very close, probably in a homosexual relationship. Devoy was an astute judge of men; every day he met people who claimed to be something that they were not. He could sense the situation and realised that Christensen had a mysterious background. The 1910 US Census has him as Norwegian, arriving in the US in 1902, and indicating that he was now 24 years of age. He married a Sadie Weaver in 1911 when she was 15 and she had a son three months later. He really was a mystery; the 1920 census shows him with a wife named Margaret and a daughter, and an arrival date in the US of 1909.

'Adler? My valet? I trust him with my life. So, if you trust me, then you can trust him. As for wanted by the police ... that might be a recommendation. But I'm sure he's wanted by a few people.' Adler fidgeted and looked at his new shoes.

Devoy tapped his fingers. 'Hmm ... There's lots of people here who tell me that they to want help Ireland ... I take them as I find them ... and I know that British Intelligence have plenty of tentacles ... there are agents ... double agents .... triple agents .... Does the name Blinker mean anything to you?' Devoy asked the question of Casement but he turned his gaze on the young man sitting alongside.

Casement frowned. 'Pardon? Blinker? Never heard that name before.'

Devoy stared at the chubby hands twiddling a hat but noted no change in rhythm, ' ... what about ... Basil ... Thomson?'

'No, why?' said Casement.

'Never mind. But you know Joseph Conrad, the writer?'

'Yes! What has he ....'

'It's just that we have a John Quinn here ... Irish born lawyer in New York ... who's very supportive of Ireland. He buys Conrad manuscripts. He and Aleister Crowley, the writer ... bit strange of course ... they're both helpful to the Irish cause. To what extent do I trust them? Well ... And then there's John Kenny who I trust 100%. Not just because he worships Tom Clarke as much as I do but also because he's the President of the US equivalent of your Irish Republican Brotherhood. John's been useful to us when dealing with Germany... d'you know why I'm telling you all this?'

'No.'

'Because I have to. I can tell that your love for Ireland is no less than mine. We need someone with your diplomacy skills and credibility. We need you to carry on with the work of John Kenny, use his contacts, and convince the Germans to help Ireland ... we're competing with others though ... It's not just Ireland wanting independence from Britain's hegemony. The rebels in India are after getting help from the Germans.'

Devoy looked out the window. He wasn't looking at the skyscrapers nor hearing the raucous New York traffic; he was thinking of when he was 27-years-old in a tiny cell of London's Millbank Prison being bashed, kicked, and abused, day after day.

'You know, I've been in the US for 40 years now ... back in 1866 ... in Ireland ... I'd organised 80,000 Irishmen in the British Army ready to mutiny but I was overruled and the troops were sent overseas. Ah well, now it's your turn ... I'm not calling you Sir Roger, damn it .... Roger, you've got to do the same as I did. Fight fer Irish independence. We'll fund your travel. I'll introduce you to von Papen[52], military attaché in Washington, who will put you in touch with Richard Meyer at the Foreign Ministry in Germany. That guy's a Jew ... you OK with that? Tough luck if you're not.'

Casement was feeling more relaxed, 'What else can you do for me?'

'I'll arrange a meeting with the Ambassador Johann Heinrich von Bernstorff. Joe McGarrity'll be there. He's like me ... wants a free Ireland, been here 20 years ... born in Ulster. Runs liquor in Philadelphia ...'

Christensen dropped his hat at the mention of Philadelphia*, and quickly picked it up. Devoy looked at him but continued speaking to Casement, 'We'll tell von Bernstorff that we can help Germany win the war, it'll mean 100,000 British troops taken out of Europe ... but we need rifles, machine guns, ammunition, troops! There'll be other guys you'll talk to, such as Karl Boy-Ed. Yeah, I know ... a lot of names ... well, you're gonna need to be aware of them ... and don't forget ... don't trust nobody.' Devoy looked again at Christensen and then at Casement.

'After meeting von Bernstorff we'll make arrangements for you two to get funding and tickets to Germany ... You'll have a passport in the name of James Landy and I suggest shaving that beard off.' Devoy sighed, 'It's going to be difficult ... I mean, persuading captured Irish soldiers to change sides and fight for Germany ...'

*

About six months later, January 1915, Devoy had another visitor from Ireland. 'Please ... sit yersel' down ... they must be crazy sending you ... look at the size of yer ... how old are yer?

---

* Christensen had a wife Sadie Anne Weaver in Philadelphia; they married in 1911 (when she was 15).

21, 22? OK, OK, none of my business ... I hear yer arrived on the *Baltic* at Ellis Island ... December 19th ... met up with a journalist writing for one of my competitor newspapers, the *Irish World* ... person known as 'John Brennan' ... and you met Jim Larkin?'

'I did, yeah.'

'Larkin? ... Yer wanna be careful of him ... He's not ... well ... I've always had my suspicions about him ... that he might be in with the Brits ... It's OK ... You obviously mustn't tell me the purpose of your visit ... It's enough for me to know that you're here with the approval of the Irish Republican Council ... and of course James Connolly.'

The visitor stifled a laugh and a choke, 'Connolly? He vouches fer me? Glad to hear that. As for Larkin? He met me when I arrived ... that's all. Most of us, yer journalist John Brennan's relatives certainly, in Ireland would trust Larkin completely. But, yeah, nobody ... not even you, are to know why I'm in the US.'

Devoy couldn't help but be almost hypnotised. He was often meeting Irish people in New York, of course. But for some reason this visitor's appearance and accent reminded him of his home in Kildare, and someone he'd known there, when he was 24.

He forced himself to focus on the present. 'OK. Understood. You're going back soon? I've got some letters that Casement has sent us which he wants passed on to people ... British Intelligence is checking the regular postage ... so we'd be grateful for your assistance. And he sent us some cash that he wants to be given to his sister. We changed that into gold. I know it's a risk for you ...'

'That's OK. I'll take it all and get it to them.'

'... and, er, the person calling themself John Brennan? Been helpful?'

'Yes, yes. Very helpful ... but I won't go into details about how helpful.'

'No, no. That's fine. It's just ... I'm amazed that they'd send someone like you ... I guess it's less suspicious. Well, I'll say Goodbye and God bless.' They exchanged a few more words and shook hands. When Devoy was alone he stood and looked out the window, anxiously looking for a last glimpse of the stranger waiting to cross the street. He couldn't get that face out of his mind.

'John Brennan' used contacts to arrange a meeting for the mysterious visitor with a Herr von Skal – an agent who worked for Count von Papen, German military attaché. The meeting resulted in von Skal being persuaded, eventually, to phone von Bersdorff in Washington. The instructions in Dublin had been that nothing was to be communicated to anybody else, no Fenians, no German attachés, no deputy Ambassador. It had to be the Ambassador. In Washington.

The German Embassy's receptionist heard the bell at the front door being tentatively rung. She crossed the room quickly, peered through a peephole but saw nothing, and heaved the great oak door open. Looking out into the frosty evening gloom, the street was empty. Nobody there, so she began closing the door. Then she noticed a shadowy shape in the darkness. Somebody small and shivering, wrapped in a thin overcoat, was standing to one side of the porch. She was moved quickly to close the door without bothering with the stranger.

'I have an appointment ... to see the Ambassador.' The Irish voice was soft, lilting and attractive. The receptionist's eyebrows lifted towards the clouds, 'Really?'

'Yes ... look at this, documentation from someone he knows. Herr von Skal.'

With reluctance and doubt, the German woman glanced at the proffered note. 'Hmmm, very well. The Count is busy. Come in. You'll have to make do with me. What do you want?'

'No. The Ambassador. I must see Count von Bernstorff. Nobody else. Sha, I can assure you ... he'll benefit from me visit.'

The receptionist stared at the extraordinary person in front of her and sighed, 'Alright ... come this way.'

The room into which they walked was warm and plush. A chandelier shone brightly and the elegant furniture was intimidating.

'Thank you for agreeing to see me, Ambassador.'

'Well ... you are very determined ... not even my closest staff would satisfy you?' His English was perfect; it helped that he had spent 11 years in England and had an American wife.

'That's because what I have brought you is of the very highest importance ...'

'Yes? Well ... please ... Where is it? You've gone to a lot of trouble. So, can I see it now?'

'No.'

'What? ... I don't understand ... What are you playing at? Ah ... Ah ... Yes, yes ... you want ... How much?'

'Nothing.'

'Nothing? But ...?'

'Just listen ... I've no documentation ... the details are here. In me head ... me memory.'

'Yes?'

'Yes ... You will want someone 100% trustworthy to take notes, though ... I have details of British information concerning your U-boats.'

The ambassador gaped. He picked up a pen and then put it down. There was a small bell at his elbow; he rang it and within about three seconds a well-dressed man entered. The ambassador pointed to a notebook and pen and waved him to sit down.

'Heinrich. Our young friend here has something that apparently needs to be documented ... Very well. Please. Start when you're ready. I trust Heinrich with my life.'

With eyes shut, there was a stream of words that had been learnt by heart from formal documentation, flowing almost robotically ... Heinrich Albert, commercial attaché at the German Embassy, struggled to write everything as it was recited.

'German U-boats will be a major weapon in the war against unarmed British cargo ships. U-boats can be attacked, with only some degree of success, by means of naval ships using depth charges. But the most effective way to destroy a U-boat is by ramming or shooting it on the surface...

... U-boats will normally allow the crew of a British ship to board lifeboats, and then use a deck gun to sink the ship. British High Command has developed a tactic to enable British naval ships to lure a U-boat into thinking it is safe and to surface ...'

The visitor paused, struggling to remember, then re-focussed. 'Telegram[53], Churchill to Commander in Chief at Portsmouth, 26 November 1914 begins: 'A small or moderate sized steamer should be taken up and fitted very secretly with two twelve-pounder guns; a few seamen and two expert gun layers will be disguised as fishermen. If a German U-Boat stops her the steamer will sink the German by gunfire. The greatest secrecy is necessary to prevent spies becoming acquainted with the arrangements.' The sudden silence in the room was weirdly both dramatic and expectant. The Count waited, then 'Anything else?' It was as if he had said nothing ... the visitor continued,

' ... U-Boot-Falle* consists of an armed British naval ship being disguised as a cargo ship flying the flag of a neutral nation. Some crew may be disguised as civilians and appear to abandon ship.

---

* 'U-boat trap'

When a U-boat surfaces and is within close range the flag is replaced by the British flag and covering panels removed from the armaments to enable the U-boat to be destroyed...

The disguised naval ships have as their home port Queenstown Harbour, Ireland; their operational name will be Q-Ships. The following are Q-ships that exist or are being converted ...

HMS Baralong cargo steamship, 4000 ton, three 12-pounder guns, built 1901

HMS Prince Charles converted collier, 274 ton, 6-pounder and 3-pounder guns, built 1905

HMS Farnborough, formerly collier steamship ship Loderer 1903, 3200 tons, being converted at Devonport, five 12-pounder guns, two 6-pounders (one each side of bridge), and a Maxim gun (centre of ship)

Decoy vessel Taranaki, trawler, to tow a hidden submarine

Cymric and Gaelic, shallow draft Iron barquentines built 1892, 230 ton

Armed trawler Nelson 61 ton 3-pounder gun built 1905

HMS Dunraven disguised as the collier Boverton, 3000 ton, 4-inch gun, 12-pounders, 2 torpedo tubes.'

The visitor stopped, eyes open, exhausted.

'Is that all?' The Count asked.

'Yes ... that's it.'

'What are you ... wanting in return for this ... You said ... Alright, we will, as you say, cut to the chase ... how much?'

'We want no money from you.'

'No money?'

'We want you to help Ireland free itself from the British curse. The enemy of our enemy is our friend. '

'Amazing! Thank you! Thank you! Yes, we'll do all we can.'

Next week the visitor boarded a ship out of New York, bound for Ireland. The Casement correspondence and gold coins were concealed in clothing. Embarking through security and disembarking through Customs were nerve-wracking times but uneventful. It had been a tiring voyage and great to be back home.

'Get that overcoat off. Come and sit down by the fire. Yer must be dog-tired.'

'I am that, right enough. Sha, it was wonderful to see Sydney Gifford* again. What a wonderful woman. She's writing articles for Devoy's newspaper, using the pen name of John Brennan. I gave her all the gos about her sisters ... Muriel and Nellie and Grace ... Oh, and I saw Jim Larkin but didn't tell him too much ... John Devoy's a quare one. Hey, I'm home and safe!'

He couldn't hold back any longer – Connolly burst into tears. 'Thanks be to God! Oh, Nora! ... We've already lost one daughter ... Come here, Nora, and give us all a hug ... I was terrified all the time yer were away. We both were. Eh, Lillie? If they'd caught yer, they'd have tortured yer and then hanged yer ... I shouldn't have sent yer ...' Nora ruffled his hair, 'Ah, c'mon ... Sha, I'm back safe ... we're all together again.' Lillie Connolly held her daughter tight and whispered, 'He kept looking at that photograph of yer ...y'know the wan? When yer got hold of a Volunteer's uniform an' put it on, had yer picture taken? *'Your soldier son'*, you wrote on the back of it ... Keeps it his wallet. We both of us knelt and prayed every night that you were alright and that you'd come back safe and sound. T'anks be to God.'

---

* Sydney Czira (Gifford) Witness Statement 909 describes meeting Nora in the US

Chapter 17 – Travellers in Germany

It was two months later when Devoy, sitting in his New York office, exploded. Joe McGarrity had only started to give him some news from Europe when Devoy shouted, 'I should'a known! I had bad feelings about that guy ... Christensen! Valet! What sort'a Irish republican needs a valet for cryin' out loud? ... Yeah! Yeah! I know ! I know! Casement is a loyal Fenian, even if he's an Oscar Wilde, and he'd die for Ireland ... but that other guy! Christensen!'

McGarrity, his County Tyrone accent mixing with Philadelphia, said, 'Apparently the European Press is callin' it the Findlay Affair after the Limey Ambassador. Nobody's gonna know the full trut'. I dunno why they travelled via Norway to Germany. Anyway, it's not all bad. The Brits look real dumb ...'

Devoy raised his eyebrows, 'OK. So, what happened?'

'Well ... In Christiania*, Christensen's told Casement that he'd been contacted by a guy from the British Legation. A promise was made, and documented, that he'd be paid five grand, pounds that is, if he fixed Casement's capture and arrest. The British officials are saying Christensen came to them first; but he says it was the other way round. He met them cup'la times, fed'em some bulldust an' collected a small fistful of cash. Casement's now using the international press to make the British Government look as dumb as.'

Devoy groaned, 'Why Norway? ... why did they go there? For just three days? Christensen's parents? What if he's playing for both sides? No, I'm not talkin' Husbands and Wives. Casement could be at risk. Thanks be to God, they're both in Germany now. Everything was going OK, or that's how it looked – von Bernstorff

---

* Name of Oslo before 1925

was even agreeable to supplying troops to support the Rising ... Whether we can take his word on that, I dunno ... And I've got my worries about Casement. How's he gonna convince those prisoners of war? A British knight? And if our Clan na Gael members hear gossip, spread by British Intelligence, that he's a faggot then we'll struggle to get funds.'

Devoy looked at McGarrity, 'Casement not only wants more dough, he's also asking you to send cash to Christensen's wife. For crying out loud! I mean, we got our work cut out helping Shyamji Krishna Varma and the Ghadar Party[*].'

McGarrity knew that the situation was reaching a crisis, 'We gotta put more pressure on the Germans. Redmond's Home Rule agreement, so called anyway, is crazy; it's gotta be all 32 counties right from the start. The British! They'd steal the white outa yer eye. 'Dere's no way the Uprising will be this year like we wanted, but it's gotta happen no matter what ... Poor old Casement didn't look well when he was here. And Christensen's written to say the guy's worse. They need someone to help 'em, so. But if they're telling the Germans that an Uprising won't happen unless there's a full-on invasion, well they can kiss help from the Kaiser bye-bye. I'll write to Dublin ... Tom Clarke ... in code of course.'

*

Plunkett left Dublin on Saint Patrick's Day in 1915. To prevent British suspicions, he travelled through France, Spain, Italy and Switzerland. The official reason for travel was 'health'; he was indeed suffering from something awful, coughing with a high fever and it wasn't helped by his smoking and drinking.

His name changed as he travelled, James Malcolm, Peter

---

[*] Indian revolutionaries, with help from Irish Republicans in the US and from Germany, were trying to end British rule in India.

Doyle, and Johann Peters. After five weeks he met Casement in Berlin. Their next few months involved devising a strategic plan for the coming Rebellion. This was in addition to meeting senior German military staff, attempting to persuade British POWs to join Casement's Irish Brigade, and Plunkett writing poetry.

The German Foreign Office building in Wilhelmstraße 76 was immense. Tall, immaculately dressed civil servants carrying folders criss-crossed the cavernous Walhalla on their way to strategic and highly secret meetings. The walls were a confusion of marble columns, statues and busts. Both Irishmen were overawed as they climbed a winding staircase and, after a brief wait, were shown into the office of Count von Wedel, their main contact in the German Foreign Office.

Neither of them looked well – they were obviously pleased to sit down. Plunkett accepted a cigar from the Count, thanked him and then coughed vigorously into a handkerchief.

The Count's face was serious, but he really didn't know whether to laugh or cry. He'd read the Casement-Plunkett Ireland Report – 32 pages with details of a proposed Irish Rebellion, and now he looked at these two. Civilians! The young one was alarmingly thin and clearly suffering from some sort of serious illness – the aristocratic Casement didn't look much better, especially around the eyes, and probably ought to be in hospital.

'Well, gentlemen ... this is quite something. I congratulate you. I was in the army for 6 years ... but neither of you have any military experience and yet you've produced this.' The ambiguity of his comment went unnoticed.

Plunkett shook his head, 'Actually, I was in the Officers' Training in school ... and I've studied as many military texts as I could get me hands on ...' The Count didn't laugh. 'Really? Yes ... Hmmm ... It's a very detailed report on how to defeat ... one of, the world's greatest military powers. Very ... er ... interesting. You have 30,000 men in Ireland ready to take up arms? ... Please, I do not doubt you ... but how do you arrive at that figure?'

Plunkett beamed, as best he could, 'I can assure you we have at least that many. Patrick Pearse has shown me detailed listings for all 32 counties. Of course, we have to keep the exact names and details under lock and key.' Casement inspected his fingernails.

The Count smiled, 'These are ... teachers and shopkeepers and such ... they are not in, shall we say, a regular full-time army? They learn to drill ... march up and down ... but firing practice? Bayonet fighting? House-to-house fighting? There are very few officers ... Obviously, you'd be aware that our Intelligence people gather information in many countries ... Hmmm ... Yes ... so ... Your report claims about ... 12,000 men in Dublin alone?' the Count's bushy eyebrows moved upwards.

'Yes ... which is why we need rifles, machine guns, and ammunition ... and ... experienced troops and officers ... from the German Army.' Plunkett stared at the German's face, desperately searching for a glimmer of promise.

The smile had disappeared, 'Ah. Perhaps, we'll deal with that in a moment ... This report doesn't touch on the Ulster issue ... that man Edward Carson has over 80,000 men ready, fully armed, to fight against a Dublin government ... ?'

Plunkett raised a finger, 'No, no, ... many, in fact most, of those have joined the British Army and are in France.'

'Some of the remainder ... may even consider ... joining with us ... ', Casement added and now it was Plunkett who inspected his fingernails.

'Hmm ... and you could rely on a substantial majority of Irish people to support a rebellion?'

'Absolutely.' Both Irishmen tried to show 100% confidence. Casement was thinking of the thousands of soldiers in the Royal Irish Rifles and the Dublin Fusiliers, plus their wives and mothers and fathers – he had doubts that they would support a rebellion against the Crown.

Nobody said anything for a few seconds. The Count placed both hands on the table, 'Look ... there is a ... how do you say ... a major stumbling ... barrier? No, block, stumbling block. Let's be honest, yes? The British Navy blockade is very effective. We'd have great difficulty transporting a large number of troops to Ireland.'

Casement couldn't resist interrupting, 'But if it meant forcing Britain to maintain, say, 200,000 troops in Ireland ... surely that would ease pressure on the German war effort in France?'

The Count shrugged, 'I don't think our High Command could spare anything like the number of troops that you're wanting ... Russia is counter-attacking in the East and then there's France ... currently at Ypres we're fighting a desperate battle ... and if we did have troops in Ireland, how could we keep them supplied? My understanding is that the Irish people have become used to ... well, deprivation and hunger. They have little enough as it is, without trying to help many thousands of German soldiers.'

Plunkett sensed that this was not going well. 'What are you suggesting then?'

'Look ... We all, including the Chancellor, recognise that both of you are risking your lives ... all Germany admires the determination of the Irish people to free their nation from British domination. We will certainly provide as many rifles ... yes, and machine guns ... and ammunition that we can spare. Also, we will provide transport for you and the munitions to Ireland ... dangerous though that will be. Perhaps we could arrange for one of our ships to take the risk of shelling an English port when the rebellion starts. As for your Irish Brigade, Sir Roger, we are willing to train them in the use of machine guns. But it may be that they will be needed to fight for Germany in Egypt or Turkey, even Russia … I know that you're trying your best to increase the Brigade's numbers … it must be very difficult?'

The next day Plunkett and Casement went again to the prison camp. A new batch of captured British soldiers had arrived and those that were Irish had been segregated; about 20 were lounging, some stretched half-sleeping on the ground, in a wooden hut when the two civilians entered with a German Sergeant. The day was hot and the place stank of urine and sweat. Each prisoner was handed a packet of Woodbines and soon the place was full of smoke. Casement towered over Plunkett but shivered slightly, suffering from rheumatic fever or malaria. Plunkett tried to stifle the coughing that was exploding in his chest.

Casement brushed some dirt from his sleeve and cleared his throat, 'I don't think any of you know me. I'm Roger Casement. And this is Mr. Joseph … Peters. We're both here because we want a Free Ireland. One that doesn't answer to England …'

Someone yawned. 'Steh auf*!' the Sergeant kicked a prone prisoner who rose slowly and leaned on the wall.

'… and we are here recruiting Irishmen that love the land of their birth … men that honour the memories of Emmet and Wolfe Tone … we are asking you to become a member of the Irish Brigade and fight for freedom.'

'You're asking us to fight for these bastards … these feckin' Jermins … the ones that have been kicking shit out a' us and tryin' to kill us … and are now half-starvin' us?' Others joined in. 'Yeah? Who are yer, anyway? Have you been out fightin', a'tall? Eh? Been in front of the machine guns spitt'en death at'cher?

---

* Steh auf= Stand up!

Puttin' yoursel' thru' the feckin' barbed wire? Yer look as if a gust o'wind'd knock der pair of youse arse over feckin tit ... Fer feck sake! G'wan ... Piss off!'

Plunkett stepped forward. 'Now, just a moment. If the British catch us we'll be bashed and tortured before being strung up. There'll be no prison camp fer us. There's no war rules fer us two. We're here because we love Ireland ... you c'n sit around beggin' the Jer'min guards for a scrap of food if yer like. Or yer c'n join our Brigade, get better food, day-sent uniforms ... uniforms that show you're proud Irishmen. We're not beggin' ... we're askin' yer to stand up fer yersels ... remember what England's done to Ireland ... even now, they're smashing Irish homes and cruelly treatin' our women and children ... there's t'ousands in Ireland now waiting to rise up ... will you be man enough to join with them?'

There was silence. Then someone from the middle pushed forward. Swaggering, slowly, he moved closer and stood less than a foot in front of Casement; not quite as tall but almost. He stared, then looked sideways and downwards at Plunkett, then back at Casement.

'No. Yer c'n feck off.' He flicked a cigarette stub to the ground, turned, and went back to the huddle.

Plunkett and Casement continued to argue, plead, and persuade. Eventually, just one man took their offer and signed to join the Brigade, before they were all dismissed.

Casement sighed, 'Joseph ... I honestly do not know whether I can go on ... these men have no love for Ireland ... I really think I'd be more use in the United States.'

Plunkett looked him in the eyes, eyes which were awfully sunken and dark, and said, 'Roger, you're doing a grand job. Don't give up now. We need you here. We'll get someone to come and provide support. I must get back to Ireland, though. Sorry ... I can see this is a hell of a task you've taken on. Devoy and McGarrity will be told that you're battling away here, making real headway, but you need some support. The people back in Dublin, Cark and yes Belfast would be proud of yer. God bless and keep you, Roger.'

The next two months of Plunkett's life are mysterious. He travelled to Switzerland, sometimes as 'Peter Doyle' sometimes as 'James Pinkerton'. In Dublin, with 6,000 others, he attended the funeral of Fenian Jeremiah O'Donovan Rossa on August 1st, 1915. A few weeks later he arrived in New York as Joseph Plunkett on the S.S. *Philadelphia* which had departed Liverpool.

The voyage must have been awful. US 'Record of Aliens Held for Special Inquiry' documentation shows 'Josef Plunkett' was detained on 8/30, hospitalised with tuberculosis and excluded on 31st August, 'returned from hospital 9/11' and admitted to the US on that date. John Devoy first, in New York, and then Joseph McGarrity in Philadelphia, met Plunkett. He gave a progress report on Casement's Irish Brigade, but its accuracy may have lacked some of the harsh truth. They were made aware, if they had not been before then, that Casement needed a senior military person to assist his credibility.

Devoy said to McGarrity, 'We'll get someone from Ireland. Tom Clarke has a fella, military background, name of Robert Monteith. Used to be in the British Army, but he's a Fenian through and through. He'll come here first to throw British Intelligence off the track before going to Germany.'

The problem was that Casement needed an officer, not a corporal. The Germans could see that he was struggling to recruit any of the prisoners of war to join his 'Irish Brigade' – their treatment in captivity did not endear them to Germany and if they signed up for Casement then they could find themselves fighting oppressed people such as Turks or Egyptians. It was October 1915 when Monteith arrived in Berlin; he was presentable enough and a good soldier, but he was not an officer, the class-conscious Germans treated him accordingly, and the prisoners gave him the same lack of respect that they would give a corporal. A brigade would normally consist of about 3,000 soldiers – the 'Irish Brigade' eventually numbered 56.

Chapter 18 – I need a job

Nellie Gifford, sister of Grace and Muriel, was a member of Connolly's Irish Citizen Army (ICA). It was Nellie that had helped James Larkin to give a speech from the balcony of the Imperial Hotel, during the 1913 lockout strike. Larkin was in the US and she'd found it difficult to get any work in the theatre, except for a play by fellow activist, Máire Perolz, but she'd been helping others to find jobs. Specifically, young Irishmen returning from England due to the threat of conscription. She was so successful at this that her mother became annoyed at the constant stream of visitors. The solution was to contact Constance Markievicz, also a member of the ICA, who offered a room at the Sinn Féin HQ.

One morning in January 1916, Nellie was working at her desk when the office door was almost taken off its hinges. A fairly tall young man, about 25 years of age, burst in and strode towards her. There were two cats stretched out on a tatty piece of carpet near the window. One got up, stretched itself and looked at Collins. Then thought better of it and laid back down.

'Mornin'. I'm told yer might be able to help me get a job?'

Nellie continued writing for a moment and then looked up. 'Yes? Are you not working at all?'

'Yeah, well … I was … in England. But it looks like they'll be conscripting fellas there …'

She wrote something. 'Umm … What type of work were you doing, Michael?'

'Financial … I was a clerk in the Post Office and then I was with the Board of Trade. Financial work … I met a fella named Frank Thornton who introduced me to …' There was a pause. He growled, 'So how did yer know me name?'

'Hmm?'

'Yer said ... Michael ... me name!'

'Oh,' she looked up, 'Well ... it's getting' like every tall dark handsome young man these days is called Michael ... lucky guess ... how long were you in London?'

He was blushing. Then he leaned forward.

'I didn't say anything about London! I said England ... could'a been Manchester or Birmingham ... or ... so how did yer ...'

'Ah ... Sha, I do a bit of acting ... in the theatre? I've a good ear for accents ... I noted your slight Cockney accent ...'

'Look! ... I'm from Cark and there's no way I've got a Cockney ...'

She laughed. 'After almost ten years in London[54]? Ah, c'mon. I'm only coddin' ya. I was talking to Seán MacDiarmada and Paddy Belton last night. They said they knew a fella that'd jus' come over who was looking fer a job. Tall, dark and young ... didn't say handsome ... from Cork ... been doing financial work in London. And they'd been telling this young Michael to get himself here, so.'

'Oh.'

She was writing on a slip of paper ... 'Yes. Well, these people ... Plunketts ... I'll give yer the address ... are wanting someone to help with book-keeping and financial stuff ...' She gave him the note, 'They're OK. The Plunketts, I mean. Irish patriots to the core, like you, me and Seán ... and Harry? Harry Boland?'

Collins was now aware that this woman had more knowledge of the personnel than he did, 'Oh. Well ... thanks.'

As he went to the door, she said 'And Michael! ... Seán said that yer like a joke but that yer preferred it when you was the one doin' the jokin' ... it's OK! ... I won't let on about the accent.'

He left the office, made his way to the obviously wealthy home of the Plunketts and pulled the chain of a bell which disappeared into a frame of ivy. After about a minute, a maid opened the door.

'I'm here to see Mr Plunkett.'

'Oh …Oh, dear! Sha, the Count's not in … nor is the missus … d'ere son, Joseph is …'

'Who is it, Bridget?' A young man, not much older than Collins, came slowly to the door. He was thin, wearing wire-rimmed glasses, stooping slightly, with an unhealthy pallor. Holding the door, as if in support, he peered at Collins and waited.

'I've come from number 6 Harcourt … '

Plunkett looked at the note that Michael gave him. 'Ah … good … yes, good. Michael Collins? I've heard a bit a'boat you. How'd yer do … I'm Joseph Plunkett. This is me parents' place. I amn't usually here … if yer know what I mean … moved out to Donnybrook. No big secret. Marlborough Road … don't ask why. Come with me. I need the exercise. We're going to Larkfield … Poddle River … Kimmage. Something I have to do.' They began walking down the tree-lined avenue; Collins slowed his pace to match that of Plunkett.

'Michael, you wouldn't have a cigarette on yer? No? OK. Never mind. Look, me parents own quite a few rental properties. My sister Geraldine needs help with the administration. You'd be doing the bookwork … Collecting rents … OK? Er, you'd also be working with me …   You've been a member of the Irish Republican Brotherhood for a while, eh? … as I have. I hear that you've been doing great work in London for us. What d'yer think of Seán MacDiarmada? And his pal Tom Clarke?'

Collins mused, 'Tom's a real Fenian from way back. Have yer seen his ears? Like an elephant's! And that great bushy walrus moustache? Like a feckin anti-macassar on the back of an armchair. What a character! Seriously though, he made a very strategic move by organising the 'Dynamite' Rossa funeral[55], yer know.'

Plunkett interrupted him, 'Matter a' fact a fella named Thomas

MacDonagh actually did most of the organising.'

'Yeah? Well, that's what I call making good use of our Fenian dead, eh? Rossa was from Cark, like me'self. But him and his family, they suffered something awful during the Great Hunger ... I must be the only one that didn't get to his funeral. I know Seán MacDiarmada ... His speeches are electrifying. Sha, all the women go woozy looking at the fella, with his dark Spanish eyes and bushy black hair. And when they know he's got a lame leg, they're all running after him. But, yeah, nice fella. He and Clarke are the very core ... or maybe the rock is a better word ... of our struggle.'

Plunkett agreed, 'Yes, if an Uprising happens it'll be because of them. What about Patrick Pearse? His speech at the funeral was incredible. He has a style of talking ... with a sort of stammer or stutter. It was perfect for that funeral speech. When he said, 'They th' th' ... think that they have for ... foreseen everything, think that they have provided against everything; but the f-f-f ...fools, the f-f-f... fools, the fools! – they have left us our Fenian dead.' It was amazing! The stammering hesitation had all of us, all the t'ousands of us, gasping to hear him finish the words ... Well, anyway ... what do you know of the others? Bulmer Hobson ... you know him?'

'Hobson was too helpful to that bastard Redmond. I've heard the other gossip ... about Seán MacDiarmada being no admirer of Pearse and he doesn't trust Arthur Griffith ... Of course, he and Tom Clarke both hate their once best friend Bulmer Hobson.'

Plunkett was finding the walk strenuous and began coughing. Collins slowed his own pace even more but carried on talking, as if trying to show the coughing was quite normal. '... and James Connolly? I haven't met him. But a lot of people tell me he's a man of strong values ... though MacDiarmada hasn't a good word for him ... probably because Connolly's socialist ideas are very much counter to his.' Collins shook his head in frustration, 'I sometimes wish we'd all agree on what it is we want for Ireland; if it varies a little ... well, who gives a damn? We all want to kick the British arses ... we can work out how to run the place after that.'

'Exactly. You're certainly up to speed on all the top people. I'm going to make use of you. C'mon. We can take this tram.'

When they arrived at Larkfield, Plunkett handed Collins over to his parents, leaving the young fella to pore through some ledgers and went to find Grace Gifford. She was in a small room, alone, working on a drawing of some kind.

'Ah, Grace ... '

'Hi, Joe ... Feeling a bit better? I won't be a minute ... dying for a cigarette. I'll just finish this cartoon it's fer Connolly's *Workers' Republic.*

He sat beside her and fidgeted. She peered at her work, 'Hmm ... hang on. That's not quite right ...'

He touched her hand.

'Don't do that Joe ... I'll be done soon ...'

'Grace ...'

'Will yer jus' wait a minute, Joe! ... I'm almost ... Have yer not got a poem to write?!'

'Grace ...'

She sighed. 'What? Oh, Joe! ... Can it not wait a ...' She sighed again. 'OK ... what is it?'

'Grace ... I wanted to ... Well ... we both know that I amn't the healthiest fella ... the doctor says it isn't TB, but I don't know what it is ... and anyway there's going to be some serious stuff goin' on with the Brits, but you know that ... people are goin' to be ... Who knows what's goin' to ... '

Grace looked at Joseph, 'What is it, Joe? What are you sayin'?'

'I want us to be married ... if you'll have me?'

She looked at him and blinked. 'Oh, Joe. Of course I will. But ... what about yer parents? Your mither's not too keen on me ...?'

'Sha, don't worry about that. I can wrap her around me finger. It's your own mither that'll be the problem.'

'Huh. Yer know very well that me mither and I haven't spoken for … oh … four or five months. And if she doesn't like me becoming a Catholic that's her lookout … as fer me marryin' you! I'd do it jus' to annoy her, even if I wasn't in love with yer. So, problems solved.'

'Oh, Grace … I love you … Bless you. But you must bear in mind what I said about me health and … well, this coming business with the Brits. You do need to take that into consideration.'

'Joe … '

'It's just that … Grace, I'd like to spend me whole life with you … a white-walled cottage in the Wicklow Mountains … with four, no five! … five children playing in the garden … you and me … growing old together … but … the chances of … '

'Joe … who knows what's going to happen in the months and years ahead? … let's just plan for the best, not for the worst, so … yes, be married … and we'll dream of that cottage and children … all living together in a free Ireland. And hope and pray that the Lord takes us into His heart and … what will be, will be.'

They kissed.[56]

Chapter 19 – D'yer Want a Rebellion or Not?

'Our Constitution ... our Irish Republican Brotherhood Constitution ... that we all swore to follow ... clearly states that there will be no insurrection when there is no public support, no adequate organisation and no chance of success. I think we all know the current situation and the conditions do not currently exist which enable a rebellion...'

There was some shuffling of papers at the other end of the table. Someone blew their nose.

'... Therefore ... that being the case ... an Uprising cannot occur.' Bulmer Hobson sat back and waited. And waited.

Tom Clarke, as he always did now, chose to ignore Hobson – 'Seán, could you please pass the water jug? Thanks. We have to move on ...' This meeting of the Supreme Council was going to be critical.

'Just a moment, Tom ...' Patrick Pearse wanted to squash Hobson's point, '... those three requirements are not separated by the word 'or'. All of them are n-n-needed at the same time to prevent an insurrection. That being the case it only needs for just one of those negatives to f-f-fail and an insurrection can occur. We have an adequate organisation and indeed, I believe, a good chance of success.'

'That depends on how we define success,' said Hobson, 'Have we identified what we want to achieve? To force the Brits out of Ireland within, say, two years? To force Asquith to negotiate new Home Rule laws so all Ireland is independent by the War's end? To occupy city areas of Dublin, Cork, and Limerick for at least three months? ... what are we trying to achieve?'

If anybody was going to support Hobson, it was Professor Eoin MacNeill. 'I have to agree. And frankly, however you define success … I'm sorry … I simply do not see it happening.'

Seán MacDiarmada was feeling frustrated, 'For crying out loud!'

'No, no, Seán … I will have my say,' MacNeill persisted, 'We all agreed on reasons for a possible insurrection. One was if Germany invaded Ireland, a second was if England forced conscription on Ireland. A third was if the War in Europe ended and we hadn't gone on the attack. None of that has happened.'

Hobson wanted to support MacNeill, 'And do we really want to focus on city areas? Where the British can use their greater numbers, locate our forces and pick them off? Surely, we should consider other ideas … such as hit and run in country areas. Guerrilla tactics as used by the Boers … or the Spanish in the Napoleonic wars?' He looked around and decided to press on, 'So you're planning on occupying City buildings? And then what? Negotiate a surrender? You leaders will be martyred, you know that, and then? … will our brave lads that are taken with you also be hanged? Or will you tell them to make a run for it and fight on?'

Tom Clarke waited and then said, 'Before you say any more, Eoin, we all know your views … you don't want an armed rebellion. So, can we move on? …'

'Oh, but I do want a rebellion … if Asquith makes the first move and suppresses us or tries to dis-arm the Volunteers.' MacNeill's cultured and authoritative voice demanded attention.

Clarke glared and said 'Sha, you may be the President of the IRB but you're not a member of the Military Council*. And the Council is very much in favour of a rebellion … as soon as possible.'

---

* Members: Pearse, Clarke, Mac Diarmada, Plunkett, Ceannt, Connolly, and (April 1916) Mac Donagh.

'Yes! Absolutely,' MacDiarmada was desperate to be heard, 'We must, must, take advantage of this War in Europe. Success? Any significant uprising would be a success. If we took the centre of Dublin and held it for ... five or six weeks ... that would have to be a success. Yes, better still, and not unlikely, if we held it for long enough to force the British Army to bring 50,000 troops here, away from France. They'd soon want to negotiate then ... And if the Jer'mins could ...' Hobson began, 'That's not going to happen and yer know ...'

Clarke broke in, 'The Jer'mins have promised to provide enough rifles and ammunition to arm 20,000 of us nationwide.'

Patrick Pearse added, 'We have the chance to follow in the steps of Emmet ... to complete the work that he started. To win recompense for the pain and s-s-suffering that he and Rossa and countless Fenians suffered ... Ireland is not going to win its freedom without blood sacrifice. This chance will not come again in our lifetime, maybe not ever again.'

Clarke summed up, 'We're agreed then. We take action. But we must find out what Connolly is up to ... he's talking about charging in with his 200-member Irish Citizen Army. If that happens, we'd have to rush in ... without any coordinated plan. Joe, you're working on a strategy for the Uprising? Best finalise it as soon as possible ... and we'll sort out Connolly. We don't want him going off half-cock.'

Plunkett coughed and coughed again but finally managed to say, 'Connolly start without us? That'd be a disaster.'

Two weeks later, Connolly was invited to attend a meeting of the members of the IRB – this was the Military Council, so MacNeill was not included; neither was Hobson. Clarke was super-security conscious and Hobson, apart from being opposed to a Dublin-centric uprising, was thought to be too talkative.

To say Connolly was invited is a slight exaggeration. He wasn't given a choice – he was practically kidnapped – but he wanted to have a meeting anyway.

Clarke lit a cigarette. 'You don't smoke, Jim?'

'No.' Connolly's main negotiating tactic was to say as little as possible.

Seán MacDiarmada was going to play the hard man. 'You're a socialist aren't you, Connolly? Which is more important? A socialist revolution or an independent Ireland?'

'What's the point of a so-called independent Ireland if it's owned by Irish capitalists and we still have slums and poverty? ... but if I need to get one before the other ... then OK, let's get the Uprising started. The sooner the better.[57]'

Clarke was never one to wait until it was his turn to speak, 'We all want a free Ireland, fer God's sake! ... so why not work to that with us?'

'Us? Does that include MacNeill? Where is he? I heard he wasn't too keen on rebellion at the moment.'

The meeting/interrogation went on for three days. It was Connolly versus the Military Council. MacDiarmada, Clarke, Pearse, and Plunkett all put pressure on Connolly to postpone any action by his Citizen's Army. He was having none of it, 'You promise to rebel soon? Why should I believe you? Face it. You're not trained soldiers, yer weak as water ... OK, not you, Tom an' not you Sean ... the rest of yer ... as the Cockneys say it ... yer all mouth and trousers.'

Clarke stubbed out a tiny tip of a cigarette and took his time rolling another. 'Jim, if you go off half-cock ... you'll alert the English and get smashed ... we'd have to go in after you, we'd have no choice ... no, plan ... unprepared ... and we'd be smashed too. It'd just be a total waste. Work with us and together we'll make hell for the British.'

Connolly rubbed his chin. 'Well ... prove it. Tell me when you're going to rise up. Are yer really serious? I need to know you have a definite date.'

This was the crux for Clarke. The ultimate secret. And Clarke hated releasing secrets. He lit another cigarette. 'OK ... but you must swear not to release this to anybody. Only we, the people that you see here, know that we will attack on Easter Sunday.'

'What? No! The end of April? Yer mad! No! I can't wait that long ...'

'You can ... you must. You know it makes sense.'

Connolly was drained. It did make sense, everyone working together in a coordinated way.

'OK ... Who else knows ... about the date?'

Clarke said, 'I told yer. As few as feckin' possible ... and certainly not Eoin MacNeill ... we'll be telling Devoy in New York. He's put Casement in touch with the Germans. If we can't trust Devoy, we can't trust anyone ... and he's practically funded the whole thing, anyway. Philomena Plunkett's goin' over there to tell Devoy what's happening.'

'It's sounding to me like half Dublin knows. Anyone else?'

Plunkett said, 'My father's going to see the Pope ...'

Connolly's chair moved sideways and he almost fell.

'... we need His Holiness to bless the Uprising ... and for him to tell the bishops here to leave off criticising us.'

Connolly wasn't convinced, 'Aye ... but does yer man in Rome really need to know the date?'

Plunkett took a deep breath as if explaining the obvious,' We have to take the Holy Father into our confidence ... if we want him to ... well, work on our side.'

'Yeah ... I guess so ... but if we're talking about secrecy ... you're gonna to tell a fella that speaks to 10% of the world's population evr'y Sunday? ... OK. I get it ... you had to tell him. And like with Devoy, if we can't trust the Pope then we're in big trouble.'

Plunkett explained how the rest of Ireland outside Dublin would take part in the Uprising. Then he went through the list of buildings in the city that were to be attacked. Connolly wanted to know how many men would be allocated to each one.

'Hang on there ...,' Connolly frowned, 'what about the Castle? How many for that?'

Plunkett knew this was going to cause some heat,'Er. No. We won't be ... attacking that.'

'Why on Earth not? The seat of administration? Lots of documents? The place where they'll be making decisions?'

'That's true ... but we considered the effort to take it would require too many of us. And even more important ... it would be just too difficult to defend.'

'Well, but for the value of propaganda! ... I mean you're going for the GPO ... great ... but to take the Castle ... even if yer only occupy part of it ... that'd be a big kick up the backside. Didn't Emmet want to take the Castle?'

'True, but ... it's sure to be packed with troops. How many? Well ... we can't be sure ... lots, though.'

Pearse had his head down, thinking of Robert Emmet's attempt to take the Castle, and aware that they had no idea of the number of troops there, but he said nothing.

Connolly sighed, 'Well, what about Trinity College? They've an Officers' Training Corp, so there'll be weapons and ammunition. It won't be full of soldiers ... we could take the place easily and defend it.'

'No. We're relying on the British to resist shelling private property, but if the College got damaged, we'd get blamed ... No ... anyway, we must use our people sparingly. There's lots'a places we'd like to take, but we can't do them all.'

'OK ... Alright, I'll be at the GPO with the main force. There'll be a group of Irish Citizen Army at City Hall, led by Seán Connolly ... no, not a relative ... Michael Mallin at St Stephen's Green and another group at the College of Surgeons.'

Plunkett was intrigued as to what Connolly planned for Countess Markievicz, 'What about Connie? She'll be in command of some of yer ICA troops?'

'No, no. It'll be Mick Mallin. I'm all for women's equality but ... well, the men don't quite get that idea yet.' He looked satisfied, 'Great ... and the rest ... I mean Galway, Cork, Wexford, Limerick ...?'

'Yeah, when the time comes they'll get orders to attack police stations and barracks. They'll be getting weapons delivered a few hours before we start. Machine guns, rifles, ammunition the lot. Coming from Germany. We've heard from Casement – he has that in hand.'

Connolly tapped on the table. 'Casement? Bit of a loose cannon ... Is that all confirmed? It's gonna be a tight schedule landing all the munitions and distributing it ...?'

'Yeah, well ... we have the fellas out in the country areas all trained up and waiting for the word. Once we get started in Dublin, the Brits will be rushing around not knowing where the next attack is gonna come from ... we've told Casement not to arrive with the weapons before Easter Sunday.'

'Sunday! Day of the Uprising? Pray to God that there's no slip up. Why're yer leaving it so late?'

'Well, look ...' Plunkett was well aware of the risk they were taking but Clarke interrupted, 'Secrecy! When the guns and stuff are being distributed, there's a huge chance the Brits will get wind of it and know the Uprising's starting ...'

Connolly wasn't convinced. 'If they don't know by now that something's gonna happen, they're more stupid than I think they are.'

Clarke put his gnarled hands on the table and looked around, 'They probably do suspect … but if there's a problem and those weapons don't arrive or fail to get handed out … well, we wouldn't want the Uprising to be cancelled just 'cos of that. Casement's not the be all and end all. I never wanted him involved in the first place. The Uprising must happen, with or without rifles from Germany.'

That was just what Connolly wanted to hear.

Chapter 20 – Powerful Friends

'The Holy Father will see you now.' Count George Plunkett placed his newspaper on a small antique table and jumped up. He'd been reading an article which said that Italy, already assisting the Allies, was considering a formal declaration of war on Germany; he knew the Pope was trying to play a neutral role but would be placed in an awkward position.

Count Plunkett had been persuaded by his son Joseph to join the Irish Republican Brotherhood. This was no small thing for a devout Catholic, least of all for someone who had been commended by the Pope. The formal position of the Church hierarchy in Ireland was that Catholics should not be members of secret societies. But young Plunkett needed his father for a special mission. One that only he could undertake and for which he would need to know the date of the proposed uprising; so, membership of the IRB was essential.

His father had said, 'How can I go against the Church teaching, Joe?'

'I'm not asking you to. You know, better than I, the teachings of the previous Pope, Leo XIII, and his encyclical *Rerum Novarum* … He referred to St. Thomas Aquinas' philosophy and showed that Catholic citizens are not obliged to obey any law which is contrary to divine or natural laws nor obliged to obey an illegitimate authority. So Catholic protest and resistance are reasonable actions against a criminal, Protestant state.'

'But Pope Leo opposed communism and preached that people must obey the law[58].'

'Yes, but not if the law was illegitimate. Dad, On March 31st Prime Minister Asquith had an audience with Pope Benedict XV. He told him that Ireland had been given Home Rule; he made no mention of the fact that it wouldn't come into effect until after the War and, even then, not the whole of Ireland. We must make sure the Holy Father knows the truth and that he tells the Irish Bishops not to condemn our Uprising. We must have his blessing.'

The Count was convinced and so now, on April 8th, he was with the Pope in his private rooms. They both spoke French and the Pope's Secretary was taking notes. Plunkett explained the Home Rule situation, Asquith's deception, and that an Uprising would take place on Easter Sunday.

The Pope frowned and pursed his lips, 'Oooh! Is there no other way?'

'Holy Father, I'm sure that you recall the thoughts of Saint Augustine. He said that Christians should punish a government's wickedness when they are forced to do so; doing nothing would be a sin; if a grave wrong could be stopped then it had to be stopped even if it meant using violence. If war was waged in obedience to the divine command, and wicked men put to death then there was no violation of the commandment, "Thou shalt not kill.[59]". Your Holiness, we ask that you give the Uprising your blessing.'

'I will bless you and all your Irish friends. You must, when you return to Ireland, speak to Archbishop Walsh.' Plunkett thanked him, kissed the Papal ring, and left.

Pope Benedict sighed and turned to his secretary.

'Take those notes ... and burn them ... Er, on the way back to your office, please ask Cardinal Gaspari to step in here.'

A few minutes later the door opened.

'Ah. Pietro. Please ... shut the door. That Irish business you were telling me about? That date which had been suggested to you? Well ... it has been confirmed.'

'Ah.'

'Yes ... as my Secretary of State ... you will be aware that information is only useful if it is used ... wisely, and discreetly, of course. That will be all.'

*

About a week later, April 14, Philomena Plunkett, one of the daughters of the Count, disembarked from the SS *St. Paul* at Ellis Island, New York. In accordance with instructions, she told John Devoy that the Uprising would be on Easter Sunday and received in return news of Casement's work in Germany. After she left, Devoy contacted the German Embassy and told them to notify Casement of the Uprising date and that the 20,000 rifles must not arrive in Ireland before Easter Sunday. This was a change to the *"Deliver between Thursday, April 20 and Sunday, April 23"* that had been agreed between Devoy and the Germans. Things were getting very confusing. In some ways, the date change was irrelevant – the SS *Aud* with the weapons had already left Lübeck (on April 9) and the ship had no radio. And Casement had already left Germany – on April 12. The chances of chaos increased.

Despite Tom Clarke's paranoia about secrecy, the number of people who knew the proposed date was escalating. Telegraph traffic between the German foreign ministry in Berlin and its Embassy in Washington was being decrypted by 'Room 40' in British Admiralty, with some degree of ease. Admiral Reginald 'Blinker' Hall, Director of the Intelligence Division, was an unconventional man and people who had a need to attend Room 40 in the Old Admiralty Building somehow always got lost. Room 40 staff included a classical historian, a music historian, an archaeologist, an actor, an expert in ancient Greek poetry, a banker, an Olympic hockey player, and a lawyer[60].

Although 'Blinker' knew the planned Uprising date, it was another thing to convince senior military members of its accuracy because he refused to disclose his source ... and he had his own reasons for not being too convincing. Nevertheless, it was obvious that something was going to happen, sometime soon. There were a few, Blinker Hall included, who considered it might be preferable to allow the crisis to come to a head. The resultant fighting would enable Irish troublemakers to be dealt with and many of their supporters could be locked away. One stream of information, though, which was promptly acted upon related to the weapon smuggling being carried out by Casement.

Chapter 21 – Going Back Home

Monteith and his senior officer, woefully ill, had done their best with the Irish Brigade. Casement had been in a sanatorium outside the City for several months but had now managed to return to Berlin. The Germans told Monteith, on March 1st, of the latest Devoy message they'd received … that the Rising was timed for next month, Easter Sunday 1916.

Casement was an exhausted man, 'I can do no more … we've got an Irish Brigade consisting of 56 men. That's the best we can do, which is next to useless. But, Bob, you've done a good job training them with machine guns.'

'There's a few good men in …'

'No! No. I'm calling an end to it. The Germans have gone back on their word. I've lost all trust in them. They refuse to provide any troops. They treat us and the Brigade lads like dirt. I think they just want us gone.'

'But, Roger, they are going to give us rifles and ammunition?'

'Yes, that's true … and they say they'll arrange transport for everything. But I'm not going to make use of the Brigade, not for an Uprising doomed to failure. And … where's John McGoey?'

McGoey, who had been sent over from the US by McGarrity to assist with the Brigade, came into the room. Casement looked at him, 'John, I want you to go to Ireland. The Germans will help with your passage. You must, I stress must, get Clarke and the others to understand that the Irish Brigade isn't viable and the Germans will not invade Ireland. The best we can do is arrange for 20,000 rifles, machine guns, and ammunition to be sent over. That will be done but … the Uprising cannot, must not, go ahead as planned. It would be a disaster with thousands of Irish men, women and children being slaughtered.'

The thought of leaving Germany was glorious but McGoey struggled to understand, 'The Germans will hit the roof when they know you've sent me back. And if they find out about you cancelling the Uprising ... they'll go berserk, Roger.'

'Ah, let me worry about that. Apart from my health, I'm still the man that I was in 1900 and I will do everything I can to stop innocent people suffering.'

McGoey said farewell to Casement on March 19th and was never officially seen again. The Germans were persuaded to use a ship to carry the rifles, ammunition and explosives on a voyage to Ireland. Casement would go to Wilhelmshaven by train where a submarine, the U20, would be provided to take him, Monteith and a man named Daniel Bailey from the Irish Brigade. The Germans agreed reluctantly but were puzzled as to the insistence on travelling by submarine rather than by ship with the weapons.

Casement was still extremely ill but managed to squash his lanky frame into a 64-metre submarine, powered by a smelly diesel engine, with the 25-man crew and two other Irishmen. They left Germany on April 12th ... but then returned to port due to a technical problem. They transferred to U19. It was nine days later, after midnight, when they arrived in Tralee Bay off the Kerry coast that an argument started.

'Kapitänleutnant, I am most grateful for your help but I must insist that you allow me to disembark,' Casement made his point although he could barely whisper. He felt close to death. The claustrophobic conditions, the tension, seasickness, stink of diesel, and symptoms of malaria, were all unbearable.

Raimund Weisbach had been watch officer on the submarine which sank the Lusitania. U-19 was his first independent command and his instructions were to take Casement, Monteith and Bailey to Tralee Bay and transfer them to a merchant steamer, *Libau,* disguised as *SS Aud,* loaded with a very small cargo of timber to disguise 20,000 high quality M1891 Mosin-Nagant rifles, 10 machine guns, and explosives.

The *SS Aud* had arrived in the bay on Thursday as scheduled months ago, but earlier than anybody in Ireland or the USA now wanted. The ship waited. There were no lights signalled from Fenit Pier where the cargo was to be unloaded, and no sign of the submarine carrying Casement. It would have helped if the *Aud* had a radio – but it didn't. Whether the Germans or Casement thought one was unnecessary or too costly or nobody thought of it ... is irrelevant – there was no radio. So, the ship waited. True, the local Volunteers had been told that the schedule had changed and the plan was now that the ship would not arrive before Sunday. But it would not have taken much initiative to have been on the alert for an early arrival due to unforeseen circumstances. Especially since they'd had no response confirming that the message changing the date had been received.

About 10 miles north of Fenit harbour, Weisbach looked at Casement, 'I'm sorry but my orders are to transfer you to the *SS Aud* ... we must get closer to the pier and wait a little ...'

'No. No, please. I must pass a message of the highest importance to the Irish High Command ...'

'Sir Roger ... we are not yet at the transfer point ... '

'I don't care! Just let us out and you can be back on naval duties. We'll find our way to Fenit.'

'Very well, as you wish. The three of you can take the collapsible boat ... good luck.'

It was two miles to the shore, the surf was rough, and it was a very small boat. Inevitably, they all fell into the water. Monteith managed to help Casement to the beach but it was decided that he was too ill to travel and the other two would try to get assistance from local Volunteers. They were on Banna Strand, 13 kilometres from Tralee – about 15 kilometres north of Fenit Pier and 5 kilometres from Ardfert police station.

Gulls and curlews sang and screamed. Casement shivered in his wet clothes, sat down and felt the sand falling through his fingers. A sudden emotion flowed through him, knowing that at last he was back home. There was the sound of someone approaching; Casement turned and looked at a policeman's face.

On Friday the *Aud* approached to within 600 metres of Fenit Pier and cruised along the coast. At 7pm it was surrounded by Royal Navy destroyers and escorted by HMS *Bluebell* towards Cork Harbour. British Intelligence had obtained access to specific details of the ship's location, along with information concerning possible submarines. Captain Spindler scuttled the ship outside the harbour and all the weapons and munitions went to the seabed.

Monteith had managed to find local rebel leader Austin Stack and told him that Casement wanted the Uprising stopped – Stack insisted on proof. They went towards Banna Strand but police were wandering along the shore; it was obvious that Casement had already been found and locked up in the small local police station at Ardfert. Bailey had also been arrested. Stack's instructions from Dublin were that there was to be no action of any kind before Sunday, so he obediently refused to try a rescue bid. Some people might have thought Casement's capture, perhaps with vital information, was a drastic enough event to force a change of plans. Not Stack. He found it more convenient to obey the earlier orders. By Saturday afternoon this was all immaterial because Casement was on the train to Dublin under police escort.

Chapter 22 – 'Throttling and Neck Breaking, Sir?'*

On Sunday morning a well-dressed man, with a white wing collar shirt in a dark pin-striped suit, sat at a desk covered with brown-paper files and documents. The interview room at Scotland Yard was tiny, sparse and smelt of pipe smoke; someone knocked on the door.

'Yes? Come in!'

A police Sergeant, with obvious contempt, brought in a tall thin-faced unshaven man; his flowing hair may have been unkempt but there was a proud alertness in his piercing eyes. When Casement strode in, despite clearly being unwell, he held his head high and stared at Basil Thomson.

'Alright, leave him here.' The Sergeant turned and closed the door. Assistant Commissioner Thomson, who worked closely with the Admiralty's Intelligence Division's Reginald 'Blinker' Hall, was now flicking through documents and reading intently. He said, without looking up, 'Sit down, Casement.' The English voice was sharp and well-bred.

It was a hard wooden chair but Casement was glad to rest. He wasn't expecting the first question though.

'Been in trouble with police before haven't you, Casement? Not your first offence, eh? Thieving! You and yer brother stole some books? In a shop? Yes, it was a while ago, but it's all here in the records … York Road Lambeth, when you were a lad, aged 11 [61]… your mother would'a been shocked and ashamed, but then she'd died three years before, eh? … only 39 years of age, poor woman … she liked a drink? Anyway … oh! Here's a letter sent

---

* *The Quare Fella*, Brendan Behan

to us from a Mr. Adler Christensen[62]. Offering to help. For a price!'

Thomson closed the folder and slapped his hands down staring at Casement. 'You're a traitor, aren't you? Persuading prisoners of war in German prison camps to fight for Germany against British troops! ... recruiting Irishmen to fight and kill loyal Irishmen? A traitor!'

'No ... I recruited them to fight for my country ... and it's their country, too. Ireland.'

Thomson ignored him, '... And Irishmen are already dead because of you.' Casement blinked.

'You didn't know? Why would yer? Even if you did, you wouldn't care ... I'll tell you though. Whilst you were making your way to Banna Strand, three men took the train from Dublin to Killarney. They stopped there and had a meal ... no doubt also had a pint or two or three. Then they met two men in cars. One was a new 20 H.P. Briscoe American open touring car and the other a Maxwell. They all headed off towards the Wireless College at Cahersiveen ... not too far from Banna Strand. One of the men, young lads really, Cornelius Keating, 22 years of age, had been a student there. He may or may not have been expelled from the College ... In Parliament Mr Ginnell on December 21st asked whether 2 students had been kicked out of the College because of their political opinions ...? It's all here in the paper work!'

He glanced down at some documents. 'Now, we know that Joseph Plunkett is fascinated by the military potential for wireless communication; he and his brother Jack are often mucking around with the bits and pieces. We also know that Keating was staying at the Plunketts' Larkfield estate with other Fenians, helping with wireless sets ... when not making bombs.'

Thomson looked up, 'You'll hang, y'know? Unless ... Perhaps

… if you plead guilty, good lawyer … an' tell us something valuable? … those local Fenians could have got you out of that police station without much effort if they'd really wanted to … You don't owe them anything … Why were the cars going to Cahersiveen[63]?'

Casement frowned, 'I really have no idea what you're talking about.'

'Well, don't worry … we know … or we can make reasonable deductions. That college would have been unguarded; they were going to steal equipment and use it … to contact the ship from Germany carrying 20,000 rifles … yes, we know about that … But the ship's captain didn't get the message about not arriving 'til Sunday.'

Casement half-laughed. 'You're not as clever as you think. This young Keating couldn't have sent a message to the ship. It hasn't got a radio.'

'Hasn't it? Ha! We'll come to that in a minute. Well, if the purpose wasn't to contact the ship, it must have been to interfere with British naval shipping communications?'

Casement raised his eyebrows, 'Really? A 22-year-old Fenian wireless operator? With access to your codes? Must be a very … precocious young man.'

'Not now, he isn't. We know that the other men might have had some expertise … Perhaps a message to Devoy in New York? Or simply steal portable sets and pass them on to … well? Who would the sets be passed to? …'

Casement scoffed.

Thomson lit a pipe, sucked and then blew the smoke before continuing, '… Donal Sheehan was with Keating and another passenger? … Was Tommy McInerney driving? As best he could, I mean. Who was the other passenger? Charlie Monahan, or

Monaghan, from Belfast? Where's he?'

'How many more times? I really have no idea what you're talking about.'

'No? I suppose I should tell you about those men … that died because of you … We know some of the details … Dublin Castle might have its leakers, but these things usually work both ways … The cars? The Maxwell was leading because McInerney didn't know the way. Probably had to allow a fair gap so as not to cause suspicions. The Briscoe only has one headlight, dark rainy night as you know … hedgerows … twisting roads …. the front car speeding through Killorglin, lest the cops pull it up, then slowing.'

Thomson shook his head as if saddened by the futility. 'But that's where the Briscoe vehicle probably lost contact so McInerney stopped; one of his passengers asked a local, young Lily Taylor, for directions, about 9:30pm. She said turn left at the church. The passenger possibly misunderstood or maybe passed on the wrong directions to the driver. How good was the chap at driving? Sober? Experienced? Let's face it … I doubt if these people had access to many cars. They certainly wouldn't have been driving those cars before. Whatever, they didn't turn at the church … they went down towards Ballykissane Quay… how fast? Who knows? But I'm betting a fair old clip … along the pier … kept going …and ended up in the Laune River. A very deep river. Cold, cold water. Keating and McInerney managed to get out but Keating drowned. Monahan? Who knows what happened to him? Do you?'

Thomson rubbed his rather large nose and stroked his moustache, 'Anyway … not much point … those rifles won't be going to your Fenian pals. Ship's at the bottom of the Bay now … Scuttled.'

Casement said nothing.

'That was another real mess wasn't it? I mean about the ship's arrival date. Didn't you get the details? From America? I think Devoy's messenger Tommy O'Connor, a ship steward, was on a slower than usual ship ... What message was he bringing to Germany? About Dublin not wanting the ship to get to Tralee Bay before Easter Sunday? But you disagreed, didn't you? Thought more time was needed for distribution? Did you get the confusing message from Count Plunkett? Saying 'Arrive in Tralee Bay not later than dawn of Easter Saturday' ... Anyway, the German ship got there too early! Nobody to meet them ... Why didn't those in Dublin realise that there was a huge risk that the message *Arrive Sunday Not Thursday* didn't get through? Why didn't anybody at Fenit use some gumption and think the ship might be early? What a joke! And yer think the Irish can govern themselves! Idiots!'

Thomson stared at Casement, 'They've left you to carry the can, matey. Pearse's people at Banna Strand could have easily helped you escape from that police station. Nobody wanted to help. Yer been disowned. Yer never were one of them, were you? Where's Monteith? He came with you, we know that. Just like Bailey ... we've got that fella. He'll swing, too. Unless he knows what's good for him ... '

Casement shrugged. He was dazed, almost falling asleep ... apparently.

Thomson snarled, 'Well?'

'Monteith? Bailey? Never heard of them.' The door opened and a small, fidgety man in a naval officer's uniform walked in, closed the door, and sat beside Thomson.

'Whoops. Clumsy of me ...', some papers fell to the floor, 'Sorry, I'm late, Basil ... timekeeping's not my strength ... Is this him? Casement?'

'Yes but being most unhelpful. Oh! Hello, Frank.' Major Frank

Hall, no relation to Captain 'Blinker' Hall, had also come into the room. He was MI5, fiercely homophobic and a committed Irish Unionist, 'Hello Basil. Reggie ... so, this is the bastard that tried to get Irish soldiers to fight and die for Germany? Sorry to interrupt. Carry on, Reggie ...'

Captain Hall was a strange, hypnotic man. Beneath enormously bushy eyebrows one eye constantly glared whilst the other was always blinking. The effect would be terrifying were it not for false teeth which seemed to have been made for someone with a larger face. He sneered, 'Casement, we obviously already have access to information ... you confirm it and we'll recommend a custodial sentence. You'd be released in a few years. Give us the names of your German contacts ... what about ... Captain von Rintelen? ... Heinrich Albert? Did you meet Brann[64]?'

'Who?'

'Oh, dear ... You really are an idiot, Casement. We had the time and date of when you left Germany. We were waiting for you to arrive. You've told him, Basil? ... That he'll hang unless ... You ever seen a man being hanged, Casement? I know you've travelled the world. Seen things that you'd prefer to forget. A hanging? No? Never seen one? Not nice. Apparently, very occasionally, the head gets torn off. Probably a quick death. Sometimes the executioner makes a botch of it ... the drop's too much ... the neck's stretched ten or eleven inches ... that happened with a soldier chap named Charles Wooldridge* ... some sort of connection with Oscar Wilde ... I saw a hanging once. Wandsworth. The canvas hood pulled roughly down over the fella's head, then quick – noose around his neck ... so quick ...

---

* Wooldridge, 31, killed his wife and was hanged at Reading Gaol in 1896. Oscar Wilde was there 1895-97.

imagine the sudden darkness and the smell of that coarse cloth hood ... the lever pulled with a clang! Trap door suddenly gone! Drop! Chap was swinging, gurgling and kick-kick-kicking for, oh ... close to 10 minutes. Fouled his trousers, of course. Choking, eyes probably bulging in the hood's darkness, blood seeping from his nose and dribbling down his chin. Gurgling and choking. Hangman hadn't done a good job ... he had to go down below and yank the fella's legs, swing on them. Oh, dear. Horrible, horrible!'

One of the Naval man's eyes wasn't quite right. It reminded Casement of Patrick Pearse and the way that an eye somehow rolled when he was excited or angry. But this man's eye was blinking, really-really blinking.

'When it's over and they take your corpse down, it'll be stripped and tossed in a pit, somewhere in the Pentonville prison yard, full of quicklime. Your bones will be alone in a shallow hole, in London .... England. We're not having any more maudlin martyr funerals. Anyway, I'm under the impression that most Irish people would prefer to forget everything to do with you ...'

Thomson sighed, 'That reminds me,' and took some objects out of his briefcase. A Letts Diary and an almanac, a Dollard's 1910 Diary, and a Cash Ledger. He placed them on the desk and looked at Casement and then at Hall.

'Reggie, old boy, have a look at these. Found in a locked trunk ... in Casement's Ebury Street lodgings.'

Casement flinched. Blinker Hall pretended to be surprised, 'Hmm? ... What's this, Basil?' flicking open one of the books. There was a brief silence, then an intake of breath.

'Oh! Oh, my goodness!? Good God! Argh! Disgusting! Is this your handwriting, Casement? Did you ... Oh, my! ... You really are a ... very ... strange ... queer ... chap.'

Casement's hands clenched, 'What have you got there? They are not mine. Where did you say you got those? I haven't been in London for ... years.'

Thomson leaned forwards, 'D'yer deny that these are yours? You know Arthur Gregory, don't yer? He's been very helpful to us.'

Casement stared at his mental torturers. 'Please ... if the Uprising takes place then hundreds even thousands, British and Irish, will be killed ... many of them civilians ... women and children ... I beg you .... allow me to send a message to Dublin. You can see it before I send it. I'll say that all the weapons from Germany have been lost and that the Uprising, if it happens, will be a disaster with enormous loss of life. I'll plead guilty ... to treason. Please! British troops will be killed too ...[65] '

Captain Hall's extraordinary eye was closed, 'No. It's beyond time to lance the boil. Irish terrorism must be dealt with once and for all. Sergeant! Get him out!'

The door closed behind Casement.

'I say, Basil old boy ... were they ...?'

'His books? Absolutely. Aren't they, Frank? ... Without a doubt[66]. I've had them for ... oh ... well, quite a while. One of my pansy helpers, chap named Arthur Maundy Gregory, told me where to find them. The contents though? Well, just between you and me, his writing is rather unintelligible so ... we may have ... added a few paragraphs ... filled some gaps ... to clarify what he was obviously thinking ... Young Frank Adcock in Room 40 was very helpful.'

Thomson sighed, 'D'yer think we should have let him send that message? To cancel the Uprising, I mean?' Frank Hall grinned, 'Better let this festering sore come to a head.'

Blinker Hall laughed, 'I meant what I said to him, about lancing the boil. True enough, there'll be quite a few deaths. Perhaps ... A thousand Irish civilians? Hundred British troops? But we're losing about 500 every day in Europe. If we can resolve Ireland ... get it off England's back ... for the loss of a hundred soldiers, we'll be able to release tens of thousands from being stationed in Ireland and send them to France.'

'So, Frank, you've notified Dublin Castle? About the insurrection ... going to start this Easter?'

'Senior people were made aware of some facts last month but whether they believed my report or what they've chosen to do about it[67] ...', he shrugged.

'They were aware the firearms were arriving, Reggie? And the Uprising was happening at Easter?

'Er, yes. Sort of. I'll tell them everything we know soon enough. Yes, yes. I will. At the appropriate time. Dublin Castle was told three days ago that a ship from Germany was arriving today ... but with a warning the information couldn't be relied upon 100%*. Anyway, I'm Navy and the people in Dublin Castle are Army. They can wait.[68]'

'But, Reggie ...'

'Basil, old boy ... the trap has only been set. I'm not going to release the trigger until I'm sure the rat is going to be well and truly killed. The more Fenians that stick their head above the parapet, the better.[69]'

---

* Royal Commission on the rebellion in Ireland. Report, Page 11

Chapter 23 – Getting Things Together

Pearse, Plunkett, MacDiarmada, and Clarke were determined that the Uprising would happen on Easter Sunday; Connolly would have preferred it months earlier but was now willing to work with the Irish Volunteers. The problem was that Eoin MacNeill, Chief of Staff of the Volunteers, was opposed to any action unless it was unavoidable; Hobson, also on the Executive, supported him.

Plunkett was therefore intent upon providing a clear reason why urgent militant action was needed and the "Castle Document" could provide that reason. A few things were stopping him from using it. Firstly, he didn't have it. Yet.

Eugene Smyth was a Fenian sympathiser and worked as a civil servant in Dublin Castle with access to high-level documentation. In April 1916 he was given a long document written by Major General Friend, Officer Commanding the Forces in Ireland. It listed the actions that would be needed if conscription was going to be enforced. They included the arrest of known Irish troublemakers and the addresses of buildings identified as being associated with those people.

Smyth later said that the Castle Document[70] was uncoded; he memorised it and then wrote out a summary. This found its way, rewritten into code for some unexplained reason and consisting of several pages, to Plunkett. How accurate was Smyth's memory, whether he made mistakes when summarising, exactly how it came to Plunkett, how many hands it passed through, whether it was coded and decoded accurately … none of this is certain and the only thing that matters is that Plunkett held it in his hands.

The second difficulty for him was the code. This was resolved as a result of a problem – he was still bedridden, after two weeks, in Mrs Quinn's Nursing Home following major surgery on his neck. One version of the truth is that a friendly waiter from the Granville Hotel had found a pocketbook containing the code; Plunkett used it to decode the document and Grace Gifford, who came to visit every day, wrote the new version[71].

As far as Plunkett was concerned it was evidence that the British Government intended taking firm action that would forestall the fight for freedom. If some of the details needed to be 'spiced up' or clarified, then he was the man to do it. For example, apparently the coded version had the Archbishop's House but the initial uncoded version showed this as Ara Coeli, Cardinal Logue's home (in Armagh). That was corrected but unfortunately, the result of 'corrections' and clarifications meant that MacNeill would later suspect, as the British Government also claimed, that the whole document was fraudulent[72]. But Plunkett? He couldn't care less.

Francis Sheehy-Skeffington, who was a co-founder with Connolly of the Irish Citizen Army (when its original role was to defend strikers), passed a copy of the 'decoded' Castle Document to a councillor who read it aloud at a Dublin Corporation meeting on the Wednesday before Easter; an uprising was now inevitable. If the British Government did not suspect this would be about to happen, then 'Blinker' Hall in Room 40 certainly did[73].

On Holy Saturday, 1916, Grace Gifford was less interested in the Castle Document than where young Plunkett might be and what he was doing. Knowing that her mother would be out, she'd managed to sneak back home and was in her room at 8 Temple Villas, Palmerston Road, in Rathmines; a very respectable semi-detached five-bedroom home typical of a solicitor and his family.

'Sha, you'll tell me where he is ... won't you?' A tabby kitten on her lap meowed. 'No! You're no help, at all. I'll be sendin' yer back to Nellie, so.' Grace reached for another cigarette, her hand shaking with knowledge that a crisis was coming. It was three hours since she'd gone to Quinn's Nursing Home to be told that Joe had discharged himself. He'd apparently told the doctor and nurses that he was needed elsewhere. They warned him that he was taking a huge risk because the wound on his neck was nowhere near healed. He'd wrapped a scarf round it, dressed himself, and left. Gone.

Grace tried her best not to cry, knowing that wouldn't help. Obviously, the marriage wasn't going to happen this Sunday as planned. Joe had told her as much. He said that they'd need to postpone it. She knew why of course. The Uprising was happening and her tears flowed. He had wanted them to marry earlier, in Lent; she knew that was permissible but even so she thought it inappropriate and wanted it later ... she wished now that she'd ... 'Oh! Where are yer, Joe? Can yer not send word? Please God, they haven't picked yer up ... and yer in the Castle or Kilmainham.' She twiddled her rosary beads and whispered a prayer. Then another one. And another.

Sleep came eventually. The house was silent when she woke just before midday and decided to try to do some drawing. The door knocker was being banged! She leapt up, wiped her eyes, and rushed to the large entrance porch. She must have left the door unlocked because there, standing on the blue-and-brown encaustic tiles, was Collins – large and awkward, fidgeting in front of the stained-glass windows.

'Grace ... sorry, the door was open ...'

'Never mind! Where's Joe? Is he alright?'

'Yeah, yeah. Busy though. He sent me ... said to give yer this.' He handed her a small automatic gun and showed how to use it, 'Be careful, now.' She shuddered, 'What? I dunno that I'm goin' to be using that! And what's wrong with yer hand? Been in the wars already?' Collins' right hand was wrapped in a bandage.

'Ha! No. One of Rory O'Connor's brilliant grenades was faulty. But, no, you be careful wid that gun, alright? Joe wants yer to have it. Just in case. And this, too.' It was a crumpled £20 note. 'Now, listen. He says he wants yer to meet him at the Metropole Hotel.'

'Now?'

'Er, later. Yeah. Later. This evening. Sorry, I've gotta go. Lots to do. Take care, God bless. Oh, almost forgot this. A letter from Joe. Bye now.' The door closed and Grace went slowly back to her room. She opened the letter; it was dated today, Holy Saturday, 2:45 pm. Joe explained that he'd been horribly busy, the gun was to be used only in an emergency and for protection, 'All my love forever, xxxxxxxxxxxxxxxxx'[74].

Joe's room at the Metropole was smaller than he would have liked. He was trying to focus on the scraps of notes that he'd been writing but his neck was aching horribly[75]. He looked at his watch and wondered when Grace would arrive. The door opened and he managed to sit up straight, but it was only Mick Collins. Joe struggled to hide his disappointment.

'Mick! Any news of those three we sent to Cahersiveen? I gotta admit I'm worried about them ...'

'Sha, they'll be fine ...'

'Yeah? ... well ... And did yer get to see Grace?'

'Yeah, I gave her everything. Told her you wanted to see her.'

'Good.' Joe looked at his watch again, 'You go to the meeting and I'll join yer later.' Collins left and Joe bit his nails. It was ten past five. He'd give her another half hour.

Allowing for an hour to get to the hotel, Grace had left home just before 5 o'clock. The Metropole in Sackville Street was next door to the General Post Office; it was originally four Georgian buildings which had been combined to give a French appearance with a typically Parisian roofline. The effect was to make the hotel one of Dublin's landmarks. Although not for much longer.

When she walked into the reception area it was almost 6pm and she saw Joe coming carefully down the stairs. He was in a green Irish Volunteers army uniform, with a white scarf wrapped around his neck and carrying a slouch hat. His hair had been shorn, and he looked tired and impatient.

'Grace! Where have you been!? …'

'Joe …'

'… I've been waiting all afternoon. I'd just about given you up!'

They found a corner away from the reception desk in which to sit. 'Joe, I was told to come in the evening. That was what Mick said. I thought you must be busy … or resting. You know that I've been worried sick about that operation on yer neck. I could have been here hours ago!'

She rubbed her nose and looked away.

'Oh.' Joe sensed that he could be in a bit of trouble himself, 'Ah. Well … you're here now. Thanks be to God. I … I was worried …' He kissed her and held her hands. 'Did Mick give you everything?'

'Yes, yes. Sha, I don't know which I was more scared of though. The money or the gun.'

Joe looked around and laughingly hushed her. 'Let's hope that you're not forced to use either.'

He paused and said, 'I'm sorry, my love. I wish now I'd made the arrangements for our wedding earlier …'

'Joe, I can wait. I know that you've not been sitting idle these past few months!'

'That's true enough. But … I want to make sure that you're in a secure position … if anything happens to me …'

'I know, Joe. It'll work out. You've got to worry about yourself, too. Getting better and … staying safe.'

Joe stood up and whispered, 'C'mon. I've still got quite a few things to do ... come in the cab with me and I'll drop yer off.'

'Joe ...'

'What, my love?'

'Joe ... I love you, Joe.'

'Sha, I know that ... and you know, Grace, that I love you.'

That was the last time that they were alone together.

Chapter 24 – 'Yes-No-Yes!'

'Pearse, yer BAStard! Open this FECKIN' door!' Michael O'Rahilly, as usual wearing an expensive suit and looking like an American film star, was doing his best to kick in a door at Saint Enda's school; he'd just been told that his friend Bulmer Hobson had been grabbed by Irish Volunteers and spirited away, lest he try to stop the Uprising.

The door opened and O'Rahilly waved a revolver in Pearse's face, 'If you've hurt Hobson … I'll kill yer!'

'Whoa! Hold yer horses, Michael. Bulmer's fine and will be released in a cup'la days.'

'Cup'la days? After the Uprising? Yer mad! Yer know that, don't yer?'

'No, look, if we wait any longer then the opportunity will be lost. We can't rely on Bulmer to keep his mouth shut. The British think that everything's cancelled because Casement's been arrested. … Connolly will attack regardless of what we do.'

'Connolly? He's only inter-rested in a communist revolution. And why has he refused to call for a rising in Belfast? Protecting his family there?'

'Rubbish. He's put his life and family at risk …'

'And you, Pearse? What are you putting at risk? No wife, no children … you're just interested in your Blood Sacrifice, aren't you? Think you're Jesus Christ? So it's got to be at Easter! Same as Joe, that fecken' Poet-Plunkett? What's he got to lose? He'll be dead from TB in a few months, so why not be a glorious martyr for Auld Ireland?'

'Look, Michael … calm down. We all appreciate what you did. T'was yerself that persuaded MacNeill to start the Volunteers and then you've funded and organised the Howth rifles. You want the same t'ing as us; an independent Ireland after 700 years of British persecution. We can't carry on putting things off. Home Rule! That's garbage. The British want to partition Ireland. After the War the Tories will win an election and either stop Home Rule or enforce the partition. We must fight ... now. This moment won't come again for decades and decades.'

O'Rahilly glared, 'Going off half-cocked like this is madness. Occupyin' the GPO, a factory or two and some houses! What's the point of that? How many rifles have yer got? Four thousand at best. The British will know exactly where you are and they'll use their machine guns, grenades, and high explosive shells to smash you out. But not just you ... hundreds, maybe thousands of young Irishmen as well, are going to get killed or mangled.'

Pearse winced. 'We'll make the Brits suffer. They won't like taking troops away from France.'

'Have yer not t'ought about the civilians that are going to be kil't? The young Volunteers that you're asking to die so that you can be a feckin' martyr? Why not take the fight to the hills? Hit and run, like the Boers? Attack barracks and police stations in Munster, Cork, and Tyrone. The British Army would need 40,000 troops to pacify the country. They wouldn't want to do that for t'ree months, let alone twelve. The US would refuse to join 'em in Europe and the Germans would be over the moon.'

'No, Michael. It's now or never.' Just then Eoin MacNeill, Chief of Staff of the Irish Volunteers and Professor of Irish History at University College Dublin, arrived and walked into the Pearse drawing room.

'Padraig, you lied to me! Who'd you get to make up that Document? O'Connor? Plunkett?'

'Eoin, you know as well as I do that the Castle people were going to come for us all sooner or later.'

'No. You've had the date fixed for ... weeks, months? And yer kept it from me. The Document is an excuse, not a reason. Well, the Uprising is not happening tomorrow. I'm having it printed in the newspaper that the Sunday manoeuvres are cancelled.'

'Eoin ...'

'The loss of Casement's firearms means it would be a disaster. It's not happening. Cancelled.' The O'Rahilly walked towards the door and then turned, 'Padraig, it's too soon. It's out of control. I'm gonna go to as many Brigades all over the country and tell them that there'll be no Uprising.'

British Intelligence saw the newspaper cancellation and assumed that there would be no action in the near future. Administrative staff at Dublin Castle could go on Easter holiday. Soldiers would take leave and officers go to the horse racing at Fairyhouse on Monday to see Jackie Lynn on 5-1 'All Sorts', trained by Richard Cleary, win the Irish Grand National by 12 lengths in front of 25,000 people. Forebodingly perhaps, "Civil War ", the horse which had won in 1914, came fourth[76].

Tom Clarke was livid, furious and devastated, and all points in between. But then he and Pearse, Connolly, Clarke, Plunkett, and other senior rebel leaders considered that the action had only been postponed – it would start on Monday regardless of MacNeill and O'Rahilly. Dublin Irish Volunteers and the Irish Citizen Army were ordered to report for duty. Messages were sent to country areas instructing them to disrupt trains on Monday; but there was still confusion outside Dublin due to both MacNeill's advertisement and to 'The' O'Rahilly, who travelled nationwide urging Volunteers not to mobilise.

On Sunday morning MacDiarmada was ready to explode, 'So, it's cancelled?' Tom Clarke, looking at Connolly, said, 'Is it hell! It's postponed. 24 hours. We go tomorrow.'

Monday, 24 April 1916 was a bright, sunny day. 50 or so Irish Volunteers crowded on to a tram at Larkfield estate with George Plunkett, Joseph's brother, paying the fares. They dismounted at Sackville Bridge and marched to Liberty Hall where they met James Connolly, Joseph Plunkett and about 150 men of the Irish Citizen Army. More Volunteers arrived. Eventually on that glorious April day there were about 1,400 men and 80 women from the Cumann na mBan, the women's auxiliary wing of the Irish Volunteers. They all formed squads with orders to occupy various locations across Dublin, and the bulk going to the GPO.

Michael ('The') O'Rahilly, who had argued and argued with Pearse, saying that the Uprising would be a disaster and tried desperately, with MacNeill, to stop it ... put on a perfectly measured green uniform, kissed his wife, Nancy, and six sons and then drove to the GPO in his De Dion-Bouton car. He stood outside shouting, 'C'mon, I've helped to wind up the clock, I might as well hear it strike[77]' and went in through a back door. Count George Plunkett, 65 years of age, went to the barricade but Joseph, his son and senior officer, told him that the offer was appreciated but he wasn't needed and ordered him to go home.

Chapter 25 – Charge!

'The misfortune of the Irish is that they rose prematurely, before the proletariat's European revolt had time to mature'*

Constable James O'Brien, forty-eight years old and six foot four inches tall, was the first to be killed when he had the top of his head shot off just after midday. He'd been enjoying the spring sunshine outside the Dublin Castle gate and was probably thinking of lunch when he perhaps assumed the approaching group to be another practice march by rather silly patriots. There were about 25 men and 9 women. Suddenly a small group broke away and tried to enter the Castle. O'Brien did his job and simply held up an arm as if to bar the way. Captain Seán Connolly, who had been newly promoted by James Connolly, shot the policeman from point-blank range. There were very few soldiers inside the Castle but several came running and Seán Connolly urged his men to enter[78].

As with all the other building seizures and sieges by the rebels that Easter, the person in command had zero or minimal military experience. A small group of Irish Citizen Army troops was led by 34-year-old Connolly; he worked in the motor taxation department of Dublin Corporation when he wasn't a part-time teacher and actor. He had no idea how many troops he was attacking nor where they would be located. One report claims that he and a few others entered the Castle, tied up six guards, and then decided to retreat. Helena Moloney was there, just behind Captain Connolly; she says

---

* Lenin, V. (1916). The Discussion On Self-Determination Summed Up. *Sbornik Sotsial-Demokrata No. 1*.
https://www.marxists.org/archive/lenin/works/1916/jul/x01.htm.

that the men that were with him appeared to be uncertain after the constable was shot; a British guard quickly shut the gate and began firing from his box[79]. A likely scenario is that Seán Connolly had been ordered to occupy City Hall next door but, on the spur of the moment, he tried and failed to enter the Castle.

The nearby Telephone Exchange was another objective but it was not taken nor destroyed[80]. The telephonists didn't leave and didn't stop working – they carried on, slept and ate there, despite being besieged and with bullets flying around, until the ending of the Rising. The British Government did pay them overtime – after deducting the cost of their meals[81].

Whilst the Castle and the Telephone Exchange were soon filled with British soldiers from Portobello Barracks, Irish Citizen Army troops quickly took over the nearby City Hall – where Seán Connolly was soon killed on the roof.

Meanwhile, former British drummer Michael Mallin with Countess Markievicz as his second in command and about 30 Irish Citizen Army men took control of St. Stephen's Green, a 22-acre park south of the River Liffey, by overpowering council workers and forcing out civilians. An unarmed policeman, Gaelic-speaking Michael Lahiff from County Clare, was standing near the Green. Two men and the Countess all aimed their guns, fired, and he fell dead.

The Green was at the intersection of several major roads, between Beggars Bush Barracks and Portobello Barracks but from a strategic point it was almost useless. British troops marching to the GPO simply detoured around it. Worse still, there were several tall buildings surrounding the Green. Thirty British troops with a machine gun, from a Reserve Cavalry Brigade, moved into the Hibernian United Service Club overlooking the western side. Near a corner was the elegant Shelbourne Hotel – Mallin said that he didn't have enough men to occupy it and, inevitably, a group of British troops with a machine gun moved in. The Irish Citizen Army soldiers dug shallow trenches on the Green using park keepers' tools. A complete waste of time and effort. They had to continually crouch and squat because of the machine guns and, after 24 hours, they abandoned the Green and ran ragged-desperate into the nearby College of Surgeons.

There was a back entrance sheltered from the machine guns and troops. Someone was in the street waving a flag and shouting for admittance. 'Hello, Margaret. Welcome,' Countess Markievicz took the Tricolour from the woman cyclist, Margaret Skinnider, a member of Cumann na mBan, 'Thanks. Come in! We'll get that put up. Hanna Sheehy-Skeffington has been in and out of here all day and Nellie Gifford is somewhere around, working like a maniac. Lily Kempson is here, too. C'mon … You'll be a great help upstairs.'

Skinnider was a 24-year-old Maths teacher from Glasgow. She was also a suffragette and bomb smuggler. Markievicz took her into a room where four men were shooting from the windows. One of them, Bill Partridge, paused and looked around, 'Madame, we've scored a few hits but the range is more than 300 yards.' He looked at Margaret and, recognising her from training at Larkfield, gave her a rifle, 'Over there … every so often a cheeky fella steps out from the barrier and fires at us.'

She knelt down and peered out, aiming at the side of a barricade where she'd seen movement and held her breath. The Tommy appeared – she fired, the recoil sending her backwards, and he seemed to duck back under cover. One of the other men in the room said to Markievicz, 'Yeah, you see. The bugger knows he's out of …' They watched as the soldier slowly re-appeared, dropping a rifle and falling backwards. 42-year-old Bill Partridge had been a member of the inaugural Provisional Army Council of the Irish Citizen Army. He glanced at Skinnider and said, 'OK, lads. This is Margaret Skinnider. She's in charge. When she tells yer to do something, you do it. Alright?'

Later that night, she suggested to Mallin that she lead a 4-person team out of the College. She wanted to attack a machine gun on the flat roof of University Church. They almost succeeded but the repetitious-chattering bullets were persistent and one Volunteer was killed; Skinnider was wounded three times so Bill Partridge carried her over his back, returning to the College, as the shots zipped around them[82].

Chapter 26 – A Republic at Last

Bernadette Higgins was walking down Sackville Street and recognised an elderly neighbour up ahead, 'Good Day to yer, Biddy!' Mrs Mulligan, an old woman with a shawl wrapped round her shoulders, spun round and almost fell over. 'Oh! Hello, Bernie. And how's t'ings going wiv' you and these two little ones a' yours?' A tattered boy of about six years of age and his slightly older sister were squabbling nearby.

'Sha, we're managing. T'anks be to God. I'm on me way to get the Separation Allowance ... Twenty-one shillings a week. The rent's gone up to t'ree shilling and sixpence. I'm paying thru'ppence for a loaf and tuppence for the pa-tayters every day ... then der's tay, milk and a bid'a bacon. So that's more than half a'me money gone already. Doesn't leave much for coal, clo'se or wot-not.'

'Ah ... I know, I know. I c'n barely get by sellin' me second-hand clo'se ... if only me son Mick woz workin' insted'a playin' his feckin' pipe all der time ... At least yer get 'dat Allowance. Have yer heard enny'ting from yer Dan?'

Bernadette sighed, 'No. T'is a worry, him being over d'ere in France fightin' dem Jermins. I've not had a letter from Dansy ... not since ... the last time.'

'Oh?'

'Yeah, when I ... Hey, what's go'an on at der Post Office? Look-now, Biddy! ... there!'

The old lady peered across the street. Trams, cars, and carts were moving up and down the wide thoroughfare as usual. She strained her aching eyes to see what Bernadette was talking about. Men, women and children were rushing, ambling, and wandering all over the broad street. Shouts and laughter, horses neighing and dogs barking, everything seemed as it always was on a Monday. Except it wasn't and never would be again.

There was a small group of men with rifles on the steps outside the GPO. One man in front of them had a hat with the brim turned up on one side and was wearing a green uniform of some kind. He was reading aloud from a piece of paper. A few of the Dubliners walking past turned to stare but most continued on. Two or three paused and stopped to listen.

As the two women walked towards the group on the steps, Bernadette said, 'I hope d'ere's not goan' to be a delay wi' me allowance. I'm behind on der rent as it is …' They could now see that many of the GPO's windows had been broken and they were close enough to almost hear some of what the man was saying. Mrs Mulligan said, 'Ah! It's jus' one of dem dopey Volunteer fellas. Well, I have to get some apples and oranges down by Patrick Street corner. It's a fair ole walk from The Coombe. I'll be seein' yer, Bernie. Bye-bye little 'uns. Next time I might have a bull's eye or sugar stick fer yer. God bless.'

The tall fella was still speaking, although the words were not really carrying far, '… readiness of its children to sacrifice … for the common good, prove itself worthy of … august destiny to which … is called.' Some of those with him cheered. A few in the green uniforms around him may have been thinking that it was strange that he didn't stammer when giving the speech.

Bernadette ignored all of them and, at the doors to the GPO, she was stopped by a young lad with a rifle, 'Sorry, Miss'us. Closed.'

'What?! Listen, sonny, I want me allowance[83] … G'wan, git out'a me way!' and she pushed his rifle to one side.

'This building has been occupied by the Irish Citizen … er, no, no … I mean, by the Irish Republican Army an' …'

'I said! ... get out of me way! ... I want ...'

'What's going on?' Connolly was rushing past but almost tripped over one of the children. Bernadette swung round, 'I want me separation money ... now!'

Connolly looked at her. 'How much d'yer get?'

'Twenty one shillin.'

He sighed and took a crushed and dirty banknote out of his pocket, 'Here's a quid ...' and then, scratching in his trouser pocket, found a florin, '... and two bob. Yer lucky day. Be off, quickly now. Mind how yer go doon the street wit' them two bairns, it'll soon start to get a bit lively.'

A short time later Connolly paused in organising the defences when his fifteen-year-old son Roddy gave him a nudge, 'Hey, Da. Who's that fella there?'

Connolly looked around. Roddy pointed at a well-dressed officer with a shiny sabre by his side, rings on his fingers and scarf round his neck, snoring on a mattress that had been thrown down in front of the Stamp Counter, 'He's not setting a very good example, is he?'

Connolly put an arm round his son, 'Roddy, that's Joe Plunkett. He's got more courage than all the other leaders of this Uprising.' A door opened and Collins, with his hand bandaged and wearing a smart uniform, poked his head into the hall and then just as quickly ducked back and closed the door. Roddy looked at his dad, 'Who was that?'

'Er. Michael Collins, I think. Joe Plunkett's aide de camp.'

'Aide de ...?'

'Don't ask ... Bit like an assistant. Helps out. He does whatever Joe tells him to do. And if you're wondering, no, I don't have an aide de camp. That reminds me ... Of course, yer want to be here with me, I know that. And I'd like that, too. But I need someone I c'n rely on to take care of yer Ma. I need yer to do that fer me. Please.' Connolly opened a side door into the street, 'It's still quiet yet ... Roddy, take care. God bless yer son.' They hugged and Roddy slipped out. Connolly waited a few seconds and then opened the door again to watch his son running off, turning a corner and then he was gone. Gone. Connolly wiped his nose.

In the main hall of the GPO Clarke was sitting at a table with a furious look on his face. He had two small and skinny teenagers standing, shivering, in front of him. They both had red hair and pimples and dark brown chocolate smeared around their mouths; one was barefooted, the other wore shiny shoes of very different sizes.

'Lootin'! Yer woz caught looting ...'

'Sha, wasn't jus us! There's lots'a others ... jus' grabbin' stuff, like.' The smaller boy started crying.

'Shut up! Stop that bawlin'. You know the penalty fer lootin' ... don't yer?'

'No.'

'Yes, yer do ... execution! Firing squad!'

'But ... I'm only thirteen an' he's jus' fourteen ... an' ... My mam'ee ...' The sobs came faster.

'Shut up! Execution. Sergeant O'Halloran! Come here! Take these two out and have them ...'

One of the lads began having hysterics, 'No, no, please ... Sir! Please! No ... no!'

'Take these two spalpeens* out'a me sight ...and have them work in the kitchen, peeling praties or summat.'

---

* *Spalpeens* = rascals

Chapter 27 – Lions and Donkeys

'Fred! ... FRED!!!!'

This was bizarre. Captain Frederick Dietrichsen, 2/7th Battalion Sherwood Foresters never expected to be going overseas (his military card shows *Home Service only*), and had just stepped off the gangway from S.S. *Tynwald*. He certainly wasn't expecting to hear someone calling his name. That it was the voice of the woman whom he loved gave him a weird feeling. He spun round, 'Beatrice?!' and rushed to hug her and his children[*], 'How did you know we'd ...'

'I didn't ... I heard about the Fenians in the City and guessed they'd be sending troops from England. We just came to see ...'

'Beatrice, it's not safe here ... I'll try to get a day's leave ... you need to go back to your parent's place in Blackrock ... love you.'

'Fred ... take care, darling! Love you, too.'

'Sorry, sir ... we ...' A soldier was saluting and talking to Dietrichsen who turned and said, 'Yes, yes ... get the men ready.' He quickly hugged and kissed his wife and children.

This was on Wednesday 26th April 1916. Earlier, on Monday afternoon, a group of 'Home Guard' elderly veterans, returning from training, had marched up Northumberland Road and come under fire from Irish rebels. If this information had been passed on to the Sherwood Foresters nobody took any notice of it.

'Fall in, you men! Come on, look lively!' A few moments before, the troops had been issued with live ammunition and some of them were still admiring it, never having seen any before. The

---

[*] They had a 4-year-old son, Christian, and 2-year-old daughter, Beatrice.

Sergeant stood glaring at the Sherwood Forester soldiers in their brand-new uniforms as they shuffled into almost tidy ranks of four. The crossing had been rather choppy and some of them were still feeling seasick.

'Squad! Squad ... 'Shun!' The men came sharply to attention and the Sergeant walked slowly along the front rank, 'All reet, we've not got much time. I know you'se were expecting this to be France. Well, it's Ireland. We're 'ere to protect local community from Fenians.' He turned, gave the orders, 'Slope Arms! Forward, MARCH!' and led the way towards Dublin Castle. The rhythmic stomp-stomp-stomp on the cobblestones made a dramatic and challenging announcement of their presence that went on and on.

The streets were lined with civilians who gaped in amazement and admiration. Slowly, there began a murmur of conversation as the smart young soldiers passed by. Then, a few people began to clap. Soon, this changed into loud applause. Someone in the crowd started cheering and then suddenly they were all cheering and clapping.

'Good Luck, Tommies!'

'Go get 'em, Lads. Shoot der Fenian bastards!'

The thousand or so soldiers grinned as they proudly marched in a brisk, tight, formation past the middle-class homes and shops, making their way up Northumberland Road. It was past midday and the sun was shining – a few householders stepped forward and offered sandwiches and cups of tea to the marching men. A few bystanders apparently tried to warn them that there had been Fenians shooting from houses in Northumberland Road – but they were ignored.

As soon as they arrived at the junction with Haddington Road a soldier fell face forward. Afterwards, the men would realise that they'd heard the shot but at the time it was so unexpected that few took any notice. Then it really started. Volley upon volley of crac-crac-crac ... crac-crac-crac. Eight, nine, perhaps ten, soldiers stumble-rolled and fell, bleeding, screaming and dying.

'Take cover! Take COVER! Get Down!' There was a disorganised rush to crouch or lie down beside hedges, garden walls, carts, or any sort of cover. This was followed by a pause until just one soldier fired wildly into the air. There were two Irish rebels in 25 Northumberland Road shooting with amazing frequency and accuracy. More and more British soldiers were being hit; several fell and lay motionless – others were wriggling and yelling on the road. The enemy's rifle fire was now coming from various directions. A corporal swore, 'King-'ell! There must be 'undreds of t' bastards. Why aren't our lads returning fire?' Another corporal shouted back, 'Cos' last week in Watford they woz learning 'ow ter march. Friday was ' first time they held a 'king rifle!'

An officer screamed, 'Sarnt! Get those men returning fire!'

'Sah! Sherwood Foresters! House with red door, 50 yards! Three rounds rapid! FIRE! And again, FIRE!' The noise from a battalion's concerted barrage of rifle shots filled the suburban street and bullets crashed into bricks and windows; choking gunsmoke billowed around and over the tiny, neat homes. Northumberland Road became a battlefield like villages in Ypres with terrified, wounded and courageous men hiding and fighting and dying. Again and again, the British troops were ordered to make a frontal attack by charging up the road. But as well as number 25, they were being hit by concentrated rifle fire from two other buildings. A Lewis machine gun would have been the most effective weapon but the Foresters only had two and they had been left behind on Liverpool's dockside. Eventually, after numerous frontal attacks, two British battalions overcame 17 rebels with the loss of four officers killed and about 200* other ranks dead or wounded. Captain Dietrichsen was one of the first to be killed[84].

---

* Documented figures vary. General Maxwell stated 234 killed or wounded. Brigade history: 165. Brigade commander: 162.

Chapter 28 – Cup'la Murders

'I never eat meat. My father never ate meat …'

'Where's my knickerbockers?! Hanna? Hanna!?! Oh. Alright, found them …' Hanna Sheehy-Skeffington was accustomed to her husband's eccentricities. As, indeed, were most Dubliners. At 37 years of age, he had never shaved, always wore boots two sizes too big, was a vegetarian, a pacifist, passionately in favour of women's rights, and a teetotaller; he distrusted cultural nationalism and thought that the Irish language was inferior to Esperanto. He was a journalist and had recently returned from a lecture tour of the US where he strongly supported Irish independence but opposed violence. James Joyce was a friend – he called Sheehy-Skeffington 'Hairy Jaysus' and said that he was the second most intelligent man at University College Dublin[85].

'Frank, Anna Haslam[86] asked me if you had read her husband's pamphlet and what you thought ...?'

'Yes, indeed. Thomas and his wife have some strange ideas ... Ha! Don't we all ... but his *Some Last Words on Women's Suffrage* is very good although I think he's a bit naïve about Asquith's promises. Pamphlets and documents can be powerful instruments. For example, the 'Castle Document' that's popped up and caused this rebellion. It's just what the British wanted, so that they can have an excuse for machine gun bloodshed. There's no chance of Germany beating Britain ... so Pearse and Clarke should stop talking nonsense about Ireland winning freedom through an English defeat in Europe … and … Hanna? I hope that you're not intending to go out to the College of Surgeons, to help Constance Markievicz? It's too dangerous.'

'I may do so, Dear … you once considered joining the Irish Volunteers.'

'That was before they chose not to take women as members

and refused to acknowledge that women should have equal rights.'

'Yes, well, I have to admit that I've always admired you for that, Frank.'

'It wasn't just that.[87]' He found a sheet of paper, 'As I wrote to Thomas MacDonagh, *'Are not the bulk of the Irish Volunteers animated by the old bad tradition that war is a glorious thing, that there is something 'manly' about going out to kill your fellow man, something cowardly about the desire to see one's end accomplished without bloodshed?'* And I told him, *'I want to see the manhood of Ireland no longer hypnotized by the glamour of the 'glory of arms' ... no longer blind to the horrors of organised murder.'**

'Yes, yes! That's all very well, Dear, but it didn't stop you from being jailed and forcibly fed for speaking against conscription at the Socialist meeting ... Oh, and I heard about what you did yesterday, by the way.'

'Hmm?'

'Don't Hmm me, you know very well to what I'm referring.'

'Not really.'

'You ran across the street and tried to help a British officer that had been mortally wounded. Whilst bullets were flying around.'

'It wasn't just me. Someone else went with me ... and anyway the chap was dragged away by some soldiers before we got to him.[88]'

'Oh, yes? And where does Don Quixote plan to wander this Tuesday during the Uprising?'

'Me? Today, Hanna? Well, there are no police on the streets

---

* https://www.cavanlibrary.ie/cavan-history/history-online/digitised-material/in-dark-and-evil-days-sheehy-skeffington-1936.pdf
Page xxiii

and there's looting going on. Women and children are risking their lives by dodging bullets and climbing through broken plate glass windows. Nobletts sweet shop in North Earl Street was a target. They're stealing chocolates, fur coats, and goodness knows what. I saw a drunken man wearing two or three sets of suits and smoking a 2-shilling cigar. Women with flitches of bacon and ridiculous hats on their heads. Barefoot urchins trying to ride shiny bicycles. There was a group of youths pushing a glistening piano down the street. Children in Sackville Street playing with golf clubs and cricket bats. We must do something. It's up to the citizenry to maintain law and order and stop people putting themselves in danger.[89]'

'I see, Dear ... and what, pray, do you propose to do?'

'I'm arranging a meeting at Westmoreland Chambers to coordinate well-meaning citizens who want to prevent the looting.'

Sheehy-Skeffington's meeting in the community hall was not too successful. He'd handed out and pasted up notices in dozens of streets but only Hanna and a couple of confused members of the public attended ... and none of them, except Hanna, wanted to be involved any further. She had to leave early to prepare dinner for their 6-year-old son Owen; everyone else had gone, so Sheehy-Skeffington wearily headed for home. It was almost sunset, the streets momentarily seemed peaceful as curfew approached, and he found himself realising not only why he loved Dublin but also why he wanted to protect everyone within it.

'Skeffy! Skeffy!' Approaching Portobello Bridge, the little man found himself being followed by a crowd of hooligans and urchins some of whom knew him by his huge red beard, knickerbockers, tweed cap and outsized boots, the large Votes for Women badge, and his public speeches. 'Skeffy! Skeffy!' they jeered as he walked down the middle of the road. Martial law had been declared and he seemed to be the cause of a crowd forming; he was arrested at a checkpoint and placed into the custody of 18-year-old Lieutenant William Dobbin, at Portobello Barracks. Australian-born but a proud British patriot, Dobbin had joined the Royal Irish Rifles in 1915 and would later be awarded a Military Cross ... and die in France aged 21.

A rather confused Sheehy-Skeffington was ushered into the guard room by weary and bored soldiers. Dobbin looked up from his official paperwork, 'Another one? Searched him?'

Lieutenant Morgan replied that he had indeed done so and then motioned Sheehy-Skeffington into the orderly room where five other miserable civilians sat on benches, 'He's been handing out these leaflets, about looters. Name's Sheehy-Skeffington. I've phoned the Castle about him and the others in there.'

'What'd they say?'

'You can release them.'

'All of them?'

'Yes ... except this Sheehy-what's his name. Dunno why, but you're to hold on to him for a while.'

He was placed in a cell and, realising that he was being detained for the night, hammered as best he could on the door with his fists and boots, shouting in desperation, 'Could someone please send a message to my wife? Let her know where I am ...Please ... she'll be worried. Please!'

A Sergeant opened the door and said, 'Certainly, sir ... would you like me to also get a Corporal to attend to yer garden 'an prune the roses at the same time? ... Listen, Paddy, Dublin is under martial law. We got fou'sands of Fenians wot's tryin' ter kill us. We ain't got time to run errands fer posh bleedin' Paddies.'

Later that evening Captain Bowen-Colthurst came into the

Guard room. He had 16 years army experience; Dobbin had less than 12 months. The Captain had been born in Ireland. He'd fought in the Boer War and been captured and now, after serving in France, he was suffering from shell-shock or post-traumatic stress. Nevertheless, a short time earlier he'd been ordered to take a squad of twenty soldiers and search a house owned by a person named Kelly.

'I want Skeffington ... Sheehy ... whatever his name is.'

Dobbin was responsible for the custody of anybody taken prisoner and said, 'May I ask why, sir?'

'I'm taking a squad of men on a raid and I want him as a hostage to protect our men.' Dobbin's mouth opened. He wasn't certain but thought this was unlikely to be in accordance with Army procedures.

Captain Bowen-Colthurst straightened his cap and pulled his shoulders back. 'Look, Dobbin, isn't it? Lieutenant Dobbin ... I'm your senior officer ... I will take full responsibility. I'm ordering you to hand him over. Damn it! Just do as you're told, old chap. Alright?'

James Kelly had a tobacconist shop at the corner of Camden Street and Harrington St. He was a Dublin Corporation Alderman, a Justice of the Peace and had once been High Sheriff of Dublin; he was a Nationalist but not involved with Sinn Féin or the Volunteers. Unfortunately, about 20 minutes away from the shop was another one owned by Thomas Kelly, a founder member of Sinn Féin, who lived in Longwood Avenue. They had obviously been confused by somebody. Possibly deliberately.

Sheehy-Skeffington was in the custody of Bowen-Colthurst, a born-again Protestant, who told the puzzled Irish pacifist to say his prayers. When he refused, Bowen-Colthurst said the Lord's Prayer for him and then tied his hands behind his back. The soldiers marched out of the barracks with Sheehy-Skeffington staggering along and Bowen-Colthurst occasionally firing his rifle at any window showing a light. After about ten minutes they stopped at Richmond Hill to interrogate some young men coming out of a church. Bowen-Colthurst said to one, 'Take that cigarette out of your mouth ... Martial law has been declared ...' But the 19-year-old, James Coade, was slow to move and said 'Has it? Sha, I didn't know ... We woz jus after ...'

'Hit him,' said Bowen-Colthurst to a soldier.

'Sir?'

'With your rifle! ... Oh! Here, I'll do it.' He swung a rifle butt into Coade's face, breaking his jaw. The young man gasped and fell to his knees, wobbled forwards, managed to stand and then began to run, as did his friend, Laurence Byrne. Bowen-Colthurst fired and killed Coade.

'Come on ... Quick March!'

Near the tobacconist's, Bowen-Colthurst whispered to Lieutenant Wilson, 'I'll take half the men while you stay here with this Skeffington chap. If we're attacked, kill him.'

There were two journalists in the shop, Thomas Dickson and Patrick McIntyre, both loyal to Britain and opposed to Home Rule. Exactly why they were in the shop late at night has never been documented. They were taken prisoner by the troops and the shop set alight. There were two other men, but these were released. It may be that one of these was Joseph Edelstein[90], a shadowy literary figure who was acquainted with the leader of Sinn Féin, Arthur Griffith. Later, there would be rumours that Edelstein, an alcoholic Jew who suffered from mental illness, had given the authorities misleading information about the 'other' Kelly.

Sheehy-Skeffington and the two journalists were taken to Portobello Barracks and handed over to Lieutenant Dobbin. But not for long. After Bowen-Colthurst had spent some time reading the Bible, he decided that the security was too weak and that the prisoners could escape.

'Lieutenant Dobbin, I'm taking charge of these three. They will be shot.'

'Sir? No, but sir … ' Dobbin was confused by the extraordinary behaviour of this senior officer. It was as if the young man were having a nightmare and there would be a sensible explanation quite soon.

'Take my word for it, old chap. It's the right thing to do. Can't take the risk. I'll need seven soldiers.'

Dobbin sent a message across the parade ground to the adjutant who responded that the execution must not take place – but it was too late. The prisoners had been led into the tiny yard and shot. They would have had no idea, it being very early morning, until the last moment what was happening. The three bodies lay in pools of blood. Sheehy-Skeffington's leg was twitching; Bowen-Colthurst ordered Lieutenant Dobbin to have four soldiers fire another volley into him.

Something had obviously occurred which was contrary to His Majesty's Regulations. Bowen-Colthurst[91] was told by a senior officer that he was not to leave the barracks – he left the barracks, taking three soldiers with him. He then captured Councillor Richard O'Carroll, an Irish rebel, in a room above a grocery shop. After a brief interrogation, a Sergeant was ordered to take him out and shoot him in the street.

Hanna Sheehy-Skeffington was confused and frantic, her husband having disappeared for three days and nobody able to help her. She was eventually told by a priest who had been to the Barracks that her husband had been executed … but that seemed too incredible. Her sisters went there and demanded to see Bowen-Colthurst. He told them that he didn't know what they were talking about and told them to clear off or they'd be in trouble. Later that evening he led 40 soldiers, with fixed bayonets, to Hanna's home and ordered them to fire at the door*. They ransacked the home, searching for incriminating evidence which could prove Sheehy-Skeffington had been involved in the Uprising. To no avail. Little Owen Lancelot Sheehy-Skeffington looked on, terrified.

The officer commanding the Barracks, Major Fletcher Vane, had been inspecting observation posts in the suburbs. On his return, after the shootings, he demanded an investigation – he was relieved of his command and his Army career ended. There were attempts to have the matter covered up. At one stage Hanna was accused by senior Army officers of 'making a fuss'[92].

A Royal Commission†was held but failed to investigate all the issues, such as Coade's death, and satisfied nobody. Bowen-Colthurst was found guilty of murder but insane. He spent 19 months in an asylum before being given a pension and emigrating with his family to Canada where he died aged 85.

---

* Hansard 14 Dec. 1916 SHOOTING OF ME. SHEEHY-SKEFFINSTON (sic).

† https://catalogue.nli.ie/Record/vtls000797084/StaffViewMARC

Chapter 29 – The End of the Beginning

Connolly was constantly slipping out of the GPO to check on barricades and firing positions. He had been wounded on Wednesday afternoon in Williams Lane when his arm was hit, and injured again on Thursday when his leg or ankle was smashed[93] by a bullet. After dragging himself more than a hundred yards he was found and stretchered back to the GPO. Cumann na mBan gave him first aid and encouraged him to sleep. The pressure was beginning to be unbearable on all the leaders.

Pearse was sitting at a desk in a small office and called out, 'Joe?' Plunkett was swaying past, barely able to stand.

'Joe, I know you've been doing your best to encourage the lads … could we talk for a moment?'

The young man walked slowly into the room. He was still wearing a sword and had sparkling rings on his fingers, but he'd lost his hat and his green uniform was no longer pristine. He was covered in dust and dirt, and the scarf that had been hiding the raw wound from his recent surgery was now filthy. He moved slowly and leaned against the door for support. Every so often they heard a British machine gun firing a short burst. Then there'd be silence until someone somewhere, dying in slow pain, began screaming. And then stopped.

'Pádraig … are you bearing up OK?'

'I'm alright. It's you that needs a rest … come here and sit … I need to talk.' Pearse chuckled, 'If I can get the words out.' Plunkett sat down, 'Well, I think the lads can cope for a while … There were a cup'la times when some of the Citizen Army lads almost got shot by our own men …'

'What?' Pearse looked up, horrified.

'All sorted, now. It was jus' that some of them had such strong London and Scots accents. But really, they've all done a grand job and I've been telling them exactly that. They don't need me.'

'How much sleep have you had, Joe? Since Sunday, I mean?'

'Sleep, Pádraig? Oh, about as much as you and all the others here.'

'Maybe, but none of us, unlike you, was in hospital this time last week.'

Joseph laughed, 'Don't remind me. I'd almost forgotten. Anyway, you an' I'll be getting plenty of rest soon enough ...'

'Joe, I haven't been much help ...'

'Sha, you did all the organising ... without you, we'd still be sittin' around talkin' a'boat Ireland's woes and how nasty England's been to Auld Ireland. You 'an Tom Clarke gave us the kick in the ole backside we had to have.'

Pearse acknowledged the compliment with a quick smile. Suddenly, there was a massive explosion somewhere above them. 'They've started with the big artillery ... incendiary shells, Joe ... Connolly thought they might not want to damage the post office after spending all that money on it ... ah well. Mind you, he was right about the Castle ... a pity my 'E' Company didn't take it with Seán Connolly's lads but they didn't mobilise in time; Willie sent the mobilisation order ... I'm not sure when ... I have to take responsibility though, as O.C. Maybe I'd have been more use there than here, leading them out to attack the Castle. What d'yer think, Joe?'

Plunkett was having a problem maintaining his balance. He sat gingerly down on a wooden chair. 'Who knows, Pádraig ... but we've given the Brits something to think about, eh? 1000 Irish men and women against 20,000 British troops, a ship, machine guns, and all their high explosive shells. 17 of ours in Northumberland

Road stopped 1500 of theirs from advancing for three days. That's nearly a hundred of them against one of us! They sent 800 young Sherwood Foresters down Northumberland Road, and, would yer believe this, most hadn't fired a rifle before ... and they marched them down in formation as if they were on the parade ground at Aldershot. What did the Germans say about the Woodbines*? Lions led by donkeys! Our Ned Daly, 25 years old, with his 200 lads in the Four Courts and North King Street? They've frustrated the British and even beaten them back. De Valera in Boland's Mill is causing mayhem. Captain Con Colbert, 5 foot tall ... he's furious at not getting enough action.'

Pearse put both hands on the table. 'Yes, but how many innocents were killed by the British in North King Street? There's civilians out there, looting and getting themselves killed, women and children! This place is going up in flames. We've got to get everybody out. Talk to Connolly if he's co ... conscious. He's out there somewhere on a stretcher. And MacDiarmada. I don't know where O'Rahilly is. He's been firing out of windows and keeping to himself.'

O'Rahilly had volunteered to take an advance party down Moore Street and search for a safe means to escape to the Williams and Woods jam factory in Parnell Street and then from there to the Four Courts. Unfortunately, the British had already taken the factory and O'Rahilly led the rush to it; the machine-gun fire was too heavy and bullets ripped into him from hip to shoulder almost as soon as he stepped out. Crawling to a doorway, he lay there in Sackville Lane for hours bleeding to death; his last act was to write a note to his wife. 'Tons + tons of love dearie to you + to the boys + to Nell + Anna. Goodbye Darling.'

---

* British troops ('Woodbines' were the brand of cigarettes issued)

Chapter 30 – Surrender? God Save Ireland!

There was a constant patter-patter, patter-patter as machine gun bullets smacked into the GPO walls. Brick dust and smoke filled the air. In the evening of Friday, 28th April, the senior Irish officers met around Connolly's bed. His eyes were bloodshot and he forced himself to stifle the agonising pain spearing through his leg, 'We've got to evacuate. They're just going to keep blasting away.' As if in confirmation, a high explosive shell exploded not far away and an injured Volunteer screamed in the next room. The others nodded; Tom Clarke stubbed out his last cigarette and said, 'If we can get to the Four Courts where the office buildings are spread out, we'd have a chance to hold on fer longer.'

Connolly being so badly injured, 21-year-old Sean McLaughlin was given command of the GPO rebels; the building was a mass of flames, smoke and falling masonry – evacuation started and soon became a panic into the streets. The door of an adjacent building was broken down ... men saw an oncoming group and they fired on each other. Irish killing Irish. A woman opened her front door and was shot[94].

A side door led into Henry Street. From there, carrying Connolly, a group made their way to a shop in Moore Street. The only way to proceed, avoiding sniper and machine-gun fire, was to tunnel through walls, building by building. They managed to reach number 16, a butcher's shop – except, now, it was a smashed shambles and unrecognisable except for the smell and the sound of rats scattering overhead.

A reconnaissance party was sent out and reported back, 'The British have control of the barbed wire barricade in Parnell Street. We could try to rush it ...?'

'They'll have it covered with dozens of machine guns ... we'd be wiped out in seconds.'

Pearse looked at his fellow heroes, 'The British have ordered no prisoners to be taken in North King Street ... anybody captured is bayoneted. These past days we've had more than a hundred men killed. And civilians? Probably three times as many, some of them women and children ... it's just too ... it can't go on. Another day, another few children die. It's got to stop. We have to surrender.'

Clarke was first to respond, 'No-no. No! We can fight on for another ... another week at least.' But Plunkett supported Pearse, 'Tom, we've made the strongest point we could make. Any more fighting will be to simply waste lives. Civilians are being caught in the crossfire.'

MacDiarmada tapped his walking stick sharply on the floor, 'Alright! There's t'ousands outside Dublin desperate to fight fer freedom ... True, it would be good to encourage 'em by keepin' the flag flyin' ... But, I'm sorry, Tom ... there's still hundreds here in Dublin that will be needed later. They're too important to be wasted.'

Connolly pulled himself up. 'I agree. We need to encourage the fight to go on in the years ahead ... and the best way to do that is by surrendering now. The lads in the Four Courts, Boland's Mills, South Dublin Union, and Jacob's Biscuit Factory on Bishop Street ... all around us ... we can't have them being killed now, needlessly, when they're the ones that'll be wanted in the years to come.'

Pearse looked at each of them. 'We've given the British Army a good hard punch in the face. More than that. We've damaged both the Army and the British Government. They'll never live this down. It might not seem like it at the moment but I believe, in years to come, this will be seen as the start of Ireland's freedom. You all know that we'll be executed. But I agree with James, we're handing the responsibility on to brave lads who've proved their ability. We must do our best so that as many of them live to fight another day.'

MacDiarmada saw that Tom Clarke was fighting back tears, 'Tom, we all know that there's been rebellions in the past and, really, they didn't achieve what they wanted. We follow brave heroic men. Our deaths may or may not be remembered like theirs. I don't obviously know. But I know that workers, men and women, will no longer put up with their children living in poverty, filth and disease. And I know we've shown that Irish people will never rest until their country is free and independent.'

Elizabeth O'Farrell, Cumann na mBan member and wearing a Red Cross uniform, walked up Moore Street with a white flag and told General Lowe that Pearse wanted to discuss a surrender. She was gone some time and Sheila Grenan, her partner, was becoming emotional; Connolly told her not to be worried – 'She's safer than you and me. The British wouldn't shoot her. They're very aware of the bad publicity that'd bring.' O'Farrell returned with a note for Pearse; they then both went and stood in front of Lowe to formally surrender. Details were carried to the various rebel locations across Dublin, at great risk, by O'Farrell and other women in Cumann na mBan.

In the Nursing Home of the South Dublin Union, a 50-acre complex of lodgings for the destitute and hospital buildings for the mentally ill, there had been hand-to-hand fighting; Cathal Brugha was second-in-command and very much involved. He was shot several times, cornered, injured by a grenade blast, and finally sat with his back to a wall – but he continued firing his revolver whilst singing,

'God Save Ireland, Said the Heroes;
God Save Ireland! Said They All!
Whether on the scaffold high,
Or the battlefield we die,

Oh what matter when for dear old Erin we fall!'[95]

The others surrendered and he lay in a widening pool of blood with an empty gun in his hand. British soldiers walked around him because they could see that he was dead – but he wasn't; he was almost dead, but not quite. It took him over a year to recover, always walking with a limp, purportedly with a rattle due to the metal that was never removed.

Connolly was taken to a temporary hospital in Dublin Castle. The rebels laid down their arms and marched to Rotunda Hospital. It wasn't far but for some it was the longest journey they'd ever taken. MacDiarmada, who had never recovered from infantile paralysis, struggled with his lame leg and Plunkett was clearly close to death.

At the Rotunda there was a small grassy area on which the grubby mass of wearied prisoners were made to squeeze together and lie down on. Whenever they needed to relieve themselves, they had to do it like animals. London-born 29-year-old Captain Perceval Lea-Wilson, of the Royal Irish Regiment 18th Battalion, was walking in amongst the rebels pushing and sneering at them. 'Ah! Look who's here! Mis-TER Clarke!' He grabbed, pulled and forced Clarke to stand up. 'Get them off! Get all your filthy clothes off!' He was intent on searching and humiliating Clarke, because he knew that he'd been the first signatory on the Republic proclamation.

58 years old and Ireland's first President, Clarke was an intelligent, courageous and inspiring man who had spent 15 years in British jails. Most of that time he was in a tiny window-less punishment cell, being bashed and kicked every week. As a result, his body was that of a man 20 years older. Three months before the Uprising Seán McGarry accidentally shot him in the arm and the wound had yet to fully heal; removing his coat was an agonisingly slow process – too slow for Captain Lea-Wilson. He

yanked at the sleeve and forced the small old man to strip and stand naked.

'Here's your President! Look! Look! A skinny little shivering old man!' Lea-Wilson turned and called up to the nurses looking down from the hospital windows, 'Look at this creature!' The men who lay crushed and cramped on the stinking wet grass watched, listened and would never forget. From within the throng someone shouted, 'If you'd suffered as much for your country as he has, that's what you'd look like!' Another voice shouted, 'Lea-Wilson! We won't forget yer!' The atmosphere around the Rotunda was heart-stopping. A few of the young soldiers on guard took a step back and fidgeted with their safety catches.

A Sergeant-Major screamed, 'QUIET! Unless yer want me to make an example of a cup'la of yer!'

It was a long and cold night for the starving men. They tried to ignore the British guards who lit cigarettes and puffed smoke into their faces. Others were nastier. 'Ey up me duk! Us'sens 'av 'ad summat ter eat ... d'you lot get owt? No? Ah, wo'rra shame! 'Appen yer'll get summat before yer executed!'

'Anybody 'ere wann'a smoke? Yeah? Oh, sorry Paddy ... yer luck's out!' The soldier laughed, 'Ne'er mind, our lads are preparing things at Kill-main'am Jail ... diggin' a great big pit fer yer! It'll be firing squad fer you'se lot ter'morra!'

Some of the rebels spoke quietly amongst themselves about past events. 'Did yer hear a'boat what happened at the Brewery on Friday night?'

'The Guinness Brewery? What?'

'British troops captured two fellas.'

'Yeah, so what?'

'And then they shot them.'

'What? Captured and then jus' shot them?'

'Yep. And would yer believe it, they caught another two and they shot them as well.'

'Holy Mary, Mother of God!'

'But, lissen ... two of the four was clerks at the brewery. Church of Ireland, Protestants. And the other two ... guess what ... they were both British officers. I wonder what they was doin' in the dark, eh?[96]'

*

Night became dawn with a reluctant slowness over Dublin's shattered city buildings, as if not wanting to remember what had been done and not wanting to know what was yet to come. Eventually the men were made to stand and form rows, four abreast. After more than an hour, a British officer marched to the front rank and stood at ease, 'I know you've had nothing to eat ... Pity. I've had some ver' nice bacon and eggs. Ne'er mind ... you might get something later. S'arnt! Get them out of my sight!'

'Quick MARCH!' British troops, with shiny-fixed bayonets, lined the streets holding back crowds of Dubliners. The Irish Volunteers did their best to march as they'd been trained but some stumbled, injured or simply weary, and only succeeded in giving the appearance of a defeated rabble. A very few wore dirty, ragged green uniforms and slouched hats, but most had old jackets or grimy raincoats. All were exhausted and filthy. The Irish onlookers jeered – booing and spitting at them. There were shouts of 'Shoot the Bastards!' 'My boy's over d'ere, fightin' Jer'mins ... why aren't you, yer Bastards?' and 'Yer should be 'shamed a yer'sells!'

It took more than two hours to cover the three miles to Richmond Barracks. Plunkett wobbled and weaved, needing help from men either side of him. Captain Lea-Wilson grabbed MacDiarmada's walking stick, whacked his lame leg, and called him a cripple.

Later, detectives identified and extracted those that had signed the proclamation, along with the commandants and other senior Irish rebels. These were taken to Kilmainham Jail but mistakes were made – Collins was left with the main group when they were shipped to English and Welsh prisons. Con Colbert, 27, small and unassuming, had been captured in Marrowbone Lane; he was not in command – but he'd been making a nuisance of himself before the Uprising and was well-known. He was tried and executed. Michael O'Hanrahan, a journalist and 39 years of age, was executed even though he was third in command under Tomas MacDonagh and John MacBride at Jacob's Biscuit Factory[*].

After very brief and rapid courts-martial, the executions began. There was confession and Holy Communion for the condemned man in his cell then, at about 3:30 am in the passage, a bandage was used as a blindfold, a white cloth badge pinned over his heart, and he was led into the yard in front of 12 soldiers, six kneeling and six standing, their rifles having been discreetly loaded by an officer, with a blank being put in one of them.

'Firing Party!' ... The rifles are raised, wavering and wobbling, most of them pointing vaguely towards the condemned man ten yards away[97].

'FIRE!'

The sound of 12 shots, almost in unison, is deafening and the man falls; an officer walks forward and, if there is any sign of life such as a leg twitching, points a revolver at the head and fires – the lifeless body jerks one last time.

'Firing Party! DIS-missed! ... Remove the body!' The corpse

---

[*] Henry O'Hanrahan, Michael's brother, was also at Jacob's and sentenced to death but this was commuted to life imprisonment.

is anointed by a priest and then taken away to be stripped and dumped with others in a pit containing quicklime.

In the early hours of May 3rd, Assistant Provost Marshal, Major Rhodes had fallen asleep at his desk. He was awoken by a noise. Whistling? Someone was whistling! He looked at his watch. 3 am. Really, this was too much. 'Sar'nt Aldridge!'

Aldridge marched into the room and saluted, 'Sah!!!'

'Sar'nt Aldridge, someone out there is whistling! That's disgraceful. A prisoner is about to be executed, and we have someone whistling? A condemned man has the right to expect some respect. Find out who's doing it and put him on a charge. I will not have it said that the British Army fails to treat condemned men with honour and respect! Give the details to Major Heathcote.'

'SAH!'

Two minutes later the whistling was continuing. In fact, it was getting louder. 'Sar'nt ALDRIDGE !!!'

'SAH! Sorry, Sir ... it's MacDonagh*... the bloke what's being done next. He's on his way to the yard now.'

---

* Thomas MacDonagh, 38, was husband of Muriel. Father of Don (3 years old) and Babilly (1 year old) whom Grace Gifford occasionally babysat.

Chapter 31 – "Tears fall from the Skies"

(Poem by Joseph Plunkett, 'I see his blood upon the rose')

Wedding rings were his speciality. 45-year-old Edward Stoker, the Grafton Street jeweller, was thinking how lucky he was not to have been affected by the looters. The fact that troops, including some Australians and New Zealanders[98], had defended Trinity College just up the road was a great help. It was closing time on Wednesday and here he was kneeling down, putting the more expensive rings into secure storage. Ada, his Belfast-born wife at 20 Hollybank Road, Drumcondra* with their daughter Gladys, would be worrying about him. He had decided that the Papists were getting out of hand – so, for a more secure life, the family would have to move back to live with Ada's parents in East Belfast.

His nerves were still on a high and he almost jumped when the doorbell tinkled; looking up, he saw that a young woman had opened the door. She had a veil almost covering her face and appeared to be hesitating.

'Yes? Can I help you? I was jus startin' ter to clos' up!'

'Sorry ... I'd like to ... would yer be having any wedding rings at all?'

'Ah! Yes, well ... Yer've come to the right place, so! These ones are very reasonably priced at ... Ten pounds. Here, try this one.'

'Oh! Er ... No, no it's a bit ... bit tight.'

'Ah! Sorry, that's the biggest £10 one that I have.'

'How much is that one ... the one over there.'

'That? Ah, it's more expensive. Better quality. Ten pounds fifteen shillings.'

---

* 1911 Census

She sighed, 'I'll try it anyway … Yes, perfect. But ten pounds fifteen! I'll try the cheaper one again. Oh well, it's almost the right size. Ten pounds? … I'll take it, thanks.' Grace Gifford, 28 years of age, had been planning to be married and she'd converted, many months ago, to become a Catholic. The only things stopping the marriage now were that Joseph Plunkett was in Kilmainham Jail and sentenced to die. She knew that Pearse, Clarke and MacDonagh (husband of her sister Muriel) had been executed earlier that day. Joe would be next.

'I'll put it in a nice little box.' Mr Stoker turned his back, fiddled with wrapping paper, and then handed over a tiny package saying, 'There yer go. I suggest yer put it in your purse straight away and don't be looking at it on the tram. In fact, not until yer safely back home!' The doorbell tinkled as the young woman left.

Mr Stoker talked to himself as he carried on securing items. 'Yeah, I know! I've had plenty buying der own wedding rings. But a Catholic with a black veil? And she's been crying? If she was younger and wasn't Catholic, I could'a sworn it was our Gladys.' He put the £10 ring back in its place. Ah, well. A sale's a sale! Amn't I still making a profit on the one that I giv' her?'

*

The jail's commandant Major W.S. Lennon had given permission for them to be married and Grace arrived there at 6pm on Wednesday 3rd May and waited. And waited. The prison smells were pervasive – human excreta and boiled cabbage – as were the screams and shouts, although as the hours passed these decreased and eventually stopped. In the near darkness and total silence, Grace sat. And waited. Occasionally she prayed. But mostly she just waited.

At last she was led into the chapel at about 11pm; she genuflected and made the Sign of the Cross, and then went to pray in one of the front pews. The darkness was made a little less by candles but only in patches and, with the eerie quietness, the atmosphere was weirdly peaceful. There were soldiers standing in the corners so she found it difficult to think and never felt more alone in her life. She looked up at Jesus suffering on the Cross and squeezed her hands. Even then, her mind strayed to what she must look like ... she was wearing a dark brown coat that Muriel had lent her. It was a size too large and fraying at the cuffs. Her shoes, which she deliberately didn't look at, were almost certainly scuffed and muddy. Not quite the bridal appearance that she'd been planning; she was glad that a veil shielded her face ... and the red, wet, eyes[99].

Plunkett was brought through a door, down some steps, and his handcuffs removed. She stood, drew back the veil and quickly wiped her face before going to the altar. He looked, with the ghost of a smile at Grace whilst she stared, wide-eyed, at him. Soldiers, all shapes and sizes and with their rifles at the ready, lined the walls. Father Eugene McCarthy solemnized the wedding; John Lockerby (Sgt 3rd Battalion, the Royal Enniskillen Regiment) was a witness. Grace and Joseph were allowed to say their wedding vows, nothing else; fingers touching briefly, very briefly, as he placed the ring on her finger. The familiar words were spoken softly, but they echoed in a mocking unreality, and it all happened so quickly – the handcuffs were replaced and Joe was led away. Grace, head bowed, was shepherded out.

Father McCarthy had found her a place to stay close by ... not the convent – they had turned her away. It was the house of a Mr Byrne, bell-ringer at Saint James' Church. She almost slept until being gently shaken at about 2am and given a message from the Commandant saying that she could visit her husband – a car was waiting.

Kilmainham Jail, a sinister place in the daytime, in those dark hours before dawn was silently sombre. Armed soldiers stood at the entrance, on landings, in the passages, and outside all doors. Grace was taken to Joseph's tiny cell. A huge and awkward key was turned noisily in the lock and the heavy door swung open. There was a bucket in the corner but no bed and no mattress – her eyes had adjusted to the darkness, and she saw Joseph getting to his feet, as best he could, from the stone floor. Several soldiers crowded in behind her and, with rifles and fixed bayonets, stood with their backs to the wall. The only light was from a candle, held by a soldier, which cast a faintly-strange yellow glow; a three-legged stool was brought in for her. Joe, handcuffed, knelt beside her. His filthy silk scarf was still wrapped round his neck, but she could see the red two-week-old wound from the operation. He looked exhausted but strangely calm.

A Sergeant held a watch near the candle, 'Ten minutes. No touching!'

Silence. Awful, awful silence. Grace looked at Joe but, shaking her head, she had no idea what to say. He whispered, 'Say the Lord's Prayer with me …'

They bowed their heads, not touching, and prayed quietly together.

'Amen.'

A soldier said it automatically with them and then pretended that he hadn't.

'Grace,' Joe said quietly, 'this isn't quite how I …'

She looked at him, 'Joe … I … it's just … all these soldiers it's … so difficult to say what I … '

'I know, Grace … I do know … strange, isn't it? When we had time to talk, we didn't always make the most of it … my fault.'

'No, no … anyway … I think I've always had … somehow … always knew what you were thinking …'

He nodded slowly and smiled. 'Yes … I t'ought yer could do that … used t'er find it a bit of a worry.' On his knees, the hard cruel floor was cramping his legs and Joe shifted his body slightly.

'No TOUCHING!'

There was silence for a while as they looked into each other's eyes.

'Joe ...'

'Yes, Grace?'

'I do wish though ... that ... I could say ... what I wanted to say ... if there weren't these soldiers ... looking at ...'

'Grace ... as far as I'm concerned ... the only face that I can see here ... is yours. I said to you once that my love for Ireland means more to me than anything else ...'

'I remember that, Joe.'

'... Well, now Ireland has had to take second place to you.' Grace said shyly, 'I don't mind sharing.' She was quiet for a moment, then, 'Joe ... you remember ... telling me that you'd like to live the rest of your ... life with me in a white-walled cottage ... with ... oh ...?'

'In the mountains, yes, my Love... I remember ... I gave you a white rose ... soon enough, we'll be together ... for the rest of eternity. You with me. I'll be waiting so there's no need to hurry. Then we'll live in God's House, the two of us with our children, forever.'

'ONE minute left!' the Sergeant rasped.

'I love you, Grace.'

'Joe, oh Joe, I love you ... Oh, Joe ... I can't ...'

'Grace ... Grá mo chroí* ... when it's time to go ... I want you to stand up, turn and ... walk straight out ... don't say anything ... don't turn round. Just ... walk out. I'll look at the floor. It'll be too

---

* Grá mo chroí = Love of My Heart

… too hard to look at each other. Alright?'

She was in a trance, there was the slightest movement of her head, 'Yes. Beannacht Libh*.'

'Time's UP! No touching!' The Sergeant moved forward, Joe ducked his head to look at the hard, filthy ground and Grace stood up. She turned and walked towards the door; there was a pause as it was opened wide; she spun round. Joe was looking at her. Their eyes met, as if they were both thinking, 'I knew you would.'

The Sergeant pushed her elbow; she stepped out and was jostled away.[100]

---

* Beannacht Libh = God bless You.

Chapter 32 – 'Well, that's something!'

'Any news of the Fenian rebellion? It has finished, hasn't it?'

Prime Minister Asquith ogled Venetia before answering, 'Yes. Well, it's now just a question of tidying things up. I sent General Maxwell to be a plenipotentiary and take charge. He's certainly wasted no time. The rebel leaders are being prosecuted and … executed. After being found guilty, of course.'

'So, they're being tried under the Defence of the Realm Act, the one that was passed at the start of the war with Germany, for assisting the enemy?'

'Yes, but in accordance with martial law.'

'What do you mean?'

'Well, martial law was introduced by the Lord Lieutenant*, who was almost certainly drunk at the time and didn't bother telling me, the day after the Rebellion started … so they're being prosecuted at courts-martial. Much quicker, of course, without the same …. ramifications of a civil court.'

'Ramifications?'

'General Blackader presided over most of the trials of the leaders – none were open to the public, no official records kept, and the accused were only given a few hours' notice of their 'trial'. The prosecuting counsel, a Mr Wylie, wanted to have the Press in attendance and for solicitors and defence counsel to be allowed[101].'

'So, were they allowed?'

'No, they were not. These are field general courts-martial, not general courts-martial. There are only three officers and no lawyer. No appeal allowed.'

'These … procedures … took place behind closed doors … in secret … was that legal?'

---

* Wimborne

'Er ... no. But Blackader could basically do whatever he pleased. And he did.'

'I see. And ... they're for use in wartime? Courts-martial? I know we're at war with Germany but this rebellion ... uprising ... that was over wasn't it, before these people were charged? No longer at war with the Irish? If indeed we were ever at war with Ireland. So why not have civil trials? Why the rush? When people are on trial for their life?'

'General Maxwell is 100 per cent responsible for what happens in Ireland. He had carte blanche to deal with the situation ... he obviously wanted to get everything under control as soon as possible... but ... yes, it does look like he's going a little too far.'

'I assume that some of the officers presiding at these trials, or whatever you call them, were involved with fighting and capturing the rebels? A potential conflict there? Rather like President Lincoln's wife being on the jury in the trial of conspirators charged with her husband's assassination?'

'Well ... er ... actually, yes. In fact, one presiding officer was Colonel Ernest Maconchy, commander of 178th Brigade, 2nd Sherwood Foresters. His young and inexperienced soldiers were decimated at the Mount Street Bridge. It does make it look bad ... risky having them as guards for the Irish prisoners and even vindictive in that they were given responsibility for executing the Irish leaders.'

'Oh dear. That doesn't sound good. And ... What were the leaders charged with?'

'Taking part in an armed rebellion, waging war against the king, hurting the defence of the realm, and assisting the enemy. Found guilty, of course. Didn't take long. Pearse gave a speech ... MacDonagh might have, as well ... perhaps ... nobody took notes. Clarke didn't say a word. Apart from claiming the Fenians treated

British prisoners well.'

Venetia stared out of the window, 'And the evidence? What did the Prosecution produce?'

'Ah! Yes, well. There's the proclamation ...'

'Oh, yes. Are there copies available?'

'Not many. A few. Our people managed to collect and destroy most of them. But the court did have a copy and it says ... somewhere in it ... about the rebels being supported by gallant allies in Europe. Gallant Allies! Germany! And ... listen to this – Pearse wrote to his mother and ended by saying '*PS. I understand that the German expedition which I was counting on actually set sail but was defeated by the British.*'

'Really, Henry? An extraordinary postscript ... he must have known that his letter would be checked before despatch. Perhaps, he was desperate to be a martyr?'

'Well. It does strike one as odd, I agree, but it's clear they were assisting the enemy.'

'Hmmm. Not to me.'

'What d'you mean, Venetia?'

'The court used a postscript written by one man to his mother, as evidence against all the others? Yes, clearly the Germans were assisting them but ... where's the proof that the rebels were assisting the Germans?'

'Well ... the wording in the proclamation ... it refers to German Allies.'

'But there wasn't an original copy of the proclamation, with the signatures? And that wording ... it just means they regarded the Germans as allies ... how were the rebels helping the Germans? Goodness, you were a lawyer once; you won the case for Parnell when he was defamed about involvement in the Phoenix Park killings. You know that the evidence against the rebels would never have held up in a civil court. Didn't they have a great banner at Connolly's HQ with *We Serve Neither King nor Kaiser but Ireland* on it?'

'Well, they were certainly causing problems for our Army, not least by shooting and killing them!'

'True. But it could be argued that the Army was shooting at them and the Irish were defending themselves? Did any of them plead Guilty?'

'Only Pearse's brother. And he could possibly have avoided the death penalty if he'd gone for not guilty. But he was determined to claim that he was a major player.'

'Yes? It's unfortunate that there was so little prior warning for the ... defendants ... and no legal advice given. How long did each of these trials or courts-martial take?'

'Not long ... William Pearse? About 15 minutes.'

'Goodness! And wasn't there a woman?'

'Oh yes. Markievicz. She was second in command to a chap named Mallin at one of the big sites. He, apparently ... there's no official notes ... he tried to claim that she was in charge and he was taking orders from her. Anyway, didn't do him any good. Markievicz though, again we can't be certain without formal records, became hysterical and screamed that we couldn't execute a woman.'

'Without court records, or journalists, we can't be sure if any of that's true? Perhaps some military people want to paint them in as bad a light as possible? ... So quite a few executed?'

'Well, all the signatories to the proclamation. Although one, Ceannt, only had his name attached ... didn't actually sign; he would have, but didn't get the chance. And most of the company commanders were also condemned to death. Ned Daly had been troublesome – his group was responsible for lots of British deaths

… but a few that were condemned, well, I'm not sure why they were singled out for execution … such as Colbert and O'Hanrahan … not too clear ... no court records kept ... all done as quickly as possible ...'

'Henry … I know they were all fighting and killing our troops but … well, they were fighting for what they regarded as Freedom and for their own Country.'

'Yes … and I must admit that I'm feeling … well, I've told General Maxwell that enough's enough. No more executions. Markievicz would look especially bad, after we criticized the Germans for killing Nurse Cavell, so we can't execute her. As for De Valera … he was born in the USA …'

'Is he a US citizen?'

'Yes, but the Americans have only just come up with a record of his birth … rather fortuitously ... but anyway we don't want to risk offending them[102]. Thomas Clarke was an American citizen as well but it's too late now and I doubt that they'll care too much about him. And I have the distinct feeling that he would have been furious if he'd not been executed.'

'What about Connolly? The socialist?'

'Oh, yes. He's in a very bad way in hospital. I've sent a telegram, on Wednesday*, telling Maxwell that there are to be no further executions.'

'But you told the Irish MP, Redmond, that you'd sent a telegram to Maxwell on Monday?'

'Hm?'

'You told Redmond you'd sent a strong telegram and that it said there were to be no further shootings?'

'Well ... the note to Redmond said that I hoped the shootings

---

* 10th May

would cease ... unless in quite exceptional cases'.

'Oh! ... But darling, you hadn't actually sent anything to Maxwell until Wednesday? At least that one was clear-cut ... No more executions to take place? ...'

'Yes, indeed. But let's not talk about that ... what about you, Venetia? Mrs Montague? How's married life suiting you? You had to convert?'

'Yes. Edwin's a dear ... I'm finding that being Jewish is rather ... special.'

Chapter 33 – A Reprieve? Yes, No

The sweet-smell was nauseating. Dr Joseph Chamney Ridgway was in a small Dublin Castle room, looking at Connolly's leg and trying not to grimace; a red-raw compound fracture of the two long bones (tibia and fibula) in their middle third. Perhaps caused by a dum dum – an illegal expanding bullet which caused severe injury and was used by both the Irish and British. Women in the GPO had done their best to sterilise the wound, dress it, and set it in splints. Ridgway had on a new clean covering, but it was a few days before Connolly was attended to by the elderly visiting surgeon Doctor Richard Francis Tobin. He operated and Ridgway applied the anaesthetic; two aluminium rods were placed alongside the leg and covered with plaster of Paris, leaving a small hole for dressing the wound.

Pearse, Clarke, Plunkett, McDonagh, and others had been executed. Lillie Connolly was almost certain that her husband would face the same punishment … but whilst he still lived, she held on to the hope that something special would happen.

A Field General Court Martial was held at Dublin Castle, on May 9th, 1916. The presiding officers were Colonel Douglas Sapte, Lieutenant Colonel Arthur Bent and Major Francis Willoughby Woodward; the accused, Connolly, was wearing pyjamas and in bed. He was found not guilty of attempting to cause disaffection but guilty of taking part in armed rebellion. The death sentence was confirmed by General John Maxwell, in command of British forces in Ireland.

In the following days Ridgway gave medical care to all the wounded rebels held in the Castle. He was on his way down a corridor when an orderly saluted and gave him a telegram. It read *'Officer Commanding Dublin Castle. The execution of James*

Connolly is postponed. Asquith'[103]. The doctor tucked it into a pocket and went to have a cup of tea[104] before passing it on to General Maxwell. He threatened to resign if there was a reprieve.

Nora Connolly, 23 years old, went to the Red Cross hospital at Dublin Castle. Small and slight, she tried to ignore the soldiers with their rifles and bayonets. Her father was in a room on his own, on a bed in the corner.

'Hello, Daddy ... oh ... oh ... Are you in pain, Daddy?'

'Och ... Well, it was pretty bad yesterday, but they've cleaned it up and given me something to ease the pain. Now, it's no too bad at all. I'm tired though. How's yer Mammy ... bearing up?'

'Well, she's pretty worried o'course.'

'Aye ... er ... I ought to tell yer ... I've been court-martialled ... so ...'

'Oh.'

'Yeah. Would yer believe, first time for ages I was sleeping and what happens ... they wake me, to tell me I'm gettin' ... done ... tomorra' at dawn. So, well, I wanted to go over some things wi' yersel.'

'Right.'

'Look. I think it'd be best for the family if you get yer'sels over to America ... we've got plenty of people there that'd help yer ... It'd be your decision of course ... but things'll be hard fer yer all here.'

'Right.'

'Oh ... and Frank Sheehy-Skeffington ... now he's a grand man ... very intelligent ... he's my literary executor.' He dropped his voice so that the soldiers wouldn't hear. 'I think he'd be of use to you and the cause .... So, make sure you meet with him ... alright?'

Nora stared open-mouthed.

'Alright, Nora?'

'Er ... yes ... Daddy.'

Later, just before midnight on Thursday 11th May, Nora and her mother were woken at home. A British officer had come in an ambulance to take them to see Connolly. Nora knew what was happening and her mother must have had suspicions though even now she was still clinging to the thought that anything was possible.

Arriving at Dublin Castle, filled with soldiers who appeared to be outside every door, they were led to Connolly's room. Two motionless guards were standing near the bed studiously looking at nothing in particular.

Connolly looked as if he were coming back from another world due to the painkillers or from lack of sleep or both. He lifted his head from the pillow and then let it fall.

They sat beside the bed.

'Lillie ... Lillie ... ' He held out his hand and grasped her's. One soldier looked questioningly at the other who shrugged.

'Lillie, I suppose yer ken wha' this means?'

Lillie's eyes widened, 'No! No, no, no. No! Don't say that Jim! ... no, no, please!' She began sobbing.

'Lillie ... Please ... I know yer canna help it ... not now, though, please ... if yer cry ... I'll ... it'll un-man me ... Lillie, oh, Lillie ... we've been through a lot together, eh? You and me? And the bairns? Some sad and some tough times, eh? But we got through them? And we had some laughs and happy times, eh? Ah'm so lucky to have had yer wi' me ... '

'Oh, Jim! Your life! ... your beautiful life!'

'Wisht, my Love ... It's been a good life. I thank God for it. Hasn't it been a full life? Isn't this a good end?'

'Time's up! No touching.' A soldier moved forward and led Nora out whilst another dragged her mother away. Not long after, a soldier came grinning with a bowl of soup containing a few pieces of pork, and a spoon. He and his pal had spent a few minutes outside in the passage spitting and emptying their nostrils into the bowl. They brought it to Connolly. 'There yer go, me-duk. No expense spared ... get stuck into it.'

'No, thanks. I canna face it.' The painkiller was affecting him.

'Oh ... yer sure?' One of the soldiers stirred the soup, 'Umm. Bits a'meat in it, smells good n'all ... ?'

'Well, leave it there fer noo, thanks. Meb-bee I'll have it in a wee while.'

A few hours later, the soldiers went into the kitchen and saw their Corporal smoking at a table laden with dirty bowls, cutlery, and dishes.

'Ay up, yo two! That Fenian bastard's in't next room. Connolly. A-ya'seen oat onn'imm[*]?'

'Yeah. We gave 'im 'is last meal ... but the weak shit din't want it.'

The Corporal looked at them and laughed, 'Ay! Ah know. Look!' Laughing even more, he pointed at an empty bowl in front of him, 'Luvv'erly! Well, ah wain't gonna let goo' food go ter waste, woz ah?'

The last to be shot, Connolly was pulled out of bed, loaded into an ambulance and taken to Kilmainham. As with the others, they did the deed at about 3:45 in the morning. He was blindfolded and a white badge pinned over his heart. There were differences though. He was wearing pyjamas and taken into the stone-breakers yard on a stretcher. They lifted him off, pulled him towards a post and tried to get him to stand up. But when they removed their hands, he slumped down in agony. The officer in charge, Major Heathcote, was getting annoyed.

---

[*] Aya'seen oat onn'imm = Have you seen him at all

'Get a chair! Go and get a damned chair! ... Go ON! From the guard room!'

A wooden chair was placed in front of the post; they sat him down – he slumped forward, his leg falling away from under him. Mouth open and his eyes closing, he groaned quietly.

'Get something to keep him up! ... I dunno! Rope or something!'

A long leather strap was wrapped around his chest, tying him to the chair. He was still leaning lopsidedly when they shot him. The officer checked for any life and then took out a revolver and fired at his head, splattering himself with blood and brain matter. After a priest anointed the body, it was stripped and taken away to be thrown into a quicklime pit with the bodies of the other executed leaders.

A few days later Lillie returned to the Castle. General Maxwell, went to meet her.

'Mrs Connolly, ...' He put out his hand – she looked down at it, then stared into his eyes. 'You don't really expect me to shake your hand? The person responsible for having the father of my children ... the man that I loved, murdered?' She stared at Maxwell, knowing that there'd be no answer, 'I'm here to collect his wallet and watch.'

'Very well. I'll arrange for someone to get them.'

She wanted to say, 'That's the least yer c'n do, yer bastard', but managed, 'Good. By the way ... I'll be requesting that our family be allowed to travel to America.'

'I see ... Well ... I certainly have no objections – I'll make my view known to Sir Robert Chalmers, the Under Secretary for Ireland. But you'll have to make a formal request and it would need to be considered by him along with comments from people in Belfast police.'

Unfortunately, the official report from the Unionist Belfast police said that the Connolly family would be very likely to start an anti-British campaign in America, and the person supporting Lillie's request was a friend of James Larkin. Maxwell changed his mind and the request was denied. Lillie did get the wallet; it contained an old, creased, photograph of herself, a £1 note and a ten-shilling note. She thought there might be another photo, but there wasn't.

Major Ivon Price of British Intelligence later interrogated Lillie at the Castle. He wanted to know about her son. 'My son? What d'yer want him fer? Isn't it enough that you've taken and kill't me husband?'

'Where is he? We want details of his whereabouts ...'

'Are yer mad or what? He's jus' a child ...'

'He's over 18 ...'

'Ah git away with yer! ... Roddy's barely 15 ... go on, wit'cha yer! ... G'wan! I amn't takin' any more of this nonsense.'

'Mrs Connolly ... We're not after Roddy ... we want your other son.' Lillie stared, clearly and honestly non-plussed, 'Lissen ... I think I know how many sons I've got; I've only had the one! Roddy. That's the only one. A young boy! And yer not gettin' him. So, yer c'n stick that where yer like!'

Major Price's mouth fell open, as confused as Lillie, 'Well ... I'm not convinced ... we'll leave it for now. If the other one ... contacts you, we'll be watching. D'yer hear? Alright, you c'n go.'

Going home on the tram, she remembered the photograph that should have been in Connolly's wallet – it was Nora, in a borrowed Volunteer's uniform, with 'Your Soldier Son' written on the back.[105]

Chapter 34 – *Let's Eat Grandma! Let's Eat, Grandma!*

Sylvia Henley had been invited to spend a weekend at the Asquiths'. Months earlier, she'd explained to her husband, now fighting in France, that she was doing her patriotic duty as much as he was. He understood. They'd named their first daughter Rosalind Venetia.

It was mid-September and the weather was glorious. A pity that Winston hadn't been able to come; he was one of the Prime Minister's favourites. While the other weekend guests were out in the garden playing tennis with his wife, Asquith had managed to inveigle Sylvia to accompany him upstairs into a bedroom, supposedly in order to discuss some books. They'd begun talking about Asquith's son Raymond, the battle that was in progress on the Somme, and 'Chaos Kitchener' as Raymond referred to the General in his letters from France.[106]

She walked nervously away from the bed, 'Were all the Fenian leaders shot?'

Asquith had other things on his mind but gathered his thoughts, 'MacDermott and Connolly were the last two. Connolly's execution in particular was probably ... excessive. There's a move by some in the Irish community to claim that Larkin, the English communist who's in America, was the main leader. Anyway, it was considered that the Government's reputation was beginning to suffer due to the number being executed. I had to pressure Maxwell to call a halt, I sent him a telegram to that effect before Connolly's, but the bugger probably thought he was on safe ground after reading the May 10th article in the Irish Independent. It said, *Let the worst of the ringleaders be singled out and dealt with as they deserve.*'

'The Independent? The Dublin newspaper owned by William Murphy? The businessman that crushed the 1913 strikers? No doubt, he later said that the article wasn't approved by him? Put the blame on the editor!'

'Anyway, Casement wasn't shot ...' Asquith whispered.

Sylvia dodged away and said 'I saw Edward Grey last week. He looked awful. Someone told me he's going blind?' The Prime Minister was momentarily off-balanced, physically and mentally, 'Who? Oh yes. His nerves are wrecked, too. Wanted to resign, but I wasn't going to allow it.'

'B-but, why not? I mean the poor chap ...'

'Yes, but damned nuisance. I need his support in Cabinet. Goodness me, the Foreign Secretary to resign!? The Press and Opposition would have a field day. Yes, well, I allowed it in the end, though. He has this weird idea about us pulling out of Ireland and leaving the Irish to sort it out themselves! He can carry on in the House of Lords. He'll have to cope.'

Sylvia sighed, 'He didn't communicate too well in 1914, did he? How on earth did this awful so-called Great War start? Was it really due to that dreadful newspaper man? I heard someone say that next to the Kaiser, Lord Northcliffe did more than any other person to bring about the war.'

Asquith shrugged, 'He was certainly very gung-ho and he does have a lot of influence at all levels of society. But, you know, little Serbia had been trying desperately for centuries to break away from Turkey.' Asquith pulled his shoulders back, chin up and proud in his stance, 'And as I told the House of Commons, England is fighting to vindicate the principle that small nationalities are not to be crushed in defiance of international good faith at the arbitrary will of a strong and overmastering Power ...[107]'

Somehow that caused Sylvia to think again of Ireland and to ask about the Fenians that had been captured following the Uprising.

'General Maxwell rounded up 3000 or so from all over Ireland. They were tried at courts-martial quick-smart, obviously found guilty of assisting the enemy, and sent to English prisons. Some were sentenced to death but all of those were commuted to 10 years. The rest got 5 years jail and sent to, oh, ... places like Dartmoor, Lewes, Knutsford, and Wandsworth. After a few months solitary in freezing cells, it was decided to put 1800 in Frongoch near Bala, North Wales.'

'Congregate them? But surely it would have been better to keep them all separate? They're likely to support each other and exchange ideas, aren't they? Why all in the same place? It's not as if we're short of prisons in England?'

'Well, it was thought a good idea from an administrative point of view, I suppose. Especially if they're out of circulation for ten years.'

Sylvia remembered her earlier question, 'What happened with Casement?' Asquith paused, 'He was hanged in Pentonville Prison. Treason. He probably wasn't grateful, but the King didn't want a public execution ... nor slow-hanging followed by decapitation. His Majesty could have insisted on that method for treason.' Another pause, thinking that the second bottle of champagne may have been a mistake, 'You know, I've always felt strongly attracted to you?'

Mrs. Henley pushed his groping hand away. He was 60, she was 34, and her sister Venetia was 29. 'Henry, I'm flattered by your attention but, please, don't do that here. Margot is downstairs ... Now, you were saying about little nations fighting for independence from great Powers? ...this Casement trial ... he was found guilty of High Treason, but which particular law does that come under?'

'Hmm? Oh. Well, the Prosecution had to carry out some research ... poring through the bookshelves, climbing the ladders in the libraries, taking down dusty tomes and scrutinising page after parchment page. Finally, one of them came upon what they needed. It was no surprise that it took so long; the Act had been written in the reign of Edward III.'

'Really? How old is it?'

'Er ... 565 years. Originally written in Norman French in the mid-fourteenth century, with little punctuation, so of course interpretation is open to debate. But they argued that it says High Treason occurred if a person ... 'adhered to the king's enemies in his realm, giving them aid and comfort in his realm or elsewhere'.

'Oh ... that sounds a little ... vague and woolly?'

'D'you think so? Anyway, Casement's defence team argued that the case rested on his words and actions whilst he was in Germany; they said that the words 'in his realm' meant that any treason act had to occur in Britain or the colonies. The Prosecution was led by Sir Edward Carson's friend, Freddy Smith. Yes, Lord Birkenhead. He argued that the words 'or elsewhere' meant that this included Germany and a Henry VIII law said that acts of treason committed outside the realm of England could be tried within England.'

'Henry VIII? Not exactly friendly to Catholics, was he? Anyway, what sort of treason did they say Casement had carried out?'

'That he'd gone to Germany and tried to persuade captured British troops to join his so-called Irish Brigade.'

Sylvia was trying to understand why all of this appeared to be so contrived and so suspiciously not quite right, 'Well, I don't know … But … hang on. The Act said giving the king's enemies aid and comfort … Casement wasn't giving the Germans anything … he was wanting them to help Ireland! Rather like England helping Serbia and Belgium.'

'Sylvia, he wanted the Irish Brigade to fight and kill His Majesty's troops in Ireland … that's certainly assisting the enemy. The fact that there were only 55 or so in the Brigade and they weren't actually used is beside the point.[108]'

'So, what did the Defence counsel say?'

'Irish chap named Serjeant Sullivan was under a bit of a mental strain … he tried arguing that Casement's actions and words were in Germany, not in the King's realm. He tried to make a thing about the old medieval statute having a comma*.'

'You're joking?'

'No, no. He went on and on about it. Prosecution said that there was a comma; Sullivan said there wasn't, so it changed the meaning. He said it could have been a dirt mark or a crease on the parchment.'

'I'm sure Casement would have preferred his chap to focus on the argument that it simply wasn't Treason[109] … Anyway, what did the judge say?'

'Judge Darling disagreed with Sullivan – he said the comma was irrelevant and the Law did apply. The jury was out long enough for a sandwich and a cup of tea – came back with 'Guilty.'

'Did Casement get a chance to say anything?'

'Yes. Quite a good speech. He said that he hadn't been a member of the Irish Republican Brotherhood, unlike all the leaders of the Uprising, but stressed that he was Irish not British. That

---

* Casement later complained from jail, "God deliver me from such antiquaries as these, to hang a man's life upon a comma and throttle him with a semi-colon."

didn't work too well because he'd accepted a knighthood, worked for the Government for decades, and had been taking a pension until fairly recently.' He paused, aware that the argument wasn't watertight and that she might raise another issue – she did.

'But one doesn't need to be British to do all that. And he hadn't actually fired a gun nor killed anybody? In fact, hadn't he tried to stop the Rising?'

'Ah ... yes ... well, that point was never actually mentioned in court ... Perhaps he didn't want to be seen as opposing the fight for independence. Anyway, I doubt that the Defence Counsel would have had any proof ...'

Sylvia was not convinced. 'No ... not unless ... someone in the British police, who initially interviewed him, was called and gave evidence about him wanting to stop the Uprising?'

'Well, we can't be certain that he tried to stop the rebellion... and he couldn't name anybody to support his assertion. It would also, of course, raise some embarrassing questions about why those Government officers didn't allow him to call for the Uprising to be stopped.'

'Embarrassing questions?'

'Well ... this is highly confidential ... one of the three interviewers was an MI5 chap[*]. Years earlier, he'd been a very senior member of the Ulster Volunteer Force; organised the Covenant signing; been willing to fight against Home Rule even if it meant fighting against His Majesty's forces; and it was he that organised the Larne gun-running.'

'And of course MI5 wanted the Rising to go ahead?! ... What about that Irish chap Bailey? The one they didn't prosecute. He was on the submarine, too. He would have heard Casement saying he wanted the Rising called off?'

---

[*] Frank Hall

'Well ... he wasn't called to give evidence.'

'Really? So, what about Casement's appeal? Against the conviction or sentence?'

'That was never going to succeed. He tried to claim that he had only done the same as Edward Carson and, yes, Smith himself. Those two had supported British officers in refusing to do their duty in 1914; they'd created a huge civilian army with German-supplied rifles and machine guns, an army that was willing to fight against His Majesty's troops. Carson had even liaised with officers in German High Command. Casement insisted that the only difference between him and Smith was that he was going to be hanged whilst Smith would become Lord Chancellor.'

Sylvia stifled a laugh, 'And Freddy Smith, the Attorney General, was there leading the Prosecution? What did he do?'

'He stomped out of the court with his hands in his pockets. Did you know that Margot once said that Freddy Smith is very clever but he lets his brains go to his head ...'

'So, Smith got his way? Casement had to hang. Was any consideration given to commuting the sentence?'

'Yes. Certainly. The Battle of the Somme was just about to start but we spent quite a massive amount of time discussing Casement in Cabinet. Day after day. Winston was even more talkative than usual. But commuting was never going to happen. We received petitions and read plenty of letters from high-profile people begging for mercy; John Masefield, Yeats, Galsworthy, Arthur Conan Doyle. George Bernard Shaw said he opposed Sinn Féin but killing Casement would make him into a martyr and be counter-productive ... Oh, and the issue of Arthur Lynch was raised.'

'Arthur Lynch? He hasn't been mentioned much ... ?'

'No. Bit awkward. Irish father and Scots mother, born in

Australia. He was a Colonel fighting for the Boers, raised a Brigade in 1900, killing British soldiers. Arrested, found guilty of treason and sentenced to hang. The sentence was commuted and he was eventually pardoned. Why? Perhaps because he's a journalist, been elected to Parliament for West Clare, and he knows Lord Northcliffe.'

'But Casement, who never held a rifle, his appeal was to no avail?'

'He was always going to hang! I thought perhaps ... a defence of insanity ... but, no. Freddy, he was Attorney General of course, refused to allow an appeal to be considered by the House of Lords. He said Irish prisoners of war who refused to join Casement's Brigade had been subjected to special acts of cruelty by their German guards; we were also led to believe that, despite being few in number, Germany planned to send the Irish 'Brigade' troops to fight in Egypt.'

'Oh? ... But wait. Freddy led the Prosecution ... and was any evidence for that cruelty by German guards or the Egypt business, produced during the trial?'

'Well, no, but during the Cabinet discussion any support that Casement got was rather ... undermined by the Black Diaries.'

'Oh, yes ... I've heard some whispers about them ... what are they?'

'Well, Casement ... preferred the company of men ...'

'What do you mean? Homosexual? What has that got to do with him being hanged, for goodness sake?'

'Well, the problem for him was that he kept a record of his ... rather perverse and depraved ... encounters with young men. Wrote the details in a very descriptive way in, well, sort of diaries. Anyway, British Intelligence got hold of them and made sure that anybody of influence was aware of the contents and saw selected copies of extracts. People such as journalists and diplomats. The Archbishop of Canterbury. His Majesty. Even people that would otherwise perhaps have called for his sentence to be commuted. The author Joseph Conrad was one of his friends once ... but he's got no wish to be suspected as being anything but masculine.[110] Herbert Ward, you know him? The sculptor? He met Casement in Africa, and he'd been a friend for 30 years, named his son Roger Casement Ward and asked Casement to be his godfather. Now he's changed the little chap's name by deed poll.'

Sylvia shook her head, 'That's incredible ... are you sure these Diaries are genuine?'

'Genuine? You think the Intelligence people may have forged them? No ... take far too long and the writing has been verified ... no, I'm as certain as I can be that they're genuine. We had to use them. The problem for us was that too many people were sympathetic to him. You know, it was even considered essential to do something about the United States ...'

'What do you mean, Henry?'

'The Irish in America were causing problems about the Uprising and claiming Casement was innocent. It's the Presidential election year. Wilson might have wanted to show sympathy to Ireland. We need the US to join us and fight the Germans. So, we made sure that their ambassador saw some photographic extracts of the Diaries.'

'We?'

'Well, alright! I showed them to him. It was essential that the President be informed so that he wouldn't be tempted to officially ask for clemency. Apparently, Margot spoke to him and said that the damned Tories were trying to wedge me on Casement so that whatever happened I'd be in the wrong.'

'You showed copies to the American ambassador? That would

be Walter Page? With the huge nose? The man who told somebody, who couldn't keep the quote to themselves, that Margot is the ugliest woman he's ever seen?' Sylvia shook her head. 'Henry, I know homosexuality is illegal ... but what on earth does any of this have to do with Casement's treason case? And let's be honest ... many, many of our friends are very much into that sort of thing.'

'Sylvia, that may be. But they do not write up the details and commit treason. And I happen to know that the Defence counsel were told about the Diaries, in case they wanted to claim insanity, the Cabinet went into this in great detail ... but the Defence refused to even look at the Diaries. There was a silly, incredible, suggestion that he'd assisted at trials of young African natives, accused of unnatural practices, and written details of that evidence in the Diaries. Anyway, Casement was terrified of them being made public.'[111]

Sylvia shook her head, 'What a mess ... was he a Catholic, by the way?' Asquith didn't answer immediately, 'His parents? It was a mixed marriage. Apparently, he was raised as a Protestant even though his mother had him baptised as a Catholic when he was five. He wanted, in jail, to have instruction and assistance from a priest ... but the Catholic bureaucracy demanded that he formally apologise for having caused a ... scandal.'

'Really? You think they knew about the Diaries?'

'I'm sure they did. Our Intelligence people made certain that the right sort of people saw some contents. Casement did write an apology but had second thoughts and destroyed it. Even so, a local priest took pity and helped him.'

They both stood looking out the window, 'Apparently, he died with great dignity ... but there was a crowd outside the gates cheering ... the Governor heard them and apparently said that it made him feel ashamed to be an Englishman.'

A telephone was ringing somewhere downstairs.

Sylvia shook her head, 'Henry, Casement may have been ... addicted to experiences which many people consider, or claim to consider, to be perverted ... but I don't believe that makes him evil.[112]' She sat down on the bed. 'Anyway ... oh, yes, I meant to ask ... did Margot enjoy Maud Allan's private performance of Salome?'

Asquith stared at Sylvia wondering how to respond. Fortunately, the telephone started ringing again. 'It's not the line from Downing Street – that phone's in the library ... must be the one in the hall. Why can I not have a peaceful Sunday? I was hoping to go for a drive with you. Never mind, someone'll answer it ...'

The ringing stopped. Asquith heard the cultured voice of Clouder the butler, 'I'm not sure where the Prime Minister ... Yes. Yes. I'll fetch Mrs Asquith.'

For a few moments there was an atmosphere of autumnal peace – the watery sun in the welkin shone into the room and a blackbird was singing somewhere in the garden. Asquith looked out the window and saw one of his sons, 14-year-old Anthony, who would be going back to Winchester College next day, laughing with the others. He could see his wife down there, sitting on the grass smiling. She had once said, 'I'm not saying that I was ever what I would call 'plain,' but I have the sort of face that bores me when I see it on other people,' nevertheless he had always known that he was lucky to have her as his wife. He watched her picking up a tennis ball and throw it to Anthony who, still grinning, caught and returned it.

Clouder marched down the path and spoke to Margot; she stood motionless for a few seconds before pulling her shoulders back and going inside with her head held high.

Asquith's mouth opened and closed. He looked at Sylvia and

then went downstairs. Margot was in the hall, putting the phone down; she turned to look at him, tears cascading down her face. He put his arm round her. 'I know… Raymond … I knew it would happen … You … don't need to say it … '

Chapter 35 – August 1916

Margot Asquith had said of David Lloyd George that he couldn't see a belt without wanting to hit below it*. Now he could smell blood and Prime Minister Asquith was forced to step down. The replacement was obvious – Lloyd George knew that he himself would be more decisive and effective.

His family household having moved into 10 Downing Street and wife Margaret now on holiday in Wales, Lloyd George was feeling relaxed. He pulled up his trousers, did up the fly buttons, and looked at his Private Secretary, Frances Stevenson. She obviously wanted to say something important …

… something Lloyd George preferred not to talk about just now. It was so much better and easier to talk politics, 'I took on the challenge of Ireland before I became PM, when I couldn't really lose. If I failed, it wouldn't have harmed my reputation. I knew that if anybody could sort it out, it would have to be me. Asquith has basically just sat on his hands and done nothing. Now I'm determined to push Ireland.'

Holding a small handkerchief, screwed tightly in her hand, she waited and could see that he was wanting to be emotionally stroked so she said, 'Asquith was a disgrace. You simply had to take over from him. Everyone's annoyed and impatient with the lack of progress in the European war. The Press, especially Northcliffe's *Times* and *Daily Mail*, was always criticising him; all the MPs could see, and hear, that his alcoholism was getting worse.'

Lloyd George shrugged, 'Northcliffe's father had been an alcoholic, so he has a hatred and contempt for drunkenness … hates Asquith. … Didn't use to like me much either, not when I

---

* Quoted by her step-daughter Violet in *The Listener*, June 11, 1953

opposed the British war against the Boers in South Africa and I even had the effrontery to increase taxes to pay for welfare.'

'But surely his newspapers say something good about you every day, darling?'

'They do now. Northcliffe knows that I was the main voice, perhaps the only one, in Cabinet arguing for war with Germany, to protect the rights of small nations ... and I took the lead, along with the Conservatives, in calling for conscription. Asquith finally came round to the idea.'

'Eventually, he did ... And do you really think you'll be able to sort Ireland out?'

'My objective is to make Ireland a non-British problem. But sort it out? Well, I always knew I could make a better attempt than Asquith ... but ... er, no. There was never a chance. I listened to the Irish Nationalist leader Redmond and told him he'd get Home Rule but he'd have to put up with Partition for a while because Ulster needed to stay as part of the United Kingdom. He accepted that. I told Carson, leader of the Protestants, that he'd have to accept Home Rule but there'd be Partition ... and Ulster would never, ever, be ruled from Dublin. He was happy with that.'

'Oh ... ? So ... you didn't quite tell them the same thing?'

'Well, no, not really. But I knew Redmond would come round to accept the reality of things ... And it would have been fine if not for the die-hard Tories. They just said no Home Rule. Full stop.'

'Ah. All your hard work, too. Wasted.' She shook the pillows and said 'David ... I've got some news ...'

He was either not listening or still thinking of his hard work, 'Well, not really wasted. Redmond ended up being vilified by his friends for agreeing to split Ireland. Carson managed to persuade his people to accept the concept of Home Rule with permanent partition. Then, blow me, if Redmond didn't come running and ask for a convention to talk more.'

'That was a bit of luck.'

'Absolutely. This can keep them talking for at least six months, maybe a year. Carson won't budge but Redmond's not going to know that ... I'm sick and tired of Ireland and just want to get on with winning the war. That means more troops, which means conscription in Ireland. Lord French says he can enforce it. I'll probably have to sweeten things with the promise of Home Rule even if it infuriates the die-hard Tories and Carson. I'm sorry, Frances ... I interrupted you.' She took his hand and said, 'David, I've got some news. I've missed again. The doctor confirmed it.'

'Oh! ... Ah, my darling Pussycat! Well ... That certainly is news. Yes indeed. Of course, as you know, I believe it's the right of every woman to be able to choose what happens to her body. In years to come, I'd like to think that every woman would be able to decide ... whether she wanted to ... do as we did last time ... but, as it is now, only wealthy couples can ... If you want ... adoption is another option ... but that means, of course, going the nine months ... and it could prove embarrassing because, well, your condition would obviously be known. We could deal with that, I suppose ... you could have a nice holiday somewhere ... abroad, maybe.' He cleared his throat, 'We'd have to find a discreet couple that wanted to adopt a child. Otherwise, if you think it best – I'll make the same ... arrangements as last time. Everything went quite well, didn't it? But ... as I say ... it's your body ... it's your choice.'

Frances turned and looked out of the window. The handkerchief was screwed tighter; tears trickled down her cheeks.

'Yes ... Yes, David. That'd be ... fine. Thank you. Yes, please ... make the arrangements.*'

---

* She had two abortions before giving birth to a daughter. Lloyd George believed that the child was his, but it is thought that his adviser, Thomas Tweed, had become Stevenson's lover.

Chapter 36 – Outlived the failure of all her hopes*

Collins worked hard in Frongoch Prison. Many inmates, some of whom couldn't read or write, had families that had been dependent on them. The wives and children had no income and those prisoners were frantic with worry. Collins wrote letters on their behalf to Susan Killeen, a girlfriend from his London days, asking her to contact Cumann na mBan and arrange for a welfare visit.

There were many instances where the rights of the prisoners were ignored or abused. Collins took responsibility for challenging the authorities and often forced them to back down.

Eight months after the Uprising, Collins and many other prisoners were released. He arrived back in County Cork just after Christmas 1916 and spent most of the next few weeks in the pub downing beers, probably because he couldn't afford whiskey, before travelling to Dublin.

The door to the tobacconist's shop at 55 Amiens Street, Mountjoy showed signs of having been battered down many times. It had barely opened before Collins stepped inside and put his arms around her. 'Ah, Kathleen! Kathleen! I heard about your loss … And for it to happen after Tom being taken from us … to have the baby die … both gone straight to be with our Lord.'

Kathleen Clarke was still crying, 'Thanks, Michael. I like to think of Tom holding the child in his arms … I suppose you know that I didn't tell him another one was on the way? I maybe should have but … well, I don't know … he was so certain that he wouldn't be coming back from the GPO. T'would've torn him apart knowing that I was carrying and that he'd not get to help me … nor see … the poor wean … and ... she died before she'd lived.'

---

* Casement speech, 29 June 1916

She sobbed. Collins held her hand and said, 'Tom would have understood your reasons for not telling him. You know that. He was the wisest man I ever met.' Kathleen smiled sadly, 'Well, he was certainly more aware of things than Pearse – I've heard some saying that the fella went to pieces in the GPO. And young Plunkett. I know the poor lad was terribly sick ... but ... Musha, there's so many things Tom would have wanted done differently.'

Collins realised he was going to have a difficult time here.

'For a start, why couldn't the rifles arrive from Germany on the day as originally planned, for goodness sake? Why mess a'boat changing the date of delivery? Craiceáilte*! And Tom always thought it would be a disaster having that madman Casement involved. Then there were those poor young fellas killed in the car ... Mother of God! Why send them from Dublin by train 'an den for them to be drivin' Killarney to Kerry at night-time in a car that the fella'd never used before? Even if he hadn't been drinking, I doubt he woz any good at the drivin'. Losing their way and drowning! Why? Because Joe Plunkett was interested in radios? If he was such an expert how is it he didn't realise the importance of cutting the telephone lines from the Castle?'

At the mention of the car crash, Collins looked away feeling very uncomfortable. The memory that he was involved in a plan resulting in three young men being killed caused him to wince. Then he gathered himself and felt a need to defend those that had been his senior officers, 'Kate, Joe Plunkett fought and died for Ireland's freedom. Pearse? He was always in control, encouraging and decisive.'

Kathleen refused to back down, 'You weren't of course in the

---

* Craiceáilte = Crazy

leadership group and we'll never know whether it was Pearse or Plunkett that decided the Castle wouldn't be taken … Did neither try to find out how many troops would be in there over Easter? Weren't Pearse's own District volunteers intended to take it? Mallin's group of the Citizen's Army was so confused they didn't know what to do so they went to dig trenches in St Stephen's Green. Trenches! Am I right or am I wrong, Michael?'

Collins opened his mouth to speak but he was too slow.

'And another t'ing … why did Éamonn Ceannt and Cathal Brugha occupy the hospital at South Dublin Union? Was there really no other useful site they could take and hold against the British? A hospital! Mother of God! Is it any wonder a nurse was kill't?[113]'

Collins said, 'As yer say, I wasn't in the leadership group but I know there were opinions *go loer** about what was the best way to move on the day. I'm guessing your Tom, Seán MacDiarmada, and Connolly would have been of the same mind. They'd have wanted to hit England as hard as possible and as soon as possible; Pearse and Plunkett were thinking of a historic event that promoted Irish freedom … and wanted to die doing it.'

Collins sensed the need to bring the conversation up to date, 'What you're doing with the Irish National Aid and Volunteer Dependents' Fund is desperately important… the men and women that were arrested after the Rising are jobless and penniless. There's many children that'd starve without your Fund.'

Kathleen took Collins' hand. 'It's not my Fund. I want you to be a part of it, now. I'm lucky that you've applied to be so active in the administrative role. The fact that you'll be going out every day to visit and support the struggling families won't do you any harm. The more people that get to know Michael Collins the better. I'm serious! … we need you to take a lead. We can't be letting the

---

* *'go loer':* plenty of

likes of De Valera get too powerful. He says he wants to support Irish families which is all very grand. But his idea of that is keeping women in their place, and it means them stuck at home having babies and answering to the men …'

Collins was finding it difficult to argue with this woman.

' … and what on earth are they doing now with these elections to the British Parliament? Yes, yes. Tom would have hated the idea of our people getting elected to the British Parliament … but … well, I don't know … Even if I'm just a woman I can think fer me'sel, yer know … It could be a great idea. Our people being elected, I mean. I cannot understand why they get that old fool George Plunkett chosen to win an election in Roscommon or wherever it is. Now that's all very good… but everyone knows he'd make himself look a complete ee'jit speaking in Parliament in London.'

Collins managed to say, 'Now hold on …' But Kathleen hadn't finished, 'And what happens next? They'll get the loikes of you an' De Valera an' the Lord knows how many others elected. Great! But then they tell you not to go to London!!! Are they mad or what? Didn't Parnell go t'er Parliament and make'em suffer, telling Gladstone and Asquith the hard truth?[114] The whole bunch of yer could be taking it up to the likes of Lloyd George and Churchill and … dem Unionists … and all a-you'se lot causing mayhem, oath or no oath. At least for a few months and then all walk out on the bastards.'

Collins gaped, speechless as she continued almost without taking a breath, 'But, no! Yer stay in Dublin and sulk and think yer making a grand gesture. I bet this'll be De Valera's cunning idea. It's because he knows that he'd be useless playing politics with those British politicians. It'd be like Jack and the Beanstalk except De Valera would talk for hours before selling the cow for

2 beans, cry a'boat it, 'den try ter buy the cow back for t'ree beans. Yer be careful of that fella, De Valera, Michael. Anyway, thanks for comin' ter see me.' Collins could see why Tom Clarke married this woman and why it had to be her that created the Volunteers' Dependents Fund. 'I'll bear in mind what yer say about Dev. Bye now. And God bless.'

'God bless yer, Michael ... please, please, never forget that yer carry Tom's inheritance. I could never forgive anybody, not even yersel', that breaks their oath to defend the republic. God bless, now.'

Kathleen Clarke's comment about De Valera came to Collins' mind when he was meeting Harry Boland a month later in the Greville Arms in Granard, Longford. Boland, a tailor and always well-dressed, was older by a couple of years but Collins treated him like a younger brother, one moment bullying him and the next protecting him. And Boland responded accordingly, one moment looking up to the Big Fella and admiring him and the next moment wanting to punch him on the nose.

Boland called to the barman, 'Musha! ... what about me feckin' change? I'm after giv'in yer five shillings!' The barman turned, 'Yeah? ... and I'm after puttin' yer change there ... on the bar.'

'Well, where the feck is it?' Boland was getting annoyed.

'I took it,' said Collins, 'I t'ought yer'd want to be donatin' it to the Dependants' Fund ... sha, they need it more'an you.'

'Yer did what? 'Gis it back, yer big ...'

'Whisht! Come over here ... we need to talk.' Collins pulled Boland into the snug. 'Yer see what that old fool Count Plunkett has done? After all the work we went to, to get him elected to the British Parliament? He wants to stay in Dublin, start his own political Party, an' go up against Arthur Griffith ... now I'm no supporter of Griffith ...'

'Ah, Mick, yer can't blame ole' Plunkett for not wanting to tramp off to London. For a start he's nearly 70 years old and Lloyd George, Carson and Churchill would tie him in knots an' make him look an eejit.'

'Yeah, well ... They'll be very happy the rich ole bastard's not drawing his 400 quid, which would've come in very handy by the way for the Fund ... and they'll be very pleased that he's not sitting opposite them, arguin' the feckin' toss ... he could have put a spoke in their wheel and made a nuisance of himself by demanding to be at the Convention they're planning for London.'

Convention? This was news to Harry. Collins explained, 'Lloyd George is tryin' to be clever with half-arsed discussions ... between Irish Catholics and Northern Irish Protestants, supposedly to negotiate agreement, just a pretence and wastin' time. They'll get nowhere for months and months but if he tries to bring conscription to Ireland that'll be the end of it because the Catholic priesthood, every political party here, and every pub-goer would be spittin' chips.'

Harry was getting worked up, 'Conscription? The feckin' British have never done any'ting fer us. When the praties were rotten an' small, we could go an' get fecked. We've got families starvin' even now in shitty slums and the ole wans coughin' their guts up ... and London doesn't give a feck. But when war comes and the Jer'mins are shootin', Churchill wants our lads to fight fer King an Cun'tree. When the submarines are sinkin' his ships from America and causing food shortages, they want our beef and pigs an ... an ... beer.'

Collins agreed, 'They might get pigs to the dock but Paddy O'Daly's lads will slaughter 'em before they can get 'em on the boats. And there's something you an' I can be doing. We're goin' to get McGuinness elected here in the South Longford by-election.'

'Joe McGuinness? The fella that's banged up in Lewes jail?

But Dev doesn't want any of our people taking part in the British so-called democracy ...'

'Harry, will yer lissen ter me ... De Valera's in Dartmoor jail. He hates not being the Big Cheese directing operations. '

'No, no, Mick! Matter of fact, I think Dev's alright ... People say that he did well commanding Boland's Mill at Easter ...'

'Yeah? That's not what I heard. I heard he was a nervous wreck. Apart from anything, I t'ink he's got an inferiority complex. Wanted to be a priest but got knocked back 'cos he couldn't be sure who his ol wan was*.'

'Mick, yer not being fair ...I t'ink he's right and we shouldn't be putting candidates in the Brits' election. If they don't get elected, we're gonna look like losers ...'

'Harry, Dev's last memory of the Irish people was 'dem screamin' abuse an' spittin' gob at us last April when we woz being loaded into the cattle ships ... politically, Dev wouldn't know his feckin' arse from his elbow.'

'Mick! McGuinness doesn't want to be a candidate.'

'I don't give a feck. I'll make sure his name is on the ballot, regardless. And he'll win.'

'Oh, yeah! And how can yer be so sure, Big Fella?!'

'He'll win because he's gonna get more votes than yer man that's running fer the Irish Parliamentary Party ... I know that because we'll be watchin' the countin' ... and findin' any missin' votes.'

Harry turned his head, 'Oh, Kitty! How's things?' Their discussion was interrupted by the appearance of a beautiful young woman, Kitty Kiernan, on the other side of the bar.

---

* A marriage certificate for De Valera's parents has not been located.

'Hello, you two hairy* rebels ... Mick ... Harry. I don't want to know what you two have been up to, do I? Is that a dirty mark under your nose, Mick? Or are yer after growing a Chaplin moustache again?' She brushed a lock of hair from her forehead and took time to look into the eyes of both men. Boland elbowed Collins, and Collins elbowed Boland.

'Any chance of some service down here?' A customer dragged Kitty's attention away.

'Did yer see the way she looked at me?'

'Yer eejit! She was lookin' at me.'

*

Sure enough, McGuinness won the South Longford election in May, with a tiny majority of 37, despite his home address being His Majesty's Prison Lewes. A bundle of ballots for the main opposition candidate was mysteriously mislaid. De Valera was released from jail shortly after and his attitude to British elections had changed. He nominated for the East Clare by-election in June and won – but Collins was too busy revitalising the Irish Republican Brotherhood to assist.

---

* *Hairy* = cunning and cute

Chapter 37 – Autumn 1917

'Nothing matters very much and few things matter at all'
(attributed to Arthur Balfour)

An Irish Republican Brotherhood member, 32-year-old Thomas Ashe, had been arrested for giving seditious speeches, sentenced to two years with hard labour, and was in Mountjoy jail on hunger strike. He was thrown into a cell with no bed, no bedding, no boots and left for five days. He refused food and water. Then the door crashed open and he was pulled from the floor blinking at the daylight, barely conscious. While other prisoners in their cells rattled mugs on the bars and shouted support, the warders dragged him down prison corridors, up and down stairs, and yet more corridors. In a small clinical room his arms were strapped to his side and his chest pinioned to a wooden chair. Hands forced his chin down and the end of a rubber hose, aided by a wooden spoon, was forced into his mouth.

He could smell the hard rubber and taste its coarseness as it was pushed past his teeth and wiggled forcefully into his gullet. He tried, unsuccessfully, not to choke – when he did, he couldn't breathe, so he choked again. A gang of five or six warders surrounded him whilst milk, into which an egg had been whipped, was forced into his throat using a stomach pump and the hose held above his head.[115] Hands were shoving and thrusting all over him. An inexperienced doctor, William Henry Lowe, 'supervised'.

'Pull his head back. Pull it! Pull his hair!'

'Hold him still! Still!'

'Force his chin up. UP!' This resulted in more choking and the sweet-rancid fluid bubbled and slopped around his mouth. Some of it may have reached his stomach, but most would have probably gone into the lungs. Despite the strapping, he was struggling and struggling, the chair scraping and leaning back and forth.

'Hold him still!'

'SWALLOW, yer bastard!'

'He's choking!'

'Shut up! Hold that hose straight! Pump some more in. MORE!' The stinking fluid bubbled around his bruised and bleeding mouth, spilling over the guard's hands. They gave it a rest for a few hours and then tried again – and yet again twice, the next day. There was much less struggling by the weakened Ashe – his lips turned blue and aspiration pneumonia followed. He was taken to hospital where he had two heart attacks and mercifully died, on September 25th, without regaining consciousness.[116]

A few days later, Lloyd George was not pleased, 'There were 50,000 at Ashe's Dublin funeral. I'll find out who did the force-feeding and have their guts for garters.' The Prime Minister was in Downing Street with a sleepy Churchill. They'd both eaten rather too much at lunch-time. No longer being a member of Cabinet, and still not the Tories' best friend, Churchill was taking the opportunity of gathering gossip. He blew a cloud of cigar smoke and sniffed, 'I hear that Collins gave a very short and disappointing speech at the graveside. He's certainly no orator ... didn't want to be compared with Patrick Pearse, I s'pose ... Anyway, how's that constitutional convention coming along? The Ulster crowd talking to the Home Rulers and Redmond?[117]'

Lloyd George pretended to be asleep. Churchill decided to speak louder, 'By-the-bye, I heard a whisper about thousands of Australian troops making trouble in France? A mutiny?'

Lloyd George fidgeted again, 'That is highly confidential ... a few hundred colonial n'er-do-wells in Etaples ... all sorted out now after a few faced a firing squad[118]. Speaking of mutinies ... that

Irish fella, Hubert Gough's going from strength to strength against the Boche, don't-cha think?'

'Yes, indeed ... I read that General Gough had a victory at some place called Polygon Wood. Funnily enough Australian troops did rather well there. Only five thousand casualties', Churchill was fully awake now. 'We ought to be thinking about what we'll do when they surrender. The Boche, I mean. Northcliffe and the hoi polloi will want to make the Jerries squeal and pay reparations.'

Lloyd George was now positively uncomfortable, 'Yes, yes. But we can't squash them too much. After the war, we'll be looking for nations to buy from us. Germany will be an enormous market.' Both men began to snooze again until Churchill's leg jerked and he woke, 'What? Oh yes! I heard that Arthur is busy on something for the Jews and Palestine ...?'

'Balfour? Yes. We owe them. The Jews worldwide have done a lot for us in this War. They can be very useful after it, too. They always do very well whenever there's a war. Millions of them in Germany, Russia and Poland. They'll prosper. I think they could have some influence in keeping the Bolsheviks with us in the War.[119] Anyway, it'd be good if we could reduce the number of Jews coming here, of course. Arthur's arranging a Declaration to give them a national home ... Palestine. Or within it. A partition. We're talking to Zionist and non-Zionists.'

'And to Palestinians?'

'Who? Oh, yes. There's not many of them, is there? Small desert and rock country. And as to who the leaders are, God knows. Civil and religious rights for all, of course.'

'And political?[120]'

'Yes, well, we've still got to get the finer details sorted out. Palestine is in a bit of a stalemate in the war ... we need to make a major military advance. Keep this quiet, but Beersheba looks a likely spot. Win there, get the Jewish State up and running, and everything's hunky-dory. All done and dusted.'

Chapter 38 – A German "Plot"

10th May 1918

'Waiter! Brandies! Another round!' Lord French, his involvement in the Curragh mutiny having been almost forgotten, had been made Lord Lieutenant of Ireland. Today, he was in his club entertaining friends from military days.

'The Germans are making a big push. Everybody knows that there's a desperate shortage of troops and we should have brought in conscription months ago, it's overdue as I told the Prime Minister – I said to him, yer know, those damned back-sliding Irish laddies wouldn't be a problem. Bit of rough discipline – that'd sort them out. I'd use armoured cars ... up an' down the streets with aeroplanes to strafe the towns and villages. After they'd been vacated of women and kiddies, of course ... I was born there, yer know. Yes, I'm Irish! Ah, the brandies. Careful with the tray! Good man, this waiter yer know! Cockney, born and bred! With me in the Sudan, weren't yer, Corporal er .... Wos-yer-name?'

'Perkins, sir. Yes, indeed, sir. Fightin' Fuzzie-Wuzzies in that 'eat. I ain't never felt so 'ot. And when I woz ...'

'Yes, yes. Leave the bottle. Anyway ... where was I? Oh, yes. That damned Lloyd George's backed off! Yes. He's decided that conscription won't be happening in Ireland. Well, they won't be getting their damn Home Rule then. The Sinn Féin can have as many meetings in Dublin's Mansion House as they like. But, I tell you, whilst I'm in charge ... the Fenian vermin will know all about it ... now, listen! This is strictly on a need-to-know basis. So, please keep it to yourselves. I'm telling you because ... well, you need to be kept abreast of things.' The others were drunkenly desperate to hear more and leant in closer.

'You remember that Fenian nancy boy that was hanged?'

Casement! ... Anyway, one of his damned Irish Brigade wallahs ... yer know, the POW traitors goin' to fight for Germany ... one of them ... was dropped off by a German submarine and got arrested in Ireland. Been interrogated a'course. He's admitted that the plan was for him to help prepare for a German invasion of Ireland.'

There were murmurs of 'Gosh!' 'I say!' and one 'Sounds a bit rum ... what sort of plan, sir?'

'Plan? Well ... I haven't seen it ... but ...' French held up a hand, 'Actually, it's a piece of luck. It'll give those Yanks something to think about. We'll tell them the Bolsheviks are involved, too. The Government's going to release details and use it as a reason next Friday for arresting about a hundred of the top Sinn Féin scum.'

There were woops and cheers as they finished the bottle. Meanwhile the ex-Corporal that had fought in Sudan continued drying glasses at the bar. As soon as the club closed, he was composing a coded message, *Sinn Féin leaders to be arrested May 17*, which was sent to Detective Joe Kavanagh in Dublin Castle – Joe told Detective Sergeant Ned Broy who had already heard a vague rumour along the same lines; he hurried to Webb's book shop on the Quays to tell Tommy Gay. Tommy, as casually as he could, went to a tailor's shop in Middle Abbey Street owned by Harry Boland and Harry passed the information on to Collins.

16th May 1918

A week later Collins looked at the meeting of senior Sinn Féiners and grinned at all of them. Eamon De Valera, their newly-elected President, humourless as ever, was at the end of the table. Collins sat next to Harry Boland who, unsurprisingly, was wearing a very smart suit. When Collins came in and sat down, Boland sniggered and gave him a nudge; Collins gave him one, much harder, in return.

Further down the table was Cathal Brugha, small but wiry and strong. As usual, he was looking serious, stern even, and determined. He wasn't a member of the Irish Republican Brotherhood, disliking its oath requirement and none too fond of either Boland nor Collins. Brugha! It was Brugha, passionate non-drinking and non-smoking, who would later formally declare Ireland to be a republic when he was acting President. He seriously planned to lead a squad into London that would assassinate the British Cabinet in Parliament. Paradoxically, he opposed the murder of civilians or non-military staff; when Collins was preparing a list of names for Bloody Sunday's killing of Intelligence officers, Brugha crossed several names off.

The deposed President, Arthur Griffith, was compulsively touching the knot of his tie and looked like he would prefer to be somewhere else – but now that he was here he'd have his say.

Collins waited for 'Any Other Business', rubbed his hand across his mouth and said, 'Those Brits, they're idiots. They should have shot yer, Dev'. He laughed and picked up a glass of sherry.

Griffith grinned and thought, *'Of course it could be that Maxwell had been told that you weren't very important, Dev.'*

De Valera rubbed his nose, drank his tea, and then proclaimed, 'Asquith got scared. Too many executions. He wanted the US to join the war and I was born in America, so he knew the Irish-Yanks would kick up a fuss.'

Collins could see the flaw in this, 'That didn't save Tom Clarke though. He was an American citizen even if he was born here in Ireland, but US citizenship didn't help him. I suppose your name wasn't on the proclamation and maybe there were too many questions being asked in Parliament about poor Frank Sheehy-Skeffington's death. Constance Markiewicz was lucky too.

Almost certainly killed a policeman but they didn't want to execute a woman. Anyway, they released me after 8 months! You, though, sentenced to imprisonment for life, had to wait a bit longer. You didn't even serve two years! The British! Idiots.'

De Valera decided the meeting was getting a little too lively, 'Well, Michael, it's not because Lloyd George was feeling kind, not after stabbing Asquith in the back. Redmond was haemorrhaging support here in Ireland having agreed to Partition – if he was going to win any seats in the coming British election he had to show the Irish public how clever and strong he is. And Lloyd George wants him and his crowd to support him in Parliament. Hence the agreement to Redmond's demand that the Uprising prisoners be released.'

They all burst out laughing. Collins shook his head as if he couldn't believe it, 'It's amazing, yer know. They arrested Irishmen that had no real interest in Ireland's independence and who none of us knew from Adam and they sent them over to Frongoch prison where we were. We used to have meetings there in the nick and those fellas ended up rock-solid patriots desperate to fight for freedom. The Brits, God bless them, did some amazing recruiting for us.'

The whole room laughed again and cheered.

Collins savoured the moment before saying, 'We really ought to send a letter of T'anks to the British Government. I mean they find us guilty of treason and murder, sentence us to execution, commuted to 10 years, beat and kick the shite out of us, throw us in water-logged cells and feed us with slops. And then release us after a few months and expect us to have changed and to be good little British boys from now on.'

De Valera knew that he had to acknowledge Griffith, 'Arthur here has changed you know. After practically kicking the door down at the GPO to join the fight and being sent away, the Brits still arrested him. He was eight months in Reading nick singing and dancing with Irish poets and authors. Now he's a republican … and Sinn Féin is gaining members like nobody's business.'

'Yeah, that was another not-clever move by the Brits …,' Collins laughed,'… accusing Arthur's Sinn Féin of being responsible for the Uprising! Now, almost every Dubliner is claiming to have been a Sinn Féiner in the GPO!'

Griffith, his eyelids flickering even more than normal, fiddled again with his tie, 'Everybody is joining Sinn Féin now. Lloyd George is desperate to get conscription here so that he can keep the Conservatives happy and send more Irishmen to die in France. The promise of Home Rule isn't fooling anybody this time around. Even the Catholic hierarchy has officially opposed conscription and the Ulster Unionists are insulted by the Home Rule idea.'

De Valera almost, but not quite, laughed, 'Well, Sinn Féin has been winning by-elections. The candidates will all refuse to go to Westminster … I'll admit I was wrong after the Uprising to oppose McGuinness running as a candidate. I didn't realise that the public's opinion had swung so much. I thought they still hated us. Anyway …

Collins raised a hand. 'Hang on, Dev. This boycotting of the British Parliament.…by our elected members. What are we achieving by it?'

Griffith was thinking that he'd really like to have a glass of whiskey. He blinked and looked at De Valera. He would have loved to have said, 'Yeah, c'mon Dev. I know I was in favour of it, but I had me reasons. I reckon they aren't the same as yours. Why don't cha' want to go to their Parliament? Is it because you're scared of London and being outmanoeuvred by Lloyd George? Or you know that you're a terrible public speaker …. or both?'

De Valera blushed and wriggled in his chair, 'The boycott was a decision agreed upon by ... senior members of Sinn Féin. It's a demonstration of our contempt for the British Parliament. We don't want to be seen working with an administration that's spent 700 years crushing the Irish.'

Collins decided to persist. 'Yer didn't think we'd be better off goin' to London and makin' a nuisance of oursel's? We could have started ... debates ... been on committees ... and spoken about the British atrocities, especially in Ulster. The newspapers would have reported what was said. The propaganda value to us and embarrassment for them would be enormous. Even if we did it for just a few months ... supporting the British Labour Party in debates ... it would have caused a hell of a problem for Lloyd George and his Tory mates. As it is, they're very happy with us not goin' to London. Why should we do anything that makes them happy?'

De Valera sniffed, 'There's no point in discussing it. It's been agreed. We would have had to swear allegiance to the King ...'[121]

Collins tried to interrupt, 'So what? Is that so terrible if it means getting their troops out of Ireland? Oath of allegiance! It's only words! I'd sell me soul for Ireland! Anyway, we could challenge the wording and ...'.

De Valera ignored him, '... how could we declare Independence from Britain whilst sitting in their Parliament? No, even if we win lots of seats at the next election, we're not going to the British Parliament and that's an end to it. We can't be going to London and having polite debates with our most vile enemies when we're conducting an all-out war with them.'

Collins was not convinced and said, 'All-out war? I thought we were done with trying to beat them at their own game. Hit and run, guerrilla style, is surely better.'

De Valera looked up at the ceiling, 'Yes, yes. That's one option but we need further discussion as to the specifics. We need to consider our reputation as a responsible government. We're not terrorists. Now ... I think it's time to close the meeting. I'm going home for a nice cup of tea.'

Everybody except one, Collins, pushed their chair back. He who always enjoyed melodrama, called out, 'Just a moment. You may want to know about something one of me sources has provided. You're all going to be arrested tonight or tomorrow... unless you make yourselves scarce ... I'll be sleeping in a safe location ... I suggest you do the same.'

De Valera groaned, 'What are you saying, Michael? Ridiculous!'

Collins could see De Valera didn't want to believe the truth, 'My informers tell me that Lloyd George and his secret service crowd have cooked up a document called 'The German Plot' accusing us of planning a German invasion. A pretext to arrest all of us.'

De Valera laughed, perhaps for the first and only time in his life, 'If the Brits did anything like that ... arresting us, at a time when they're trying to impose conscription here ... it would be propaganda madness ... Look, you do what you want. I'm goin' home.'

Cathal Brugha went out and cycled, with some difficulty due to his leg, away down the Dublin streets; the green Pierce bike swished through the rain but he wasn't going towards his home. Next day, Griffith and De Valera and most of the other leaders were in jail. Brugha was in a secret safe house.

Harry Boland had vanished with Collins. The pair of them were so alike they could have been brothers. When they arrived at a gathering the women would stop talking and gape. Charismatic, decisive, and ruthless, they were both also attracted to the same woman: Kitty Kiernan. But they had their differences. Boland supported De Valera; Collins didn't. Boland was always well-dressed; Collins wasn't bothered one way or the other.

A month later, after midnight, they strolled through the sleeping suburban streets and stopped at 1, Brendan Road, Donnybrook, Dublin. It was as peaceful as any other well-to-do home and obviously empty. Collins led the way to the front door and entered as if he knew it would be unlocked. Boland elbowed him aside and went straight upstairs. 'Janey Mack! It's cold out there … Me granny used ta say when it gets really really cold that means Spring's comin'. Mind you she used ter talk ta the spiders. Thank goodness, the fire's lit,' he strode to the warmth and rubbed his hands over the flames. Collins followed and gave a great shove pushing his friend aside.

'Argh! … yer big bully,' Boland grabbed Collins round the waist and tried to toss him to the floor. They grappled and rolled on the carpet, first one and then the other was on top. Boland was annoyed that his jacket would be crumpled but more than happy to wrestle. Collins grunted and tried to twist the other man's arms. Neither wanted to give in because they were both evenly balanced in weight and size. Intermittently they groaned, threatened and ordered each other.

'Will yer leave …'

'Let go of that …!'

'I'll hurt yer if yer don't …'

'D'yer … give … let GO!'

'Stop that or I'll …'

It went on for at least 10 minutes until Boland said, 'OK, OK! Enough! Yer ruining me jacket.'

They crawled to chairs and sat down. Collins said, 'Ah … that was good fun. Now. We're going to be busy. You, Cathal Brugha, and me. There'll be a General Election soon and we need to get as many Sinn Féin candidates elected as possible, regardless of whether they're in jail, and despite Dev not wanting them to go ter London. Of course, we'll have to get De Valera out of Lincoln nick.'

Boland agreed, 'Soon we'll have our own Government in Dublin ... we'll be needing finance, so. Dev's got contacts in the US. Devoy and McGarrity have the potential for organising collections ... mind you, they can be very jealous of anybody muscling in.'

'Well, Harry, you'll be going there with Dev and using your charm ... while I stay here and set up some sort of Loan Scheme.'

Accordingly, despite the British having jailed most of the senior Sinn Féin, the wheels of Independence began turning and then spinning. Faster and faster.

Shortly after the end of the Great War there was a General Election. Sinn Féin won 73 seats but, as De Valera wanted, they refused to attend the British Parliament (making the Tories there very happy). Instead, they created their own Irish Parliament. Boland became President of the Irish Republican Brotherhood and, with Collins, helped De Valera to escape from jail. In 1919 Harry went with De Valera to the USA soliciting funds and, whilst Dev managed to annoy Devoy and other Irish-Americans, he was popular at the vast meetings.

Ambitious Judge Colohan was born in America; he was both anti-President Wilson and opposed to the League of Nations. He and John Devoy earnestly promoted Ireland's fight for independence, so they welcomed Fenian friends from Ireland. But as the popularity of the Boland-De Valera partnership at the mass rallies increased, so did the enmity of Devoy-Colohan for the two young Irishmen. Whenever De Valera, a man who often spoke without bothering to think, gave a Press interview he somehow managed to say something that displeased Colohan. The media-savvy Judge tried to belittle Boland when introducing him to a large rally by asking him what University he'd attended. Boland replied, 'The University of Cell 941, Dartmoor Prison,' and there was a massive roar of approval – Colohan was furiously speechless.

De Valera wanted to raise a loan of $10 million through selling bonds but Colohan thought the idea was both stupid and probably illegal because the Republic of Ireland was not a legally recognised nation. De Valera argued that it would be recognised if it began issuing bonds; Colohan wanted money for his and Devoy's Victory Fund run by 'The Friends of Irish Freedom' and would provide a portion of that to the 'republic'. De Valera tried to get the U.S. Republican Party to formally recognise the Irish Republic but instead they offered to recognise the Irish people's right to self-determination. De Valera, annoyed that he was not getting what he wanted, refused the offer. His twisted logic was that it would somehow make him, the republic's President, appear to be a puppet. The tour resulted in five million dollars donated but much of that would not flow into the republic for several years due to legal wrangles.

Chapter 39 – Saint Enda's: The Sequel

Dublin 1919

'Ow! This tea's too hot. And this table ... it's wobbly! No, no. Never mind.' The Englishwoman was talking to Kathleen Houlihan but not looking at her. She was peering through the café window trying to catch sight of Grace coming back from the Dáil Bonds Loan raising at Saint Enda's. She called the waitress over and ordered a slice of cake, dripping with cream and covered with raspberry jam.

At St. Enda's School, Collins was feeling tired. He'd given the speech, now he was accepting money from Notabilities and giving receipts. After Mrs Pearse, mother of Patrick, came a confused-looking Count Plunkett followed by his wife, then various mothers and widows of the 1916 executed rebels, Patrick's sister Margaret Pearse, then came Grace. It was being filmed and Collins felt self-conscious.

For each 'Notability', he hands over a bond and a signed receipt. To most of them he gives a quick smile and a couple of words; but for a few favoured ones, there's a special just-between-us chuckle. An old biddy drops her receipt and bends to pick it up – Collins looks away.

Nora Connolly stands to one side, self-consciously holding a one pound note; Collins moves the ink pot closer and, head down, takes her money and then hands her a Dáil bond and receipt whilst saying something to O'Hegarty. She softly says, 'Thank you'. Collins has barely, if at all, noticed her. Perhaps he was still thinking of the good-looking sister of Michael Hanrahan who preceded her.[122]

Nora, daughter of James Connolly, the tiny very young woman who went alone to New York with vital information stolen from the British, gave it to German Ambassador Count von Bernstorff, and returned with gold and secret messages, moves shyly out of camera shot without looking up and stands near Grace, whispering 'Well, that was ... interesting.' Grace looked at Nora and responded, 'I don't think I feel like chatting to this lot. But it's been good catching up with you. I'd better be taking those two rascals back.'

Nora looked at the little ones and whispered, 'Oh, God! They've lost their Ma and Da! But you and yer sister Kate are looking after them?' Grace blew into a handkerchief, 'We are, yeah. At the moment. But ... Well, we've got a problem. Tom's eldest sister is a nun and wants to make sure that they're brought up in a Catholic family ...'

'Yeah? Well, you're Catholic now ...'

'I am ... But I've no husband and Muriel's mother, my mother, is Protestant. So Sister Francesca is looking for a good Catholic foster family to take care of them ...' Nora frowned, 'But ... Fostered? I don't understand ... haven't yer got lots of sisters and brothers ... most of the Giffords have young families?'

Grace looked down, 'They're Protestant and Sister Francesca is the eldest MacDonagh ... she wants to be sure Babilly and Don are raised Catholic. There's four or five brothers on the MacDonagh side, but the elder sister makes the decision ... Anyway, we best be off. God bless yer.' They hugged and Nora kissed the children, 'I hope it works out for you. Goodbye, God bless.'

At the café, Mrs Bull was excited. 'Oooh. Yes! There she is! Looking as though butter wouldn't melt in her mouth.'

Kitty watched Grace wearily walk past with two toddlers, and quietly voiced her own thoughts, 'Sha, Grace has had her share o'trubles, right enough. I hear she's having no luck getting a Widow's pension ...'

Mrs Bull sitting opposite was jerked to attention and her

eyebrows bounced up as she looked at Kitty, 'Widow's pension? Yes! That might have been one reason why she was so desperate to get married to young Plunkett. But ... My dear ... well, I don't spread gossip, never have done, however I have it on good authority from senior people that I know in Dublin Castle ... they tell me that ... that young woman was expecting! ... pregnant! ... when she rushed to get married.'

Kitty's mouth opened. She'd heard the same rumours but said, 'M'am, those children are her sister Muriel's. Grace doesn't have a child.'

'Really? Oh. Yes! Of course ... apparently ...' the Englishwoman dropped her voice, '... apparently, after the Uprising she was being cared for by one of Plunkett's sisters, and one morning ... a ... er ... tiny ... you know ...covered in blood ... was found in a bucket under her bed. Nothing was said, the bucket was emptied, and after a while she began going out and seeing people again.'

Kitty stared and eventually said, 'Baby? She was a devout Catholic! Are you sayin' that she deliberately ...'

This was met by a smile, of sorts. 'No, no. No! It could have been an unfortunate ... maybe convenient, even so ... medical incident ...' Kitty stared, waiting to hear if there was anything more to be said.

'... but, of course, we can't be sure that Plunkett was the father anyway.' The woman's face had the same impression as someone that had proven the square on the hypotenuse is equal to something obvious.

Kitty looked at the café clock, 'Oh my! Is that the time?! Sorry, M'am ... I must rush ... been nice seeing yer again.' She stood up leaning on the table to steady herself, but it shifted, her hand slipped and somehow flipped the plate on which sat a large slice of delicious cream cake, covered in jam and yet more cream. There was a gasp and an 'Argh!' followed by Kitty saying, 'Oh! Oh, dear, oh dear! I'm terribly sorry. Oh! What a mess. Sorry ... Ooooh! I really do need to catch that tram.' The plate slid to the floor but the delectable slice was upside-down in the well-endowed lady's lap and her coat was covered with cream and sticky raspberry jam.

*

Not far away, Collins had sent Paddy O'Daly with instructions to murder Alan Bell, the accountant who was chasing the Dáil Funds; Jameson, or Byrnes whatever his real name was, would be dealt with later. Now, Collins was back doing administration tasks at his desk, checking some figures. Ireland was desperately in need of funds.

It still annoyed him to think of Count Plunkett and that Kelly-fella going to Paris to attend the Peace Conference. To do what? There was no way that the major powers were going to take any notice of Ireland. Oh, sure! Britain, France, and the US wanted to help the small nations. But Ireland? No, not a chance. Our two people didn't get to see anybody. Nothing except dinner with a communist pastry cook. A complete waste of £4,000. No receipts of course. Argh, what Collins could have done with that! The door opened behind him and he slammed the ledger shut.

'It's OK, only me,' Harry Boland wasn't his usual chirpy self. 'Dev and me ... we got back from the US yesterday ... I thought I'd call in 'an see if yer was wantin' a drink, at all?'

Collins sensed something was out of order ... Harry wasn't usually so hesitant. And he knew that Collins was always open to having a drink, so why ask?

'Harry! Come'ere, Bai. Sit yersel' and tell us about the US... what's that yer've got there in yer bag? Lots of dollars fer me? I hear Dev's been busy raisin' funds from the Yanks, eh? Min' you, those speeches by Archbishop Mannix* must have gee'ed up the crowds. C'mon, tell me all a'boat it.'

Boland put a Gladstone bag down at his feet. 'I got things to tell yer, alright. The tours were grand; we got promises of funds. T'ousands and t'ousands of dollars ... could be 5 million if they all pay up. Dev's secretary Seán Nunan is arranging transmission of the money.'

Collins grinned, 'Well, that's all good ... But Dev didn't get on too well with Devoy? What the feck was Dev doing telling the newspapers that Ireland was going to be to England the same as Cuba is to the US? Fer feck's sake! I heard that Devoy told him he was crazy ... and I agree with him. Cuba? Crazy! Anyway ... Yer got some'ting else ter tell me?'

Boland ran his hand through his hair, 'Er ... Yeah ... it's like this ... Dev's been working hard to get recognition of Ireland. Globally, I mean. Of course, yer knew that. Anyway ... well, er, we had meetings with ambassadors an' stuff, but nobody wanted to know. Then didn't we meet the Russian representative-fella in New York, named Ludwig Martens. There's an arrangement being ... um ... negotiated and we might be able to get Russian rifles via the US†. Great, eh? But, anyway, well, he offered to coordinate recognition of Ireland by Lenin's Russian Government. So ... James O'Mara, Trustee of Dáil Éireann he ... er ... and this is with Dev's approval, OK? ... he ... he accepted these ... in the bag.'

Collins frowned, 'What? What's in the bag?' Boland opened it,

---

* Archbishop Mannix from Australia toured the US, whilst De Valera was there, and criticised the British.

† Patrick Moylett, Businessman, Witness Statement 767: A shipment of 50,000 Russian rifles was prevented by US.

saying, 'It's collateral. Jewels. They must be worth t'ousands and t'ousands. Diamonds, sapphires, rubies. Lots and lots ...'

'Collateral? For what, Harry? ... what did yer ....?! ... what did Dev give the Bolsheviks?'

'We giv' em a loan ... A loan to Russia, I mean ... $20,000. These jewels are security for the loan! Sha, we'll get the money back whenever we axe fer it ...'

Collins screamed. 'Yer didn't – Yer didn't! Tell me yer jokin'! Argggh! ... Oh, No! Good God! Have yer had 'em valued? No, of course not. How many diamonds, how many ... rubies ... d'yer even know? Valuable? Yeah, maybe in a jeweller's shop. But if yer sell 'em, yer'd be lucky to get ten per cent of their true value. A loan? $20,000? For us, that's massive. For Russia? That's loose change! He probably needed it to buy some stationery. They're dealing in 100s of millions! As for 50,000 rifles ... if yer ber-lieve that, yer outta yer feckin mind! $20,000 fer jewels. Holy Mary, Mother of God!'

'C'mon, Mick ... we got recognition ... fer the Republic, from Russia[*] ... an' it's really costin' us nothin' ... that's just collateral ... it's fer until we get the money back ... I brought the jewels so's yer can look after 'em fer us...'

Collins stared, 'Jewels! Where did this Russian fella get them ... Oh, God! I know ...they're from the Romanovs! The Tsars. The murdered family. They killed the children!' He picked up a handful and threw them at Boland, 'Stick these up yer feckin' arse. I amn't havin' 'em! They're blood-stained. Them Bolshevik bastards murdered the Tsar and his wife and all their children. In a cellar! Then they stole these ... Take'em away! G'wan! Get out of me feckin' sight!'[123]

---

[*] Russia (USSR) did not officially recognise Ireland until 1973

Chapter 40 – Just Stop

'The forces of evil are going to win.' Until now, Churchill had always refused to admit defeat, but here he was sitting in his favourite armchair, reading ministerial papers and he could see that all hope was gone. The fighting would continue for a few months at best before the Bolsheviks' Red Army smashed through General Wrangel's White Army in Crimea. Churchill, as Secretary of State for War, had supported the Whites and tried to supply them with munitions but the London dock workers refused to load the cargo. Parliament had never formally approved his actions. With hindsight, it was inevitable that Russia's Civil War would end this way. Churchill took an extra-large mouthful of champagne and sighed.

Clemmie and he had only just moved into 2 Sussex Place, near Hyde Park. They couldn't really afford it, but they'd manage somehow. She had, though, reminded him that Freddie Smith was a bad influence, so he'd promised to cut back on the gambling. Yes, and perhaps the drinking … but what the playwright Shaw had said[124] about alcohol is true … cut back? Well, maybe later.

So peaceful here … and yet, not far away, British people were killing each other. He began reading about the riots in Belfast. Inspector Oswald Swanzy, Royal Irish Constabulary, had been shot by the IRA when he left Christ Church Cathedral in County Antrim. It was a reprisal for the murder, six months earlier, of Tomás Mac Curtain, Lord Mayor of Cork, who had been killed in front of his wife and son. After the murder, hooded men ransacked the home – Swanzy was known to have been responsible and the local coroner passed a verdict of wilful murder against Prime Minister Lloyd George.

Churchill guessed that Collins had ordered Swanzy's death. Now there were riots by Protestants in the North; 35 people killed, Catholic homes and businesses were torched and 5,000 were driven out of Belfast. Churchill rubbed his eyes, feeling very tired.

'Winston, could you please spare a few minutes?'

Churchill, feeling slightly uncomfortable and wondering what this could be about, put the glass of champagne down, 'Of course, Clemmie ... is it Marigold*? She's feeling better, isn't she?'

His wife sat with hands clasped, 'I think she's over it. Whatever it was ... her birthday's coming up. Two years! ... No, no. I want to talk about something else. Winston ... I've never tried to influence you in your work before ... I think that would be intolerable ...'

'And I'm very grateful to you for ...' Churchill began but, for one of the few times in his life, he allowed himself to be interrupted.

'... Until now. Yesterday, at the dinner party I couldn't help but hear the Chief Secretary of Ireland, Hamar Greenwood, talking about officially approved reprisals in response to Sinn Féin outrages.'

Churchill would have liked to pick up the champagne glass but instead said, 'My dear, it is simply not possible to fight guerrilla tactics with kid gloves. Reprisals, properly approved, must be considered as an option ...'

'Is that what happened at Balbriggan? Two policemen get into a drunken argument in a pub, and are shot by the IRA, so 100 British troops attack the town, burn down 49 homes, and kill two men that had nothing to do with the argument? Asquith has compared it to the acts of violence carried out by the German army on Belgian civilians.'

'Asquith's changed his tune now he's a backbencher. Actually, they were not British troops who did that in Balbriggan. They were

---

* Marigold Churchill died just short of her 3rd birthday of sepsis (the very young may have a weakened immune system causing injury to tissues and organs).

temporary police constables, also known as Black and Tans. Most are ex-Army, some are Irish. They do behave poorly sometimes, which is why I have recommended using men who have been officers, known as Auxiliaries.'

'Oh yes? I think it was a lorry-load of those Auxiliaries that thought it would be jolly fun firing rifles as they drove through Galway? A young mother, sitting on a lawn in front of her home, baby in her arms, probably didn't think it funny when she was shot and killed.'

Churchill swallowed all of the champagne before saying, 'A Military Court of Inquiry found that incident to be death by misadventure. The Auxiliaries were firing as a precautionary measure as they rounded a bend.'

'I see. So ... these intrepid British men thought that a woman with a baby in her arms, out in the open, could have been participating in an ambush? And so, taking no chances, they shot her?[125] Winston, you've said previously that our troops are getting out of hand.'

'Yes, a few troops have been acting unlawfully ... so, better by far, that there is a formal process within the Army for authorising ... reprisals. And the Prime Minister agrees ... but he wants to wait until after the American presidential election is over before he allows them to occur.'

'Winston, I know you take a great deal of interest in our American Cousins. I assume that you have read the New York Times article concerning a discussion between King George and Lloyd George?'

'Clemmie, that was ...'

'The article reported that the King had said, *'Are you going to shoot all the people in Ireland? ... This thing cannot go on. I cannot have my people killed in this manner.'* I think it was sourced to Mr. Steed, editor of the London Times.'

'My dear, it was also supposedly traced to Lord Northcliffe. And he has denied ever quoting the King in that way.'

'Authorising reprisals? Is that what you said just now? Do I have to remind you that all Irish people are citizens of His Majesty? And have as much right to British protection as people living in Oxford or Kent? Reprisals? Will that stop Sinn Féin from killing? I'm sorry, Winston, I know that if you were the leader of Sinn Féin then you wouldn't be intimidated by cruelty or reprisals, which often impact the innocent as much as the guilty. I feel sad and disappointed when you're tempted to act like an iron-fisted Boche …'

Churchill's mouth was open, but nothing came from it. He took out his handkerchief and pretended to blow his nose.

Chapter 41 – Three Events, November 1920

Event #1   *Just A Lad Of Fifteen Summers ... Fifteen?!*
Yeah, a medical student having missed one of his first-year examinations at University College could be in a spot of bother. 18-year-old Kevin Barry knew that of course, which was why he said he had every intention of sitting the next one at 2pm on Monday, 20th September 1920. But Seumas Kavanagh, the Commandant of the Dublin Brigade, wasn't convinced.

Barry grinned his boyish charm, 'Look, it's not until two and the Monk's bakery ambush is at 11. I can do both. Yer know yerself what happened at that King's Inns job. Wasn't it meself that got the Lewis gun for all of you'se?'

'Well, I dunno ... Let me t'ink ... Oh! Yeah, alright. Your enttwos-ey-as-um is worth its weight in gold, Kevin. We'll be meeting at the Sinn Féin Club in Ryder's Row at 9 on Monday. First, though, we'll get our'sels sorted out as to who's doin' what. C'mon, the others are almost certainly in Vaughan's.'

They walked across Parnell Square and Kavanagh shepherded the twenty or so Volunteers over to the meeting hall at Number 41.

'OK, lads. It's been approved. A half dozen or so British troops in a lorry go to Monk's Bakery in Church St every Monday morning at 11. We want their rifles and we'll be waitin' fer 'em.' There were whoops and cheers.

'Now lissen! There'll be 23 of us and here's the plan.' Each man was told whether he'd be in the bakery, outside the pub, or at one of the street corners. 'I'll be in the pub doorway and I'll make the Go signal with a handkerchief, blowing me nose. Then we rush the lorry and shout Hands Up! Rifles Down! When they surrender, we grab their rifles and load 'em into our van. If they start any shootin' ... Er, the nearest ones of yer will fire back but the barracks is too close by, so we'll back off and retreat. OK? See you'se all here tomorra at 0900.'

If anybody noticed a lack of clarity, such as the importance of not opening fire unless attacked or ordered to do so, or who was the person responsible for cancelling the attack, and how that would be done ... they didn't mention it.

By the time Barry arrived the revolvers were already being issued and he missed out on his favourite Webley. 'Never mind, Kev. Here yer go ... a Parabellum! You'll get used to it.'

Church Street was crowded with shoppers, children, and businesspeople. The Volunteers merged in with them and waited. And waited. At last, they heard the unmistakeable broom-broom-BROOM of an army lorry, gears being fiercely changed and the squeal of brakes.

Kavanagh was looking out of the pub window, with Frank Flood by his side. 'How many, Seumas?'

'I dunno, Frank. More than usual, I'm thinkin'. A lot more.' The Volunteers outside were wondering why it was taking so long ... then the handkerchief appeared and they ran the short distance towards the lorry.

'Hands up!' someone shouted. Confused, a few of the soldiers squashed in the lorry stood and wobbled into each other. Most put their hands up; somebody fired a gun at point-blank range; more shooting; three soldiers crammed together, all fell, one screaming; several soldiers were shooting at nobody in particular. The Irish Volunteers peeled away, one slightly wounded, running for safety and seclusion – except for Kevin Barry who dived under the lorry.[126]

He was tried for murder, not in a civil court but by general courts-martial and found guilty. He refused to recognise the court and made no statements in his defence. Sentenced to death, he was to be hanged on November 1st, All Saints Day, a holy day of obligation in the Catholic Church calendar.

General Macready signed the death warrant. There was huge pressure from high-profile personalities for the sentence to be changed. IRA propagandists stressed Barry's youth and publicised the allegation that he'd been tortured. The Mountjoy Jail medical officer insisted that, apart from a slight muscle strain, he was in good health but Barry, with some encouragement from the IRA, made a sworn statement that he had been tortured. He would certainly have been questioned under severe pressure, with a promise of incarceration instead of hanging if he gave names of his comrades; the men, he would have been reminded, who had run and left him behind. But he refused to answer questions.

General Macready was determined that the hanging would occur. Army discipline and the illegal reprisals by troops were appalling; if the British authorities could demonstrate judicial processes were effective then army morale would improve and reprisals would cease. He hoped.

To strengthen the case for hanging, the British Army let it be known that the ages of the soldiers killed were very similar to that of Kevin Barry's. In fact, unfortunately for Macready, the age of Private Harold Washington[*] could not be revealed without causing official embarrassment. He shouldn't have been allowed to enlist because he was hardly more than a child and only 15 years old when a rebel's bullet tore into him.

IRA plans to enable Barry to escape from jail were cancelled because his mother was hopeful that the sentence wouldn't be carried out and she was fearful, with some justification, that the escape plan would fail. If it was successful, he would always be on the run and, if captured, there'd be no chance of a reprieve for which she prayed right up to the last minute.

Barry was hanged on November 1st. Full use was made by the IRA of propaganda; strong allegations of torture, his refusal to

---

[*]Duke of Wellington's West Riding Regiment

name other offenders, the fact that he died with great dignity and the question as to why, since there had been a military court martial, he was hanged rather than shot. Newspaper articles referred to Kevin Barry as a schoolboy and included a photograph of him in his rugby jumper. A song was written for him, sung in pubs, and said to be popular with British troops in later years. There are no photographs of young Harold Washington, it's not recorded what school he went to, nor whether he played any sport. Nobody has written a song about him.

Event #2   *A Game in The Park*

'G'wan! It's cold out there in Parnell Square! The team leaders have got their instructions – let's us three have one more fer the road. Yer don't want to get back home too early. Yer might catch the missus up'ter mischief wid the fella from next door!' Collins was in the smoking room of Vaughan's Hotel with Dick McKee and Peadar Clancy, Commandant and Vice-Commandant of the Dublin Brigade.

'It'll be an early start for the lads tomorrow, Mick. Tis a long list of British secret agents we're goin' fer. Yer people did well finding out their addresses. Some of them are real bastards. None worse than the fella with one leg. When he interrogates, he does it slowly and causes as much pain as possible...' McKee finished his drink and looked across the bar. Apart the three of them there was just a young well-dressed man sitting on his own. Clancy whispered, 'D'you know him?' Collins chuckled, 'He's alright. I checked him earlier. A salesman. Would yer believe he's Archbishop Clune's nephew!'

The pub door opened with a crash and Joe O'Reilly rushed in, 'Quick! It's a raid. Auxies coming!' Collins jumped up, 'The pair of yer! Out now 'an down the alley. Joe! With me, upstairs an' out the skylight!' Seconds later, the pub was filled with Auxiliaries looking at Archbishop Clune's nephew ... the only customer in the bar. He hadn't registered in the hotel, so he was grabbed and taken to Dublin Castle. Collins and O'Reilly escaped to a safe house; McKee and Clancy headed for Lower Gloucester Street in the red-light area of Monto ... but were followed by an informer, John 'Shankers' Ryan. A few hours later they were arrested and taken to the Castle.

Next evening McKee was sitting handcuffed, bruised and battered in a windowless dungeon; the door opened and in strode an under-sized British officer. Captain Hardy, DSO, MC and bar, was a 26-year-old war hero. He'd fought in France, wounded twice, been captured and escaped. He had a toothbrush moustache and one leg. The other was rotting somewhere in France. He always walked quickly, trying but failing to disguise the fact that there was anything wrong.

'McKee? You know who I am, don't you? Captain Hardy. I've been interrogated by Germans. Their ... techniques were not nice. Mine are worse. I'll be talking to Clancy and the other chap later. I was going to offer you the chance to give me the address where Collins is skulking. In exchange for a quick death.' Hardy's coal-black pupils were almost popping from his sinister blue eyes as he waited for a response.

'Get fecked.'

'Yes, well, I thought that'd be the response. But now that option's not available anyway. Not after what your scum did this morning. You're all going to die of course but first you'll suffer. Horribly. You call yourselves soldiers? I've fought alongside real Irish soldiers. Connaught Rangers that had genuine courage in the face of machine guns and German bayonets. You? You're pathetic. Your cowardly civilian murderers, as you planned, sneaked into the bedrooms of my friends and shot them whilst they slept. Fourteen. Murdered. Captain Newberry's pregnant wife saw him being shot. A few of the murders of course were mistakes ... you got the wrong ones. Others, like me, were missed. You wanted more, but your people were too bloody useless.' The interrogation was over. He punched McKee's already bleeding face. Again and again. Clancy and Clune, both handcuffed, were brought in by Captain William 'Tiny' King. Over six foot tall, he had various implements including pliers and a hammer. The Chief of Intelligence, Ormonde Winter, followed him and all three of them removed their jackets, replacing them with leather aprons.

It took more than half an hour to hose down and clean out the room. The three prisoners, barely alive, were dragged into a yard and shot, it was officially stated, whilst trying to escape.

Earlier that day Jerome O'Leary, 39-year-old accountant, had kissed his wife, Ellen, when he left their home 69, Blessington St., Inns Quay. She called to him, 'Did yer ask Mary if she wanted to go with yer?'

'Of course. But she's a girl and almost 15. Not inter-rested in watchin' football ... is she, Jerry?' He looked down at his 10-year-old son, Jerome.

'Well, make sure Jerry stays warm ... and bring him back if he gets tired ... it's a twenty-minute walk to Croke Park.' She tried not to molly-coddle the lad but she'd never got over losing her first son, John, at three months of age.

Father and son joined the crowd heading for the Gaelic football game. Dublin versus Tipperary. The boy felt excited and grown-up despite holding his dad's hand. The atmosphere was buzzing electric as they passed through the turnstiles, Mr O'Leary paying his shilling then walking shoulder to shoulder with some of the other 10,000 supporters, all noisy and many of them beery. The boy looked up at his dad who strode knowledgeably to a position behind the Canal End goal, 'We'll get the best view from here, Jerry.' He helped his son to sit on a low wall, 'You can stand up when the game starts ... I'll hold yer. Look! They'll be comin' out-a there soon enough.'

There was a soft-loud growl when the teams ran out at 3 o'clock, the start having been delayed by the size of the crowd. The whistle blew and in amongst the oooh-ing and ahhh-ing of those around them, O'Leary began trying his best to explain the basic rules to Jerry.

'Daddy, when that fella got the ball and ...'

'Hang on, Jerry ... watch this ... that's Michael Hogan. Captain of Tipperary.' The ball had been kicked high high high into the air and a player was running, sprinting, to its imminent arrival; he caught it, shrugged a tackle, and swerved away from another. Then he, Hogan, bounced the ball and grabbed it again, all the time running, and then kicking towards the goal. The Dublin crowd couldn't resist roaring in appreciation.

A mixed force of British soldiers, police and Auxiliaries suddenly arrived in trucks and moved quickly to all the exits. After ten minutes of play the game stopped. There was a strange hushly silence. Then rifle shots crackled out, more and more of them, a disorganised rattling and spluttering. The tail board of a truck was lowered revealing a seated soldier behind a Lewis machine gun, pointing at the crowd and soon tut-tut-tutting. A slight pause. Then more tut-tut-tut. Again and again, monotonous and unemotional. Tut-tut-tut. Croke Park became reminiscent of a WW1 poem where rifles patter out bullets like prayers.

Young Jerome fell backward off the wall, out of his father's grasp; one of the first to be hit, a bullet boring its relentless way through the boy's barely grown head.

The crowd rushed for the blocked exits, stampeding and

crushing. Police linked arms to stop them. The shooting lasted over two minutes. Apart from Jerome, thirteen others were killed including Michael Hogan. 14 lay dead and almost 100 were wounded. Not quite as many as at Amritsar in India where, a year earlier, a British officer had ordered troops to fire into a peaceful crowd, killing more than 300 trapped in a walled enclosure[127].

Event #3   *We Surrender ... No, not really*

Exactly one week later, just before sunset, two Army lorries were travelling through the countryside near Kilmichael, Cork. The first one had nine Auxiliaries. It slowed and stopped when the driver saw, in the fading light, what he probably thought was a British soldier standing in the road. In fact, it was an IRA man, wearing an Irish Volunteer's uniform, who threw a Mills bomb into the lorry's cab; the explosion killed the driver and a passenger. A whistle sounded and twenty IRA men began shooting. After violent hand-to-hand fighting, all nine troops were dead or dying. Hearing the explosion, nine Auxiliaries in the second lorry had quickly dismounted and began returning fire at another dozen rebels; these were soon joined by those who had attacked the first lorry.

The IRA version of the event describes the British troops as surrendering, laying down their rifles, and then several of them using revolvers as IRA men approached, killing one. The IRA leader then ordered, 'Rapid fire and do not stop until I tell you!'; any further attempts to surrender were ignored. The British version is that the troops put their hands up but were butchered to death and The Times reported it as being a brutal massacre. In Cork a week later there was a huge funeral procession by the British military. The following week, the centre of Cork was set on fire by British Auxiliaries. 300 homes, the City Hall, and 40 business premises were destroyed. The smell of smoke and wet ashes was everywhere suspended in the desolation. But in London people were beginning to think about Christmas ...

*

Frances Stevenson turned to Lloyd George, shaking his shoulder, 'Goodness, look at the time! C'mon. We'd better get up and get dressed.' He groaned, 'Umm. Yes.'

'David ... David? It's Christmas next month I hope you've got your wife's present arranged.'

'Yes ... Yes, all done.'

'Good ... I suppose there's no likelihood of a truce? No, not with your wife! With Sinn Féin, I mean.'

'Actually, my Love ... this month there were three events which have probably increased the chances considerably.'

'Not long ago you were saying that the British Government had got Murder by the throat?'

'Yes, well ... those events this November have proved me wrong. They've turned the whole situation upside down. A truce won't be immediate, but Sinn Féin is proving to be the Voice of the Irish which can't be ignored. It's obvious that sometime next year we'll have to call a truce and begin negotiating. We're allowing De Valera to move around freely – he's basically got immunity – unless some idiot decides to arrest him. In which case, I'll have to arrange a discreet release. Arthur Griffith has already put out a peace feeler. Alfred Cope*'s coordinating things[128].

'Who?'

'Cope. He's a street-wise Cockney civil servant that Warren Fisher[129] found and rapidly promoted[130]. He walks the streets of

---

* Cope was a senior civil servant sent to Dublin Castle by Warren Fisher.

Dublin as if he was in Brixton market and exchanges information with Collins. Cope enjoys not treading but stamping on people's toes. So of course, the Dublin Castle Intelligence wallahs hate him. If anybody can arrange a truce, it will be him. We do though have to get the Northern Ireland Parliament in place first ... otherwise things would ... come apart.'

'You mean Ulster would scream blue murder?'

'Exactly ... So, the campaign against terror must continue ... the terror by the Irish, I mean ... whilst we hold on to the possibility of peace talks. We've introduced martial law; reprisals can be legally authorised. British troops are sometimes required to carry out tasks which appear to be distasteful ... but if we are to maintain the greatest Empire that ever existed, then that is what must be done. With courage, determination, and belief in British justice.' Lloyd George pulled his shoulders back and for a moment he imagined himself at Question Time being cheered by the whole House, Liberals and Tories alike.

British justice means different things to different people. Whether it is dispensed or received can depend upon a place of birth, an accent, or ancestry. Major Arthur Percival was the Intelligence Officer for the Essex Regiment located in Cork. In April 1921 his troops ordered Irish neighbours to burn down a farmhouse at Woodfield. The owner was absent at a local council meeting and his wife had recently died from TB. On the day of destruction eight children, the eldest being 12 years old, in the care of a maid, watched as their home and belongings went up in flames. The owner was named Johnny, Collins' brother, and Woodfield was where they'd both grown up.

Chapter 42 – You Go and Talk to Them

'Michael, what the British did to your home and your brother's place in Cork was appalling. At least we've had success at the Custom House ...', De Valera looked across at the other senior members of Sinn Féin. He was taller than most of them but unnaturally so, as if he'd grown five inches more than God had actually intended. He sat there, like an ancient and supercilious bird of prey, and surveyed the room looking for signs of disagreement. In some ways he would always be a schoolteacher[*] – expecting people to do as they were told and then being surprised when they didn't or, worse still, argued.

Collins glared, 'Johnny and I are not being treated any differently from others who have been victimised. We'll get over it ... the Custom House, though! I hope you're not calling that a victory?'

De Valera cleared his throat, 'C'mon, Michael. After 3 months of detailed planning by Oscar Traynor, we've burnt that place down. The HQ of the Local Government Board, the administrative heart of the Civil Service machine, tax files! We all agreed that there had to be a major full-scale event to show the world that the Irish people have a national government and an army capable of taking it to the British ...'

'I didn't agree! An army capable of taking it to the strongest nation in the world! Yer crazy! Hadn't we been doing well with quick, short, sharp attacks using grenades and handguns, hit-and-run guerrilla tactics like in the Boer War, not just in country areas

---

[*] De Valera was a Teacher of Mathematics

but in the towns and cities as well.'

'Michael, the propaganda value of the destruction of the Custom House has been enormous.'

'Really? Documents going back 400 years burned? The New York Times called it 'Priceless Records Lost' ... That's apart from us losing close to a hundred men. Five killed. Jim Slattery's hand had to be amputated. At this very moment, the ones that were captured are getting the living shite kicked out of them in Kilmainham jail.'

Oscar Traynor, Brigadier of the Dublin Brigade and one of the planners of the attack, couldn't stay silent. 'Hang on, Collins! We altered the plan because you wanted to reduce numbers ... The British troops swamped us. We were lucky to do the two million pounds worth of damage that we did.'

Collins shouted, 'Sha, it's a pity we didn't keep more of our fellas back. Those that were sent didn't have enough ammunition and some didn't even have guns. 100 of 'em killed or captured! We've been decimated! We'll have to carry on with hit-and-run.'

'Fer Christ sake, shut up!' Traynor shouted, 'The British are going to be screaming fer a truce now.'

Collins stared at him, 'If they call fer a truce, it'll only be due to the USA, the Press and British public figures being sickened by the reprisals. Lloyd George couldn't give a feck a'boat the Custom House.'

De Valera looked around proudly, 'Well, I've news. A letter from the English Protestant religious leaders to *The Times* deploring the British reprisals, had an effect. The King[131] has also expressed his disapproval, apparently, and his speech to the new Northern Ireland Parliament wasn't critical of us at all. So ... Lloyd George wants to meet me and talk about a settlement ... We do have a truce.' The applause that De Valera apparently expected didn't eventuate.

Collins certainly was not surprised. He knew that more than four weeks ago British civil servant Alfred Cope, a passionate pursuer for peace, had met Sinn Féin intermediaries. The King's speech had undoubtedly been conciliatory, no thanks to Ulster's James Craig whose advice and suggestions were ignored. In fact, Lloyd George's Private Secretary Edward Grigg was responsible; he wrote it in association with General Smuts, the South African leader, and crafted a speech which met the King's wishes and the needs of the time perfectly.

Collins also knew that Lloyd George had invited both Craig and De Valera to London, but De Valera didn't want to give the Ulsterman any recognition as being an Irish leader, so he declined. Smuts told Dev a truce could be arranged, as well as a meeting which Craig would not attend if that was his wish. The result was De Valera telegraphing London and agreeing to go to London. But he didn't simply respond with, 'Yes, where and when?' No, no! Not, him. It was, he replied, to be a meeting *To discuss on what basis such a conference as that proposed can reasonably hope to achieve the object desired*. De Valera would never choose to speak succinctly if he had the option to muddle and obfuscate.

'Yes! A truce.' He was slightly disappointed that there was no applause. But Arthur Griffith, trying not to cry, took out a handkerchief and cleaned his pince nez.

'A truce?' Collins had to admit it, 'Well ... That's good news at last, anyway. The Irish people are sick and tired of all the killin' ... they'll be celebrating this ...'

Griffith straightened his tie knot, even though it was quite happy as it was, 'Yer right there, Mick ... most of Ireland will be over the moon. Problem for us, is that d'ere's a noisy, powerful, minority that's desperate to keep fightin' ... Ernie O'Malley,

Oscar Traynor over here, and Rory O'Connor fer example. They think the British are almost beaten! Nonsense! Thinking they'll either get everyt'ing they want or else destroy all Ireland to spite the King.'

Traynor was about to explode but Cathal Brugha, always the one to raise an awkward point, 'We're not giving an inch on the republic! ... *We want a Republic here in Ireland!*' he sang the words. The others stayed silent. De Valera tried to calm things and continued, 'There's no hurry ... I'll string Lloyd George along for a while. The coal miners are on strike and lots of people in England think a revolution is a possibility. Lloyd George's getting desperate. He can wait until I'm good and ready; then I'll tell him that the unity of Ireland is paramount. We want Dominion status like Canada ... the whole of Ireland, united. Otherwise, we demand complete independence here in the South ... external association or a republic ... Certainly, no oath of allegiance.'

Griffith was aware that De Valera was almost as bad as O'Malley and that he hadn't listened to a word that he himself had said before Brugha's interruption, so he shouted, 'Dev! ... Exactly what's meant by Dominion status is going to be an issue ... Lloyd George is never going to get the Protestants to agree to Dublin's governance over Ulster ... and Craig has the British Tories in his pocket. Without them, Lloyd George's Coalition will fall.'

'That's Lloyd George's problem. And I don't care about Craig or what he wants.' As a negotiator, De Valera was a good Mathematics teacher.

A few weeks later, his meeting in London went as well as could be expected of any at which he was in attendance. Edward Grigg, on behalf of Lloyd George, prepared a proposal where Ireland, without Ulster, would have Dominion status. De Valera said he wanted a unified Ireland but added that if Ulster was not included then it had to be total independence for the South. Lloyd George refused to compel Ulster to be under a Dublin government and he leaked a letter to the Press concerning the offer of Dominion status. De Valera was furious, as he always was whenever somebody was wanting to steal his role as headline maker.

He reported the meeting's results to the Sinn Féin leaders – in his own words, that is, and ended by saying, 'The truce continues.'

'But at least, you agreed on the need for another meeting?' Collins asked and reminded everyone, 'Craig's after grabbing Fermanagh and Tyrone for his Ulster, isn't he? ... counties where there's more Catholics than Protestants. Did you, er, touch on that with Lloyd George, Dev?'

De Valera gaped at Collins. 'Fermanagh, Tyrone? ... No! No, of course not. Why would I be after going into those low-level details? Sha, I was focused on reminding him of the appalling treatment England's given us these past 700 years and why we want all Ireland to be free. Those technical issues can be covered later. Now ... the next meeting of delegates in London ... '

Austin Slack blurted, 'Count me out. I'm not going ... the thought of discussing an oath of allegiance with Churchill!' Cathal Brugha looked at Collins first then at the others and said, 'Me? I'm not going either!'

Collins grimaced, 'Argh! Some of us have to take up the task. OK. I'll go with yer, Dev.'

De Valera shook his head, 'No! No, I'm not going. You'll be chairman of the delegation, Arthur. You'll be the head of a party of plenipotentiaries. Alright?'

'But ... Why aren't you going to lead the delegation?' Griffith asked the obvious question.

'Look. There's plenty of reasons ... we need 'a symbol of the Republic' ... something ... or someone that represents all of us.

That person must be 'untouched' by the negotiations and stay here.'

Griffith couldn't help but silently wonder, '*Symbol of the republic? Untouched? Noli Me Tangere*[*]*? Who does he think he is? Jesus Christ or the French republic's Marianne?*'

De Valera rubbed a cloth on his spectacles, 'You'll go to London, see what they're proposing, raise issues and make sure they're not pulling a fast one ... if they do, then we can pick it up when you report back to me. That way, we'll have a final court of appeal ... me. If I was there and the talks broke down ... well, that would be an end to it. Finished. All over.'

Collins frowned, 'We'll be plenipotentiaries? So, we make decisions as to ... '

'Yes, yes!. But major issues will be referred back to me here.'

'If we're to be plenipotentiaries ...', Collins began but was cut off by Griffiths, 'And ... The British are going to present us with a set of proposals for a treaty... ?'

'Yes. I hope so!' De Valera laughed as if that were too obvious to even be doubted.

Now Griffiths was confused, 'Shouldn't we prepare proposals for what we want?'

De Valera was getting annoyed, 'No! No, no. Let them show themselves. We'll keep our cards to ... er, to ... our chest.'

'But,' Griffith was determined to get some clarity, 'Are there some items for us that are a 'must have'? So that we're all clear, shouldn't we document them ... for our own knowledge? And shouldn't we be discussing amongst ourselves those areas which we might be willing to negotiate ... I don't know ... the words of

---

[*] Noli Me Tangere = 'touch me not' Jesus said to Mary Magdalene when she recognized him after His resurrection.

an oath of allegiance … an All-Ireland Parliament, Ulster making some decisions that relate to itself … and … under what conditions the Royal Navy can access our ports …'

De Valera interrupted, 'Look! Let's see what they come up with and then we'll decide what we're willing to accept. That way we'll get a sense of what we can force them to agree to.'

Chapter 43 – Get Together In London

The Anglo-Irish Treaty draft details which the British and Irish delegations began discussing in October 1921 were almost the same as those that they had in front of them two months later. In between, there were meetings and yet more meetings. A British strategy was to persuade the Irish to accept the concept of more efficient talks – what might be called 'divide and conquer'. Sometimes they were made up of all the delegates, sometimes it was only Collins and Lloyd George and Griffith; sometimes only Lloyd George and one of them.

Another strategy was that Craig, soon to be the first Prime Minister of Northern Ireland, was not directly involved in the Treaty-making. Given that he was the main obstacle to peace in Ireland, this absence might be considered a case of wilful cowardice by all the delegates. However, Lloyd George made sure the Ulsterman was not only kept informed but also able to provide comments to the Prime Minister's team, privately of course.

Unfortunately, Craig had the habit of telling Lloyd George that he was happy with something … and then changing his mind – usually after he'd spoken to hard-line Ulstermen. For example, he once proposed that Northern Ireland should also have 'Dominion status'. Later, he was on the verge of agreeing to an All-Ireland Parliament but then decided against; the reason being that Churchill and Henry Wilson promised to allow the dregs of the Ulster Volunteer Force (Orangemen and Protestants) to 'maintain order' in a separate Ulster.

Lloyd George had negotiated the UK's share of Germany's colonies at the 1919 Paris Peace Conference. Churchill, Austen Chamberlain, and Lord Birkenhead, formerly F.E. Smith, had contested and negotiated the 1916 Irish Home Rule Act. They all had bargaining skills, experience, and artfulness from decades of arguing and debating. The Irish delegation was made up of an unqualified accountant (Michael Collins), a farmer (Robert Barton), a journalist (Arthur Griffith, in poor health) who left school aged thirteen, and lawyers (Duffy and Duggan); men that had, at best, a few months parliamentary experience in the Dáil where there was no formal Opposition to challenge or debate them.

In addition to the five delegates, the Irish had a huge support team of four secretaries, 28 advisers, secretarial assistants and staff, 13 security bodyguards, seven dispatchers, two chaperones, and 12 key members of the household staff. Nobody knows now how much drinking and partying went on. Many of the Irish personnel, including Collins, would have had friends and relatives in London. It's impossible to believe that no alcohol was consumed; Harry Boland in a letter, July 1922, to Joseph McGarrity in the US, referred to *a drunken treaty drunkenly arrived at*.[132]

One advantage that the Irish could have had over the English was that they all slept under the same roof, meeting to eat breakfast, lunch and dinner together. It would have been an advantage but one of them chose to opt out. Collins. He insisted on being in another building[133]. Why? Nobody has ever said, but it obviously allowed him to stay out all night, visit old friends ... and meet privately with British negotiating operatives such as Alfred Cope.

10 Downing Street would have been heavy with the smell of cigars, affluence, and power. At the first meeting the Irish delegation tried their best not to show it, but they must have felt a range of emotions as they stood waiting in the reception room. They were kept there only long enough to make them aware that

they were being kept waiting, before being taken to meet and shake hands with the Prime Minister in the Cabinet room. There, waiting for them, were some of the British representatives including Lord Chancellor Birkenhead, Austen Chamberlain, and Winston Churchill.

Chamberlain, Trinity College graduate and an MP for 28 years, was the Leader of the House of Commons. Opposite him was Collins, a farmer's son from Cork who left school aged 15 and had worked in the lowest level of the Civil Service. Arthur Griffith had been a printer and was educated by the Irish Christian Brothers. What thoughts went through Arthur Griffith's mind as he looked across the huge shiny table at the famous lion-headed Lloyd George? He wouldn't have known that one of the Prime Minister's own friends had said, 'You can't rely on what Lloyd George says ... he may not actually tell a lie, but he'll lead you to believe something which will cause you to do what he wants.'

Prior to the first meeting Lloyd George would have made it clear to the British team that the sole objective was to reach a settlement, but an essential requirement was that the demands of Craig's Ulster would be protected ... the Irish delegation might suspect this but could not know for certain that it was a sine qua non. There were other important issues for Lloyd George such as keeping Ireland within the Empire and British access to ports. But whatever Ulster, specifically Protestant Ulster, wanted was the priority.

Thomas (Tom) Jones left school in 1884 when he was aged 14; he became a Professor of Economics in 1909, joined the Civil Service and was now Deputy Secretary to the Cabinet. It helped that he could speak Welsh – he and Lloyd George exchanged ideas during the Treaty Talks without anybody else being aware of them.

It was Jones who suggested smaller meetings of 2 or 3

delegates. It was Jones who reminded Collins and Griffith that Lloyd George might be forced to resign, possibly resulting in the Catholic-hater Bonar Law becoming Prime Minister. It was Jones who told Collins and Griffith of Lloyd George's idea, using the pretence that it was Jones own suggestion, that a Boundary Commission could be part of the Treaty. It was Jones who went to see an emotional, possibly drunk, Griffith at midnight in December and heard him plead for Lloyd George to give the delegates something to take back to the Dáil – anything, for example that Ulster might be considering Irish unity, in return for an Independent Ireland agreeing to stay in the Empire. It was also Jones who told the Prime Minister about the late night visit and enabled Lloyd George to make a dramatic manoeuvre on the final day in December.

The talks throughout July to December swung perilously from near breakdown to virtual collapse. Tom Jones, often through stratagems and half-truths, always brought the parties back together.

The final meeting in December did not start well. How much had the various men, English and Irish, drunk the night before?

In the Cabinet room, Lloyd George singled Arthur Griffith out for attention with his melodic Welsh accent rising in volume, 'You … You, Arthur, have already agreed with me on the Ulster question. We discussed a Boundary Commission … Ulster was to decide whether it wanted to be part of an Irish Free State … if it didn't, there would be a Boundary Commission. You agreed, Bach[*]!'

Griffith was surprised and confused. He had indeed met with Lloyd George early in November, discussed the issue and of course drunk a whiskey or two. It had been in the luxurious Park Lane apartment of parliamentary private secretary Sir Phillip

---

[*] Bach = Mate, Pal

Sassoon. However, Lloyd George was distorting what was agreed and taking Griffith's words out of context. It didn't matter though because, as Griffith struggled to recall what was said, Lloyd George shouted, waving a sheaf of notes, 'Surely, you're not going to go back on your word? You agreed! Look! Tom Jones summarised everything that was said. Are you going to let me down?'

Griffith agreed that he had indeed made a promise not to criticise the proposal which Lloyd George intended to make to Craig; but he recalled that he'd also stressed that he wanted to know Ulster's response before committing himself; furthermore he could not, at that time, guarantee its acceptance by the other delegates because they knew nothing of it.

Griffith could have now said, 'Mr Jones has drawn up a memorandum* based upon that meeting. Tentative suggestions. Yours. Not mine. I haven't noted that I agree with this memorandum.'

He could have taken the high ground by requesting Lloyd George not to shout, saying that until now they'd been having dignified and respectful discussions. But he didn't say any of that.

Lloyd George, the Welsh Wizard negotiator, moved quickly to another issue and the meeting proceeded to discuss the Oath of Allegiance, Finance and Defence. But Griffith had been shaken – his sense of honour had been doubted by the Prime Minister of Great Britain. When Ulster was again raised, he said, 'Regardless of what Craig will do, I gave me word ... I will therefore sign the Treaty.' It might have been at that point when Collins or Barton should have said, '*No. Wait a moment. We need to take a break here.*' – but they didn't.

---

* https://www.difp.ie/volume-1/1921/tentative-suggestions-for-a-treaty-presented-by-thomas-jones-to-arthur-griffith/197/#section-documentpage

They could have said, 'We've given way on Ireland becoming a republic ... we've recognised that Ireland has an association with England, yes and to the Crown. We've allowed for the fact that parts of Ulster want to be independent of Dublin ... You've always said that Ulster would not be coerced in any way. Fair enough. But what of Fermanagh and Tyrone with their majority of Catholics? Are they to be coerced into Ulster? We've given way on so much ... what have you given way on? Anything of substance? The Boundary Commission? It's essential that the Treaty ensures Irish nationalists in Fermanagh and Tyrone, yes and in Belfast, have their voices heard and protected. We want plebiscites, the same as you yourself allowed small nations in the Versailles Treaty! We want assurance that Catholics will be protected and get justice under a Northern Ireland government. We want certainty that the Boundary Commission will be independent and effective and ... that the Northern Ireland Government must comply with it.' They could have said all that. They didn't.

Lloyd George could scent victory. He looked at the Irish delegates. 'You were all in Dublin two days ago ...talking to De Valera. You all knew, as he did and as he acknowledged two months ago, I'm sure, that a British Government would never agree to an Irish republic. Never.'

Lloyd George waited to allow the point to resonate. Then, 'Obviously, I don't know what issues De Valera spoke about. Possibly the wording of the Oath and what was acceptable to him. Anyway, he again refused to come here as leader of your delegation; you know better than me his reasons. Arthur is your Chairman. We have always assumed, and none of you tried to disabuse us of this, that when he speaks, he speaks on behalf of you all.' Collins looked at Barton. Barton looked at Collins. Collins had no major objections to the Treaty as it now was, but Barton had reservations.

Lloyd George, using all the authority that his position of Prime

Minister gave him, stood up. Both hands on the table, he leant forwards and glared, 'You're plenipotentiaries. You must decide ... war or peace? Which is it? How much longer are you willing to accept the violence and killing? Brave young men dying in muddy ditches or stinking back lanes. The deaths of innocent men, women and children as a result of mis-directed shootings, speeding lorries, and carelessly laid bombs? ...Your friend, your Chairman, has agreed to sign ... but every delegate here must sign or there is no agreement.'

He moved a folder; underneath it were two envelopes. Picking both up, his voice low and slow, 'One of these contains a letter saying that a Treaty has been agreed and you are recommending that the Dáil accept it. The other contains a letter saying negotiations have collapsed. Which one do you want me to send to Sir James Craig in Belfast? You must come back before morning with a decision. War or peace. You choose.'

The delegation knew they'd be criticised for not telephoning De Valera. But, considering his comments the last time they met in Dublin, they knew he'd never agree to them signing. He would have raised the same issues and insisted on the delegates returning for further discussions covering them all again. There had never been any recognition by De Valera that Lloyd George might have his own ideas as to what was acceptable and what was unacceptable. The Prime Minister could be bluffing when he threatened war ... but if De Valera prevented them from signing, then there could be thousands of deaths and no break from England whatsoever. Collins and Griffith thought that they'd got all that they would ever be able to get – the oath could be re-worded and there would be independence equivalent to that of Canada's. The alternative to signing was a return to war with Britain and they knew that the Irish military resources were no match. Signing would mean British troops leaving; a Boundary Commission would mean that a Northern Ireland government, without Tyrone and Fermanagh, would be financially forced to remove Partition. True, they were not getting a republic – but they were never going to get that.[134]

A few hours later, at 02:15 on December 6th, all those present at the final meeting signed the Treaty; the Irish signatures consisted of Arthur Griffith, Michael Collins, and Robert Barton. George Gavan Duffy. Éamonn Duggan signed the Irish copy a short time later at 22 Hans Place where all but Collins were staying.

Duggan then took the copy to Dublin; British representatives arrived in the afternoon at Hans Place with the British copy of the Treaty – they wanted the signatures of Duffy and Duggan. Duffy signed but Duggan was on the ferry to Dublin; his signature was snipped from an autographed copy of a programme from a reception dinner held for the delegates at London's Royal Albert Hall in October, two months earlier, and this was pasted onto the British copy. It was a wonderful example of initiative and imagination, but whether it was legal is debatable. Furthermore, the Irish delegates decided that they wanted the word 'Treaty' added to the 'Articles of Agreement' title and the British Cabinet agreed to this at 12:30pm. Unfortunately, of course, the copy held by Éamonn Duggan and passed to De Valera did not include the word 'Treaty'.

The response from De Valera and his friends in Dublin was fury*. Rory O'Connor, member of the Dáil, demanded loudly and publicly, 'The delegates? They should be arrested as soon as they step off the ship at Dún Laoghaire.'

The Mansion House debate on whether to accept the Treaty was long and spiteful. De Valera was furious that the delegates had

---

* You tell him to bring back a cow, and he brings you a donkey (Quoted by Clare Sheridan, '*In Many Place*', page 49)

signed it. Constance Markievicz, fists waving, screamed and bansheed, 'You sold out! Ireland can never be half-free! Jackeens!'

There were shouts of anger like those from tormented souls who had been cheated and condemned to eternal damnation, 'What happened to our Republic?' 'Yer filthy Shoneen thicks', 'Swear an oath to the King of England? Never!, 'Up the republic, Damn the empire!'

Cathal Brugha yelled, 'Traitors! ... Michael Collins? Look at him, swaggering around. Fresh from being the big celebrity in London, with all the women gasping after him. What did he do in 1916? Never fired an angry shot!'

Insults and abuse were thrown by just about everybody. Harry Boland joined with De Valera in condemning the Treaty and turned against Collins.

The man from Cork stood, pushed a lock of hair to one side and waited for silence. 'It's true! The Treaty doesn't give us all that we wanted. But it gives us freedom, not the ultimate freedom that all nations desire and develop to, but the freedom to achieve it.' To a journalist, Clare Sheridan, he later said 'Lenin and Trotsky were unwise to have gone so far at the beginning. They should have been content with less and would have attained their goal in time.'[*]

Brugha's violent condemnation of Collins was counter-productive; a few members that were leaning to the anti-Treaty side changed their minds and voted for it. The final vote was in favour of acceptance 64 votes to 57. The losers stormed out. Then they came back and sulked. Most of the nation, impatient for peace, was in favour of the Treaty and there had been a democratic vote in the Dáil, with a clear, albeit not large, majority following a lengthy debate. Clearly, some in the Dáil were simply bad losers and wanted to 'spit the dummy'. The meeting ended in uproar.

---

[*] Sheridan, C. (1923). *In Many Places,* Page 32

Chairs tumbled and everyone was shouting as they left, streaming for the exits.

Brugha opened a door, almost bumped into Collins, and snarled, 'Yer an idiot, Collins! Lloyd George was desperate for a Treaty. Yer could'a squeezed him ... did yer not remind him that 70,000 troops in India, 30,000 in Egypt and 50,000 in Ireland are costing the British taxpayer a fortune? They'd have removed the oath to get a Treaty if it meant getting their troops out and save £200,000 a week!'[135] His voice spluttered in anger, 'If ... if ... if you think I'm swearing allegiance to an English King ...' Despite being almost 12 inches shorter than Collins he managed to wave his fist in his face.

'Yer feckin' idiot, Cahileen[*]! There was never any chance of us gettin' a republic. That was always a non-starter. The British were never goin' to negotiate the point. De Valera always knew that. As for the oath! I'd swear an oath of allegiance to the devil himself if it meant gettin' the feckin British Army out of Ireland ...'

'Don't use that foul language with me, yer great oaf!'

'Ah, feck off ... G'wan, go an ... sit in a pool of blood and sing a patriotic song. Well may yer sing *God Save Ireland* because if feckin' De Valera ever gets to govern the country nothing will save Auld Ireland!'

Four days later Arthur Griffith and the pro-Treaty members created a provisional government. De Valera refused to be part of it and produced his own idea of a Treaty, calling it Document No.2 – instead of Ireland staying within the Empire there was reference to 'external association' but few, apart from De Valera, knew quite what that meant. In fact, only he and Erskine Childers understood Document No.2 or thought it worth reading at all.

In the South of Ireland people either supported the Treaty or hated it. Friends argued with friends, sisters and brothers ceased

---

[*] Collins' nickname for Cathal Brugha

talking to each other, neighbours crossed the street even quicker than usual to avoid neighbours. Disputes became fiercer and arguments crescendoed into fighting and outright hatred.

Chapter 44 – Well, I'm Happy
'*Armies of playboys, playing with fire*'*

It was different in Ulster where Sir James Craig, Prime Minister of Northern Ireland since June 1921, sat in his imposing home and was reasonably content. He rubbed his soft, chubby hands in front of a roaring fire, 'Well, we'll of course be opting out ... there's no way Ulster will be part of an Irish Free State. And you, Henry? We've got work for you to do.' Field Marshal Sir Henry Wilson was retiring from his position of Chief of the Imperial General Staff. He'd been selected for the ultra-safe electoral seat of Ulster's County Down in the coming by-election.

'As soon as you're elected[†], I need you to take on the role of military advisor to our government.'

Wilson's famously ugly face crinkled in pleasure, 'Perfect. A few weeks back I told Churchill that simply protecting the North-South border wasn't going to be enough. The only solution to the Irish problem is reconquest ... he didn't like it of course. I told him ... I said, Winston, this is what needs to be done: send a large number, 5000 or so, special constables ... yes, Ulster Volunteer Force people ... across the border and teach the South how to behave. He nearly had a fit! Oh, and he had a chat with Collins about reducing ... border conflicts!'

Craig looked into the fire's exploding flames, 'We of course had no involvement in the Treaty ... we didn't officially agree to anything ... we may well eventually say that the Boundary Commission has nothing to do with us ... that we're just not interested.'

'But you won't mention the Commission yet?'

---

* 'In Many Places', Clare Sheridan, page 45

† February 1922

'No, we won't… They've got a hell of a problem finding out the wishes of the Border County inhabitants, as stated in the Treaty, and adjusting so-called economic boundaries. We'll sit back and wait for them to make the first move. And then tell them we're happy as we are, thank you very much.'

Wilson edged forward, 'You've spoken to Churchill about the partition?' Craig's crocodile smile appeared, 'Oh yes. He told my wife that England would defend every inch of Ulster soil. Ulster will not be disadvantaged, whatever happens.'

Wilson reflected Craig's smile, 'And Collins? Churchill is arranging meetings for you two? What happened in that first one, in January? On the 21st wasn't it?'

'Yes. Interesting meeting. Our feelings for each other are, of course, mutual. I hate him and he hates me. We did eventually start a discussion. As far as we here are concerned, there's going to be maybe a few very minor border adjustments, but Collins was wanting massive changes. Griffith and he only signed the Treaty because they thought Ulster would be too small and wouldn't be able to survive economically! He thinks he'll get Tyrone and Fermanagh! No, no … not a chance! Not an inch! We'll have them and get financial subsidies from Westminster. It'll be the Dublin government that'll struggle for decades economically.'

'Did you agree on anything? Anything at all?'

'Well, the Treaty originally said that there'd be three people involved in the Boundary Commission. One of Collins people, one of us, and one from the British. We both decided that the British representative was … not needed.'

Wilson was amazed, 'What? Collins agreed?'

'Yes! I was surprised, too. I told Collins that Ulster no longer trusted London … he may or may not have believed me and perhaps thought his side would be better off without the English continuing to interfere. Perhaps gambling on his side being better at negotiating ... Mind you, I very much doubt if the Boundary Commission ever actually comes to life.'

'But, I mean, taking the British representative out ... how can you and Collins get away with that? Altering the Treaty? It's been signed?! Anyway, I thought Collins was brighter than that ... maybe he's up to something?'

'Maybe ... Anyway, he promised to stop the boycott of Belfast goods ... and I agreed, after a few minutes of shilly-shallying, to deal with the Belfast shipyard problem ... where Catholic workers have been locked out at Harland and Wolff unless they signed a promise not to support Sinn Féin.'

Wilson choked on some whisky, 'You agreed? To help Catholic workers get their jobs back?'

'I, er, undertook to facilitate ... in every possible way ... their return to work.' Wilson had started laughing when Craig spoke about 'facilitating' and carried on laughing.

'No, no, no!' Craig said, 'I will ... honestly, I will ... in every possible way ... but I doubt that I'll be successful ....'

'You obviously got what you wanted from that meeting?'

'Yes. Two things. An acknowledgement that the Treaty, in which we were not involved, can be altered. And ... secondly, by meeting me, a recognition that they accept the Northern Ireland Government. Let's see what happens at the next meeting ... '

Wilson finished his whisky, his voice slipping into an Irish accent, 'Don't forget to axe him how Lady Lavery was ... the last time he saw her. Plenty of gossip about d'ose two, if yer know what I mean,' he managed a drunken wink.

*

A few weeks later, February 1922, two murderers looked at each other. Neither had actually pulled a trigger in anger, but they were both complicit in activities resulting in people being killed. Collins ordered IRA executions to take place; Craig would have known the names of people in Protestant assassination squads and did nothing to discourage them from their brutal gore.

Now the two men were looking into each other's eyes, unblinking, confident that they knew what the other was thinking. Craig held a glass of whisky and said, 'Are you drinking this stuff or are yer still on the sherry?[136]'

Collins shook his head, 'I wouldn't be drinking your feckin family firm's piss, anyway. I'll have a Jameson. OK, to business, you haven't done anything to get Catholic workers back into the shipyards? 10,000 workers expelled from their workplace on account of their religion? What sort of government are you running? One where so-called law enforcement bodies, like yer 'B' Specials*, smash down innocent people's doors and shoot their children? Club them on the head with a sledgehammer? Is that your government's justice?'

'Now hold on there. You've no proof of that. I, on the other hand, have documented reports of instances where your IRA murderers have thrown bombs at trams carrying Protestant workers to shipyards.'

There was a pause whilst they each re-filled their glasses.

'Talking of the IRA ... tell me, Mr. Collins, how's your friend Harry Boland? Still on talking terms with him? Oh, and Kitty Kiernan ... are you engaged to her? Or is he? No, alright, none of my business. I just wondered. But I did hear that you had quite a good time in London ... in between negotiating the Treaty ... meeting old friends ... Lady Lavery, Mrs Llewelyn-Davis?'

'As you say, Jimmy, that gutter gossip is nothing to do with you.'

---

* Belfast 'B' Specials, drawn from Ulster Volunteer Force, 19,000 part-time and unpaid Constables independent of Royal Irish Constabulary.

'Fine, fine. Your time with the ladies is your business, and if you also like ... wrestling with the young fellas like Harry Boland, that's your business, too. Anyway ... how's that little fella of yours ... what's his name? O'Reilly. Yes, Joe O'Reilly. Still taking care of all yer needs? No chance of him gettin' engaged, eh? Well, not to a lassie! Oh, that reminds me. Is it true that you had drinks with Birkenhead and he asked you to look at the Casement homosexual diaries ... and you verified them as genuine? Difficult to believe ... after all, you're not a handwriting expert and in 1916 yer were not much more than a message boy!'

Collins' face was reddening as he clenched his fists, 'What are you blithering on about? Is it to avoid discussing Tyrone and Fermanagh and their Catholic majorities? Yer know full well Lloyd George promised the Boundary Commission would result in counties with high numbers of Catholics coming to us in the South.'

Craig coughed as he swallowed some whisky. 'Rubbish. The British assured me that there'd only be minor border changes. Boundary Commission? What's that? Oh, yes. Your Treaty mentions it ... the Treaty that I had no involvement with and certainly didn't sign. Anyway, what makes you think Catholics in Ulster want to come under a Dublin government?'

'Well, the way your cops and Special Constables attack Catholic homes, setting them on fire, shooting innocent Catholics and killin' children, might have something to do with it.'

Craig's eyes sharpened as he leant towards Collins, 'Listen ... you know as well as I do that the IRA is struggling to get Catholics in Belfast to support them. There's many Catholics there ... and in Londonderry and Armagh ... turning their backs on your precious IRA ... even informing the police about your people.'

Collins glared, 'I know that your thugs have intimidated and terrified people into thinking the safety of women and children is more important than a unified Ireland …'

Craig shouted back, 'There's thoush-ands of Catholics willing to help police and keep their communities sh'cure. They know the IRA kills in-der-scriminately an' that Northern Ireland is proshperous. They didn't like the idea of the IRA helping the Germans in the War and they sher-tainly don't like them helping Bolshshevik Russia now. Catholics in Tyrone and Fermanagh look at yer De Valera and yer IRA and they're happy to sh-tay with things as they are.'

Both men sat in silence for at least two minutes before Collins said, 'OK. We've got that out of the way. Now what?'

Craig said, 'We can at least agree on two things? First, the border needs to be sorted out … obviously … so, we need bilateral discussion in the coming months on that.'

Collins didn't believe a word of it but knew the importance of maintaining the pretence, 'What else? I'd say … all this killing ... women and children, for God's sake! … There has to be greater protection for Catholics in Belfast.'

Craig said, 'Well, I was going to say the killing has to stop … and yes, we can discuss ways to deal with it.' The meeting ended. Both of them knew it had been a waste of time.

Catholics and Protestants in Belfast continued to be killed; sometimes it's a police officer, sometimes it's a Sinn Féin, sometimes an innocent civilian. Occasionally a child. Homes, pubs, and businesses continued to be bombed or set on fire. The Northern Ireland government requested more funding from the British to pay for Ulster Special Constables. Tom Jones in Downing Street formally documented his concerns that such expenditure could be illegal and that the British Government could face criticism for providing monies being used to fund a private army. His comments were noted. And ignored.[137]

Feb 11th 1922

Collins, without telling others in Dublin, created an Ulster Council branch of the IRA. It kidnapped about 40 important Loyalists and Special Constables and took them to the South as hostages; the aim was to have Monaghan footballers, and three condemned men in Derry's jail, released. Border tensions were high and 19 Ulster Constables were ordered to travel by train from Belfast to Enniskillen.

The train stopped in Clones, Monaghan, population of about 1500 and just inside Southern Irish territory. A large group of IRA attacked and in the firefight about 20 people, most of them civilians, were killed or wounded. Churchill suspended the evacuation of British troops and, under pressure from Sir Henry Wilson, ordered three battalions to go North. Belfast erupted in violence with 27 Catholics and 16 Protestants killed.

March 23rd

Two Special Constables were killed by the IRA. Next day a group wearing police uniforms and masks used a sledgehammer to break into the McMahon family home in a middle-class Protestant-Catholic suburb of Belfast. The strong suspicion was that the men were Royal Irish Constables led by District Inspector John Nixon. They told eight males in the house, only one of whom had Sinn Féin connections, to kneel – they killed six and wounded two, one of them a 12-year-old boy.

March 29th

Churchill met with Craig and Collins and devised a pact titled Peace is Declared; Collins agreed to call for IRA attacks in the North to stop. There would be action taken to ensure that Ulster police did not abuse their powers, and units consisting of equal numbers of Catholics and Protestants would police mixed areas of

Belfast. Almost immediately the Peace Pact fell apart. People like Sir Henry Wilson in Ulster didn't like the mixed policing idea and Belfast Sinn Féin didn't want to recognise the authority of the Craig government.

Two days later a Protestant home was bombed; a two-year old was killed and two other children seriously injured – one later died. A police constable in Belfast was shot. A few hours later ten police officers climbed into an armoured car and went to a Catholic area, Arnon Street, where they broke into a house and shot the householder, then went next door and killed a man asleep in bed. At another home they killed a 70-year-old man in front of his grandson. Next door they used a sledgehammer to kill a man in bed while his small son and daughter were beside him. The 7-year-old boy was shot ... and killed.

It seemed as though that it was only Collins amongst senior Sinn Féin leadership who was thinking about Belfast. Only he that cared about the border areas of Ulster where Catholics were in the majority. He was trying to build up Irish National troop numbers in the North whilst sending weapons, that had been supplied to him by the British, to Sinn Féin in Belfast – he couldn't care less that the firearms passed through Anti-Treaty hands. He was determined to do something, anything, to stop Catholics being murdered in Belfast. But in the South the bulk of the Irish fighting men were anti-Treaty, anti-Collins, and anti-Griffith – they were not too bothered about Belfast.

Outside of Dublin, IRA units planned their own operations and financed themselves. Their leaders were elected and supposedly answerable to the Minister of Defence, Richard Mulcahy[*]. The Irish Republican Army might have been 'democratic' and

---

[*] Mulcahy was a firm Collins supporter.

effective as a guerrilla force, but Ireland now had a Provisional Government and most of its Army units were dysfunctional and rudderless. They told Mulcahy that they wanted a convention to discuss objectives, including a rejection of the Treaty, and to elect a leader – he initially agreed but then decided to ban the meeting. They chose to have it anyway.

Rory O'Connor, the explosives 'expert' responsible for organising grenades which were occasionally effective during the Uprising, had met Collins at Plunkett's Larkfield estate in 1916. Now in 1922 they were enemies and O'Connor was elected chairman of a 'military council' formed by dissident anti-Treaty IRA members. He immediately arranged for the illegal occupation and lock down of the Four Courts in Dublin – Irish home of law and justice.

Chapter 45 – The Split

'First item on the agenda of any Irish organisation is the Split'[*]

April 1922

'Collins isn't a leader; he's an opportunist and a bully ... Hang on, d'yer want a cuppa tea? I'll call fer a pot – I can hear the ole black kettle boiling.' 39-year-old Rory O'Connor was talking to a journalist, Clare Sheridan of the *New York World*[†]. She'd managed to get him to agree to an interview by the simple expedient of phoning the number of the Lord Chancellor of Ireland whose office, until O'Connor moved into it, was in the 'Four Courts', Dublin. The place was a secure area but Sheridan didn't need to tell anybody that she had an appointment with O'Connor – she gained entry to the buildings by chatting to the anti-Treaty guards and fluttering her eyelashes. The lads of about fifteen years of age almost fell over each other to let her through the gates.

O'Connor had majestically ensconced himself in the antiquated office, portraits of bewigged forgotten fogies on the walls, and was lounging on a Hepplewhite chair behind a vast polished desk. There were two revolvers resting ostentatiously in front of him with a small pile of bullets beside them. While he was talking, he would pick up a bullet and roll it lovingly between his fingers, place it down and then pick up another – arranging them into neat warlike dispositions.

There was an immediate, almost sexual, connection between this Dublin-born Irishman, and the tall, socialite Englishwoman.

---

[*] Brendan Behan, quoted in a speech by President of Ireland, at City Hall, Cork, Friday, 1st February, 2019

[†] *'In Many Places'*, C. Sheridan, pages 45-48

Women often found O'Connor attractive; a thin face that was finely structured and a slow voice, deep and rich whilst carrying with it something close to an almost evangelical passion. Sheridan was a seriously-beautiful, highly intelligent woman who had travelled the world, meeting powerful politicians and asking them provocative questions in her English-rose accent while daring them not look into her world-weary intense blue eyes*.

'So ... you're the leader here? Aren't there some other senior ... anti-Treaty ... Liam Lynch and Ernie O'Malley ...?'

'No, no. They're commanders of ... individual brigades. I'm the overall leader, making the key decisions. Such as invading the North, defending the republic and opposing the General Election that Collins is planning. What else d'you want to know?'

She didn't tell O'Connor that her family home, Innishannon House in Cork, had been burnt down the year before by the IRA and that Fred Stenning, the gamekeeper, was murdered when he tried to stop them. Her lips moved slowly as she simply asked, 'Do you love Ireland so much that you hate England?'

There was a pause as he half smiled in return, 'Hate? No. True, whilst Ireland is unfree, we'll always be a menace to England. The way to stop that is for us to be free because, unlike as it is now, an Irish republic wouldn't be a threat ... far from it, we could live side by side defending each other against France, Germany or Russia, or whatever.'

O'Connor had a degree in engineering and worked in Canada constructing rail lines across and through the Rockies. It was this knowledge of, and experience with, explosives that he used when he later worked with Joseph Plunkett at the Larkfield Estate. He

---

* A one-year-old daughter died in 1914; her husband died in WW1; a lover died 3 years later.

also assisted with altering the so-called Castle Document which helped inflame the Easter Rising, and afterwards he coordinated, with Collins, IRA escapes from British jails.

Fascism was beginning to jack-boot and crush its way in many nations. In a few years there would be Irishmen wearing Blue or Black uniforms, determined to enforce their beliefs violently if need be. O'Connor said in a press conference, before occupying the Four Courts, that 'Armies have overthrown governments in many countries' and 'Suppression of the Press and stoppage of elections' were possibilities. Someone asked if he wanted a military dictatorship and he replied, 'You can take it to mean that.'

Sheridan was aware of her impact on this man and his self-importance. Was there some jealousy here? She probed further, 'I met Collins ... in Cork. He seemed ... genuine enough. You said that he's a bully?'

He smiled, 'But I don't mean that in a derogatory sense ... being a bully is sometimes necessary. A way to get things done ...' Sheridan thought to herself, 'Well, yes, dictators often feel and enjoy the need to be a bully. Whether it's really required or the extent to which they go about it, well ...'

He was indeed charismatic and passionate; he knew what he wanted – an independent republic, free from grasping capitalists. But now that he'd forged his way into leadership of determined rebels, he was obviously vague with regard to the next step. Whilst fiddling with the ammunition on the desk, he instructed Sheridan as to why there was no reason an Irish republic needed to have factory stacks; it could be perfectly happy as a rural economy. It was obvious to her that his political ideals, although high-minded, lacked realism.

She looked into the dark eyes and asked him what he was going to do when the shelling started. Here was an opportunity to display his patriotic masculinity – he shrugged, indicating that an attack by the British was what he wanted and said, 'I'll go down in the ruins or in the flames.' He was perhaps already thinking about the collection of explosives being stored nearby. Guy Fawkes with an egomaniac complex, thought Sheridan.

It was ironic that Clare Sheridan would cable her article about O'Connor from the offices of the *Freeman's Journal*. A few months earlier the newspaper had printed an article referring to him as a potential military dictator – in the early hours of the following morning he led sledgehammer-wielding thugs in an orgy of destruction, smashing the newspaper's presses and linotype machines. Some may have said this was rather an extreme expression of reader disapproval.[138]

Chapter 46 – We Did the Right Thing

'De Valera's a pure slíbhín*! Collins looked up from the stack of papers he was checking and realised that Griffith was standing at his side. 'Arthur! Take a seat, Bai. I need a break. Sha, my guts are playin' me up again … Joe O'Reilly insisted I at least have a 'biled egg … I'm thinkin' it may not have been a good idea … but, er, yer not looking too grand yersel' if yer don't mind me sayin' so.' The two men rarely agreed on strategies, nor indeed on anything, but Griffith knew the importance of them working together. He winced, 'I do have a bit of a head …' Collins pulled a drawer open and took out a bottle of whiskey, 'Well, a hair of the ole dog might help, eh? Not too early in the day?' He poured two very large whiskies, 'Sláinte.'

'Saol fada chugat†, Mick.' Griffith's hand shook slightly as he picked up his glass, swallow-gulped, and ran his tongue round his lips.

'De Valera, sly? Yer not wrong there, Arthur. He's claiming to be a humble soldier for the anti-Treaty boys and gone on the run. We're goin' to have a problem fer a while with that lot … they're all over the country … d'ere's more of them than we have in the new National Army. Still, we'll build up numbers. And at least our fellas stayed loyal to us outside the Four Courts – I wasn't certain that they would. We had to take back those offices … Churchill was threatening to use his troops if we didn't. God knows what would have happened if he'd had his way. He got insistent after that bastard Henry Wilson was killed in London by the two Irish fellas … on instructions from Rory O'Connor … I'm sure that's what Churchill thought …,' he looked at Griffith to see if he had

---

* Slíbhín = sneaky, sly, and untrustworthy person

† *Saol fada chugat* = Long life to you

any other ideas as to who had ordered or encouraged Dunn and O'Sullivan, but there was no reaction, so Collins continued 'there was a danger of Churchill convincing himself that we and De Valera had got back together.'

Griffith laughed, 'It must have looked like that when De Valera agreed to have a national election and we didn't oppose his candidates. And you had that new Constitution drafted supposedly creating a republic.'

Collins had the grace to look just a little embarrassed, 'Ah! I know yer didn't like the election pact but De Valera fell for it ... and the electorate mainly voted for our Pro-Treaty candidates. On election day, we distributed the draft Constitution with no reference to a republic, so Lloyd George and Churchill were happy. In fact, Churchill's speech in the House of Commons gave a complete account of the Irish situation including a defense of the Collins-De Valera Agreement and the good faith of the Free State Government!'

Griffith's eyes were tired and watery. He looked at the whiskey bottle, 'De Valera couldn't have been too pleased when you issued the new Constitution?'

'I couldn't give a feck! The long streak a'shite tried to send me ter the US so he'd get more control in Dublin. Then he went to meet Lloyd George but would he take me? Nah! And he got nowhere by nagging at the sneaky Welsh bastard.'

Griffith wanted to know why Collins didn't include a reference to the Republic in the new Constitution.

'Arthur, the British would never put up with it. No chance. They'd keep their army here and we'd be fecked. As far as I'm concerned though, as soon as the British Army are out and we're governing ourselves that Constitution will be changed to suit the Irish people. Oath of allegiance! ... well, that's just a jumble of words for politicians to mouth.' He looked at Griffith and spoke from his heart, 'De Valera's not the greatest of leader of men. The anti-Treaty boyos, O'Connor and the rest, they ignore him and go their own way. As a political strategist, he's not too good either. He doesn't seem to realise that the whole of Ireland can get its independence and more if things are handled carefully and patiently.'

A clock tick-tocked softly. Collins said, almost to himself, 'We have time on our side. Lloyd George'll be gone soon. In ten, maybe twenty, years there'll be another war. Churchill can't help himself – wars are attracted to him, like bloody moths to a flame. Might be the Roo'suns or the French. Germany again? It's a big nation but it'll take them twenty years to recover. Whichever one it is, when England's at war again, Ireland won't be neutral. They'll need our ports, troops, and landing strips[139]. That's when we can really negotiate. A republic with no oath. No tariffs on Irish goods for a hundred years, plebiscites for Tyrone and Fermanagh, and no more funding of 'B' Specials in Northern Ireland.' But Collins was talking to himself.

Griffith was still thinking back to the battle for the Four Courts, 'I heard that Churchill was offering to send aircraft! They supplied the two 18-pounder field guns, and our men got .... What? Cupla hours instruction on how to load and aim them guns? No wonder they almost hit the British troops in Phoenix Park. Emmet Dalton[*] used his experience to take charge, didn't he? I hear he loaded some of the shells himself.'

'Yeah, the young fella did well. A great General. And what a'boat Paddy O'Daly? The anti-Treaty crowd's leaders couldn't make up their minds on ... anything. They had no option but to surrender there. Did yer hear the explosion? All those ancient papers destroyed ... O'Connor says it was an accident! Like hell,

---

[*] Emmet Dalton, MC, fought in France during WW1 in the 7th Battalion Royal Dublin Fusiliers, later with 9th Battalion, RDF, 16th (Irish) Division, and 6th Battalion, Leinster Regiment

it was!' There were a few minutes silence. Griffith poured himself another drink, 'Cathal Brugha ... killed at the Hammam Hotel.'

Collins looked out the window, 'Argh! That was bad. A brave man. Cahileen ... wife and six children. Yer know that he didn't want this business of Irish fighting Irish? He argued against O'Connor's idea for a military coup and stopped them from attacking British troops!'

'Cathal was right, Mick. I'm no pacifist but violence for no purpose with no hope of success, is immoral and stupid. It's ridiculous to think that a few thousand poorly armed Irishmen could defeat a British government that was willing to use hundreds of t'ousands of troops to fight and die in Europe in a war costing hundreds of millions. Most English people hate and despise the Irish, so d'yer think their Government would ever allow the Irish to win?'

They lapsed into whiskey-thought.

'Arthur, we had to sign that Treaty. Dev, being Dev, wanted to be the one that made the decision. All that garbage about the oath? He couldn't really give a feck*. The Treaty we brought back's not much different from his dopey Document Number 2, written of course by Childers. As for saying we should have got approval from our Cabinet in Dublin? Nonsense. We were plenipotentiaries ... elected representatives and answerable to the Dáil. In a democratic parliamentary system the Cabinet is subordinate to parliament and accountable to it, not to a feckin' President or Prime Minister.'

'Unfortunately, Mick, some didn't see it that way ...'
Collins poured another two whiskies, his eyes blinking, 'Yep ... Harry Boland being one ... and now he's dead ... because of me.'

---

* In 1927 De Valera took the Oath, saying that he was simply signing a piece of paper so that he could be admitted to the Dáil. Archbishop Mannix agreed with his views.

'Mick! Other good men have died because of De Valera ... and, yes, because of Archbishop feckin' Mannix[140]. Maybe if Mannix hadn't supported Dev and if he'd instead condemned the anti-Treaty people for killing Irishmen, then Harry would still be alive. Harry made a decision to side with De Valera and he was arranging for weapons to fight our democratic government. He got caught and tried to fight it out.'

'Yes ... That's what they say. We're not gonna know the truth because he died in hospital refusing to say who shot him.[141]'

Chapter 47 – Trip Back Home
Go raibh maith agat, My Laughing Boy*[142]*

Collins was going home, County Cork, to inspect military sites. But that included Clonakilty, with maybe a quick visit to the remains of the family house at Woodfield.

'Yer sneezin'? Yer got a cold, Mick?' Johnny Collins clapped an arm round his brother. 'Anyway, it's wonderful to see yer again.'

'A cold! Yeah, Sean, an' isn't it me guts playin' up a'gin as well … Getting' older! Ah well, there's always someone worse off. Isn't that what Ma used to say? … but what about yersel … is that hand still givin' yer a hard time?'

'Ah, I'm grand, Mick … but listen …' He directed Collins to the pub's snug, 'Listen, now. What were yer thinkin'! Coming to Cark? Sha, yer must know the anti-Treaty fellas are infesting the whole county?'

'I'll be fine, so. C'mon, drink up and I'll get yer another pint o' Wrastler†. I'll have one more ball o' malt … Don't worry. Yer can see I brought plenty of troops with me. An armoured car, too. Anyway, if I amn't safe in the County where I was born and bred, where can I be safe?'

'Alright … but just take care. Well, c'mon. Tell me about yer time in London. Was that Lloyd George a slíbhín or what?'

Collins laughed, 'Sha, wern't they all loike that. But, yeah, he was der worst. Did yer know he grew up in his uncle's house? A shoemaker? That's why he can talk a load of old cobblers.' Collins laughed at his own joke, but Johnny stared having no idea what his

---

* *Go raibh maith agat* =Thank you

† Wrastler=Beer popular in Cork

brother meant. 'That's Cockney slang ... never mind. No, they didn't trust us and we didn't trust them. I was surprised though ... I couldn't help but likin' Birkenhead and, yeah, even Churchill. Neither of them pretended to be what they weren't, if yer know what I mean. They both had a job to do jus' like I had mine. They certainly know how to drink, that's fer sure. I could barely keep up with der pair a' them.'

'You agreed to sign the Treaty after Griffith said that he would?'

'Yeah, well, ... Arthur ... he did surprise us. But, yer know, I thought *'Why not? We've got as much as we're gonna get. In London, I mean.'* We were losing the war ... running short of weapons and ammunition ... and men. Of course, I knew that they'd twist the Treaty to suit themselves after signing it ... but I knew we could do the same, too. The Boundary Commission was always going to be the contentious bit. I didn't think they'd be so blatant though ... allowing Craig to get his way so quick.'

'So, is this just a visit to see the family and build morale?'

'Sha, who knows when I'll get to see me big brother again! ... but yeah ... just between you and me ... we've gotta stop this nonsense of Irish fightin' Irish; the anti-Treaty lads and us need to sort things out. I'll be meeting ... well, I won't say who, but I'm determined to make peace with them. Then we can move North, all of us, and deal with Craig's Ulster Special Constabulary thugs. They're good at smashing up homes and scaring women and children ... I doubt they'll put up much of a fight.'

'But Churchill ... he'll send over t'ousands of Tommies.'

'Yes. And we'll hit and run like we did before signing the Treaty. The USA won't support them. We've got to do something to help the Belfast and Derry Catholics. The British won't simply give us Fermanagh and Tyrone ... we're gonna have to fight for them. And then? Once we have them, as Griffith always said, Northern Ireland won't be able to survive with just 4 counties. Who knows, we can maybe force Craig to stand down and we'll have all 32 counties in the Republic. This fighting amongst ourselves! ... God, I wish we hadn't let Liam Lynch and the others walk free from the Four Courts. Just because they promised not to continue the fighting ... lying bastards.' He looked at his brother and blinked, 'Well. I'll be sayin' Goodbye and God bless to yer, Johnny ... Take care of yourself, now ...'

Collins went into the main part of the pub, 'Patsy! Come here to me. Did I tell yer a'boat de old fella that went to see his cousin, Dan, in New York? They went for a trip up to Niagara Falls ... and Dansy says, 'There! Wadda yer tink a'dat?' an de ol wan he sez, 'What? That? Sha, isn't that like Clonakilty on a wet day.' Collins grinned when everyone laughed, even though they'd all heard it a few times before.

'C'mon, then ... we best be off. Jasus! Will yer look at the time, would yer! Quick, quick, finish yer drinks. We need to get to Rosscarbery, Skibbereen and Clonakilty. If yer lucky, I'll stand yer another at each. Then, depending on a few things ... Crookstown, and back to Bandon. Yeah, yeah. The way we came ... can't be helped.'

Several times, everywhere they stopped, Collins was quietly warned about the likelihood of an ambush, and several times he said, 'Ah, sha, they'd never attack me here in Cark.'

'Another, Mick?'

'Yeah, g'wan. We've bags a'time, so.'

Everybody, including the motorcyclist and the drivers, had been drinking throughout the day. Sitting next to Collins in the Leyland Thomas touring car was 24-year-old Major-General Emmet Dalton[143]. Some people, incredibly, thought he worked for

British Intelligence. He'd been with Collins and the delegation to London when the Treaty was negotiated. Now they were both dozing, on and off, as the car moved fitfully through the narrow County Cork country roads. The sun hadn't quite gone down on this late-summer early-autumn evening. It had been a dry day but, as always, there was an agricultural smell of greenness. In a far-off field a cow, separated from its calf, was calling hopelessly and mournfully. The sun was slipping slowly away, leaving streaks of carmine across the cloudy horizon. An owl hooted.

Collins opened his eyes, stared at the familiar hills and farms and wiped his nose. 'Yer know ... Emmet ... I love this country.'

'Yes, Mick. I know.'

'*Into my heart an air that* ... ah, ah ... something.'

'*kills* ... Mick.'

'Yer know it?[144] ... Not bad, eh. And yet didn't I waste more than half me adult life in yon far feckin' Country! D'yer know that other soppy English poem ... Read it when I was at the Civil Service School[145] ... the one that starts '*The curfew tolls the knell of parting day*'? This Celtic Twilight reminds me of it.[146]' He glanced at Dalton, needing to check whether he was smiling or, worse, sneering.

'Yes, Mick, *Now fades the glimm'ring landscape on the sight, And all the air a solemn stillness holds, Save where the beetle wheels his droning flight, And drowsy tinklings lull the distant fold.*^{*}'

Collins half-smiled, 'We won't tell anyone we discussed it, eh? Did yer learn that at school?'

'Nah! Yer jokin! I read it when I was in the trenches on the Somme. Apparently, when England was at war with France in Canada, a General recited it to his officers the night before a big

---

* *Elegy Written in a Country Churchyard,* by Thomas Gray

battle.* Me? Learn it at school!? Sha, I was taught by the Christian Brothers! They wouldn't have touched that English stuff. O'Connell School, Drumcondra[147]. Tom Kettle went there, too. He died in my arms on the Somme. Éamonn Ceannt, Ernie O'Malley, Seán Heuston, Con Colbert, John Devoy; they all went to that same school. Out of the, what, 1300 that took part in the Easter Rising, more than a hundred† went there, yer know?'

Collins laughed, 'I sometimes think the Christian Brothers did more damage to England than any of us!'

'Mick, d'yer know any-ting of a fella by the name of Brendan Bracken ... I was there at that school, same time as Brendan. Christian Brothers![148] They didn't spare the rod there, I can assure yer. They enjoyed plying the ole wand! But young Brendan was a little too much even for them – he was that awkward and bad, he got kicked out. Mick, guess where I last saw Brendan Bracken?'

Collins rested a rifle across his knees, 'No idea.'

'London. Not long before the Treaty talks officially started. I saw Churchill leaving the House of Commons and I was going to catch him up but a young fella – tall, red-haired – started speaking to him. I stood to one side, pretending to look at the traffic, and earwigged. Winston says, *'Brendan! Are you alright, dear boy?'* I heard the tall fella speaking in a sort of Australian accent, *'Actually, I need ... a reference ... d'you know ... someone ... such as ... a headmaster of a good school?'* Churchill looked surprised, *'Let me think ... well, your middle name's Rendall, isn't it?*

---

* General Wolfe was killed in 1759 at Quebec, aged 32. Collins was 31.

† At least 134 participants in the Uprising had attended the O'Connell school. A comparison could be made with England's Winchester College and its influence on Irish affairs.

There's Montagu Rendall at Winchester ... But why? What are ...' He stopped and looked around, saw me, and said, '*Hello, Emmet ... er, Emmet Dalton ... this is Brendan Bracken ... young friend of mine ...* '. Dalton chuckled as he thought back, 'So I say, '*Brendan! We were at O'Connell School together!*' But yer know what? He denied it and rushed away; probably because his family were Fenians and Catholic.'

Collins looked at Dalton, 'Churchill with a Fenian connection? I can believe it ... they're all crazy in London ... MI5, MI6, Cope ... secrecy and shadows ... who know's which fella of our's is workin' fer 'em ... Arthur Griffith always thought Erskine Childers woz ... But what made yer think of Brendan Bracken?'

'Ah, well, Mick ... I was thinking of the London Treaty meetings ... to talk peace ... and now, you're looking to have a meetin' with the anti-Treaty people here? Yer must be otherwise, why are we driving to all these places? Rosscarbery, Skibbereen, Bandon, Clonakilty... and Crookstown!?'

'Yeah, I know ... you're quick on the uptake, Emmet. It's no secret though that I'm desperate to negotiate a truce with De Valera. I just wish I knew where he was ... I was told he might be interested and that for some reason he's around here, close to Clonakilty. Clonakilty, God help us! ... I mean ... if he is here, then why? Why would he come to this area where he knows I'd be, if not to have a meetin' with me?'

Dalton lifted his own rifle and looked at it. 'Mick, it could be a trap ... enticing yer to come down here? De Valera? You know that I've never trusted him. When they took over the Four Courts why did he insist on being just an ordinary private sol'jer in the anti-Treaty Army? Nobody's ever explained that. I can only think it's because he knew that, with him not being a leader when they were forced to surrender, we wouldn't be able to execute him like the Brits did to our leaders in 1916.'

'Look, Emmet, I know De Valera can't be trusted... but I have to take the risk. This civil war's ridiculous. We should all be up North, doing what we can to help Belfast. If we don't stop fighting each other down here... if we don't get this border situation sorted out and a unified Ireland ... there'll be troubles in Belfast and Derry for years, decades, to come. It won't just be soldiers dying, never is ... it'll be innocent men, women and children. I'm determined to stop that.'

Crack-crack! Crack-crack-crack! The sound of rifle shots made them stare at each other. The convoy had stopped. Dalton shouted, 'Drive on! Drive like hell!'

Collins shouted, 'No! Stop! Stop the car! We'll fight it out.' The Vickers gun mounted on the armoured car was already rat-ta-ta-tatting. Collins and his men jumped down from the vehicles. They took cover as best they could in a ditch and began firing at gun flashes, less than 200 yards away, in the bushes on either side of the boreen*. The armoured car was trundling slowly backwards and forwards, machine gun bullets sweeping the verges ... and then silence. The gun was jammed. Collins took cover next to the armoured car. Nobody from the convoy was returning fire now and for a brief moment there was an eerie silence. He began walking towards the bend in the road[149].

Dalton called, 'Mick! Come back ... get down!' But Collins was trotting down the road and shouting, 'There they go!' He waved towards a couple of rain-coated figures running up a slope. He was aiming and firing his rifle as he slowed to walking; then he was out of sight, round the bend. What was going through his mind? To stand up during an ambush when he had no idea where

---

* *Boreen* = narrow, country road

all the enemy were? Was it the whiskey that he'd been drinking all day? Was he thinking of the accusations, especially those by Cathal Brugha and Seumas Robinson during the Treaty debates, that he'd never been a real soldier ... never fired a shot in anger? Was he determined to prove that he was a fighter, like them? An Irish soldier?

Crack-thump! Dalton ran and saw that Collins had fallen, face forward. The back of his head was a mass of pulsating dark redness and blood was spouting onto the road. There would be those who would insult his memory by attributing sugary-sentimental 'last words' to him. But it's difficult to know how anything can be said by a person that has had a high-velocity, probably dum-dum, bullet smashing through their brain. Dalton held a small bandage to the wound but it was useless. An Act of Contrition was whispered in Collins' ear and he was lifted into the car. A final shot from somewhere wounded the motorcyclist as he rested the body beside Dalton.

They drove with great difficulty down dark lanes and byways, some of them still blocked by the remains of a barricade; they almost crashed when arriving at a broken bridge, then had to cross a muddy field and became bogged. Meeting a solitary walker, they sought guidance to a priest's house. As usual, lies were later told about what occurred when they arrived there in the darkness.

One version is that the priest came down the garden path, by the light of a small torch, and peered over the garden railing into the car – shocked at the sight, he returned whence he'd come without saying anything, leaving the men to shiver and wait for nothing. It was said that a soldier then fired a shot in anger at the house. Another version, the priest's, is that he said an Act of Contrition, some prayers and made the Sign of the Cross, before telling them that he needed to get the Holy Oils – when he returned, they had all gone. Well, that's what he said.

Another version: the men in the gloomy roadway looked at each other ...

'Where's that fella gone?'

'Is he coming back?'

'Did he say something?'

'I thought he did, but I didn't catch it.'

'He was after crossing hissel', but I didn't think he said anything.'

'Has he gone to get something?'

'I don't think he's comin' back.'

'The feckin bastard!'

They waited. And waited.

'Come on, we'll get the Big Fella back to Cark.'

Eventually, long past midnight, the body was delivered to Shanakiel, the military hospital in Cork, to be stripped and cleaned by the British staff, some of whom had been born perhaps in Oxford or London or Leeds. Then it was transported by ship to Dublin. In the months and years to come there were suspicions and private confessions as to who had fired the fatal shot. Many consider Sonny O'Neill responsible – if so, it would assist those who want British involvement because he was a former British soldier. He was said to be a 'sniper' but there is no evidence to support this; in fact, most soldiers would be confident of scoring a hit at 200 yards. O'Neill had been injured in the arm during WW1 and some people argue that he'd be unlikely to be able to fire a rifle with any accuracy – if so, why was he there? There were attempts to blame both the British and the Treaty supporters; whispers that Dalton, on behalf of British Intelligence, had fired the shot. There were also suggestions of a ricochet, or a 'stray' shot – either of which would imply that the killing of Ireland's

Laughing Boy was somehow not intentional.

As had become usual, there was a wonderfully sad funeral in Dublin attended by hundreds of thousands. But conveniently, there was no autopsy and no death certificate. And nobody rushed to ask awkward questions – until later, when the accusations were made.

The uncivil Civil War continued. In the tradition of the times, captured people were summarily killed if they were on the 'wrong' side, or even if they only appeared to be. There were reprisals … and then reprisals for the reprisals. The Provisional Government authorised executions, without trials, because they could. And these were followed by yet more executions; Dalton resigned in disgust. Meanwhile, Catholics and Protestants in Northern Ireland rioted and killed, the Protestant police participated, and the Craig government did nothing – apart from demanding, and getting, funds from the British Government to pay Special Constabulary wages.

In the South, as well as killing, songs were sung in the pubs and De Valera bided his time. For him, Craig's Northern Ireland Parliament was illegitimate but there was nothing that he would do except sometimes mouth sympathies for Catholics suffering there. England? The English thought how good and comfortable it was now, not to be involved anymore – and felt pleased that they would no longer be tangled up in the sticky bloody web of Irish "Troubles". They were wrong.

"The moment the very name of Ireland is mentioned, the English seem to bid adieu to common feeling, common prudence, and common sense, and to act with the barbarity of tyrants, and the fatuity of idiots."

Sydney Smith, 1771–1845, English Anglican clergyman and essayist. Educated at Winchester College.

Biographical and Nomenclature Appendix

General Sir William Thomson Adair (1850–1931): Even though he was a serving officer in the Royal Marines, he also became commander of the Antrim Division of the Ulster Volunteer Force and was responsible for supervising the importation of arms at Larne, Co. Antrim.

Frank Adcock (1886-1968) Cryptographer worked for the Intelligence Division Royal Navy in Room 40. Professor of Ancient History at Cambridge University between 1925 and 1951.

Heinrich Albert (1874-1960) German civil servant, diplomat, politician, businessman. Suspected of illegal activities at Embassy in Washington.

Maud Allan (1873 – 1956): Canadian lesbian dancer who performed topless in Oscar Wilde's Salome to private audiences. Margot Asquith paid the rent of Allan's apartment near Regent's Park for twenty years. Allan sued British MP Noel Pemberton Billing for publishing an article which accused her of being an associate of German WW1 conspirators. (He wrote that people who attended her performances were included in a Black Book and were being blackmailed by the German government.) As a witness at the libel trial, she said that the name of the trial judge, Charles Darling, was in the Black Book. He was a judge in the Roger Casement case.

The **American Committee for Relief in Ireland**: created to give financial assistance to civilians in Ireland who had been injured or suffered financial hardship due to the Irish War of Independence.

Ancient Order of Hibernians: An Irish Catholic organization. Members must be male, Catholic, and either born in Ireland or of Irish descent. Its largest membership is in the United States. Original purpose was to act as guards to shield Catholic churches from anti-Catholic forces. Strongly opposed to the non-religious Irish Republican Brotherhood (the IRB). Opponents, such as Jim Larkin called it the "Ancient Order of Catholic Orangemen".

Herbert H Asquith (1852–1928): Liberal Prime Minister 1908 -1916. Won honours at Oxford. Lawyer, not wealthy, before becoming MP. His

Liberal reforms were opposed by the House of Lords. His Parliament Act, August 1911, ended the Lords' veto power over financial legislation. 1914 Home Rule for Ireland legislation was passed but postponed until end of the World War. In May 1915 he formed government in coalition with Conservatives. His alcoholism worsened as he became older. Following the death of his son and press criticism over war strategy and Ireland, he handed over to Lloyd George in December 1916.

Referring to WW1, he said 'We are fighting to vindicate the principle that small nationalities are not to be crushed, in defiance of international good faith, by the arbitrary will of a strong and overmastering Power.' Some thought this ironic in that Ireland is a small nationality which had been subject to an overmastering power (England) for more than 600 years.

Margot Asquith (1864 – 1945): wife of Prime Minister Asquith, married in 1894 (his first wife died 1891). Opponent of women's suffrage. Devoted defender of her husband. Step-mother of Raymond, Herbert, Violet, and Arthur.

Raymond Asquith (1878–15 September 1916): barrister and eldest son of Prime Minister H. H. Asquith. A member of the fashionable group of intellectuals called The Coterie known for unconventional lifestyles and extravagant hospitality. Went to Winchester College (as his two brothers did) like Jack White but he was one year older. Won a scholarship to Oxford. Tall, handsome, brilliant barrister intending to become an MP but enlisted during WW1. Became a staff officer but requested active duty with his battalion and fought at Battle of the Somme where, on 15 September 1916, at Flers-Courcelette, he was shot in the chest. It's said that he lit a cigarette to hide the seriousness of his injuries. He and his wife Katherine had 3 children; son Julian was born a few months before Raymond's death. Katherine converted and all three children were brought up as Roman Catholics.

Herbert Asquith (1881-1947): younger brother of Raymond. Service with the Royal Artillery in WW1. Lawyer, poet, novelist. Educated at Winchester College.

Arthur Melland Asquith (1883-1939): younger brother of Raymond. Wounded three times in WW1. Wounded during fighting near Beaucamp and evacuated to Britain where one of his legs was amputated.

Violet Asquith (1887-1969): Her best friend when young was Venetia Stanley, who had a very close and intimate relationship with her father, PM Herbert Asquith. She, like brother Raymond, was a member of the intellectual, social, group The Coterie. She was Sir Winston Churchill's closest female friend, apart from his wife Clementine, and at one point they were thought to be engaged. She married Maurice Bonham-Carter.

Saint Augustine: Bishop of Hippo (now Annaba, Algeria) from 396 to 430; one of the most influential thinkers in history and influence on St Thomas Aquinas. He has been sometimes called "the Father of Roman Catholicism." He described the doctrine of a 'just' war to defend innocents and preserve peace.

Daniel Julian Bailey, alias Beverley (1887- 1968): Born Dublin. 5ft 4in tall. Joined 2nd Battalion Royal Irish Rifles 1904. Prisoner of War in Germany April 1916, joined the Irish Brigade, made a Sergeant. In German submarine with Casement and Monteith. On trial with Casement, 26 June 1916. He gave information about the gun-running plot. Found not guilty of any crime (Prosecution offered no evidence). Returned to Army service, mentioned in Dispatches by General Allenby. Died in Canada.

Balbriggan: Village just over the border in County Meath. There was a British army camp in Gormanstown about three kilometres from Balbriggan. On September 20th, 1920, Sergeant William Burke of Glenamaddy, Co Galway and his brother Peter (Royal Irish Head Constable) had a fight in a pub with locals. Later that night, they were both shot by IRA volunteer Michael Rock, Commander of the Fingal Brigade. Within an hour, three lorry loads of Black and Tans, Auxiliaries and RIC entered Balbriggan and looted four pubs before burning them down. They then travelled up and down the village shooting at and attacking 49 homes, setting fire and destroying a factory, and grabbed known Irish patriots; these they bashed and tortured. Seamus Lawless was beaten with the butt of a rifle, bayoneted and then shot along with John Gibbons. Their bodies were dumped in the street.

The atrocity drew international attention, debate in Parliament and Press criticism of government policy. Labour's Arthur Henderson called for an independent inquiry, saying British forces seemed to have "a policy of military terrorism, totally opposed to the best traditions of the British people". Chief Secretary for Ireland, Hamar Greenwood said Henderson had been misled by IRA propaganda and he opposed an inquiry because the police and military needed to know the British government and people were fully behind them. The Labour Party established a commission, and an American Commission on Conditions in Ireland was created.

Major George Joseph Ball (1885-1961) Educated at King's College School, Strand, and at King's College, London. [Note: Michael Collins attended King's College School, Strand, but probably a year after Ball. Served as a private in the Irish Guards. Worked for MI5 and MI6, he became acquainted with Basil Thomson.

Kevin Barry (1902-1920): Born Dublin. Family owned a farm in County Carlow and a dairy business in Dublin. Medical student at University College Dublin. Member of the IRB. He was a late addition to the Dublin Brigade squad which planned to ambush a lorry carrying British troops in Dublin. The action was a debacle when a firefight resulted and most Volunteers quickly fled but left Barry behind. He was captured, possibly tortured, tried and hanged.

Robert Barton (1881-1975): Reluctant Treaty signatory and was later supporter of anti-Treaty De Valera. Born into a wealthy Protestant Irish family. Cousin and close friend of Erskine Childers. Educated in England, British Army officer but resigned after Easter 1916 and joined Irish Republican Brotherhood.

Edmund Musgrave Barttelot (1859 –1888): Brutal and deranged. Casement's friend Herbert Ward went with Barttelot into darkest Africa. Barttelot treated the natives savagely and was killed. Joseph Conrad's ivory trader Kurtz (Heart of Darkness) is possibly based upon him.

Alan Bell (1858-1920): Born County Offaly, Central Ireland. Irish Protestant probably involved in conspiracy to smear Parnell using forged letters. Later he investigated funds flowing into Michael Collins' Dáil Loan scheme. He confiscated over £71,000 from Sinn Féin. Magistrate and policeman, probably a member of the British Secret Service, answering to Basil Thomson and 'handler' of John Byrnes/Jameson. His murder was ordered by Michael Collins; he was dragged off a tram – his wife lodged a claim for £10,000 with Dublin Corporation.

Patrick Belton (1884-1945): Irish Nationalist born County Longford. Went to Kings College London about same time as Michael Collins with whom he became friends. Devout Catholic and ant-communist (became very Right-wing and antisemitic). Like Collins, very involved with Irish National Aid Association, the Irish Volunteer Dependants' Fund. De Valera hated him, and vice versa.

Brigadier-General Charles Guinand Blackader (1869-1921): He suppressed colonial conflict in Sudan and Egypt. using courts-martial and internment. Commanded Territorial brigade in Dublin during the Easter Rising of 1916. Presided over a number of the resulting courts-martial, including those of Patrick Pearse, Éamonn Ceannt, Thomas Clarke, Thomas MacDonagh, and Joseph Plunkett. Following the trial of Pearse he is quoted as saying,' I have just done one of the hardest tasks I have ever had to do. I have had to condemn to death one of the finest characters I have ever come across.'

Augustine Birrell (1850-1933): Liberal politician, Chief Secretary for Ireland from 1907 to 1916. Took some responsibility for theft of the Irish Crown Jewels from Dublin Castle. Helped tenant farmers to own their property, and enabled more university education Catholics, but was considered to have failed to take action against the rebels before the Easter Rising. From 1912 Birrell's second wife Eleanor was suffering from a brain tumour, causing her to be mentally ill.

Bishop of Killaloe (1859-1955): **Michael Fogarty,** born County Tipperary. Archbishop 1904-1955. After 1916, protested against the "hideous atrocities" perpetrated by the triumph of British culture on Irish nationalists. Served as vice-president on Maynooth (Catholic university) to the then president and future Archbishop of Melbourne, Daniel Mannix who was known for his nationalist strong sympathies. Opposed conscription being introduced to Ireland. Trustee for the first Dáil loan. Held talks on peace proposals in Dublin with the Archbishop of Perth (Australia), Patrick Clune, promoted by Archbishop Mannix (Melbourne). Criticised De Valera and anti-Treaty propaganda.

Harry Boland (1887-1922) President of the Irish Republican Brotherhood from 1919 to 1920. Very close friend of Michael Collins until 1922 when he opposed the Treaty and eventually fought against Collins in the Irish Civil War. Went to USA as aide to De Valera.

Bonar Law (1858-1923): Canadian born, fiercely pro-Ulster. Leader of the Conservative Party. Chancellor of the Exchequer in David Lloyd George's Coalition Government. Very anti-Home rule and claimed that Ulster Protestants would have the right to go to war against the London Government if Home Rule was imposed because, he argued, Home Rule would itself contravene the constitution.

Pope Benedict XV (1854-1922): In WW1 he was neutral and tried to promote peace but Germany distrusted him. Count Plunkett went to see him in April 1916 telling him about the Uprising and, Plunkett claimed, the Pope blessed the Irish Republic. This was later (in 1933) denied.

Maurice Bonham-Carter (1880-1960): Married Violet Asquith, daughter of Prime Minister Herbert Asquith. Educated at Winchester College (as were the Asquith brothers and Jack White). Principal Private Secretary to the Prime Minister H. H. Asquith, accompanied Asquith to Ireland in 1916 following the Uprising.

Johann von Bernstorff (1862-1939): German ambassador to US, 1904-17. As a child for 11 years lived in England. In Prussian Army for 8 years. Wife was German-American. Financed intelligence and sabotage operations in US, assisted by Captain Franz von Papen, Heinrich Albert and Karl Boy-Ed.

Karl Boy-Ed (1872-1930): Naval attaché at the German Embassy in Washington. He and von Papen (military attaché in US) established an effective spy and sabotage network. Expelled, as was von Papen, from the US in December 1915.

Brendan Bracken (1901-1958): Born Tipperary, Catholic family (he lapsed). Father was a passionate Fenian. Attended Christian Brothers' O'Connell School in North Richmond St (as did numerous children who later became members of Sinn Féin). Misbehaved and sent to Victoria, Australia, aged 14. Teacher at Wolaroi Grammar (Protestant) School, New South Wales. Returned to Ireland 1919 then to England, persistent liar about his background; worked as a journalist. The source of his wealth is unknown. Became a politician, 1929. Confidant of Churchill who insisted that he be a privy councillor (June 1940). Lived in Churchill's home during WW2. Minister of Information. LYSAGHT, C. (1979). Brendan Bracken: The Fantasist Whose Dreams Came True. In: *Brendan Bracken Memorial Lecture* (2001) Brendan Bracken Memorial Lecture. Cambridge: International Society, https://winstonchurchill.org/publications/finest-hour/finest-hour-113/brendan-bracken-the-fantasist-whose-dreams-came-true/. p.13.

Fischer, T. (2002). The rise and rise of a failed jackeroo. *Australian Financial Review*. 15 Feb. https://www.afr.com/politics/the-rise-and-rise-of-a-failed-jackeroo-20020215-k1h5n.

Alice Brady (1898-1914): Shot during the 1913 Dublin Lock-out when she joined a crowd screaming at scabs delivering coal during 1913 strike. Lived in Asylum Yard near Townsend St, close to the Magdalen Laundry (1911 census). Died from tetanus.

John Brennan (Pseudonym of Ms. **Sydney Gifford,** quo vide) (1889-1974): Journalist. Wrote for New York Sun and the Irish World. Youngest of 12 children, sister of Grace, Nellie and Muriel. Father was Catholic and her mother a Protestant. Daughters raised as Protestants. Unlike her parents, she was very radical and joined Sinn Féin. https://bmh.militaryarchives.ie/reels/bmh/BMH.WS0909.pdf#page=2

Ned Broy (1887-1972): Eamon "Ned" Broy. Member of the Dublin Metropolitan Police who worked as a Detective Sergeant in the intelligence branch. Copied sensitive files for IRA. He smuggled Collins into a police building at Great Brunswick Street where Collins obtained details of "G-Men", six of whom were killed by the IRA. Commissioner of the Gardaí 1933 to 1938.

Cathal Brugha (1874-1922) Born Charles Burgess. Protestant father and Catholic mother. He was head of a candle manufacturing company. Non-drinker, non-smoker, did not swear – strongly opposed to women being involved in military activity. Left the Irish Republican Brotherhood after the 1916 Easter Rising, once the Republic had been declared. Sinn Féin member. Severely injured in Easter Rising. He proclaimed the Irish Republic, as Acting President, when De Valera was in USA and made it mandatory for IRA members to swear allegiance to Irish Parliament. Minister of Defence in Provisional Government and often clashed with Michael Collins (Minister of Finance and Director of Intelligence). Worked on plans to kill British Cabinet members. Agreed with De Valera on need for large scale battles with British forces, rather than guerrilla attacks as proposed by Collins. Very anti-Treaty, a committed republican and opposed to Oath of Allegiance to the Crown. Killed in 1922 fighting for anti-Treaty forces. Had six children; wife Caitlín was committed to Irish independence and strongly loyal to Brugha.

John Byrnes/ Jack Jameson (1885-1920): attempted to infiltrate IRA. Almost certainly worked for British Intelligence and was shot dead by Collins men, on Ballymun Road in Glasnevin, 7 March 1920. Born John Charles Byrne, 38, he was from Romford in Essex.

Lord Byron (1788-1824): Poet. Byron joined the Greek War of Independence . He said of John Philpot Curran (Lawyer and father of Sarah Curran, Rober Emmet's lover) 'I have heard that man speak more poetry than I have seen written'.

Edward Carson (1854-1935): Born in Dublin to a rich Protestant family. Lived at 25 Harcourt Street Dublin (later Michael Collins, Minister for Finance, had an office at No. 6). As a young Crown prosecutor, he'd walked alone through a huge mob of angry Irishmen after 3 of them had been shot by police in Mitchelstown. This fool-hardy bravery had been widely reported and not only raised his profile enormously but also resulted in a powerful friendship with the Conservatives' Arthur Balfour, Secretary for Ireland. Following the Mitchelstown Massacre, 'Bloody Balfour' issued instructions that if police with batons failed to control a mob then a detachment with rifles was to use bayonets; if that failed, they could shoot to kill – depending upon the circumstances, of course. The Carson-Balfour alliance was brutally successful in crushing civil disobedience.

Carson had been a barrister acting for a newspaper in a libel case brought by the Cadbury chocolate family; an article had been printed describing how slave labour was used in producing cocoa. Carson lost the case but made his name because Cadbury was awarded only 'contemptuous damages' of one farthing. Another case was where he proved the innocence of a 13-year-old boy, from a Catholic family (Archer-Shee), who had been dismissed from the Royal Naval College after being accused of stealing a postal order (Terence Rattigan based his play *The Winslow Boy* on this.).

Irish unionist politician, Attorney General and First Lord of the Admiralty. Strongly opposed to Home Rule. Friend of F.E. Smith (Lord Birkenhead) until the Anglo-Irish Treaty.

Roger Casement (1864-1916): Human rights campaigner. Born in Dublin, father's family was from Antrim (N.I), mother was Anglican but Casement was baptised Catholic. His grandfather went to Australia. Some of his childhood was spent in London. His mother died when he was 9, his father when he was 13, moved to Northern Ireland. Left school aged 16. He was helped to expose cruelty and exploitation in Africa and South America. He supported, using his own money, Edmund Dene Morel's Congo Reform Association (CRA). Retired from Diplomatic Service in 1913 and tried to persuade N.I. Protestants to support Irish Independence. Asked for troops and munitions from Germany for Irish rebels. Converted to Catholic before being hanged in 1916.

Graham, C. C., & van Dopperen, R. (2016). Roger Casement on Screen: The Background Story on an Historical Film Opportunity, 1915–1916.

Historical Journal of Film, Radio and Television, 36(4), 493–508. https://doi.org/10.1080/01439685.2015.1100386 Casement, R. (1918). The Secret Diplomacy of England.

The Irishman.https://drpatwalsh.com/2017/02/15/the-secret-diplomacy-of-england/ 15/02/2017 Dr. Pat Walsh.

Éamonn Ceannt, Edward Thomas Kent (1881-1916): Galway, the son of James Kent, an officer in the Royal Irish Constabulary. Devout Catholic, he attended the O'Connell Schools on North Richmond Street. Met Patrick Pearse and Eoin MacNeill. He became a fluent Irish, expert player of uileann pipes; socialist; 1907 joined Arthur Griffith's new political party, Sinn Féin. Irish Republican Brotherhood by Seán MacDiarmada . co-opted to the IRB Military Council. Ceannt and 120 men of the 4th Battalion of the Irish Volunteers, who reported for duty, occupied the South Dublin Union, a workhouse/ hospital. Executed by firing squad in Kilmainham Jail on 8 May. His brother William was a colour sergeant-major in the Royal Dublin Fusiliers (British army) stationed in Fermoy, Co. Cork.

Austen Chamberlain (1863-1937): Chancellor of Exchequer under Lloyd George. One of the British group, with Churchill and Lord Birkenhead, negotiating the Irish Treaty. Awarded the Nobel Peace Prize in 1925. Wore a monocle due to poor eyesight (much to Michael Collins amusement).

Sir Robert Chalmers (1858-1838): Following Easter rising of 1916 he became Ireland's under-secretary (senior Civil Servant). Contemptuous of Ireland and Irish people. Refused to allow the Connolly family permission to go to US after 916 Uprising.

Erskine Childers (1870-1922): English-born Irish nationalist. Orphaned, he grew up on aunt and uncle's 15,000 acre Glendalough (County Wicklow) estate. Privately educated and Cambridge. Fought in Boer War. As a young man loyal believer in the British Empire. Wrote the novel *The Riddle of the Sands*. In the British Navy and, later, the Air Force. Wife Molly was a major persuasive influence in him being a believer in Irish Independence. His ship Asgard was used to transport weapons in 1914 for the Irish Nationalists. Attended Treaty talks and continually raised concerns but as he was a Secretary not a Delegate. Arthur Griffith thought he might be a British spy. Knowledgeable in tactics of the Boer guerrillas. Some people thought he had written De Valera's 'Document No.2' (opposition for the Treaty). Fought on the anti-Treaty side but was never trusted due to his English background and his military experience was ignored. The pro-Treaty forces suspected him to be the leader of anti-Treaty forces. Captured and executed 1922.

Molly Childers (1875-1964): American born. Wife of Erskine. Very pro-Independence and a major influence on her husband. She was at the helm of the *Asgard*, 1914, used to transport weapons to Howth.

Eivind Adler Christensen (1890-1930?): Aide/valet and probably homosexual partner of Casement. Involved in the 1914 'Findlay affair' in Christiania (Norway). Used aliases, for example Olaf Olsen. Believed by some people to have been a double agent. Life after 1916 is uncertain.

Winston Churchill (1874-1965): Politician, soldier, journalist. Conservative but joined Liberals (later went back to Conservatives). Agnostic but preferred Protestants to Catholics.

Clan na Gael (1867): Irish republican organization, founded in the United States in late 1900s, aligned with the Irish Republican Brotherhood.

Peadar Clancy (1886-1920): Vice-commandant of the Dublin Brigade, IRA. Member of Collins' "Squad". Took part in in prison escapes; rescued nineteen prisoners from Mountjoy prison and five from Manchester prison. Captured, with Dick McKee, by the Auxiliaries on night before Bloody Sunday; tortured and shot the next day.

Kathleen Clarke (1878-1972): Founder member of Cumann na mBan wife of Tom Clarke and sister of Ned Daly, both of whom were executed after the Rising. She was pregnant when she visited them before they were executed. She had a miscarriage. Helped to set up the Irish National Aid Fund to aid those who had family members killed or imprisoned following the Easter Rising. Worked with Michael Collins to rebuild networks after the Rising. Supported the anti-Treaty IRA. She disliked

Pearse and Casement.

Tom Clarke (1858-1916): Born in England to Irish parents. Father was a sergeant in the British Army and sent to Ireland, where Clarke grew up. Joined the IRB, Irish Republican Brotherhood, when he was 20 and went to USA but returned to UK, with the name "Henry Wilson", on a dynamite mission – arrested and sentenced to life imprisonment. Released after 15 years and went to USA; became a naturalised American citizen. Worked for John Devoy's Clan na Gael (Irish republican organization in USA). Returned to Ireland and bought a newsagent shop (possibly funded by Devoy). Intent on Irish independence rather than socialism. He and MacDiarmada through the Military Committee of the IRB planned for the Uprising. Continually liaised with Devoy in the USA, especially regarding supply of weapons from Germany.

Conor Clune nephew of Archbishop of Perth (Australia) (1893-1920): Not an active member of the Irish Volunteers. Manager of a seed and plant nursery, he was at the Vaughan Hotel (but hadn't registered as a guest) to meet a friend; Collins and his team were upstairs preparing for Bloody Sunday next day. Clune was arrested along with Dick McKee and Peadar Clancy – all these were killed, probably after being tortured, 'attempting to escape' November 1920.

Patrick Joseph Clune Australia's Archbishop of Perth, (1864-1935): Born County Clare. Archbishop in 1913. Strong supporter of WW1 and conscription: Lloyd George trusted him. Shocked by the murder on Bloody Sunday (21 November 1920) of his nephew Conor Clune while in British custody. He met Michael Collins and later Arthur Griffith (acting president of Sinn Féin whilst De Valera was in US) in Mountjoy Jail. The meetings were arranged by Bishop Fogarty of Killaloe. He also met Lloyd George. A temporary truce was negotiated but opposed by Bonar Law and Winston Churchill because they wanted the IRA to surrender their weapons.

Michael Collins (1890-1922): Irish revolutionary, soldier and politician. 1906-15 worked in London. Studied for a short time for Civil Service

Exam at Kings College, London[150]; he joined the Geraldine Hurling Club when he was 17 and was active as a committee member. He spent other leisure time in pubs. He was elected to the London County Board of the Gaelic Athletic Association. In 1909, after meeting Patrick Belton, he joined the IRB and became active in London on its behalf and on direction by Seán MacDiarmada. Through his cousin Nancy O'Brien, he met Susan Killeen with whom he kept in contact for several years but became less close. His brother Pat in Chicago urged him to join him there[151]. He chose instead to go back to Ireland in January 1916.

He was aide de camp to Joseph Plunkett during the Rising. Later, Minister for Finance and Director of Intelligence of the IRA. In 1921 he was one of the five plenipotentiaries that negotiated a Treaty. He secretly provided support for an IRA offensive in Northern Ireland but this was disrupted by the Irish Civil War between Pro and anti-Treaty forces. Some women said that he was arrogant. Engaged to Kitty Kiernan, but never married – almost certainly had girlfriends and adulterous affairs. Various suggestions have been made that he was a virgin, a man that had numerous sexual encounters, and that he was bisexual but no evidence for any of this.

John (Seán) Collins (1878-1965): Born in Cork, elder brother of Michael Collins. Member of Irish Republican Brotherhood. Farmer in Cork, father of 9 (one died aged 2). Elected to the Cork Council in the 1920; wife died in 1921. After their home was burnt down he was arrested, leaving the children homeless and parentless, and jailed for 8 months.

Captain Bowen-Colthurst (1880–1965): Born in Cork. Went to Royal Military Academy and was second in his class. An intense Christian. At Mons in WW1 he refused to retreat and later tried to lead his company in a suicidal attack which had not been authorised. Possibly suffering from post-traumatic stress disorder. During the Easter Rising he was convinced all Irish civilians in Dublin were untrustworthy. He arrested several innocent civilians and had them shot and possibly shot one himself. Tried for murder, he was found guilty but insane and committed to Broadmoor Mental Asylum. After about 18 months he was declared sane and released. He went to Canada with his family and died aged 85. Maume, P. (2009a). Colthurst, John Colthurst Bowen-. In: Dictionary of Irish Biography. Dublin: Royal Irish Academy. https://www.dib.ie/biography/colthurst-john-colthurst-bowen-a1885.

James Connolly (1868-1916): Socialist but had his own philosophy, not antisemitic. Joined British Army but little is known about this. He may have joined the Royal Scots or the King's Liverpool Regiment. Later learnt German in order to read political literature, also Esperanto and some Gaelic. Very strong on equality and rights for women. Regarded Irish Language movements and Literary Societies of little benefit. The US 1910 Census shows him living in the Bronx, occupation 'Journalist'. In US worked as a salesman for insurance companies but became a union activist – he met with Elizabeth Gurley Flynn (American labor leader) and Mary G. Harris Jones ('Mother Jones', "the most dangerous woman in America" Union organizer).

Lillie Connolly (1867-1938): socialist and trade union organiser. Born County Wicklow, Protestant family. Initially domestic servant, later governess to stockbroker's family. Married James, had seven children. Helped him with speeches and writing. Lived in tenements. Family moved to US then back to Belfast. She was distraught when she visited James before his execution; she became a Catholic on 15 August 1916.

Nora Connolly (1892-1981) she was a founding member of the Young Republican Party. Also helped to found the Belfast branch of Cumann na mBan, the women's section of the Irish. She helped courier ammunition and firearms. With nine other Cumann na mBan members she left Ulster to go to Dublin to help the Uprising. Trains were disrupted so they began to walk, arriving after the surrender. After the Uprising she ignored the authorities' prohibition on her travelling and went to the US, using a pseudonym, where she met Seamus O'Brien and later married in Ireland. She wrote a book that was banned in the US. She was on the anti-Treaty side in the Civil War.

Diana Cooper (1892-1996): Possibly in love with the married Raymond

Asquith; she became close friends with both him and his wife, Katherine. Diana and friends were 'wild young things', earning the censure of the older generation and newspapers of the day as they played, flirted, motored, and partied. Raymond's death in WW1 devastated her, followed by the loss of other men in her circle: Edward Horner, Charles Lister, Julian and Billy Grenfell and Shaw-Stewart in the war.

James Craig (1871-1940): Fought in Boer War. Received a £100,000 legacy from his father's will (son of a wealthy Belfast whiskey distiller). One of the main organisers in preparing an armed resistance in Ulster to an all-Ireland parliament; he was created a baronet in 1918. Co-founded the Ulster Unionist Council to in loyalist opposition to Irish Home Rule. He supported Major Frederick Crawford to arm the Ulster Volunteers (UVF). He replaced Edward Carson as leader of the Ulster Unionist Party. Argued for only 6 of the 9 Ulster counties – he did not want Donegal, Cavan and Monaghan which had large numbers of Catholics. Prime Minister of Northern Ireland.

Major Fred Crawford (1861-1952): Began work in Harland and Wolff's shipyard as apprentice, qualified as an engineer. Returned from Australia in 1892. Fought in Boer War. Failed to import 10,000 rifles into Ulster. Founder member of the Ulster Volunteer Force (UVF). In 1914, he arranged to arm the UVF (20,000 rifles and 2,000,000 rounds of ammunition) smuggled from Germany. Members of the UVF were incorporated into the Ulster Special Constabulary and he was appointed commandant of the South Belfast B Specials.

Aleister Crowley (1875-1947): Inherited wealth. A drug user, bisexual. English novelist, occultist, philosopher, political theorist, mountaineer, and painter. May have worked for British Intelligence whilst in the US where he campaigned for the German war effort against Britain. Educated at Trinity College, Cambridge.

Cumann na mBan (1914): "The Women's Council". Objective: advance the cause of Irish liberty, by use of force if needed. Women's paramilitary organisation. Recruits were mainly well-to-do, professional women, with just a few were from the poorer suburbs. Many acted as nurses and messengers during Rising; but some also took part in shooting. Over 70 were arrested afterwards and imprisoned in Kilmainham.

Curragh Camp: The Curragh, in County Kildare about 30 miles SW from Dublin, with a wide expanse of flat land, has historically been a military assembly area. Barracks were built in 1879. The Irish Free State took over the Camp in May 1922. It was then used as an internment camp for 1,300 people on 10 acres. 7 were executed there in December 1922. 3,390 went on Hunger Strike in 1923 and 4 died.

John Curran (1750-1817): Irish barrister. Lord Byron said of Curran, "I have heard that man speak more poetry than I have seen written". Karl Marx described him as the greatest "people's advocate" of the eighteenth century. Curran argued for Catholic emancipation, reform in the Irish Parliament and was defence counsel for United Irishmen facing charges of sedition and treason. He refused to defend Emmet because his daughter, Sarah, was in a romantic relationship with him. He disowned Sarah, who died five years later of tuberculosis. A few days before he died, he burst into tears at the mention of Irish politics.

Sarah Curran (1782-1808): she and Emmet were secretly engaged in 1803. Her father disapproved and she had to live with friends in Cork. 5 years after Emmet was executed she died of tuberculosis; she had wished to be buried in her father's garden in Dublin, beside her sister Gertrude, who had died at the age of twelve, but her father refused to allow it.

Dáil Éireann: Lower House of Irish Parliament.

Emmet Dalton (1898-1978): The 1911 Census has his name spelt Emmet not Emmett. Born in USA. Educated by the Christian Brothers at O'Connell School. Joined the Irish Volunteers but was a British Army Captain, fought at Somme and saw Tom Kettle (nationalist Member of Parliament) die there. April 1919 joined IRA. Agreed with Collins in accepting the Anglo-Irish Treaty. Successful in commanding troops at Four Courts against anti-Treaty forces and in Cork. He travelled with Collins on the day he was killed. Some people, without evidence, suggest that Dalton killed Collins. He was rumoured, again without evidence, to be working for British Intelligence. Disagreed with the execution of anti-Treaty prisoners in the Civil War and resigned.

Ned Daly (1891-1916): Brother of Kathleen Clarke (Tom's wife). He commanded the battalion at the Four Courts. Intense fighting in the Church Street, North King Street and North Brunswick Street area. Aged 25 when executed by firing squad on 4 May 1916.

Mrs **Moya Llewelyn Davies**, nee Mary Elizabeth O'Connor, (1881-1943): . Husband was adviser to Lloyd George. Republican activist in War of Independence; Gaelic enthusiast. Most of her family died after eating contaminated mussels. Raised funds for Casement's legal defence. During the Irish War of Independence she spent some time in Mountjoy prison and Collins sent her flowers There are suspicions she and her husband, who suggested the words for the oath in the Anglo–Irish Treaty, were British agents. She later claimed to be Collins' mistress. She strongly disliked Éamon De Valera. Suspected, by some, as being Michael Collins' obsessive lover. She bought a house in Dublin and allowed him to stay there. Patrick Moylett (1952). Bureau of Military History 1913-21, Statement by Witness 767.

Alexandre Delcommune (1855-1922): Belgian explorer and officer of the *Force Publique* Congolese army, he was ordered to get the local chiefs to accept Belgian sovereignty. He later claimed he disagreed with the brutal techniques used.

John Devoy (1842-1928): He went to Christian Brothers' O'Connell School in Richmond Street, Dublin; joined the Irish Republican Brotherhood (IRB); in 1866 he was jailed for five years with hard labour but exiled to the US in 1870. (So, his planned marriage to Elizabeth Kenny never happened – she eventually married Thomas KilMurray in 1884.) Organised the rescue of Fenian prisoners from Western Australia in 1876. He argued and broke with other Fenians and factions, including (very strongly) with De Valera.

He wrote, July 20, 1916, about Casement "We knew he would meddle in his honest but visionary way to such an extent as to spoil things, but we did not dream that he would ruin everything as he has done. He took no notice whatever of decisions or instructions, but without quarrelling pursued his own dreams." Also, "It is not true that the Germans treated us badly; they did everything we asked, but they were weary of his [Casement's] impracticable dreams and told us to deal directly with them here. He had no more to do with getting that shipload than the man in the moon. The request was made from Dublin, and we transmitted it from here." Schmuhl, R. (2016). Roger Casement and America // Articles // breac // University of Notre Dame. breac.nd.edu.: https://breac.nd.edu/articles/roger-casement-and-america/.

Éamon De Valera (1882-1975): Born in USA. Father was a Spanish artist. Raised by his Irish grandmother, Elizabeth Coll. Teacher of Mathematics, but he had considered being a priest. He was Commandant at Boland's Mill during the 1916 Easter Rising; After 1922 he became the political leader of anti-Treaty Sinn Féin. With Childers he created 'Document Number 2' and urged that it be used instead of the Anglo-Irish Treaty – the Document was broadly disliked by almost everyone. He opposed an oath to the Crown but later signed a document which included one. Pulju, A. (2009). De Valera Performs the Oath: Word, Voice, Book, and Act. In: Crossroads: Performance Studies and Irish Culture. London: Palgrave Macmillan, pp.129–130.

Thomas Dickson (1885-1916): Convicted fraudster. Produced a periodical The Eye Opener which was pornographic, anti-Semitic and libellous. He is said to have told lies about businessman Joseph Issacs and playwright Joseph Edelstein. He was conservative and pro-Home Rule.

Lieutenant William Leonard Price Dobbin (1897-1918): Born in 1897 at Maldon, Victoria (Australia) but grew up in Belfast. Commissioned in June 1915 as a Lieutenant in the Royal Irish Rifles and assigned to the 3rd Battalion. He was on duty, aged 18, in Dublin during the Easter Uprising. Transferred to the 2nd Battalion RIR and deployed to France, he was brought back to Dublin to testify at a Royal Commission into the actions during the Uprising. On 1st January 1918, he was awarded the Military Cross (MC) for bravery; killed in action, aged just 21 years, on

21st March 1918, during the second battle of the Somme at Contescourt.

Mrs. Seán O'Donovan (nee Kathleen Boland) (1889-1954): Sister of Harry Bolland. The family was strongly Irish Nationalist. She hid some of the Russian crown jewels, collateral against a loan organised by Harry to the new Russian government, at the family home. The jewels were handed to the Irish Government in 1938. "the original loan of $20,000 was repaid, and the collateral returned to the Soviets. The transaction was completed on 13 September 1949. "

O'Keeffe, H. (2020). How Russian crown jewels went from the Romanovs to Harry Boland. *RTE.ie*. doi:urn:epic:1115356.

D.O.R.A. Defence of the Realm Act. When WW1 began, emergency legislation was enacted without debate. It allowed the government to exercise a wide range of powers to ensure the security of the nation, including prohibition, rationing, the introduction of British Summer Time, widening of police powers, ban meetings, search premises for anti-war publication and prosecute anyone who was deemed to be helping the enemy.

Joseph Donnelly:Nellie Gifford's husband. After 1916 Nellie lectured throughout America. While there she married Joseph Donnelly, of Omagh, County Tyrone in 1918. In 1921 she and their year-old daughter Maeve left him to return to Ireland

Nora Dryhurst (1856-1930): Irish writer, activist. Friend of the Gifford sisters. Attended the International Anarchist School set up in Fitzroy Square in London by Louise Michel (Anarchist). A police raid on the school uncovered explosives in the cellar probably put there by Auguste Coulon, an agent working for Special Branch. Coulon was later responsible for entrapping anarchists in Walsall.

Reginald Dunne (1898-1922) (the spelling of his name varies): Born London. Battalion Commandant of the London Battalion, IRA. Fought for British Army in WW1. He and Joseph O'Sullivan killed Sir Henry Wilson, June 1922 – it is unknown whether it was their own idea or on the orders of Collins or orders of anti-Treaty leaders who were besieged in the Four Courts. Dunne said 'The same principles for which we shed our blood on the battle-field of Europe led us to commit the act we are charged with.' Hanged.

George Duffy (1882-1951): Born Cheshire, England. solicitor and practised in London. He defended Sir Roger Casement at his trial . 1918 elected as a Sinn Féin MP. Attended Paris Peace Conference on Ireland's behalf but failed to achieve anything and declared *persona non grata.* He protested against signing the Treaty but did so reluctantly, becoming the last person to sign. Friend of Erskine Childers.

Eamonn Duggan (1878-1936): Born Armagh. Solicitor. Fought at North Dublin Union during Uprising. IRA director of intelligence 1918–1920. In Mountjoy jail with Arthur Griffith (qv) where they and British civil servant Alfred Cope (qv) had talks that would eventually lead to the truce and Treaty. With De Valera (qv), in London, he met with Lloyd George in July 1921. He was signatory of the Treaty and persuaded Barton to also sign.

Robert Emmet (1778-1803): From a wealthy, Protestant, Dublin family. Irish Republican, orator and rebel leader. Formed the United Irish organisation and tried to start a rising in Ireland with French help. When gunpowder in their Dublin store was accidentally detonated, Emmet issued a Proclamation and the rebels decided to storm Dublin Castle but their numbers were too few. Emmet escaped but then tried to contact his fiancée Sarah Cullen. He was tried and sentenced to death. His speech from the dock is often remembered. Percy Bysshe Shelley wrote a poem about him. For a few years his memory was derided but then Fenians and Partick Pearse honoured him and poems and plays recall his actions.

Joseph Edelstein (1886-1939): Born Portobello, Dublin; supporter of home rule, pro-suffragist. Secretary of the Judaeo-Irish home rule association. Wrote newspaper articles on Jewish faith and customs, and in the 1930s he worked on behalf of Jewish refugees. May have suffered a mental illness.

At the inquiry into murders committed by Captain John Bowen-

Colthurst (q.v.), Edelstein was accused of collaborating with Councillor J. J. Kelly in relation to the scandal sheet, The Eye-Opener. He was also accused of giving false information to the authorities about the use of Kelly's premises by rebels, leading to the arrest of two men, Dickson and McIntyre, who were found there during a raid and were subsequently murdered by Bowen-Colthurst. Edelstein denied these accusations and insisted on giving evidence in rebuttal; he said his life had been threatened as a result of the allegations and that his only contact with the military during Easter week had been when he tried to arrange safe passage of bread to the civilian population.

Joseph Edelstein, (ed.), Echo of Irish rebellion 1916 – verbatim report of the proceedings before the royal commission – vindication of Mr Joseph Edelstein, n.d. [1933]; Louis Hyman, The Jews of Ireland (1972)

Four Courts: Large complex. Originally housed four courts of justice. Easter Rising: Ned Daly's battalion fought here in 1916. On 14 April 1922, the complex was occupied by anti-Treaty forces, with Rory O'Connor in charge. On 28 June the new National Army commanded by Dalton attacked. Two days later, on the day of surrender the Irish Public Record Office was obliterated in a huge explosion. Some of those present said that the archive was used to store ammunition, and the explosion was caused by accidental detonation. (Comment: the amount of 'ammunition' would been huge and the fact that Rory O'Connor had a fascination for explosives suggests an element of intention. Nobody was injured implying that people knew the explosion was going to happen.)

Mansfeldt Findlay (1861-1932): British diplomat in Oslo ('Christiania'), Norway. In October 1914, details of what happened in differ – Casement says that his valet Christensen was taken to the British legation and that Findlay offered him a reward if Casement was "knocked on the head". However, British security services disagree. They suggest that Christensen went to the Legation with a plan to betray Casement, was given a small amount of money, and was offered a large amount for help leading to Casement's capture. Casement made a formal complaint to the UK government.

Sir Norman Fenwick Warren Fisher (1879-1948): British civil servant. Permanent Secretary to the Treasury and Head of the Home Civil Service; some say he was one of the most influential British civil servants of his generation. He investigated the efficiency and effectiveness of Dublin Castle's administration, reported major failings, and made many changes in personnel and processes. He was critical of the strongly Unionist and anti-Catholic attitudes (Ronan Fanning, Fatal Path, pp. 228-229). He promoted Alfred Cope (q.v.) who liaised with Michael Collins and played a major role in the Treaty process. (James Mackay, Michael Collins – A Life, pp. 202-203). Educated at Winchester College.

O'Halpin, E. (1981). Sir Warren Fisher and the Coalition, 1919–1922. The Historical Journal, 24(4), pp.907–927. doi:https://doi.org/10.1017/s0018246x00008268.

The Friends of Irish Freedom 1916: Created in US to 'encourage and assist any movement that will tend to bring about the National Independence of Ireland'. Supported the Uprising and raised $350,000 to assist dependents of those who fought. In the Irish War of Independence, the Friends of Irish Freedom raised over $5,000,000 in Dáil loans for the newly declared Irish Republic through the promotion of Bond Certificates. De Valera founded a rival organisation-the American Association for the Recognition of the Irish Republic and the result was that most of the five million were returned to the original donors.

Field Marshal **John Denton Pinkstone French** (1852-1925): Born in Kent but always regarded himself as "Irish". Chief of the Imperial General Staff (CIGS) – resigned over the Curragh Incident/Mutiny. May 1915 he leaked information about shell shortages to Lord Northcliffe (and PM Asquith resigned shortly after). Became Lord Lieutenant of Ireland in 1918.

Moreton Frewen (1853-1924): Entrepreneur and writer on monetary reform, Member of Parliament. Gambled and lost a fortune on a two-horse race; went to US and founded a huge cattle ranch in Wyoming but lost it due to frost. Had homes in London and 3,000 acres at Innishannon in County Cork. Opposed Home rule. Father of Clare Sheridan.

Ruby Frewen (1881-1966):Born Kensington, London. Married Edward Carson 1914 when she was 33 and he was 60.

Stephen Frewen (1857-1933): Trinity College Cambridge. Long military career. 16th Queen's Lancers in 1878. Aide-de-Camp to the Inspector-General of Cavalry in Ireland, 1888-1890. Boer War. JP for Galway. Father of Ruby who married Edward Carson. Brother of Moreton Frewen.

Frongoch Concentration Camp (1914): Merionethshire, North Wales. German POWs held there until May. In June, Irish rebels arrived. They claimed to be POWs, the British called them detainees. Most of the 2,000 had not been tried in court. About 500 had been grabbed off the street and had not actually been involved in the Uprising. It came to be known as The Republican University because the prisoners spent time discussing Irish Independence. After attempts to conscript inmates failed they were all released (Dec. 1916) mainly to pacify world opinion when Lloyd George became P.M.,

https://webbs.substack.com/p/britains-first-concentration-camp

Cardinal Gaspari (1852-1934): the Cardinal Secretary of State under Pope Benedict XV. The Secretariat of State performs all the political and diplomatic functions of the Holy See and the Vatican City State. The secretary of state is sometimes described as the prime minister of the Holy See.

Tommy Gay (1884-1953): Controlled the main spy network (e.g. Neligan, Broy and Joe Kavanagh, policemen at the Castle) for Michael Collins. Librarian at Capel Street Library in Dublin.

Ghadar Party: political movement founded by expatriate Indians in the western United States and Canada. Formed in 1913 allied with Germany, to oppose British imperial rule in India.

Grace Gifford/ Plunkett (1888-1955): Born Dublin. Wealthy family. Catholic father and Protestant mother, both Unionists. Raised as Protestant. Went to Slade School of Fine Art in London (1907), Cartoonist for many activist journals including Irish Review (of which Joseph Plunkett was an editor). Notice of engagement to Joseph Plunkett appeared in Irish Life magazine (11 Feb. 1916). Short time later she converted to Catholicism. After the Rising, for a short time, she lived in the Plunkett family home where, her sister-in-law Geraldine claimed, she suffered a miscarriage (Grace and the Plunkett family were not on good terms). anti-Treaty during Civil War. Had low income until she got a pension in 1932. In 1934 she settled her claim through her husband's will.

Nellie Gifford (1880-1971): Born Dublin. Wealthy family. Catholic father and Protestant mother, both Unionists. Raised as Protestant and remained a Protestant. Active in the Dublin lockout and the Irish Citizen Army and in Uprising.

Muriel Gifford (married Thomas MacDonagh) (1884-1917): Born Dublin. Wealthy family. Catholic father and Protestant mother, both Unionists. Raised as Protestant. Mother forced her to leave her home. Nurse. Wife of Thomas (executed 1916), sister of Grace). Mother of Donagh/Don and Barbara (Bairbre/Babilly). Always in poor health (rheumatic fever and phlebitis). Died when swimming, in attempt to place an Irish flag on an island.

Sydney Gifford (1889-1974): Born Dublin. Wealthy family. Catholic father and Protestant mother, both Unionists. Raised as Protestant. Journalist using the pseudonym John Brennan. Later, a radio broadcaster.

Laurence Ginnell (1852-1923): Irish nationalist politician, lawyer and Member of Parliament (Irish Parliamentary Party, IPP) became an Independent after questioning IPP accounts. After the Uprising he accused Prime Minister H. H. Asquith, of "Murder". At the 1918 general election he was elected for Sinn Féin. He opposed the Anglo-Irish Treaty.

David Lloyd George (1863-1945): Liberal Chancellor. His welfare reforms were blocked by a Conservative House of Lords – the Parliament Act 1911 removed this blocking ability. Prime Minister from 1916 to 1922, latterly in coalition with Conservatives.

William Gladstone (1809-1898): Began as a Tory then became a Liberal and was Chancellor of the Exchequer four times. Prime Minister for 12 years. Persistent supporter of Home Rule.

John McGoey (1883-1924): Born in Scotland, Irish parents. Went to

USA – businessman and Fenian supporter Joseph McGarrity sends him to Casement in Germany, as support, where he joins the Irish Brigade. Casement sends him to Ireland with a message that any Uprising will fail but McGoey disappears after leaving Germany.

General Hubert Gough (1870-1963): Fought at Ladysmith where he met George White (father of Jack White, founder of Irish Citizen Army). Favoured by Commander-in-Chief of the British Expeditionary Force on the Western Front. In 1907 he was the youngest lieutenant-colonel in the Army. The main Army 'mutineer' in the Curragh Mutiny.

Sir Edward Grey (1862-1933): British Foreign Secretary. Agreed with exclusion of Ulster. Frustrated with Ireland, eventually wanting British troops simply pulled out and the Irish left to deal with their problems. His eyesight became worse until he was almost blind.

Alice Stopford Green (1847-1929): Born County Meath, near Dublin. Close friend of Casement and supported his Congo Reform movement. Spoke at same meeting as him and Jack White, to Protestants about Home Rule. Supported the pro-Treaty side.

Hamar Greenwood (1870-1948): Born in Canada. Liberal imperialist, supporter of Lloyd George. Chief secretary for Ireland, 1920-1922. He did not start Irish coercive policy but was seen to be an apologist, dismissing accusations of misconduct by Ulster police and Black and Tans – refusing to investigate or punish lest morale suffered. Teetotal; took a minor part in Treaty talks.

Arthur Maundy Gregory (1877-1941) Blackmailed senior people that were homosexual. Worked for Basil Thomson, the head of Special Branch. Socialist MP Victor Grayson named Gregory as placing the 'black' diaries in Casement's lodgings. Grayson disappeared after entering Gregory's one night in 1920.

Sheila Grenan (1883-1972): Irish nationalist, republican, suffragette, socialist and member of Cumann na mBan; one of the last to leave the GPO in 1916. Elizabeth O'Farrell's partner; the two women are buried together in Glasnevin Cemetery, and their gravestone reads "... And her faithful comrade and lifelong friend Sheila [Julia] Grenan". All their adult life was spent together, the two girls being childhood friends and growing up together. They were, it seems obvious, in love.

Edward Grigg (1879-1955): Military secretary to Edward, Prince of Wales from 1919 to 1920, then became private secretary to Prime Minister David Lloyd George. He ensured that the King's Speech to Northern Ireland Parliament had no involvement from Craig, that it laid the groundwork for Treaty negotiations and he played a major part in the Lloyd George – De Valera communications. Educated at Winchester College.

Arthur Griffith (1871-1922): Born Dublin. His great-great-grandfather was Welsh. Irish writer, newspaper editor and politician who founded the political party Sinn Féin. He opposed Larkin and socialism. Once argued that Ireland should become a separate kingdom alongside Great Britain, the two sharing a monarch but separate governments, He led the Irish delegation at the 1921 Treaty negotiations. Died at the age of 51, ten days before Michael Collins.

Abraham Gudansky (1873-1945): cantor in the Lennox Street synagogue, who is said to have helped Michael Collins hide from the Black and Tans; wrote to John MacDonagh praising the positive depiction of the Jewish Lord Mayor in his play The Irish Jew. Earls, M. (2024). The Irish Jew. *Dublin Review of Books*. https://drb.ie/the-irish-jew/.

Frank Hall (1876-1964) Born in County Down. Educated at Harrow and joined the Army in 1895. Retired in 1911 – Edward Carson used him to reorganise the Ulster Clubs. Military Secretary of the UVF. MI5 Officer. With Reginald Hall and Basil Thompson, interrogated Casement.

Admiral **Reginald 'Blinker' Hall** (1870-1943): He and Sir Alfred Ewing were responsible for the establishment of the Royal Navy's codebreaking operation, Room 40, which decoded the Zimmermann telegram. Room 40 intercepted at least thirty-two messages from the US concerning German support for the Nationalist movement. He was called "Blinker" because one of his eyes blinked furiously. His daughter thought this was due to childhood malnutrition.

May have suffered from developmental coordination disorder (dyspraxia) resulting in clumsiness, poor time management, and dyslexia.

Involved in the Zimmerman Telegram incident (secret diplomatic communication issued from the German Foreign Office in January 1917 that proposed a military contract between the German Empire and Mexico) and in 1924 Hall was suspected of leaking the Zinoviev letter from Russia (forged document published by the British Dáily Mail) just before an election. It is thought that Arthur Maundy Gregory, had forged the letter and that Major George Joseph Ball passed it to Hall who hated Bolsheviks and became a Conservative MP.

Simkin, J. (1997b). *Reginald Hall*. Spartacus Educational. https://spartacus-educational.com/SShallW.htm [Accessed 2 Nov. 2024].

Captain Jocelyn Hardy (1894-1958): Born London but his father was from County Down. Hardy was a war hero (DSO, MC and bar) and had been severely injured in France, having a leg amputated. Ruthless and effective British intelligence officer, interrogating prisoners in Dublin Castle. Worked with Captain William Lorraine King, MC who was cleared of executing two IRA members. Hardy was suspected of murdering Conor Clune and IRA members Dick McKee and Peadar Clancy shortly after 'Bloody Sunday' (Hardy was on the Fenian list to be killed).

Anna (1829-1922) and Thomas **Haslam** (1826-1917): They shared a belief in equality for men and women and he supported Anna's campaigns. He wrote about prostitution, birth control and women's suffrage.

Fred Henderson (1867-1957): English socialist writer, poet and journalist, and a Labour Party politician. Sentenced to four months imprisonment for incitement to riot after groups of unemployed workers looted food shops.

Commandant Leo Henderson (1894?): In Civil War he was responsible for anti-Treaty IRA units stealing vehicles. Captured by Frank Thornton (Pro-Treaty) – in response to this General JJ 'Ginger' O'Connell was captured and held at the Four Courts garrison.

Sylvia Henley (1882-1980): She married Colonel Anthony Morton Henley in 1906; her sister Venetia became friends, possibly lesbian relationship, with Violet daughter of Prime Minister H.H. Asquith. Asquith was besotted with Venetia. When Venetia married, Sylvia Henley became her replacement. She told her husband she was doing her "patriotic duty".

Seán Heuston (1891-1916): Executed aged 25. Commanded 25 rebels in the Mendicity Institution (Charity for the poor); for 3 days they prevent 350 British troops going to the Four Courts.

Bulmer Hobson (1883-1969): Born Belfast, Quaker family; great friends with Casement and insisted that Casement was not gay. Writer. Member of the IRB supreme council. With Constance Markievicz he created a republican boy scout movement, Fianna Éireann. He supported Redmond, and thus clashed with Tom Clarke, and opposed the Rising preferring guerrilla warfare. He urged Eoin MacNeill to stop the Rising and was thereafter shunned by the other rebels.

Kathleen Ni Houlihan: Used in literature to represent Ireland as a personified woman. The figure of Kathleen Ni Houlihan has also been invoked in nationalist Irish politic. Also "Shan Van Vocht"), the Poor Old Woman needing the help of young Irish men willing to fight and die to free Ireland, usually resulting in them becoming martyrs. Roger Casement (q.v.) told a Catholic priest that he was resolved to die in the religion of Kathleen O'Houlihan. Cronin, J. (1951). *BUREAU OF MILITARY HISTORY,1913-21.* https://bmh.militaryarchives.ie/reels/bmh/BMH.WS0588.pdf.

Ho Chi Minh, Nguyễn Ái Quốc, (1890-1969): Vietnamese communist revolutionary; worked as either a chef or dishwasher in London, pastry chef on cross-Channel ferry; as a member of The Group of Vietnamese Patriots in Paris he sought to have an influence at the Versailles peace talks. When told in 1920 of hunger striker Terence MacSwiney's death, he was said to have burst into tears saying "a country with a citizen like this will never surrender".

Dwyer, R. (2019). *Death of MacSwiney had enormous significance as prisoners hunger strike drew global coverage*. Irish Examiner. https://www.irishexaminer.com/lifestyle/arid-30943591.html [Accessed 9 Dec. 2024].

Irish Citizen Army (ICA) Founded in 1913 by James Larkin, James Connolly and Jack White as a workers militia to defend the union movement from attacks by the police during the 1913 Lockout. About 220 members took part in the 1916 rebellion at the General Post Office (GPO), St Stephen's Green, City Hall. During Civil War ICA was anti-Treaty

Irish Boundary Commission: created 1924 to settle the border between Northern Ireland and the Irish Free State. In 1921 Lloyd George had caused the Irish delegates at the Treaty negotiations to believe that a Commission would adjust the border so that Catholic majorities would come under Dublin's control. Northern government refused to cooperate in 1924, so the British government chose a Belfast newspaper editor to represent Northern Irish interests. Irish nationalists expected a significant transfer of land to the Free State, because most border areas had Catholic majorities. But recommendations were for relatively small transfers, and in both directions. In fact no changes were made, the existing border was confirmed by W. T. Cosgrave for the Free State, Sir James Craig for Northern Ireland, and Stanley Baldwin. Outstanding financial disagreements (the sum due under the Imperial debt had not yet been fixed, but was estimated at £5–19 million annually) would be wiped.

Irish Republican Brotherhood (1858-1924):
A secret organisation aimed create an "independent democratic republic" in Ireland. Opposed by Catholic Church.

Irish Parliamentary Party IPP (1874-1922): objectives were legislative independence for Ireland and land reform. 'Home Rule'. Sinn Féin ran in the 1918 election; IPP's representation fell from over 70 seats to just 6.

Irish Republican Army (IRA) the "old IRA", was raised in 1917 from members of the Irish Volunteers and the Irish Citizen Army. Became the official army of the first Irish Parliament, Dáil Éireann. In later years it split into factions.

Irish Volunteers (1913): formed in response to the formation of its Irish unionist/loyalist counterpart the Ulster Volunteers. Members were from Ancient Order of Hibernians, Sinn Féin and the Irish Republican Brotherhood. 200,000 members but these split when Redmond urged them to fight in WW1. A small number refused and stayed as Irish Volunteers. Their Leader Eoin MacNeill said there would be armed resistance only if the Dublin Castle administration started repression against Irish nationalist movements, or if they tried to introduce conscription in Ireland.

Alfred Lewis Jones (1845-1909): Started as a ship's apprentice, became a clerk in the firm of Fletcher and Parr, shipping agents, and became manager. Joined the firm of Elder Dempster, shipping and general trade of the West African coast. Ship owner and chairman of the Bank of British West Africa. Known as the 'uncrowned King of West Africa. Roger Casement worked for same firm, Elder Dempster.

Thomas /Tom Jones (1870-1955): His working-class family was Welsh speaking. British civil servant and educationalist, once described as "one of the six most important men in Europe", and "keeper of a thousand secrets". First-class honours in economics from the University of Glasgow in 1901. Deputy Secretary to the Cabinet under four Prime Ministers including David Lloyd George.

Lev Kamenev (1883-1936): leading figure in the early Soviet government, one of Lenin's close associates. He and Zinoviev aligned with Trotsky against Stalin. Met Clare Sheridan (q.v.)

Tom Kehoe (1899-1924): Very tall and known as 'Long Tom'. Fought at Jacob's Factory. As one of "The Twelve Apostles", involved in Bloody Sunday. He and Ben Byrne shot James "Shankers" Ryan, who enabled the capture of O/C Dublin Brigade, Dick McKee and his Deputy, Peadar Clancy, following Bloody Sunday. He was injured in the fire at the

Custom House in 1921, the largest action in Dublin by rebels since 1916, and died aged 23.

James Kelly (1871-1954): Dublin Corporation Alderman, a Justice of the Peace and had been High Sheriff of Dublin. Owned a tobacconist shop on the corner of Camden Street and Harrington Street. A Nationalist but not a member of either Sinn Féin or the Irish Volunteers. May or may not have been mistaken for another person also named Kelly – he was arrested shortly after Captain Bowen-Colthurst took a squad of troops to his shop (Kelly was not present) ransacked it and arrested two journalists. He was imprisoned, beaten, held for two weeks then released.

Elizabeth Kempson -McAlerney (1897 – 1996): Trade union activist; aged 16, during the Dublin lock-out, she was arrested and imprisoned for two weeks. Joined the Irish Citizen Army. At St Stephens Green one of the rebels attempted to leave – she pointed a revolver at him and told him no one was leaving. Went to the US after the 1916 Easter Rising. She died on January 21, 1996, at 99 years of age in Washington state, Seattle, where she had married a fellow Irishman, Matt McAlerney. They had seven children, 34 grandchildren, and 116 great-grandchildren.

John Kenny (1847-1924): Associate of John Devoy in US, with whom he assisted six Irish prisoners to escape from jail in Fremantle, Western Australia. Leader of Clan-na-Gael – he swore in Thomas Clarke, involving him in a London bombing campaign. Kenny worked closely with the IRB leaders in Dublin and tried to arrange for weapons from Germany.

Tom Kettle (1880-1916): Irish economist, journalist, barrister, writer, war poet, soldier and Home Rule politician. Reformed alcoholic. Member of the Irish Parliamentary Party. Irish nationalist. A classmate of James Joyce and Francis Sheehy-Skeffington, a friend Patrick Pearse. Joined the Irish Volunteers in 1913 and, serving alongside Emmet Dalton, fought with Dublin Fusiliers in France where he died. His 'wife and comrade', Mary Sheehy Kettle, was the sister of Hanna Sheehy-Skeffington.

Kitty (Kathleen) Kiernan (1892-1945): Granard County Longford

(1901 Census). The Greville Arms and Kiernan's store in Granard burnt out by the Tans on 3rd November 1920 (RIC inspector Kelleher killed 31 Oct). Engaged to be married to Michael Collins.

Susan Killeen (1891-1950):15 Vicarage Gate, Kensington, London, Born Molosky, County Clare. Post Office Clerk (1911 Census). One of Michael Collins (maybe his first) girlfriends. Met him in London.

Captain Franz Dagobert Johannes von Rintelen (1878-1949): Agent for German Imperial Navy Intelligence wing of which operated in WW1 covertly in the then-neutral United States. He operated under German Foreign Office cover, receiving funds and orders directly from the Admiralty in Berlin. His job was to prevent American corporations from sending military supplies to the Allies, using sabotage if need be.

James Larkin (1874-1947): Born Liverpool, Irish (Ulster) parents. Irish republican, revolutionary socialist and trade union leader. Like his ally (although later they had disagreements) James Connolly, he did not steal gamble, drink, or smoke. Focussed on the unskilled labour force as opposed to tradesmen. Tall with very big hands, inspiring orator, promoted social equality and justice. Clashed with other socialists and unionists. Went to the US and opposed American entry to World War I, acclaimed the Russian revolution and was imprisoned for almost three years. John Devoy in US turned against him and even suspected Larkin of being a British agent. Larkin returned to Ireland; opponent of the Free State.

Lady Lavery (1880-1935): Born in Chicago, Irish background. Rumoured to have had affairs with Michael Collins and Kevin O'Higgins (Minister for Justice from 1922 to 1927). She and her husband lent their house in South Kensington, London, to the Irish delegation during negotiations for the Anglo-Irish Treaty in 1921. Famed for her beauty, her face was on Irish bank notes for many years.

Captain Perceval Lea-Wilson (1877-1920): Born in Kensington London; Royal Irish Regiment. After the Uprising, during which he mistreated prisoners, he was Wexford police district inspector. In June 1920,

Collins sent Liam Tobin and Frank Thornton to meet with Joe McMahon, Michael McGrath and Michael Sinnott. Wearing civilian clothes, Lea-Wilson bought a newspaper as normal. The IRA men pretended to be repairing a car and shot him 7 times.
(Educated at Winchester College.)
Lady Londonderry (1856-1919): Theresa Susey Helen Vane-Tempest-Stewart,Marchioness of Londonderry. Born Staffordshire. "Queen of Toryism". She organised a petition of 20,000 women from Ulster to oppose the 1893 Home Rule and created the Ulster Women's Unionist Council. Very forceful and persuasive, she was not faithful to her husband.
Cardinal Logue (1840-1924) Archbishop of Armagh, Primate of All Ireland. Loyal to Britain in WW1. Told priests to obey legitimate authority but opposed conscription. Supported the Treaty.
General Lowe (1861-1944): OIC British Forces in Dublin in 1916. He ordered the Sherwood Foresters to continue frontal advance on Mount Street Bridge with a high cost in casualties.
Arthur Lynch (1861-1934): Born Victoria, Australia. Recruited an Irish brigade and fought for the Boers. (cf. Roger Casement) Elected as an Irish MP but then arrested for treason – found guilty and sentenced to be hanged. This was immediately commuted to a life sentence, and a year later he was released. Volunteered for British Army in WW1. Became a doctor in London.
Józef Teodor Konrad Korzeniowski, (1857-1924): **Joseph Conrad,** author. Born Ukraine. Became a British subject. Met Roger Casement in Africa in 1890. Novels include Heart of Darkness (1899), Lord Jim, Nostromo. Gave no support to Casement during his trial and refused to be involved in calls for clemency.
Dr. Charles MacAulcy (1887-1956): Born Belfast. Surgeon in Dublin and friend of Eoin MacNeill and Pearse. Treated Joseph Plunkett and Irish rebels.
Seán MacDiarmada (1883-1916): Born County Leitrim. Joined Sinn Féin, the Irish Republican Brotherhood (IRB), the Ancient Order of

Hibernians, Irish Volunteers. Afflicted by polio. With Clarke, he supported the 1913 Lockout strike and planned the Uprising. Executed aged 33.

John MacDonagh (1879-1961): Nationalist, brother of the 1916 patriot Thomas MacDonagh. Was with his brother in Jacob's factory in 1916. Wrote script for DW Griffith's The Fugitive (1910). Manager of The Irish Theatre Company; strong dislike for plays about Celtic past and peasant life. Wrote songs including 'Did Santa Claus come from Ireland?' Filmed Collins issuing republican loan bonds. He wrote The Irish Jew, a comedy play. Rabbi Abraham Gudansky (who was said to have helped Collins escape from Black and Tans) wrote to him praising the play.

Joseph MacDonagh (1883-1922): Born County Tipperary, brother of Thomas (executed) and John. Sinn Féin MP. Organised the boycott of Belfast goods in 1920. Strong debater, he opposed the Anglo-Irish Treaty. Died whilst refusing medical treatment in prison during Civil War.

Muriel MacDonagh: See Muriel Gifford

Thomas MacDonagh (1878-1916): Born County Tipperary. Teacher. Husband of Muriel (sister of Grace Gifford). Friend of Eoin MacNeill and Patrick Pearse. Taught Gaelic to Joseph Plunkett. Joined the Irish Volunteers, deputy commandant of the Dublin Brigade during Uprising, at Jacob's Biscuit Factory. Executed 1916.

Joe McGarrity (1874-1940): Born Tyrone; went to Philadelphia when 18; borrowed to buy pub and joined Clan na Gael. Raised $20,000 for the Irish Volunteers; funded purchase of arms brought into Howth. Involved in German assistance to Ireland during WW1. Opposed to Partition. Supported De Valera against Devoy; anti-Treaty. Organised 495 Thomson sub-machine guns to Ireland (but they were seized in the US).

Eoin MacNeill (1867-1945): Gaelic revivalist, nationalist. Born County Antrim, BA degree in economics. Helped formed the Irish Volunteers. Opposed armed rebellion, but initially agreed to 1916 Uprising; tried to cancel the Uprising when he learnt Casement had failed to bring weapons. Interned after the Uprising. Pro-Treaty.

General Macready (1862-1946): In 1910 responsible for army discipline and the use of troops in aid of the civil power. Supportive of the right to strike and favoured Irish home rule. Threatened to resign if the UVF was recognised. Politically astute – refused to deploy British forces against the republican-occupied Four Courts.

Terence MacSwiney (1879-1920): Writer and poet. Sinn Féin Lord Mayor of Cork; guilty of sedition and jailed in Brixton Prison. Died after 74 days on hunger strike.

Archbishop **Daniel Mannix** (1864-1963): Born in Cork. the Archbishop of Melbourne for 46 years. Strong supporter of De Valera and vocal critic of British Government. He campaigned against conscription in Australia. In 1921, British security forces refused him entry into Ireland.

" ... the campaign of armed resistance and civil war which the Carsonites had been allowed to preach and prepare for within the past few years. Their leader, instead of being sent into prison, was taken into the British Cabinet." 29.4.16 reported Sydney Morning Herald, 1.5.1916.

Constance Markievicz (1868-1927): Socialist. Born Buckingham Gate Westminster. Strongly republican. Formed Na Fianna Éireann (Soldiers of Ireland), in which young boys were trained to be nationalist soldiers, a republican organization based on the Boy Scouts. Sentenced to be executed but commuted. anti-Treaty. When elected to the UK Parliament she refused to swear allegiance to the King.

Ludwig Martens (1875-1948) Head of Russian Soviet Government Bureau in New York. Julius Hammer worked for him and used illegal sales of smuggled diamonds through the Allied Drug company to provide funds for Soviets. Soviet contracts with American companies were worth more than $300 million by May 1920.

Michael Mallin (1874-1916): Born Dublin. In British Army for 7 years. Irish republican, Socialist and devout Catholic. second-in-command of the Irish Citizen Army under James Connolly. OIC at St Stephen's Green in the Uprising. He faced a court martial; no jury in the court, and no independent observers or members of the public were permitted to attend;

he was executed. Some documentation tries to discredit Mallin by asserting that he claimed Countess Markievicz was senior to him.

Tomas Masaryk (1850-1937): A Czechoslovak statesman, political activist; first president of Czechoslovakia. In exile in 1914, he began organizing Czechs and Slovaks outside Austria-Hungary. He could be considered a parallel figure to Casement in that he formed the Czechoslovak Legion in Russia as a fighting force for the Allies in World War I, using prisoners of war that had been conscripted into the Austria-Hungary army and captured by Russia. He lectured at the School of Slavonic and East European Studies (founded by Robert Seton-Watson in 1915, as a department of King's College, arguing that on both moral and practical grounds the United Kingdom should support the independence efforts of "small" nations such as the Czechs. Nobody in the UK seemed to have seen the similarity with Ireland, another a "small" nation wanting its independence.

General Maxwell (1859-1929): Born Liverpool, Protestant. At Easter 1916 he was made temporary military governor of Ireland. He was ordered by Asquith to make a military "solution" to what was a political problem. Coordinated the trials and executions of the leaders of the Easter Uprising. He said that the courts-martial would be held *in camera* and without a defence counsel or jury. This was illegal. Some officers who conducted the trials had commanded troops involved in suppressing the rebellion; again, this was illegal. Asquith promised to publish the court martial proceedings, but transcripts were not made public until 1999. Maxwell arranged for Captain Bowen-Colthurst to be tried for the murders of Thomas Dickson, Patrick MacIntyre and Francis Sheehy-Skeffington by court martial rather than by civil court.

He was responsible for execution of rebel leaders and was fully supported by Asquith's government in London. Promoted in June 1919 to full General.

In a letter to his wife, he says that the British establishment made a grave error in not clamping down on the UVF in 1913 and this failure caused the Rising and its aftermath. May 4, 1916, to his wife: "Ever since they

winked at Ulster breaking the law they have been in difficulties." Sloan, G. (2013). *The British State and the Irish Rebellion of 1916: An Intelligence Failure or a Failure of Response?* Intelligence and National Security, 6(3), p. 355.
DOI: http://dx.doi.org/10.1080/02684527.2012.735079
Source cited: Foy and Barton, The Easter Rising, Stroud Gloucestershire: Sutton Publishing,1999, p233
https://centaur.reading.ac.uk/25318/3/THE_BRITISH_STATE_1916_R EBELLION_final_%281%292.pdf Page 39

Dick McKee (1893-1920): joined the Irish Volunteers in 1913; involved in attempt to assassinate Lord French; sent to Derry to organise response to riots by armed loyalists; captured, along with Peadar Clancy the night before Bloody Sunday, on information passed to the police by James 'Shankers' Ryan. They were both tortured before being shot 'attempting to escape' at Dublin Castle.

Elizabeth 'Lily' Mernin (1886-1957) a short-hand typist at the garrison adjutant's office in Dublin Castle. Spied for Michael Collins. "She was employed as Typist in Command Headquarters of Dublin District, the intelligeon branch of which was under the control of Colonel Hill Dillon, Chief Intelligence Officer." Frank Thornton Page 9 BMH.WS0615.pdf

Louise Michel (1830-1905): A teacher; involved in the Paris Commune (1870). Transported to New Caledonia; became anarchist. First user of of a black flag 1883. Her International Anarchist School for the children of political refugees opened in 1890 at 19 Fitzroy Square London; it was closed when explosives were found, put there by a Special Branch agent.

Helena Moloney (1884-1967): actress and a journalist; first Irish female political prisoner of her generation. Smuggled guns into Ireland before the rebellion. Using theatrical make-up, assisted Nellie Gifford to disguise James Larkin when he spoke at the Imperial Hotel, 1913. She was opposed to the dual-monarchist policies advocated by Sinn Féin's Arthur Griffith. At Uprising she marched with nine other women and Seán Connolly's group of Irish Citizen Army men on Dublin Castle. Her witness statement describes what she remembers (Connolly kills a

policeman and the group then moves on to occupy City Hall).
https://bmh.militaryarchives.ie/reels/bmh/BMH.WS0391.pdf

Edwin Montague (1879-1924): Montagu was a "radical" Jewish Liberal that married; not initially part of Lloyd George's inner circle; married Venetia Stanley (with whom Asquith was enamoured).

Dora Montefiore (1851-1933): English-Australian women's suffragist, Jewish socialist. Born in middle-class Tooting, London, and married George Montefiore. Joined Charlotte Despard (sister of Lord French) and other socialists in the Women's Freedom League. When she tried to help starving Dublin children she was charged with kidnapping and subjected to an anti-Semitic attack by G. K. Chesterton

Allen, J. (1986). Dorothy Frances (Dora) Montefiore (1851–1933). In: *Australian Dictionary of Biography*. Canberra: Australian National University. https://adb.anu.edu.au/biography/montefiore-dorothy-frances-dora-7626/text13329.

Lord Morley (1838-1923): Lord President of the Council, supported Home Rule (Major-General Henry Wilson hated him); assisted John Seely with regard to rewriting the 'Curragh Mutiny' two paragraphs.

Robert Monteith (1879-1956): Met Tom Clarke and joined Irish Volunteers. Went to USA where John Devoy sent him with Adler Christensen to Germany via Norway. He tried to assist Casement in recruiting for the 'Irish Brigade'. Returned to Ireland with Casement but police were alerted and only Monteith escaped.

Patrick Moylett (1878–1973): Businessman who arranged supplies of armaments. He met British officials during the initial negotiations to end the Anglo-Irish war, briefly served as president of the Irish Republican Brotherhood. A successful businessman in County Mayo and County Galway, a close associate of Arthur Griffith and Cathal Brugha; he travelled to London acting on behalf of Sinn Féin. He distrusted Erskine Childers and disliked De Valera. In the 30's and 40's he associated with an anti-Jewish Pro-Nazi party.

Richard Mulcahy (1886-1971): Irish Volunteer and Irish Republican Brotherhood; at Uprising (with Thomas Ashe) responsible for defeat of

Royal Irish Constabulary at Ashbourne. Interned at Frongach. He was pro-Treaty and gave strong support to Collins. He ordered that anti-Treaty activists carrying firearms were liable for execution. "Some people feel that General Mulcahy and Mr. Dillon, with their willingness to play a full part in the British Commonwealth, may yet be the ones to end Partition." (JF Kennedy, at the Crosscup-Pishon American Legion Post, Boston, Massachusetts, November 11, 1945.)

William Murphy (1845-1919): Affluent Catholic Cork family. Very successful businessman; built tramways and light rail in Britain and overseas. Part owner Clery's department store and the Imperial Hotel. Had friends in the Irish Parliamentary Party. Associates said he did 'unostentatious' works of charity. Owner of Ireland's best-selling newspaper. Larkin organised a strike and Murphy persuaded other employers to force employees to undertake that they would not join, nor support Larkin's union – each man hated the other. Organised 1913 lockout. When there was a move to send starving children to temporarily live the UK, Murphy's newspapers, whipped up fear of an anarchist/Protestant plot affecting Catholic children. After 4 months Murphy had won. Supported Home Rule but was regarded as a "West Briton" for his support of the Crown and WW1. Opposed Partition but agreed with Connolly's execution. His will of £264,005 included £2,000 to charity.

Maume, P. (2009b). Murphy, William Martin. *Dictionary of Irish Biography*. doi:https://doi.org/10.3318/dib.006106.v1.

John Nixon: Born into Methodist family, Cavan. District Inspector Royal Ulster Constabulary, member of Orange Order. Strongly Loyalist and anti-Catholic. Considered by many as being responsible for assassination 'reprisals' including Owen McMahon and his sons, and the Arnon St murders of 4 men and a boy. Awarded an MBE by the Northern Ireland Government.

Lord Norbury (1745-1831): "The Hanging Judge"; John Toler. Born Co. Tipperary. Lawyer (Trinity College, Dublin); Member of Parliament. Despite having very little knowledge of the law, he became Chief Justice mainly due to his willingness to please the Government. He interrupted and abused Emmet throughout the trial before condemning him to be executed the next day. Lysaght, M. (1975). Norbury, 'The Hanging Judge' (17451831).

doi:https://doi.org/10.2307/30087176 Read to the Old Dublin Society.*Dublin Historical Record*, 30(2), pp.58–65.

Lord Northcliffe (1865-1922): **Alfred Harmsworth**. Has been called ′Britain's greatest press baron′ and megalomaniac. Mother was very ambitious for him; his father was alcoholic. Grew up in genteel poverty in Dublin. He said, "News is something someone wants to suppress. Everything else is advertising." He was fascinated by technology; workaholic, cruel and enjoyed power; Empire Loyalist; focus was on cheap, but clean, sensational journalism. After WW1 he demanded, in his newspapers, a punitive settlement upon Germany. Had extramarital affairs; antisemitic; he was certain that only he knew what was best for people; obsessive desire to interfere in politics. Lloyd George insinuated he was mad. A joke at the time was "the PM has resigned, and Lord Northcliffe has sent for the King". He died 8 days before Michael Collins.

James O'Brien (1868-1916): Unarmed policeman (born County Limerick) was on duty at the Cork Hill entrance to the upper yard of Dublin Castle when he was shot dead by Seán Connolly between 11am and midday on Easter Monday, April 24th. First victim of the Rising. An Irish Times article quotes Jim Herlihy's 2001 book, *The Dublin Metropolitan Police, A Short History* as referring to Police records which state 'a Volunteer rode up on a bicycle' – this seems to be unsupported by any other evidence which makes no reference to a bicycle. Keena, C. (2013).

https://www.irishtimes.com/culture/heritage/first-victim-of-the-rising-1.1402766 [Accessed 21 Jan. 2025]. *First Victim of the Rising*. The Irish Times.

May Oblong (May Roberts) 1878 -1925 Brothel keeper "Queen" May Oblong in Dublin's Monto (Montgomery St) district. Celebrated in songs like "Dicey Riley" and in Finnegan's Wake.

Cunningham, S. (2003). Historic Irish brothel to be bulldozed. Iol.co.za. https://www.iol.co.za/news/world/historic-irish-brothel-to-be-bulldozed-104607 [Accessed 4 Dec. 2024].

Councillor Richard O'Carroll (1876-1916): left school at 14 to enter the building trade; an active trade unionist, 1907 elected as an independent Dublin Corporation councillor; involved in planning funeral of Jeremiah O'Donovan Rossa. The official details are not documented but it appears, during the Uprising he was captured, disarmed and then illegally shot in the chest by Capt. Bowen-Colthurst (who shot Francis Sheehy-Skeffington in cold blood on the same day). He died 9 days later, leaving a wife and 7 children.

General "Ginger" O'Connell (1887-1944): served two years in the US army (1912–14). Irish Volunteer; communicated the countermanding order from Eoin MacNeill in Cork to stop the Rising. Pro-Treaty. Captured by anti-Treaty IRA from the Four Courts garrison.

Paddy O'Daly (1888-1957): soldier and counter-intelligence officer; leader of the "Squad", Michael Collins' assassination unit.(Michael Collins: A Life by James Mackay, p. 132); responsible for the killing of many British intelligence office; sided with the pro-Treaty party; Daly and his men were implicated in a series of atrocities against anti-Treaty prisoners.

Elizabeth O'Farrell (1884-1957): Born Dublin. Midwife. Educated by the Sisters of Mercy. Cumann na mBan member. Under fire, she left GPO with a white flag to deliver surrender note. Later went to various units to communicate the Surrender. Lifelong, from school, partner of Julia (Sighle, Sheila) Grenan; they were the last women to leave the GPO in 1916. Opposed the 1921 Anglo–Irish Treaty.

Diarmuid O'Hegarty (1892-1958): Born County Cork. Civil servant and revolutionary. Active in Uprising, afterwards a key figure in the reorganisation of the Volunteers and IRB and central figure in Kathleen Clarke's prisoner support group, the Irish Volunteer Dependents Fund. Very close to Michael Collins and Harry Boland.

Murphy, W. and Coleman, M. (2009). O'Hegarty (Ó hÉigeartuigh),

Diarmuid. In: *Dictionary of Irish Biography*. Dublin: Royal Irish Academy. https://www.dib.ie/biography/ohegarty-o-heigeartuigh-diarmuid-a6802.

Kevin O'Higgins (1892-1927): A 'conservative' rather than socialist. Supported Treaty side in Civil War. As Minister for Justice he signed death warrants for 77 anti-Treaty prisoners including Rory O'Connor who had been his Best man when he married. He was later assassinated in retaliation.

Nora O'Keeffe (1885–1961): revolutionary and feminist from County Tipperary. The War Office in London described her as 'one of the most notorious dispatch riders' in Ireland. Partner of Margaret Skinnider (q.v.)

Ernie O'Malley (1897-1957): anti-Treaty. Irish republican and writer. Went to same O'Connell Christian Brothers School as Emmet Dalton and Brendan Bracken.

Timmy O'Mahony (1866-?): Hall Porter. Granville Hotel, Sackville St. Grace Plunkett in her Witness Statement says a Hall Porter from the Granville gave her James Plunkett's pocketbook.

Sonny O'Neill (1888-1950): Born in County Cork. Thought by many to have killed Michael Collins, "a first-class shot and a strict disciplinarian" and "undoubtedly a dangerous man,". His pension application states "We accidentally ran into the Ballinablath [sic] thing. We took up a position, and held it there until late in the evening,"

Phelan, S. (2014). *Irish Independent*. Oct. 2014 Available at: https://www.independent.ie/irish-news/Michael-collinss-killer-met-him-twice-before-beal-na-blath-ambush/30632271.html. 'Denis O'Neill and the road to Béal na Bla Information in the Military Service (1916-1923) Pensions Collection.' https://www.militaryarchives.ie/fileadmin/user_upload/Documents_2/News_Documents/Denis_O_Neill_article___scans.pdf

Michael, The O'Rahilly (1875-1916): He liked to be known as 'The O'Rahilly'. Born County Kerry, Gaelic language enthusiast. He was one of the founders of the Irish Volunteers in 1913 and active in obtaining weapons. Opposed to the Uprising but went to the GPO. He was killed nearby. Married Nancy Brown, wealthy New Yorker (After 1916, She was on the Committee of Irish National Aid and Volunteers Dependents Fund, as was Michael Collins.

Col. Joe O'Reilly (1893- 1943): Born Co. Cork (like Collins). Thin, small, religious and very energetic. Confidential messenger or 'aide de camp' to General Collins – devoted to him. He went to London in 1911 at the age of 15 where they met. They were together in the GPO, 1916, and were later in the same jails (Stafford, then Frongoch).

Joseph O'Sullivan (1897-1922): Born in London, father from Bantry, County Cork. Joined British Army as soon as he could; leg amputated at Ypres. Joined IRA and believed to have killed British spy. He and Reginald Dunne killed Sir Henry Wilson.

Orange Order Also known as Loyal Orange Institution, a conservative, British unionist and Ulster loyalist organisation commonly known as the Orange Order, is a Protestant fraternal order based in Northern Ireland associated with Ulster Protestants. It is a fraternity sworn to maintain the Protestant Ascendancy in Ireland. Opposed to Irish nationalism/republicanism. Orange marches through Catholic neighbourhoods are controversial and have often led to violence. The Orange Order, the British Conservative Party and unionists in general, were totally opposed to Home rule. There was a strong overlap between Orange Lodges and Ulster Volunteers. The Orange Order had control of the new state of Northern Ireland. From 1921 to 1969, every prime minister of Northern Ireland was an Orangeman.

General Sir Arthur Henry Fitzroy Paget (1851-1928): Partly responsible for the Curragh Incident/Mutiny. In 1911, when he "commanded" one of the forces on the Annual Manoeuvres, he did not actually attend, and his Brigadier-General, chief of Staff had to tell him on the train what happened so that he could talk in the de-brief. His military career progressed due to friendship with Prince of Wales (later King Edward VII). Pompous, not too bright, tendency to hyperbole – predicted Ireland 'would be in a blaze'. In 1915 he was appointed commander in the Salisbury training centre.

Emin Pasha (1840-1892): Born Isaak Eduard Schnitzer in Silesia. Governor of the Egyptian province of Equatoria on the upper Nile. Named 'Pasha' by Ottomans.

Charles Parnell (1846 – 1891): Born in Wicklow, wealthy Protestant English family. Land reform agitator and founder of the Irish National Land League. MP for Irish Parliamentary Party. Held the balance of power in 1885 and helped force Home Rule legislation. Richard Pigott forged letters linking him to murders of British politicians by Fenians. Pigott committed suicide in Spain after admitting his crime. Parnell's reputation soared but was then crushed by revelation of an adulterous love affair.

Margaret Pearse (1857-1932): Mother of Patrick and William, Margaret and Mary. Housekeeper at St. Enda school and ran it after 1916. Joined Sinn Féin after the Rising. In 1921 she was elected to Dáil Éireann as a Sinn Féin candidate. Strongly opposed the Anglo-Irish Treaty.

Patrick Pearse (1879-1916): Mother was from Dublin, his father was from Birmingham and had a Dublin stonemasonry business . Pearse was obsessed with Gaelic culture and its revival. He had unconventional ideas about education and started a bilingual school for boys, St. Enda's School. Leader of the Uprising and executed.

Thornley, David. "Patrick Pearse." Studies: An Irish Quarterly Review, vol. 55, no. 217, 1966, pp. 10–20. JSTOR, http://www.jstor.org/stable/30088626. Accessed 10 Sept. 2024.

Lieutenant-General **Arthur Ernest Percival** (1887-1966): In 1921 Major Arthur Percival was Intelligence Officer for the Essex Regiment which burnt down homes in Cork, including the childhood home of Michael Collins. He was undoubtably 'ruthless' in doing what he thought necessary. In 1942 Percival chose to surrender a British Empire fortress, Singapore, defended by 85,000 Commonwealth troops to 35,000 Japanese troops on bicycles, who were 3,000 miles from their homes, and desperately in need of food, water, and ammunition.

Máire Perolz (1874-1950): Champion of the rights of women Born in Limerick city. Close to Countess Markievicz and James Connolly, member of Cumann na mBan and the Irish Citizen Army. She was registered owner of the Spark, a nationalist weekly printed by Connolly. Actress.

Captain **Guy Vickery Pinfield** (1895-1916): Royal Irish Rifles. The Irish Times, 23 May 2013, states that at Dublin Castle 'The guardroom of the complex was rushed by a number of armed Volunteers' and 'From these posts' the Irish rebels 'kept up a relentless fire. It states Pinfield was 'killed in Dublin Castle'. But the website www.hertsatwar.co.uk says 'Not far from Saint Patrick's Cathedral, he was mortally wounded.'

Grace Plunkett (nee Gifford) (1888-1955): Cartoonist for various journals. Married Joseph Plunkett, widowed 7 hours later; never re-married. Had legal battle with her parents-in-law who disputed the validity of Joseph's will. She was anti-Treaty and this resulted in her imprisonment in Kilmainham; she lived in near poverty until 1932, the De Valera government agreed to a pension.

Joseph Mary Plunkett (1887-1916): Republican, poet and journalist (The Irish Review). Interested in Irish heritage and the Irish language. Educated at the Catholic University School (CUS) and by the Jesuits at Belvedere College in Dublin and later at Stonyhurst College, in Lancashire, England where he may have acquired military knowledge from the Officers' Training Corps. Studied Esperanto. One of the founders of the Irish Esperanto Association. Had tuberculosis (TB) at a young age and so went to Mediterranean with his mother. In Algiers he studied Arabic literature and composed poetry in Arabic; he enjoyed roller-skating. His brothers George and Jack fought in the Uprising. On the first day of the Uprising he put a bomb into an empty tram on Earl Street, ran towards the GPO, and then fired a shot at the bomb resulting in the tram blocking the street. A signatory to the Proclamation of the Irish Republic. Executed (aged 28) seven hours after marrying Grace Gifford.

Major **Ivon Price** (1866-1931): Dublin born, Protestant. Royal Irish Constabulary, 1891; Director of military intelligence, 1914. Claims to have shot a Citizen Army member at Dublin Castle at the start of the

Uprising, but there is no independent evidence. Some sources assert that he was awarded the Distinguished Services Order, but this is a military decoration for active service in wartime. Price is also sometimes shown as being a Lieutenant-Colonel, a commissioned officer rank in the armed forces, but Price was always in the police service.

John Quinn (1870-1924): Born Ohio, parents Irish. Financial lawyer, very interested in literature and Irish cultural revival. He admired Patrick Pearse but thought the Uprising was lunatic and megalomaniac. He initially defended Casement until learning of the Diaries. Owned manuscripts of Joseph Conrad.

John Redmond (1856-1918): Wealthy, Wexford, Catholic family. After Parnell, he was leader of the Irish Parliamentary Party and argued for Home Rule but had a good personal relationship with Edward Carson. Opponent of votes for women. He supported WW1 and campaigned for Irishmen to join the Army. His call to the Irish Volunteers to enlist in WW1 caused them to split. Attended the Irish constitutional convention 1917-1918 which came to nothing. He was persuaded to accept Partition on a trial basis for 6 years, but this never eventuated.

Montagu Rendall (1862-1950): Teaching for 37 years at prestigious Winchester College; headmaster from 1911 to 1924. He promoted literary, moral and religious standards, which he considered supremely important.

Mary Spring Rice (1880-1924): Born Co. Kerry, wealthy family. Friends of Casement, Childers and Stopford Green. She suggested using a private yacht to transport weapons to Irish Volunteers at Howth.

Lieutenant General Sir **George Richardson** (1847-1941): led the final assault on Peking during the Boxer Rebellion. Commander of the Ulster Volunteer Force.

Dr Joseph Chamney Ridgway (1880-1959): Treated James Connolly in Dublin Castle. His witness statement records that he passed a letter to Mrs Connolly. Also states that he was given a telegram from Asquith to the effect that Connolly's execution was to be postponed but General John Maxwell refused to comply. His description of Connolly's injury conflicts with that of others. (See Endnote #94)

Room 40: the cryptanalysis section of the British Admiralty during the First World War. One of the main issues causing its creation was a captured German naval codebook that Britain's Russian allies passed on to the Admiralty. The Russians had seized it from the German cruiser SMS Magdeburg when it ran aground off the Estonian coast August 1914. Also, the Royal Australian Navy seized, from the Australian-German steamer Hobart on 11 August, a codebook used by German naval warships, merchantmen, naval zeppelins and U-boat. A short time later, a British trawler recovered a safe from the sunken German destroyer with the German code used to communicate with naval attachés, embassies and warships. But Admiralty insisted the decrypts were to be analysed only by Naval specialists … so the operators were not allowed to understand the meaning/impact of what they had produced.

https://dn790006.ca.archive.org/0/items/room40/Room%2040%20%3B.pdf.

Beesly, P. (1984). *Room forty Room 40: British naval intelligence 1914-1918*. San Diego New York London: Harcourt Brace Jovanovich, p.188.

Hines, J. (2008). Sins of Omission and Commission: A Reassessment of the Role of Intelligence in the Battle of Jutland. *The Journal of Military History*, 72(4), pp.1117–1154. doi:https://doi.org/10.1353/jmh.0.0092.

William Rooney (1873-1901): Born Dublin. Irish nationalist, journalist, poet and Gaelic revivalist. Established, (with Arthur Griffith) Sinn Féin in 1905. Educated by the Christian Brothers North Richmond Street. Died, aged 27, from TB.

Jeremiah O'Donovan Rossa (1883-1915): His death in the USA gave the Irish Volunteers a chance to stage manage his funeral in Dublin, and Patrick Pearse to give an emotional address. Rossa had been released from prison in England in 1870 and sent into exile in the US by the British government. There, he organised fundraising for Irish nationalist causes and a dynamite campaign in England in the 1880s, for which the Americans refused to extradite him to the UK.

Sir Philip Sassoon (1888-1939):Wealthy politician and aristocrat. Jewish family. Unionist MP in 1912. Openly gay. Fought in WW1. Parliamentary Private Secretary to David Lloyd George in 1920

John Seely (1868-1947): Initially a Conservative MP but became a Liberal. Fought in Boer War. Secretary of State for War 1912-14. Resigned after Curragh "Incident" (Mutiny). Friend of Churchill. He met various Nazis and in 1935 he said that Hitler that was 'absolutely truthful, sincere, and unselfish'.

Seton-Watson, Robert William (1879-1951) D.Litt. Oxon 1910; Hon. Ph.D. Prague, Zagreb, Bratislava, Lecturer at King's College, London 1915; Intelligence Bureau 1917-18. Friend of Czechoslovak philosopher and politician Tomáš Masaryk

Frank Shackleton (1876-1941): Brother of Antarctic explorer Ernest, prime suspect for stealing Irish Crown Jewels (value today several million euro) from Dublin Castle. They went missing on 6 July 1907 stolen shortly before the visit of King Edward VII from a strong room. Ulster King of Arms, Sir Arthur Vicars, was responsible for custody. There were frequent drunken parties. Lord Haddo took one of the safe keys, stole the jewels and returned them to Vicars by post as a prank. Vicars was also known to show off the jewels to impress visitors. He shared a house with Captain Richard Howard Gorges and arranged for Shackleton to have a job at the Castle. Shackleton was short of money (declared bankrupt in 1910) and may have been mastermind behind the theft; his associate/lover Gorges was thought responsible, the investigation was inconclusive but Vicars was blamed. Gorges was never charged for the theft; he was later found guilty of manslaughter for killing a policeman who tried to arrest him for "indulgence in illegal sexual practices". Jewels remain lost.

Francis Sheehy-Skeffington (1878-1916): A friend and schoolmate of James Joyce. He wrote that "Gaelic" was irretrievably dead and "the study of Esperanto would be more useful to the youth of Ireland". He denounced smoking, drinking, and vivisection. Joyce based "MacCann" in his novel A Portrait of the Artist as a Young Man on Sheehy-

Skeffington. In accordance with his feminist ideals, he took his wife's name of Sheehy when they married (they had been classmates). A pacifist, suffragist, vegetarian, journalist and Irish nationalist. Jailed for six months in prison for campaigning against recruitment to the British Army in WW1. He and wife Hanna had a son, Owen, whom they refused to have baptised. Being a pacifist, Francis distanced himself from the Irish Volunteers when he saw they intended a military confrontation with Britain. Murdered by a British officer who was declared insane but later allowed to emigrate. https://www.anphoblacht.com/contents/25871.

Moloney, M. (2016). On this day 1916 – The Portobello Barracks murders. *Anphoblacht*, (1), 26 Apr.

Gordon Shephard DSO, MC (1885-1918): He became a Brigadier-General in the RFC and was aged 32 when he died. He suffered no sanction for his role in the 1914 Howth gunrunning for the Irish Volunteers. His father left a sum of money in trust to award annual prizes for essays on reconnaissance and related subjects submitted by RAF officers and airmen (The Gordon Shephard Memorial Essay Prize – it seems have ceased to be awarded.)

Adams, D.T. (2020). Who was Gordon Shephard – the man who never was. The Dragon's Voice.

https://www.nwwfa.org.uk/index.php/newsletters/2020/july [Accessed 4 Nov. 2024].

Clare Sheridan (1885-1970): The daughter of Moreton Frewen. Her mother was the elder sister of Lady Randolph Churchill, making her a cousin of Churchill. She was encouraged to write novels by Henry James and Rudyard Kipling. Her husband died in the war. In 1924 she went by motor cycle sidecar 6,600 km across Asia. She sculpted Churchill, Vladimir Lenin, Leon Trotsky, Felix Dzerzhinsky, and Lev Kamenev and had sex with at least one of them; she was possibly working for British Intelligence. She had an affair with Charlie Chaplin. As a journalist she interviewed Michael Collins and Rory O'Connor (leader of anti-Treaty rebels), Mussolini, and Kemal Ataturk.

Sinn Féin: 'We Ourselves'; founded in 1905 by Arthur Griffith and

William Rooney. Initially, it was conservative and advocated an Anglo-Irish dual monarchy, similar to the Austro-Hungarian Compromise. Most members later joined the Irish Volunteers. In 1916 the British Press used the terminology 'Sinn Féin' when referring to those involved in Easter Uprising – in the following years its membership increased. It split in 1922 in response to the Anglo-Irish Treaty which led to the Irish Civil War.

Major Sirr (1764-1841): Irish-born soldier, member of Orange Order. Dublin's 'chief of police' in 1796, with informers and spies, he pursued potential rebels, arrested Robert Emmet, 1803, and accosted Sarah Curran. Much despised by Dubliners. https://www.dib.ie/biography/388al-henry-charles-a8099 [Accessed 30 Oct. 2024]. Kleinmann, S. (2009). *Sirr, Henry Charles*. Www.dib.ie.

Joyce, J. (2012). *Dubliners*. Penguin UK. Ivy Day In The Committee Room.

FE Smith/Lord Birkenhead (1872-1930): Strongly opposed to Irish nationalism. Smith won a scholarship to University College, Liverpool but rarely spoke of it (at that time students were awarded external degrees) then studied Law at Oxford.

In a murder trial he was defence counsel for Dr. Crippen's mistress, Ethel Le Neve. The doctor was hanged; she was found not guilty. Smith, as he knew for certain and everybody else expected, would become Lord Chancellor. He was, like Carson, the typical Conservative but that didn't prevent him from wearing a pink shirt when he married the daughter of Reverend Henry Furneaux, fellow of Corpus Christi College, Oxford. He always did and said whatever he wanted to do and say – and to hell with anybody else.

He led the prosecution in 1917, as Attorney-General, of peace activist and socialist Alice Wheeldon (seller of second-hand clothes) charged with conspiracy to murder David Lloyd George. Evidence came from an undercover agent (not named) who had lied to her and who was not questioned in court; evidence included poison sent to her by post. She was found guilty and jailed for 10 years but released on licence, at the request of Lloyd George, after 9 months.

Became a wealthy lawyer, Conservative politician, barrister, and Lord High Chancellor (as he always knew he would). Died aged 58 from pneumonia caused by cirrhosis of the liver.

Eugene Smyth (1881-1959): Passed the civil service entrance exam aged 17, appointed to the Post Office as a Sorting Clerk and Telegraphist in September 1898, Dublin. Source of "Dublin Castle" document which assisted in justifying the Dublin Easter Uprising.

His older brother Partick was a policeman (a 'G' man) and killed in 1919.

Margaret Skinnider (1893-1971): Born Glasgow. Maths teacher. Expert rifle sniper. the only woman combatant wounded in Uprising. She and Nora O'Keeffe (q.v.) were lifelong lovers.

Wilfred Spender (1876-1950): Educated at Winchester College (1892). Edward Carson asked him to help organise the Ulster Volunteer Force, a paramilitary group opposed to Home Rule. He resigned from the army and assisted in the Larne 1914 gun-running. In WWI, he returned to the army. In 1920 he was appointed head of the reconstituted UVF and helped organise the civil service in the Northern Ireland government – opposing any discrimination on religious grounds (but had little success in this). He never joined an Orange Lodge.

Captain Karl Spindler (1887-1951): According to Spindler he was to take a ship re-named the Aud (Libau) and Casement and two companions to Ireland but Casement had expressed a very strong objection against going in the Libau, it was finally decided to place a submarine at his disposal. The submarine was to meet the Libau and transfer the 3 to the ship in Tralee Bay, and Spindler was then to proceed in under his instructions.

The Aud arrived in Tralee Bay at the previously agreed time on Thursday 20 April, but her signals went unanswered. The ship took shelter amongst near the Blasket Islands but in the evening of Good Friday, 21 April, the Aud was stopped by the Royal Navy. While being escorted to Queenstown in Cork Harbour the crew sank the ship on Saturday, 22 April.

Bruno Spiro (1875-1936): Hamburg-based weapons dealer, owner of the firm Benny Spiro, founded in 1864. Sold rifles, etc. to UVF. Later sold weapons to the Haganah (organization to protect Jewish settlements in Palestine). Arrested in Hamburg in 1936 by the Gestapo, sent to concentration camp and reported as committing suicide.

Lorenz, I. (n.d.). *THE TRIAL AGAINST DAVID SEALTIEL IN HAMBURG (1937)*. https://www.xn--jdischer-friedhof-altona-vsc.de/img/biographien/sealtiel_david-trial.pdf.

Austin Stack (1879-1929): Born County Kerry. Irish republican and politician. Irish Republican Brotherhood. In 1916, as commandant of the Kerry Brigade of the Irish Volunteers, He prepared for the arms sent by Roger Casement from Germany. Casement was arrested; Slack did not try a rescue bid (he said that he'd been ordered not to cause an alarm before the Rising). He was anti-Treaty in the Civil War.

Henry Morton Stanley (1841-1904): Born illegitimate. Grew up in Workhouse for the Poor; sexually abused. Fought in the US Civil War on both sides. Welsh-American explorer, journalist, soldier, colonial administrator, author and politician. Searched for explorer David Livingstone. King Leopold II of the Belgians' agent for the occupation of the Congo region. Commanded the Emin Pasha Relief Expedition.

Venetia Stanley (1887-1948): Youngest of the seven children, wealthy family. Friend and later lover of Violet Asquith, the daughter of Prime Minister Asquith (who became very close and intimate with Venetia). Venetia married, out of convenience, wealthy Liberal Party MP, Edwin Montagu. Prime Minister Asquith discussed domestic political events with Venetia and told her "the sudden outburst of the Great War" had been the greatest stroke of luck in his political career.

Frances Stevenson (1888-1972): Mistress, personal secretary, confidante and second wife of Prime Minister David Lloyd George. After two abortions she gave birth to a daughter.

Charles Stokes (1852-1895): Born Dublin. Missionary/trader in Congo. The commander of the Belgian forces, Lothaire, learnt that Stokes had been trading firearms to enemies; Stokes was subject to a 'drumhead trial' and hanged. Belgium was forced to put Lothaire on trial, but he was found not guilty. However, the affair resulted in the Congo's exploitation being investigated.

Jim Sullivan (1873-1935): Born in Kerry, raised in US. American Ambassador to Santo Domingo; pro-Irish and anti-British. His film company used motion pictures as propaganda vehicles for Irish Independence from 1913. He was arrested and charged with complicity in the Rising,

Felter, M. and Schultz, D. (2004). James Mark Sullivan and the Film Company of Ireland. *New Hibernia Review*, 8(2), pp.24–40. doi:https://doi.org/10.1353/nhr.2004.0041.

Schultz, D. and Felter, M. (n.d.). The Making of an Irish Nationalist: James Mark Sullivan and the Film Company of Ireland in America. *screening the past*, (33). https://www.screeningthepast.com/issue-33-knocknagow/the-making-of-an-irish-nationalist/.

Doctor Lieutenant-Col **Richard Francis Tobin** (1843-1919): Surgeon St. Vincent's Hospital Dublin. Operated on James Connolly prior to the execution.

Basil Thomson (1861-1939): He had a long career which involved interrogating spies and communists, but he also wrote crime novels. His department came under criticism for over-spending; he was defended by Reginald Hall. Later, Thomson was arrested and found guilty of committing an act in violation of public decency in Hyde Park with a prostitute. (Wikipedia)

Oscar Traynor (1886-1963): In the Uprising he was leader of the Metropole Hotel garrison; led the attack on The Custom House in 1921. He was anti-Treaty and organised guerrilla activity in south Dublin against Collins.

Ulster Special Constabulary "B-Specials", Ulster Protestants; James Craig wanted a volunteer constabulary (on duty for one evening per week) raised from the Loyalist population, organised on military lines and armed for duty within the six county area. They were drawn from the Ulster Volunteers (UVF), the militia formed in 1912 by Carson and

Craig. They carried out several reprisals against Catholic civilians, 1920–22. The IRA said that any Catholics who joined the Specials would be treated as traitors.

Ulster Unionist Party (1905): originally Ulster Unionist Council, a political party in Northern Ireland. A Protestant organisation. Formed 1905 by Carson as unionist opposition to the Irish Home Rule movement. Following the partition of Ireland, it was the governing party of Northern Ireland. Strong association with the Orange Order.

Ulster Volunteers (1913-1922) Protestant Irish unionist, loyalist paramilitary organisation created to block Home Rule.

Major Sir **Francis Vane** (1861-1934): Dublin born. He led 150 troops to attack the South Dublin Union Workhouse where rebels were preventing the progress of troops from the Curragh military garrison. After the Uprising, he was ordered to hand over his duties to the murderer Captain Bowen-Colthurst. Vane tried unsuccessfully to have senior officers at the Castle investigate the murders, so he went to Lord Kitchener in London. He later wrote to the press stating that the rebels had observed the laws of war and tried to avoid civilian casualties. He visited Hanna Sheehy-Skeffington and showed all the sympathy he could to her and young son, Owen. He took the boy to Dublin Zoo and then to the Gresham Hotel for supper. Vane suggested that he try the chicken. Owen said, 'No, I never eat meat. My father never ate meat ... my father can't eat even vegetables now'. Vane founded the Boy Scouts in Italy and was an underwriter at Lloyds.

Quinn, J. (n.d.). Sir Francis Vane's quest for justice after Easter Week. *History Ireland.* https://historyireland.com/sir-francis-vanes-quest-for-justice-after-easter-week/.

Shyamji Krishna **Varma** (1857–1930) an Indian revolutionary, who founded the Indian Home Rule Society.

Ambassador Count **Von Bersdorff** (1862-1939): Born London. In the Prussian Army for eight years in an artillery unit. Married a German-American. German ambassador to the United States. Financed intelligence operations and sabotage in US, assisted by Captain Franz von Papen, and Captain Karl Boy-Ed, a naval attaché, and commercial attaché, Heinrich Albert.

Hugh Wallace (1860-1929): Born Co. Down. Fought against Boer guerrillas. Senior Freemason, political activist, Orangeman. Very close to James Craig and Edward Carson. A founding member of the Ulster Unionist Council. Organised drill training for members of the Orange order.

Herbert Ward (1863-1919): Aged 15 travelled to New Zealand and Australia. In Africa, adventurer and explorer. In the Congo 1884-9, working first for H M Stanley in the Congo Free State; later with him on the Emin Pasha Relief Expedition (1887-9). In 1890 Ward married a rich American, Sarita Sanford (1860-1944), and became an author and lecturer and sculptor. Enlisted in the Ambulance Corps in WWI. For 30 years a close friend of Roger Casement. Casement was described by Ward but broke with him in 1916 due to Casement's time in Germany. Changed the name of his youngest son (Casement's godson) by deed poll from Roger Casement Ward to Rodney Sanford Ward.

Harold Washington (1904-1920): 15-years of age from Salford, Manchester. Private in 2nd Battalion, Duke of Wellington's West Riding Regiment. Killed, along with Privates Thomas Humphries and Marshal Whitehead, by a group of Sinn Féin that included Kevin Barry which was intent on stealing their rifles.

Raimund Weisbach (1886-1970): Casement first boarded the U-20, but it had to turn back with rudder problems and instead was taken on the U-19, commanded by Raimund Weisbach, who had previously served as torpedo officer on U-20 and had launched the torpedo that sank Lusitania. During his brief command of U-19, Weisbach delivered Roger Casement along with Bailey and Monteith to Banna Strand, Ballyheigue Bay, County Kerry.

Field Marshal Sir **George White** (1835-1912): Born Londonderry. Fought at Peshawar during the Indian Mutiny. Awarded the Victoria Cross. Governor of Gibraltar. Father of Jack White.

James 'Jack' White (1879-1946): 1st Batt. Gordon Highlanders 1899;

Capt. 2nd Batt. 1904; fought in South African War (despatches, medal with five clasps, King's medal with two clasps, D.S.O.); A.D.C. to Governor of Gibraltar 1902-5; resigned his commission 1909; helped to raise Irish Citizen Army, Dublin 1913. He used his own car as an ambulance in WW1 in an Australian unit. He was administrator of the 2nd British Medical Unit, Spain 1936 and author of "Significance of Sinn Féin" in 1919. He was educated at Winchester College (some years overlapping with Raymond Asquith, Edward Grigg, and a British political activist and historian Robert William Seton-Watson who was involved in European border decisions relating to small nations at Versailles after WW1.

https://www.rte.ie/centuryireland/articles/punching-the-wind-captain-jack-white-the-misfit-of-the-irish-revolution. Mulhall, E. (n.d.). Punching the Wind: Captain Jack White, the misfit of the Irish Revolution.

Irish Labour History Society. (n.d.). Captain James Robert (Jack) White DSO, 1879-1946. *Saothar – Labour Lives 15 J White* https://www.irishlabourhistorysociety.com/wp-content/uploads/2022/08/LL-15-J-White.pdf.

Major-General **Henry Wilson** (1864-1922): Born County Longford, Ireland. Regarded as a political intriguer for agitating for the introduction of conscription and the Curragh incident of 1914. In 1917 informal military advisor to Prime Minister David Lloyd George, and Permanent Military Representative at the Supreme War Council at Versailles Peace Conference. In 1918 Wilson served as Chief of the Imperial General Staff (the professional head of the British Army). Member of Parliament, and as security advisor to the Northern Ireland government. Irish unionist politician.

Lieutenant Colonel **Francis Willoughby Woodward** (1872-1926): A Major in September 1914; was acting Lieutenant Colonel, commanding a service battalion of Manchester Regiment when he was a presiding officer at James Connolly's court martial.

President **Wilson, Woodrow:** (1856-1924) Democrat. Narrowly re-elected in the 1916 election. Took US into WW1 after much hesitation. In late 1916 he secretly promoted a compromise peace; but both Britain Germany rejected it. Main creator of League of Nations (but US was not a member). He became ill and his wife and doctor took control – US policies alienated German- and Irish-American Democrats and the Republicans won the 1920 election. His paternal grandparents came from County Tyrone. He and his family were Presbyterian.

Count **von Wedel** (1862-1943): Chief of the English Department of the German Foreign Ministry; Advisor in the Political Department. Assisted Roger Casement.

Lord Lieutenant, **Wimborne** (1873-1939): fought in Boer War. Like Churchill, changed to being a Liberal from Conservative. He was made Lord Lieutenant of Ireland in 1915 and wanted Under-Secretary Nathan, prior to the Uprising, to arrest rebel leaders but Nathan awaited Chief Secretary Birrell's permission. Notorious womanizer.

Winchester College: Considered one of the most prestigious schools in the world; independent boarding school in Hampshire for pupils aged 13-18. About 600 pupils in 1900. The following people were educated at Winchester (some of them being contemporaries of 'Jack' White): –

- Raymond Asquith (born 1878), son of Prime Minister. **At Winchester 1892-1897**
- Sir Norman Fenwick Warren Fisher (born 1879): British civil servant. Permanent Secretary to the Treasury and Head of the Home Civil Service. **At Winchester 1892-1898**
- Edward Grigg (born 1879), private secretary to Prime Minister David Lloyd George. **At Winchester 1892-1898** (N.B. He would have known Fisher very well.)
- Robert William Seton-Watson (born 1879) a British political activist and historian who was involved in border decisions at Versailles after WW1. Worked in the Intelligence Bureau of the War Cabinet in the Enemy Propaganda Department 1917-1918. Friend of Thomas

Masaryk. **At Winchester 1893-1898**
- Sir Maurice Bonham-Carter (born 1880) – he was Prime Minister Asquith's Principal Private Secretary 1910 to 1916 and went with him to Ireland after the Uprising. Married the Prime Minister's daughter, Violet Asquith (at one point she was thought to be engaged to Churchill). **At Winchester 1893-1898**
- Wilfred Spender (born 1876) He signed the Ulster Covenant even though he was an officer in the Army. Close friend of Edward Carson, he helped organise the UVF. **At Winchester 1889-1892**
- Jack White (born 1879) helped create Irish Citizen Army. **At Winchester 1892-1896**
- Captain Perceval Lea-Wilson (born 1887) killed 1920 on the orders of Michael Collins (Lea-Wilson had victimised and publicly abused Thomas Clarke after the Easter Rising. At **Winchester 1900-1906**

Brigadier-General Sir **Ormonde de l'Épée Winter** (1875-1962): OIC of intelligence operations in Ireland during the Anglo-Irish War / Irish War of Independence. In 1904 he and another officer were being attacked by youths whilst boating, Winter killed one with an oar – he was acquitted of manslaughter. With two Auxiliary Division officers, Captain Hardy and Captain King, he interrogated Clunes, Clancy, and McKee who were arrested just before Bloody Sunday. All 3 were almost certainly tortured before being shot whilst 'attempting to escape'. Winter later joined the British Fascists.

General **James Wolfe** (1727-1759): Born in Kent but his family was Anglo-Irish. he took part in the suppression of the Jacobite (Catholic) Rebellion. Died due to injuries from three musket balls when leading his forces and defeating the French at Quebec. Theobald Wolfe Tone (Irish patriot) was born 4 years after James Wolfe died. Theobald Wolfe was named in honour of his godfather, Theobald Wolfe of Blackhall, County

Kildare, a first cousin of Arthur Wolfe, 1st Viscount Kilwarden.

Charles Wooldridge (1865-1896) Royal Horse Guards Trooper. Contrary to Army regulations he married a younger woman. Unable to live together, the marriage crumbled and he suspected his wife of adultery – they quarrelled and he killed her. Oscar Wilde was in Reading Gaol when Wooldridge was hanged.

Bibliography and Reference List

The Life and Times of Michael Collins. (2021). *London Years.* https://web.archive.org/web/20210624205614/http://www.generalMich aelcollins.com/life-times/1905-to-1915/ [Accessed 10 Nov. 2024].

Adams, D.T. (2020). *Who was Gordon Shephard – the man who never was? The Dragon's Voice.* https://www.nwwfa.org.uk/index.php/newsletters/2020/july [Accessed 4 Nov. 2024].

Ainsworth, J. (2002). Kevin Barry, the Incident at Monk's Bakery and the Making of an Irish Republican Legend. *The Historical Association*, 87(287), Jul., pp.372–387. https://eprints.qut.edu.au/247/1/Ainsworth_Kevin.PDF.

Alberge, D. (2021). *Sworn enemies: the real story of Old Bailey clash that ruined Oscar Wilde.* the Guardian. https://www.theguardian.com/uk-news/2021/jan/24/oscar-wilde-old-bailey-libel-trial-grandson-bbc-edward-carson-and-the-fall.

Allen, J. (1986). Dorothy Frances (Dora) Montefiore (1851–1933). In: *Australian Dictionary of Biography.* Canberra: Australian National University. https://adb.anu.edu.au/biography/montefiore-dorothy-frances-dora-7626/text13329.

Andrew, C.M. (2012). *The Defence of the Realm.* Penguin Group.

Andrews, H. (2011). Roger Casement: The Gay Irish Humanitarian Who Was Hanged On a Comma. *First Things.* https://www.firstthings.com/blogs/firstthoughts/2011/11/roger-casement-the-gay-irish-humanitarian-who-was-hanged-on-a-comma.

Baker, M. (2019). *The Laughing Boy.* poetscorner.blog. https://poetscorner.blog/2019/03/20/the-laughing-boy/ [Accessed 28 Oct. 2024].

Barkham, P. (2009). The Brothers grim. *The Guardian.* 28 Nov. https://www.theguardian.com/world/2009/nov/28/christian-brothers-ireland-child-abuse [Accessed 28 May 2020].

Beesly, P. (1984). *Room 40: British naval intelligence 1914-1918.* San

Diego New York London: Harcourt Brace Jovanovich, p.188. https://dn790006.ca.archive.org/0/items/room40/Room%2040%20%3B.pdf.

Bennett, G. (2018). *The Zinoviev Letter*. Oxford: Oxford University Press.

Bhabha, Homi. "Of Mimicry and Man: The Ambivalence of Colonial Discourse." *October*, vol. 28, 1984, pp. 125–33. *JSTOR*, https://doi.org/10.2307/778467. Accessed 6 Dec. 2025.

Birrell, A. (2011). *The Project Gutenberg eBook of Res Judicat by Augustine Birrell*. Gutenberg.org. https://www.gutenberg.org/files/37159/37159-h/37159-h.htm [Accessed 22 Oct. 2024].

Boland, H. (1922). *placing 'on record the events that have led up to this British manufactured war on the Republic'*. Drunken treaty.

Brennan-Whitmore, W. (1968). *'Collins murdered by a British Secret Agent'*. Orwellianireland.com. http://www.orwellianireland.com/collins.jpg [Accessed 7 Nov. 2024].

Burtenshaw, R. (2018). *Connolly at 150*. Jacobin.com. https://jacobin.com/2018/06/james-connolly-ireland-socialism-iww-labor [Accessed 3 Nov. 2024].

Casement, R. (1916). *Speech of Roger Casement from the dock*. https://doi.org/10.48495/pn89d807q.

Casement, R. (1918). The Secret Diplomacy of England. *The Irishman*. https://drpatwalsh.com/2017/02/15/the-secret-diplomacy-of-england/ 15/02/2017 Dr. Pat Walsh.

Catalogue.nli.ie. (1914). *Context: Copy of a letter from Eoin MacNeill to Edward Carson on behalf of the Irish Volunteers Executive, regarding co-operation between the Irish Volunteers and the Ulster Volunteer Force, with copy of a resolution regarding same,*. https://catalogue.nli.ie/Record/vtls000365415 [Accessed 6 Nov. 2024]. Collection: Bulmer Hobson Papers, 1905-1968.

Chris Dalton (2017). *Emmet Dalton remembers: The Irish Civil War, Michael Collins, Beal na Blah, Ardmore Films*. YouTube.

https://www.youtube.com/watch?v=SLrGnImYCwU&list=PLCVN7OI 0vnzzaSm4zxk_tveVWLzocx7CH [Accessed 8 Nov. 2024].
Churchill, W. (1960). *The Second World War ; [part I]: The Gathering Storm*. London: Penguin Books.
Collins, D. (2024). *Rivals in the Storm*. Bloomsbury Publishing.
Collins, J. (1923). *'Short account of Michael's life in London' to Piaras Beaslai*. [Letter].
Collins, L. (2015). *Rising Poems: 'I See His Blood Upon The Rose' by Joseph Plunkett*. Irish Independent. https://www.independent.ie/irish-news/rising-poems-i-see-his-blood-upon-the-rose-by-joseph-plunkett/34143648.html [Accessed 4 Nov. 2024].
Collins, M. (1906). *King's College London arithmetic examination papers and answer papers completed by Michael Collins*. UCD Digital Library. https://digital.ucd.ie/view/ivrla:10965 [Accessed 8 Nov. 2024].
Collins, P. (1915). *Letter from Patrick Collins (brother) to Michael Collins concerning the possibility of Michael going to Chicago*. UCD Digital Library. https://digital.ucd.ie/view/ivrla:11519 [Accessed 8 Nov. 2024].
Cork, U.C. (2021). *Civilian Frederick Charles Stenning*. The Irish Revolution Project. https://www.ucc.ie/en/theirishrevolution/collections/cork-fatality-register/register-index/1921-177/ [Accessed 17 Nov. 2024]. Cork Fatality Register.
Costigan, G. (1955). The Treason of Sir Roger Casement. *The American Historical Review*, 60(2), p.283. doi:https://doi.org/10.2307/1843187 pp. 283-302.
Cronin, J. (1951). STATEMENT BY WITNESS. *BUREAU OF MILITARY HISTORY, 1913-21.STATEMENT BY WITNESS*. https://bmh.militaryarchives.ie/reels/bmh/BMH.WS0588.pdf.
Cunningham, S. (2003). *Historic Irish brothel to be bulldozed*. Iol.co.za. https://www.iol.co.za/news/world/historic-irish-brothel-to-be-bulldozed-104607 [Accessed 4 Dec. 2024].
Deleuze, M. (2016). 1916: Dublin Youths' Sweet Revolution. In: *2016*

– *Food and Revolution*. Dublin: Dublin Gastronomy Symposium, p.Page 3. https://arrow.tudublin.ie/cgi/viewcontent.cgi?article=1074&context=dgs.

Denis O'Neill and the road to Béal na Bla Information in the Military Service (1916-1923) Pensions Collection. (n.d.). https://www.militaryarchives.ie/fileadmin/user_upload/Documents_2/News_Documents/Denis_O_Neill_article___scans.pdf.

Dolan, A. and Murphy, W. (2018). *Michael Collins The Man and the Revolution*. Cork: Collins Press.

Dudgeon, J. (2016). *Roger Casement: a campaigner, not a conspirator or even an Ulster Protestant*. The Irish Times. https://www.irishtimes.com/culture/books/roger-casement-a-campaigner-not-a-conspirator-or-even-an-ulster-protestant-1.2680244 [Accessed 9 Nov. 2024].

Dungan, M. (n.d.). The 1916 Courts-martial and the Dublin Executions. *Essays on the Court Martials*. https://courtmartial.nationalarchives.ie/1916-court-martial-and-the-dublin-executions.html.

Dwyer, R. (2019). *Death of MacSwiney had enormous significance as prisoners hunger strike drew global coverage*. Irish Examiner. https://www.irishexaminer.com/lifestyle/arid-30943591.html [Accessed 9 Dec. 2024].

Earls, M. (2024). The Irish Jew. *Dublin Review of Books*. https://drb.ie/the-irish-jew/.

Edgerton, D.L. (2018). *The Rise and Fall of the British Nation: a twentieth-century History*. London: Penguin Books.

Egan, D. (2022). Solving the Murder of Michael Collins The Conclusive Evidence. https://www.irishpcople.ie/solving-the-murder-of-Michael-collins-the-conclusive-evidence/ [Accessed 7 Nov. 2024].

Éirígí For A New Republic (2022). *The Coming Generation*. The Connolly Archive. https://eirigi.org/latestnews/2022/7/20/the-connolly-archive-the-coming-generation 'Worker's Republic' July 15th 1900.

Fallon, D. (2016). *Nurse Margaret Keogh, the first civilian fatality of the Rising*. independent.ie. https://www.independent.ie/irish-news/nurse-margaret-keogh-the-first-civilian-fatality-of-the-rising/34510459.html [Accessed 28 Oct. 2024].

Fanning, R. (2013). *Fatal path: British government and Irish revolution ; 1910-1922*. London: Faber And Faber.

Fanning, R. (2014). *Ronan Fanning: Why commemorating the Home Rule Bill would be unwise*. IrishTimes.com. https://www.irishtimes.com/news/politics/ronan-fanning-why-commemorating-the-home-rule-bill-would-be-unwise-1.1898370 [Accessed 22 Oct. 2024].

Felter, M. and Schultz, D. (2004). James Mark Sullivan and the Film Company of Ireland. *New Hibernia Review*, 8(2), pp.24–40. doi:https://doi.org/10.1353/nhr.2004.0041.

Fintan O'Toole (2021). *We Don't Know Ourselves: A Personal History of Modern Ireland*. London: Head of Zeus, pp.116–117.

Fischer, T. (2002). The rise and rise of a failed jackeroo. *Australian Financial Review*. 15 Feb. https://www.afr.com/politics/the-rise-and-rise-of-a-failed-jackeroo-20020215-k1h5n.

Foster, R.F. (2015). *Vivid faces: the revolutionary generation in Ireland, 1890-1923*. UK: Penguin Books.

Fox, S. (2023). *Chronology of Irish History 1919 – 1923*. Irishhistory1919-1923chronology.ie. http://irishhistory1919-1923chronology.ie/March%201920%20-%2002-%20Alan%20Bell%20Star%20Chamber.htm [Accessed 20 Oct. 2024].

Franz Von Papen (1952). *Franz von Papen: memoirs*. Translated by B. Connell. London: Deutsch, p.35.

Garden, A. (2017). 'Leaving hardly a sign-and no memories': Roger Casement and the Metamodernist Archive. *Modernism/modernity Print Plus*, 2, Cycle 4(4). doi:https://doi.org/10.26597/mod.0032.

Gifford, S. (1953). Witness Statement 0909. *Witness Statements*, p.9. https://bmh.militaryarchives.ie/reels/bmh/BMH.WS0909.pdf#page=2.

Glandon, V.E. (1984). Arthur Griffith and the Ideal Irish State . *Studies:*

An Irish Quarterly Review, 73(289), pp.26–36.
https://www.jstor.org/stable/30090941.

Griffen, J. (1986). Daniel Mannix (1864–1963). *Australian Dictionary of Biography*, 10(305). https://adb.anu.edu.au/biography/mannix-daniel-7478/text13033.

Hahessy, E. (2022). A forgotten alliance that shaped Ireland. *The Irish Revolution Project*. https://www.ucc.ie/en/theirishrevolution/feature-articles/a-forgotten-alliance-that-shaped-ireland.html First published: Irish Examiner Supplement 'Civil War: The conflict that ripped the county apart', published 13 June 2022.

Hansard.Parliament.uk. (1920). *Galway Fatality – Hansard – UK Parliament*. https://hansard.parliament.uk/Commons/1920-11-04/debates/66fa768a-8505-47b5-aee1-5ccccf230286/GalwayFatality?highlight=lawn#contribution-f9463a02-d9be-4a4c-aff7-106723e7656d [Accessed 28 Oct. 2024].

Haslam, T. (1916). Some Last Words on Women's Suffrage. *Some Last Words on Women's Suffrage*. https://catalogue.nla.gov.au/catalog/1943612 Ormond Printing Co., Ltd. (Dublin).

Higgins, M. (2016). *Speech at a Reception to Mark the 102nd Anniversary of the Irish Citizen Army*. media-library. https://www.president.ie/en/media-library/speeches/speech-by-president-higgins-at-a-reception-to-mark-the-102nd-anniversary-of [Accessed 3 Nov. 2024].

Hines, J. (2008). Sins of Omission and Commission: A Reassessment of the Role of Intelligence in the Battle of Jutland. *The Journal of Military History*, 72(4), pp.1117–1154. doi:https://doi.org/10.1353/jmh.0.0092.

hÍomhair, P.Ó. (2022). *Éirígí For A New Republic*. Éirígí For A New Republic. https://eirigi.org/latestnews/2022/7/20/the-connolly-archive-the-coming-generation [Accessed 20 Oct. 2024].

Hughes, B., Campbell, B. and Schreibman, S. (2017). Contested Memories: Revisiting the Battle of Mount Street Bridge, 1916. *British Journal for Military History*, 4(1).

https://journals.gold.ac.uk/index.php/bjmh/article/view/769 [Accessed 21 Nov. 2024].

Ingen (2020). *'God Save Ireland!' – Irish Patriotic Anthem*. YouTube. https://www.youtube.com/watch?v=J_KEcfmHeN0 [Accessed 22 Dec. 2024].

Intelligence report about an armed rising in Ireland. (1916). *Éamon de Valera Papers: British documents relating to 1916*. Dublin: UCD Library, University College. https://digital.ucd.ie/view/ucdlib:53987.

Irish Labour History Society. (n.d.). Captain James Robert (Jack) White DSO, 1879-1946. *Saothar – Labour Lives 15 J White*. https://www.irishlabourhistorysociety.com/wp-content/uploads/2022/08/LL-15-J-White.pdf.

John Dorney (2013). *Today in Irish History – August 31, 1913 – Labour's Bloody Sunday – The Irish Story*. Theirishstory.com. https://www.theirishstory.com/2013/08/31/today-in-irish-history-august-31-1913-labours-bloody-sunday/ [Accessed 24 Oct. 2024].

John_Dorney (2015). *'Glorious Madness' – The Life and Death of Michael O'Rahilly – The Irish Story*. Theirishstory.com. https://www.theirishstory.com/2015/04/09/glorious-madness-the-life-and-death-of-michael-orahilly/ [Accessed 24 Oct. 2024].

Jones, N. (2014). *Peace and War*. London: Head of Zeus.

Joyce, J. (2012). *Dubliners*. Penguin UK. Ivy Day In The Committee Room.

Keena, C. (2013). *First Victim of the Rising*. The Irish Times. https://www.irishtimes.com/culture/heritage/first-victim-of-the-rising-1.1402766 [Accessed 21 Jan. 2025].

Keogh, D. (2013). William Martin Murphy and the Origins of the 1913 Lockout. *Saothar*, pp.28–30. https://www.irishlabourhistorysociety.com/wp-content/uploads/2022/08/William-Martin-Murphy-and-the-origins-of-the-1913-Lockout.pdf.

Khalidi, R. (2020). *Hundred Years' War on Palestine: a History of Settler Colonial Conquest and Resistancesistance, 1917-2017*. S.L.:

Picador.

Kildea, J. (2003). Called to arms: Australian soldiers in the Easter Rising 1916. *Journal of the Australian War Memorial*, (39). https://www.awm.gov.au/articles/journal/j39/kildea.

Kleinmann, S. (2009). *Sirr, Henry Charles*. Www.dib.ie. https://www.dib.ie/biography/sirr-henry-charles-a8099 [Accessed 30 Oct. 2024].

Kumar, A. (2022). *Michael Collins hid from Black and Tans among Dublin's Jews*. Irish Examiner. https://www.irishexaminer.com/news/arid-40822321.html [Accessed 15 Jan. 2025].

Lenin, V. (1916). The Discussion On Self-Determination Summed Up. *Sbornik Sotsial-Demokrata No. 1*. Jul. https://www.marxists.org/archive/lenin/works/1916/jul/x01.htm.

Linder, Professor, D. (1995). The Trials of Oscar Wilde: An Account. *The Trials of Oscar Wilde: An Account*. https://www.famous-trials.com/wilde/327-home UMKC School of Law.

Little, P. (1941). *A 1916 DOCUMENT THE MYSTERY OF THE DUBLIN CASTLE CYPHER*. The Capuchin Annual, Dublin: Irish Capuchin Franciscans, pp.454–462. https://designrr.s3.amazonaws.com/mbyrne_at_actonbv.com_141156/mbyrneactonbvcom_CA-1942-CA1699364021.pdf [Accessed 23 Oct. 2024].

Lorenz, I. (n.d.). *THE TRIAL AGAINST DAVID SEALTIEL IN HAMBURG (1937)*. www.jüdischer-friedhof-altona.de. https://www.xn--jdischer-friedhof-altona-vsc.de/img/biographien/sealtiel_david-trial.pdf.

Louis, W.R. (1965). The Stokes Affair and the Origins of the Anti-Congo Campaign, 1895-1896. *Revue belge de Philologie et d'Histoire*, 43(2), pp.572–584. doi:https://doi.org/10.3406/rbph.1965.2576 Stokes Trial 573-574.

Lynch, R. (2022). Ireland's Other Civil War: Ulster January-June 1922. *www.rte.ie*. https://www.rte.ie/history/ira-

convention/2022/0209/1278754-irelands-other-civil-war-ulster-january-june-1922/.
Lysaght, C. (1979). Brendan Bracken: The Fantasist Whose Dreams Came True. In: *Brendan Bracken Memorial Lecture*. Brendan Bracken Memorial Lecture. Cambridge: International Churchill Society, p.13. https://winstonchurchill.org/publications/finest-hour/finest-hour-113/brendan-bracken-the-fantasist-whose-dreams-came-true/.
Lysaght, M. (1975). Norbury, 'The Hanging Judge' (17451831). *Dublin Historical Record*, 30(2), pp.58–65. doi:https://doi.org/10.2307/30087176 Read to the Old Dublin Society.
machree01 (2008). *Grace – Anthony Kearns*. YouTube. https://www.youtube.com/watch?v=G6Oi7CdBc78 [Accessed 22 Dec. 2024].
MacNeill, E. (1914). *On behalf of the Irish Volunteers Executive*. [Letter] Co-operation between the Irish Volunteers and the Ulster Volunteers. Collection: Bulmer Hobson Papers, 1905-1968. https://catalogue.nli.ie/Record/vtls000365415 [Accessed 6 Nov. 2024].
Mannix, P. (2011). *The Belligerent Prelate*. Cambridge Scholars Publishing.
Maume, P. (2009a). Colthurst, John Colthurst Bowen-. In: *Dictionary of Irish Biography*. Dublin: Royal Irish Academy. https://www.dib.ie/biography/colthurst-john-colthurst-bowen-a1885.
Maume, P. (2009b). Edelstein, (Eli) Joseph. In: *Dictionary of Irish Biography*. Dublin: Royal Irish Academy. https://www.dib.ie/biography/edelstein-eli-joseph-a2878.
Maume, P. (2009c). Murphy, William Martin. *Dictionary of Irish Biography*. doi:https://doi.org/10.3318/dib.006106.v1.
McAleese, M., Senator (2013). *Report of the Inter-Departmental Committee to establish the facts of State involvement with the Magdalen Laundries. gov.ie*. Dublin: Department of Justice. https://www.gov.ie/en/collection/a69a14-report-of-the-inter-departmental-committee-to-establish-the-facts-of/?referrer=https://www.justice.ie/en/JELR/Pages/MagdalenRpt2013.

McElhatton, S. (2022). Civil War 1922: Darkness descends. *RTE.ie.* doi:urn:epic:1305408.

McGarrity, J. (1923). *Context: Note in Joseph McGarrity's handwritting listing the names 'of those who murdered brave Harry Boland in his hotel at Skerries, Ireland',.* Catalogue.nli.ie. https://catalogue.nli.ie/Record/vtls000588256 [Accessed 22 Dec. 2024].

McGarry, F. (2016). Essay, The courts-martial of the 1916 leaders. *Essays on the Court Martials.* https://courtmartial.nationalarchives.ie/court-martial-of-the-1916-leaders.html.

McHugh, R. (1956). Thomas Kettle and Francis Sheehy-Skeffington. *University Review*, 1(9), pp.6–18. https://www.jstor.org/stable/25504394.

McNamara, K.J. (2016). *Dreams of a Great Small Nation.* PublicAffairs.

McNeill, R. (2004). *Ulster's Stand For Union.* Cambridge University Press. https://www.gutenberg.org/files/14326/14326-h/14326-h.htm.

Miller, I. (2016). *'The Instrument of Death': Prison Doctors and Medical Ethics in Revolutionary-Period Ireland.* A History of Forced Feeding. https://link.springer.com/chapter/10.1007/978-3-319-31113-5_3 OnLine ISBN 978-3-319-31113-5.

mise me fein (2016). *Grace – Jim McCann.* YouTube. https://www.youtube.com/watch?v=A8LVlJ1I5pQ [Accessed 4 Nov. 2024].

Mohr, T. (2019). Irish Home Rule and Constitutional Reform in the British Empire, 1885-1914. *Revue française de civilisation britannique*, XXIV-2 2019(XXIV-2). doi:https://doi.org/10.4000/rfcb.3900.

Moloney, M. (2016). On this day 1916 – The Portobello Barracks murders. *Anphoblacht*, (1), 26 Apr. https://www.anphoblacht.com/contents/25871.

Morrison, G. and Tim Pat Coogan (1999). *The Irish Civil War -its Origins and Course.* London: Weidenfield and Nicholson.

Mulhall, E. (n.d.). Punching the Wind: Captain Jack White, the misfit of the Irish Revolution. *Punching the Wind: Captain Jack White, the misfit of the Irish Revolution.* https://www.rte.ie/centuryireland/articles/punching-the-wind-captain-jack-white-the-misfit-of-the-irish-revolution.

Murphy, F. (1984). *Dublin slums in the 1930s.* [Read to the Old Dublin Society] https://www.jstor.org/stable/30100635 [Accessed 29 Oct. 2024]. Page 106 refers to Asylum Yard.

Murphy, G. (2018). *The Great Cover-Up.* Cork: Collins Press.

Murphy, W. and Coleman, M. (2009). O'Hegarty (Ó hÉigeartuigh), Diarmuid. In: *Dictionary of Irish Biography.* Dublin: Royal Irish Academy. https://www.dib.ie/biography/ohegarty-o-heigeartuigh-diarmuid-a6802.

Murray, Sean Patrick. (2024) "The Case for Eamon de Valera's Birth and Baptismal Records Being Forgeries." *Iarmhí: Journal of the Westmeath Archaeological and History Society*, vol. 1, no. 4 debanked.com/pdfs/deValeraBirthRecordForgeries.pdf.

Nationalarchives.ie. (2024a). *National Archives: Census of Ireland 1911.* https://www.census.nationalarchives.ie/pages/1911/Dublin/Pembroke_West/Lotts_Road__South/10339/ [Accessed 12 Nov. 2024]. Residents of a house 70 in Lotts Road, South (Pembroke West, Dublin) James Connolly aged 43 and family.

Nationalarchives.ie. (2024b). *National Archives: Census of Ireland 1911.* https://www.census.nationalarchives.ie/pages/1911/Dublin/Trinity_Ward/Asylum_Yard/87701/ [Accessed 12 Nov. 2024]. Alice Brady family.

Newsinger, J. and Newsinger, J. (1986). 'As Catholic As The Pope': James Connolly and the Roman Catholic Church in Ireland. *Saothar*, 11, pp.7–18. https://www.jstor.org/stable/23195983.

Newsinger, J. (1983). James Connolly and the Easter Rising. *Science & Society*, 47(2), pp.152–177. https://www.jstor.org/stable/40401707 [Accessed 25 May 2019].

Niall O'Dowd (2023). *The Easter Rising and a day at the races for my*

Irish grandfather. IrishCentral.com. https://www.irishcentral.com/roots/history/easter-rising-races-grandfather [Accessed 27 Nov. 2024].

Ó Néill, J. (2018). *Where, oh where, is our James Connolly: #Connolly150*. The Treason Felony Blog. https://treasonfelony.wordpress.com/2018/06/05/where-oh-where-is-our-james-connolly-connolly150/ [Accessed 21 Oct. 2024].

O'Callaghan, M. (2009). *Pigott, Richard*. Www.dib.ie. https://www.dib.ie/biography/pigott-richard-a7335 [Accessed 10 Nov. 2024]. DOI: https://doi.org/10.3318/dib.007335.v1.

O'Callaghan, M. (2016). Ireland, Empire and British Foreign Policy: Roger Casement and the First World War. *Breac: A Digital Journal of Irish Studies*. https://breac.nd.edu/articles/ireland-empire-and-british-foreign-policy-roger-casement-and-the-first-world-war/#_edn28.

O'Connor, R. (2021). *"Who was Grace Gifford Plunkett? The heartbreaking true story behind the song 'Grace*. irishpost.com. https://www.irishpost.com/life-style/who-was-grace-gifford-plunkett-the-heartbreaking-true-story-behind-the-song-grace-205281 [Accessed 4 Nov. 2024].

O'Keeffe, H. (2020). How Russian crown jewels went from the Romanovs to Harry Boland. *RTE.ie*. doi:urn:epic:1115356.

O'Siochain, S. (2005). *Roger Casement's Vision of freedom*. mural.maynoothuniversity.ie. https://mural.maynoothuniversity.ie/1136/1/RCSOSRIA.pdf [Accessed 3 Nov. 2024].

O'Halpin, E. (1981). Sir Warren Fisher and the Coalition, 1919–1922. *The Historical Journal*, 24(4), pp.907–927. doi:https://doi.org/10.1017/s0018246x00008268.

Player, A. (2016). *Republican Loan Film*. IFI Archive Player. https://ifiarchiveplayer.ie/historical-material-republican-loans/ [Accessed 24 Oct. 2024].

Pletcher, K. (2019). Jallianwala Bagh Massacre | Causes, History, Death Toll, Importance, & Facts. In: *Encyclopædia Britannica*.

https://www.britannica.com/event/Jallianwala-Bagh-Massacre.
Plunkett, G. (1949). *Index of /reels/bmh*. Militaryarchives.ie.
https://bmh.militaryarchives.ie/reels/bmh/BMH.WS0257.pdf [Accessed 23 Oct. 2024].
Plunkett, J. (1915). *Plunkett, G. G. Letter (how happy he is and how much he loves her)*. [Postal] https://catalogue.nli.ie/Record/vtls000652679.
POPE LEO XIII (1891). *RERUM NOVARUM*. [Encyclical].
Pulju, A. (2009). De Valera Performs the Oath: Word, Voice, Book, and Act. In: *Crossroads: Performance Studies and Irish Culture*. London: Palgrave Macmillan, pp.129–130. https://link.springer.com/chapter/10.1057/9780230244788_11.
Quinn, J. (2009). *Crawford, Frederick Hugh ('Fred')*. Dictionary of Irish Biography. https://www.dib.ie/biography/crawford-frederick-hugh-fred-a2158.
Quinn, J. (n.d.). Sir Francis Vane's quest for justice after Easter Week. *History Ireland*. https://historyireland.com/sir-francis-vanes-quest-for-justice-after-easter-week/.
Harrington, Ellen Burton. "*Homosexuality in the Life and Work of Joseph Conrad: Love between the Lines* (Review)." *Conradiana*, vol. 42, no. 1-2, 2010, pp. 171–177, https://doi.org/10.1353/cnd.2010.0008.
Sara (n.d.). *Sara's Michael Collins Site – A Grisly Business*. SarasMichaelcollinssite.com. https://sarasMichaelcollinssite.com/a_grisly_business [Accessed 7 Nov. 2024].
Schmuhl, R. (2016). *Roger Casement and America // Articles // breac // University of Notre Dame*. breac.nd.edu. https://breac.nd.edu/articles/roger-casement-and-america/.
Schultz, D. and Felter, M. (n.d.). The Making of an Irish Nationalist: James Mark Sullivan and the Film Company of Ireland in America. *screening the past*, (33). https://www.screeningthepast.com/issue-33-knocknagow/the-making-of-an-irish-nationalist/.
Sheehy Skeffington, H. (1916). *British Militarism as I Have Known It*.

[1916-1917 – delivered at numerous fundraising events across the United States] https://speakingwhilefemale.co/war-sheehy-skeffington/.

Sheehy-Skeffington, F. (1915). *Against Militarism*. [Published in the 'Irish Citizen'] https://www.irishtimes.com/opinion/francis-sheehy-skeffington-open-letter-to-thomas-macdonagh-1.2580899.

Sheridan, C. (1923). *In Many Places*. London: Jonathan Cape, p.Chapter 3 Rory O'Connor. Pages 29-33 Michael Collins. https://ia800100.us.archive.org/20/items/in.ernet.dli.2015.37719/2015.3 7719.In-Many-Places.pdf.

Sheridan, C. (2018). *Russian Portraits*. The Project Gutenberg, p.109. https://www.gutenberg.org/cache/epub/58009/pg58009-images.html [Accessed 18 Nov. 2024].

Simkin, J. (1997a). *Clare Sheridan*. Spartacus Educational. https://spartacus-educational.com/Clare_Sheridan.htm [Accessed 18 Nov. 2024].

Simkin, J. (1997b). *Reginald Hall*. Spartacus Educational. https://spartacus-educational.com/SShallW.htm [Accessed 2 Nov. 2024].

Simon, J. (1916). *Report of the Royal Commission on the arrest and subsequent treatment of Mr. Francis Sheehy Skeffington. Mr. Thomas Dickson, and Mr. Patrick James McIntyre.* *https://archive.org/details/op1256532-1001*. UK: University of Southampton. Report of the Royal Commission on the arrest and subsequent treatment of Mr. Francis Sheehy Skeffington. Mr. Thomas Dickson, and Mr. Patrick James McIntyre.

Skeffington, F.S. (1936). *In Dark and Evil Days*. Dublin: JAMES DUFFY, p.xxiii. https://www.cavanlibrary.ie/cavan-history/history-online/digitised-material/in-dark-and-evil-days-sheehy-skeffington-1936.pdf.

Skinnider, M. (2016). *DOING MY BIT FOR IRELAND*. US: Gutenberg. https://www.gutenberg.org/cache/epub/52740/pg52740-images.html.

Sloan, G. (2013). The British State and the Irish Rebellion of 1916: An Intelligence Failure or a Failure of Response? *Intelligence and National*

Security, 6(3), pp.328–357.
doi:https://doi.org/10.1080/02684527.2012.735079.

Sloan, G. (2017). Hide seek and negotiate: Alfred Cope and counter intelligence in Ireland 1919–1921. *Intelligence and National Security*, 33(2), pp.176–195.
doi:https://doi.org/10.1080/02684527.2017.1329118.

Smyth, E. (1950). *Index of /reels/bmh*. Militaryarchives.ie. https://bmh.militaryarchives.ie/reels/bmh WS334.

South, A. (2018). *Room 40: Cryptanalysis during World War I*. Navy General Board. https://www.navygeneralboard.com/room-40-cryptanalysis-during-world-war-i/.

Stafford, D. (2020). Clare Sheridan: 'The nearest thing to a sister that Winston ever had.' 23 Mar. https://winstonchurchill.hillsdale.edu/clare-sheridan/ Adapted from David Stafford's book Oblivion or Glory: The Making of Winston Churchill 1921.

Sweetman, R. (2019). *Defending Trinity College Dublin, Easter 1916: Anzacs and the rising*. Dublin, Ireland: Four Courts Press.

Talbot, H. (1923). *Michael Collins Own Story*. Ireland: Hutchinson & Co. http://www.generalMichaelCollins.com/on-line-books/Michael-collins-own-story-index/.

Taylor, A.J.P. (1987). *The First world war: an illustrated history*. Harmondsworth: Penguin Books, p.146.

Thomas, C. (2019). *'Take them to hell': The curious tale of the hidden Russian jewels and Dev's deal with the Bolsheviks*. TheJournal.ie. https://www.thejournal.ie/russian-jewels-state-papers-4942636-Dec2019/ [Accessed 21 Nov. 2024].

Toibin, C. (1997). A Whale of a Time. *London Review of Books*, 19(21), 30 Oct. https://www.lrb.co.uk/the-paper/v19/n19/colm-toibin/a-whale-of-a-time.

Towell, N. (2016). *Anzacs and the Easter Rising 1916: Australia's role in Ireland's past*. The Sydney Morning Herald. https://www.smh.com.au/national/anzacs-easter-rising-and-the-20160317-gnl5oo.html [Accessed 24 Oct. 2024].

Townshend, C. (2022). *The Partition Ireland Divided, 1885-1925.* Penguin Books.

Venning, A. (2017). *Winston Churchill's cousin was a seductress and SOVIET SPY.* Mail Online. https://www.dáilymail.co.uk/news/article-4502608/Winston-Churchill-s-cousin-seductress-SOVIET-SPY.html

Virtual Treasury (2022). *Clare Consuelo Sheridan.* YouTube. https://www.youtube.com/watch?v=7VOQ0y0GYEM [Accessed 24 Nov. 2024]. Actor Shona Gibson reads from Clare Consuelo Sheridan's Diary as part of 'Inside the Railings: A Portrait of Life within the Public Record Office of Ireland'.

Walsh, M. (2016). *Bitter freedom: Ireland in a revolutionary world 1918-1923.* London: Faber & Faber.

Ward, H. (1910). *A Voice from the Congo.* CHARLES SCRIBNER'S SONS, p.233. https://ia600102.us.archive.org/2/items/voicefromcongoco00ward/voicefromcongoco00ward_bw.pdf.

Wikipedia Contributors (2024a). *Edmund Musgrave Barttelot.* Wikipedia. https://en.wikipedia.org/wiki/Edmund_Musgrave_Barttelot.

Wikipedia Contributors (2024b). *Strand School.* Wikipedia. https://archives.kingscollections.org/index.php/strand-school-london-1897-1979 King's College London Archives.

Winchestercollegearchives.org. (1895). *PDF.js viewer.* https://winchestercollegearchives.org/PDFViewer/web/viewer.html?file=%2fFilename.ashx%3ftableName%3dta_wykehamist%26columnName%3dfilename%26recordId%3d370%23page%3d5&searchText=cromwell [Accessed 4 Nov. 2024]. Page 141 No. 316-OCT. 1895.

Www.cso.ie. (2017). *Census and People of the 1916 Rising Life in 1916 Ireland: Stories from statistics – Central Statistics Office.* https://www.cso.ie/en/releasesandpublications/cp/p-1916/1916irl/cpr/cmp/imp/ [Accessed 18 Jan. 2025].

www.lurganancestry.com. (n.d.). *Lurgan Ancestry ~ The Irish Land War.* https://www.lurganancestry.com/landwar.htm [Accessed 10 Nov. 2024].

Www.rte.ie. (1913). *Larkin makes dramatic appearance before arrest | Century Ireland.* https://www.rte.ie/centuryireland/articles/larkin-makes-dramatic-appearance-before-arrest [Accessed 5 Nov. 2024].

Yeates, P. (2001). The Dublin 1913 Lockout. *History Ireland.* https://historyireland.com/the-dublin-1913-lockout/.

Acknowledgements

I acknowledge the assistance provided by the wide range of books, blogs, and articles identified in the bibliography. In particular:

Ronan Fanning's Fatal Path – British government and Irish revolution ; 1910-1922,

R.F. Foster's Vivid Faces: the revolutionary generation in Ireland, 1890-1923.

There is, obviously, a massive amount of useful information available on the internet and I accessed many sites. I'm sorry that I do not have space to thank all the authors. I should though mention the following people's whose podcasts I found especially informative and, indeed, inspiring ...

Professor Patrick Geoghegan: *'Ireland in Rebellion: 1782-1916'* lecture series, Department of History, Trinity College Dublin

Prof. Michael Laffan: *'The Civil War: A Centenary Perspective, Address to the Galway Archaeological and Historical Society'* (April 2022) and *'Nationalism in Ireland 1900-1916: Home Rulers Separatists and Protestant Nationalists'*.

Staff at Winchester College, National Library of Ireland, and King's College London were extremely helpful, making suggestions and giving guidance on how to access data:-

- Suzanne Foster, College Archivist at Winchester College, provided crucial information about Jack White (a founder, with James Connolly, of the Irish Citizen Army). This led me, with her assistance, to learning about other Winchester College pupils who had involvement with events detailed in this book.

- Joanne Carroll, Archivist National Library of Ireland, assisted me with accessing information concerning the executions following the Uprising.

- King's College London staff: Oliver Snaith, Archives Assistant, Professor Richard Kirkland (English Dept.), Doctor Michael Collins (Reader in American Studies). These people gave me advice and assistance concerning Michael Collins time in London before 1916.

- As well as making use of his podcast, I took the opportunity to email Professor Patrick Geoghegan, Department of History, Trinity College Dublin. He provided useful advice regarding the Uprising and Michael Collins.

I also acknowledge the support and patience of my wife (Lorraine), especially when I was continually promising that the book was almost finished, and our friend Robin Thepsiri who made some valuable comments.

Any errors or omissions are my responsibility.

INDEX

Adcock, Frank, 174

Albert, Heinrich, 133, 172

Alfred Lewis Jones, 48

Allan, Maud, 245

Ancient Order of Hibernians, 108, 112

Aquinas, Saint Thomas, 159

Asquith, Herbert, 61, 62, 66, 81, 83, 85, 86, 87, 89, 90, 91, 102, 103, 107, 111, 113–18, 151, 152, 159, 223, 230, 236–46, 247–50, 264, 265, 279

Asquith, Margot, 245

Asquith, Raymond, 70, 95–97, 113, 115, 116, 235, 246

Augustine, Saint, 80, 124, 160

Australia, 25, 242, 276

Bailey, Daniel, 164, 165, 166, 171, 240

Balbriggan, 279

Balfour, Arthur, 259

Bandon, Cork, 60, 63, 330, 333

Barry, Kevin, 282–85

Barry, Kevin - Introduction, 2

Barton, Robert, 300, 303, 304, 306

Barttelot, Edmund, 47

Behan, Brendan, 44, 167, 319

Bell, Alan, 275

Bell, Alan - Killed, 32–36

Belton, Patrick, 146

Birrell, Augustine, 87, 89, 93, 113

Birrell, Augustine - King George V, 82–86

Birrell, Augustine - Wife, 80–82

Birrell, Eleanor - Augustine, 80–82

Blackader, Charles, 223, 224

Bloody Sunday, 264

Boland, Harry, 146, 255, 263, 268, 275, 300, 307, 313, 314, 326

Bonar Law, Andrew, 91, 113–15, 118, 302

Bowen-Colthurst, John, 201–4

Boy-Ed, Karl, 129

Bracken, Brendan, 332, 333

Brady, Alice, 76

Broy, Ned, 263

Brugha, Cathal, 211, 253, 264, 268, 269, 295, 306–8, 326, 335

Bull, Mrs, 9–18, 273

Byron, Lord, 14

Carson, Edward, 13, 65, 83, 85, 86, 87, 89–92, 106, 107, 108, 109, 113–15, 116–19, 139, 238, 241, 248, 256

Carson, Edward - Covenant, 416–17

Carson, Edward - F.E. Smith "Dinner Talk", 57–65

Carson, Edward - Land Evictions, 42

Casement, Roger, 46–51, 70, 110, 125, 126, 127, 128, 129, 130, 135, 136–44, 155, 157, 158, 173, 182, 236–46, 251, 252

Casement, Roger - Introduction, 2

Casement, Roger - Jack White meet, 69–70

Casement, Roger - New York, 125–29

Casement, Roger - Return to Ireland, 161–66

Cave of the Golden Calf, 95

Ceannt, Éamonn, 226, 253, 332

Chalmers, Robert, 233

Chamberlain, Austen, 299

Childers, Erskine, 22, 110, 326, 333

Christensen, Adler, 136, 137, 168

Christensen, Adler - New York, 125–29

Churchill, Clementine, 88, 278–81

Churchill, Marigold, 279

Churchill, Randolph, 60

Churchill, Winston, 60, 63, 86, 89–91, 92, 93, 95, 97, 103, 133, 235, 254, 256, 260, 261, 278–81, 279, 299, 301, 310, 311, 316, 323, 325, 329, 332, 333

Churchill, Winston - Clementine, 88

Clan na Gael, 137

Clarke, Kathleen, 251, 255

Clarke, Tom, 105, 107, 108, 111, 118, 126, 128, 137, 143, 147, 148, 151–55, 157, 158, 161, 163, 176, 184, 193, 198, 207, 210, 212, 218, 224, 227, 229, 255, 264

Clune, Archbishop, 25

Colbert, Cornelius, 208, 215, 227, 332

Collins, Johnny/Seán, 291, 328

Collins, Micheal, 20–31, 145, 147, 148, 149, 192, 215, 253–58, 260, 263, 272, 275–77, 278, 291, 296–302, 303–18, 323, 326

Last Trip Home, 328–37

Collins, Micheal - Bolland, 263–70

Collins, Micheal - Introduction, 2

Connolly, James, 2, 52, 53, 54, 55, 70, 130, 135, 145, 148, 149, 176, 177, 182, 184, 185, 186, 192, 206, 207, 208, 210, 211, 212, 227, 235, 253, 272

Connolly, James – Castle Hospital, 229–34

Connolly, James - Larkin, Nellie Gifford, 71–74

Connolly, James - Lockout, 77–79

Connolly, James and Mallin, 105–12

Connolly, James 'Kidnapped', 153–58

Connolly, Jimmy - 'Boyhood', 37–40

Connolly, John, 37

Connolly, Lillie, 52, 53, 54, 55, 56, 71, 106, 135, 229, 231, 233, 234

Connolly, Nora - St. Enda's, 20–27

Connolly, Seán, 157, 186, 187, 207

Conrad, Joseph, 51, 128, 243

Cooper, Diana, 95

Cooper, Majorie, 95

Cope, Alfred, 1–3, 290, 300, 333

Craig, James, 86, 92, 106, 118, 295, 296, 299, 301, 303, 305, 310, 312, 329, 337

Craig, James - Covenant, 416–17

Crawford, Fred, 109, 110

Crawford, Fred - Firearms, 65–68

Crippen, Dr, 91

Cullen, Tom, 31

Cumann na mBan, 112, 185, 188, 206, 211, 251

Curragh Mutiny/Incident, 94, 118, 262

Curran, John, 14

Dáil Éireann, 276

Daly, Ned, 208, 226

Darling, Judge, 239

De Valera, Eamon, 208, 227, 254, 255, 257, 258, 263–71, 276, 290, 292–98, 304, 305, 306, 307, 308, 315, 324, 326, 327, 333, 334, 337

Devoy, John, 136, 137, 143, 155, 156, 161, 163, 169, 171, 270, 271, 276, 332

Devoy, John - Casement, 125–29

Dickson, Thomas, 203

Dobbin, William, 201–4

Donnelly, Joseph, 72

Dryhurst, Nora, 119

Duggan, Eamonn, 300, 306

Dunne, Reginald, 104

Edelstein, Joseph, 203

Edward III, 238

Emmet, Robert, 13, 14, 25, 36, 141, 153, 156, 325, 333, 334

Esperanto, 55, 56, 198

Ewart, Adjutant-General, 99, 100, 101, 102

Fisher, Norman, 96, 290, 291

Fisher, Warren, 70

Four Courts, 208, 210, 318, 319, 321, 323, 325, 330, 333

French, Field Marshal, 90–94, 97–103, 179, 262, 263, 297

Frewen, Moreton, 60

Frewen, Ruby, 60

Frongoch, 237, 251, 265

Gaspari, Cardinal, 160

Gay, Tommy, 263

Gifford (Plunkett) Grace, 272–75

Gifford, Grace, 18, 19, 20–27, 119, 120, 121, 122, 123, 124, 135, 145, 149, 150, 177, 180, 181, 216

Gifford, Grace - Marriage, 217–22

Gifford, Nellie, 71, 73, 79, 135, 145, 188

Gifford, Nellie - Connolly, Larkin 'Meet', 71–74

Gifford, Sydney, 135

Gifford, Sydney 'John Brennan', 130, 131, 135

Gifford-MacDonagh, Muriel, 21, 119–22, 120, 135, 145, 216, 218, 219, 273

Gladstone, William, 276

Gorges, Richard, 17

Gough, Hubert, 93, 94, 101, 102, 103, 109, 261

Granville Hotel, 9, 10, 28, 29

Greenwood, Hamar, 279

Gregory, Arthur, 174

Grenan, Shiela, 211

Grey, Edward, 51

Grey, Lord, 236

Griffith, Arthur, 22, 24, 72, 76, 111, 112, 148, 203, 255, 264, 266, 268, 290, 293–306, 308, 317, 323–27, 329, 330, 333

Grigg, Edward, 70, 96, 294

Gudansky, Rabbi Abraham, 26

Hall, Frank, 66, 67, 172, 174, 240, 364

Hall, Reginald, 161, 162, 167, 172, 173, 174

Heathcote, Major, 216, 232

Henley, Sylvia, 237

Henry VIII, 238

Heuston, Seán, 332

Ho Chi Minh, 28

Hobson, Bulmer, 106, 148, 151, 152, 153, 176, 182

Houlihan, Kathleen Ni, 11, 12, 14, 272

Howth, 109, 182

Innishannon, Cork, 60, 320, 360

Irish Citizen Army, 70, 77, 78, 105, 108, 145, 153, 154, 157, 177, 184, 185, 187, 188, 189, 253

Irish Republican Army, 191, 317

Irish Republican Brotherhood, 107, 108, 111, 126, 128, 147, 151, 159, 239, 258, 259, 264, 270

Irish Transport and General Workers Union, 70, 74

Irish Volunteers, 106, 107, 108, 109, 111, 112, 116, 118, 119, 176, 180, 183, 184, 185, 198, 199, 214

Jameson, Jack, 29, 30, 31, 275, 313

Joyce, James, 198

Kavanagh, Joe, 263

Kavanagh, Seumas, 282

Kehoe, Tom, 33

Kell, Colonel, 1

Kelly, James, 202

Kenny, John, 128

Kettle, Tom, 332

Kiernan, Kitty, 22, 257, 268, 313

Killaloe, Bishop of, 25

Killeen, Susan, 251

King George, 280

King George V - Birrell, Buckingham Palace, 82–86

Lady Londonderry, 66, 68, 91

Lady Londonderry- Covenant, 416–17

Lahiff, Micheal, 187

Larkin, James, 70, 71–76, 108, 112, 130, 135, 145, 234, 235

Larkin, James - Lockout, 77–79

Lavery, Lady, 312, 313

Lea-Wilson, Perceval, 370, 371, 396

Lenin, 186, 276, 307

Leopold, King, 46–51

Lloyd George, David, 3, 61, 62, 86, 87, 89, 90, 113, 247, 254, 256, 260–62, 265, 266, 267, 268, 278, 290, 293, 295, 296, 299–306, 308, 314, 324, 325, 328

Logue, Cardinal, 177

Lowe, General, 211

Lynch, Arthur, 241

Lynch, Liam, 320, 330

MacDiarmada, 235

MacDiarmada, Seán, 107, 146, 147, 148, 152, 153, 154, 208, 210, 212, 214, 253

MacDonagh, John, 21

MacDonagh, Joseph, 22

MacDonagh, Thomas, 119, 199, 216

MacNeill, Eoin, 106, 118, 119, 151, 152, 153, 154, 176, 177, 183, 184, 185

Maconchy, Ernest, 224

Macready, General, 284

Magdalen Laundry, 76

Mallin, Micheal, 157, 187, 189, 226, 253

Mannix, Daniel, 276, 326, 327

Margot Asquith, 247

Markievicz, Constance, 71, 72, 145, 157, 198, 226, 227

Markievicz, Constance During Uprising, 187–89

Martens, Ludwig, 276

Masaryk, Tomas, 70

Maxwell, General, 23, 197,
223, 224, 227, 229, 230,
233, 234, 237, 264

Maxwell, General John, 228

McDonagh, Thomas, 229

McGarrity, Joe, 129, 136, 137,
143, 163, 270, 300

McGoey, John, 163, 164

McIntyre, Patrick, 203

Michel, Louise, 120

Moloney, Helena, 2, 186

Montague, Edwin, 95, 228, 237

Montefiore, Dora, 75

Monteith, Robert, 143, 144,
163, 164, 165, 166, 171

Morel, Edmund, 50

Morley, Lord, 102

Mulcahy, Richard, 317, 318

Murphy, William, 74

Nixon, John, 316

Nora, Connolly, 119, 135, 230,
231, 234, 272, 273

Norbury, Lord, 14

Northcliffe Lord, 236, 242,
247, 248, 261, 281

O'Brien, James, 186

O'Brien, Nancy, 43

O'Connor, Rory, 119, 295,
306, 319–22, 323, 325, 326

O'Connor, Tommy, 171

O'Daly, Paddy, 28, 32–36, 275

O'Farrell, Elizabeth, 211

O'Hanrahan, Micheal, 215, 227

O'Hegarty, Diarmuid, 27, 28, 272

O'Malley, Ernie, 294, 295, 320, 332

O'Mara, James, 276

O'Reilly, Joe, 24, 314, 323

O'Sullivan, Joseph, 104, 324

Oblong, May, 45

O'Neill, Sonny, 336

Orange Order, 68

Paget, Arthur-
   Curragh, Mutiny/Incident,
   90–102

Parnell, Charles, 32, 225, 254

Partridge, Bill, 188, 189

Pasha, Emin, 47

Patrick Traynor, 77

Pearse, Patrick, 16, 17, 106,
   107, 118, 125, 126, 139,
   148, 151, 153, 154, 156,
   171, 173, 176, 182–85, 198,
   206–12, 218, 224–27, 229,
   252–53, 260, 272

Pearse, Willie, 27, 207

Percival, Arthur, 212, 291

Perolz, Maire, 145

Plunkett (Gifford), Grace, 272–75

Plunkett Grace - Marriage.
   Gifford, Grace - Marriage

Plunkett, Count, 22, 159, 160,
   171, 185

Plunkett, George, 185

Plunkett, Joseph, 18, 19, 22,
   29, 118, 119, 120, 121, 137–
   44, 146–49, 148, 153, 154,
   155, 156, 157, 168, 176,
   177, 180, 182, 184, 185,
   192, 206, 207, 210, 212,
   214, 218, 229, 252–54, 255,
   256, 272, 275, 318, 320

Plunkett, Philomena, 161

Pope Benedict XV, 159, 160

Price, Ivon, 1, 234

Quinn, John, 128

Redmond, John, 82, 83, 87, 89,
   107–10, 111, 113, 114, 115,
   116, 118, 137, 148, 248,
   260, 265

Rendall, Montagu, 333

Rhodes, Major, 216

Rice, Mary Spring, 110

Richardson, George, 109, 110

Ridgway, Joseph, 229

Robinson, Seumas, 335

Room 40, 161, 174, 177

Rossa, Jeremiah, 143, 147, 153

Sassoon, Philip, 303

Seely, John, 91, 92, 93, 97,
   100, 101, 102

Curragh Incident-Mutiny, 90–102

Serjeant Sullivan

Casement Trial, 239

Seton-Watson, Robert, 70

Shackleton, Francis, 17

Sheehy-Skeffington, Francis, 79, 177, 200, 230, 264

Sheehy-Skeffington, Hanna, 188

Sheehy-Skeffington, Hanna - Murder, 198–206

Shephard, Gordon, 110

Sheridan, Clare, 60, 307, 310, 319–22

Sherwood Foresters, 194, 196, 208, 224

Sirr, Major, 11

Skinnider, Margaret, 188, 189

Smith, F.E (Lord Birkenhead) - Carson, 59–65

Smith, F.E. (Lord Birkenhead), 63, 86, 89, 95, 238, 241, 278, 299, 301

Casement's trial, 238

Smith, F.E. and Carson - "Talk", 57–65

Smith, F.E., Lord Birkenhead, 329

Smuts, General, 294

Smyth, Eugene, 176

Spender, Wilfred, 70, 110

Spindler, Karl, 166

Spiro, Benny, 67

Stack, Austin, 166, 169

Stanley, Henry, 47, 48

Stanley, Venetia, 61, 92–98, 113, 114, 116, 223, 225, 237

Stanley, Violet, 95, 247

Stevenson, Frances, 247, 290

Stokes, Charles, 50

Stopford Green, Alice, 110

Sullivan, James, 22, 391

Swanzy, Oswald, 278

The Aud, 166

The Friends of Irish Freedom, 271

Thomson, Basil, 30, 127

Tobin, Richard, 30, 229

Tom Jones, 302, 303, 315

Tralee Bay, 164, 165, 171

Traynor, Oscar, 292, 293, 295

Traynor, Patrick, 77

Trotsky, 307

truce, 293–306

Ulster Special Constabulary, 329

Ulster Volunteer Force, 70, 299, 310, 313

Ulster Volunteers, 90, 91, 107, 108, 116

Valera, Eamon, 323–27

Vane, Francis, 67

von Bersdorff, 131, 273

von Kuhlmann, 115

von Papen, Count, 129, 131

von Rintelen, Franz, 172

von Skal, 131

von Wedel, 138

Wallace, Hugo, 68

Wallace, Robert - Covenant, 416–17

Washington, Harold, 284, 285

Weisbach, Raimund, 164, 165

White, George, 69

White, James 'Jack', 70, 77, 78, 96, 108, 278

White, James 'Jack' - Casement meet, 69–70

Wilde, Oscar, 17, 57, 58, 91, 136, 137, 172

Wilson, Henry, 52, 90, 91, 102, 103, 104, 113, 212, 213, 214, 299, 310–12, 316, 317, 323

Wilson, Woodrow President, 23, 27, 243, 270

Wimborne, Lord Lieutenant, 223

Winchester College, 69, 70, 96, 245, 333, 338

Winston Churchill, 78

Wolfe, Tone, 141

Woodfield, County Cork, 291, 328

Woodward, Willoughby, 229

Wooldridge, Charles, 172

End Notes

Introduction

1 Alfred Cope joined the Civil Service aged 14 and was rapidly promoted. He was one of a select team created by Warren Fisher (q.v.) sent to Dublin Castle in 1920 to improve the chaotic and corrupt administration. He was an agent in the truce and Treaty discussions; a 'firm believer in self –government for Ireland.' Sloan, G. (2017). Hide seek and negotiate: Alfred Cope and counter intelligence in Ireland 1919–1921. Intelligence and National Security.

"The negotiations which he (Cope) undertook at considerable danger to himself were approved by his superiors and he was able to bring about a state of affairs whereby the treaty of 1921 could be signed." The Times 14th May 1954 quoted in Sloan, G. (2017). Hide seek and negotiate: Alfred Cope and counter intelligence in Ireland 1919–1921. Intelligence and National Security, 33(2), pp.176–195.

Chapter 1 – Dublin, November 1919

2 Belfast was 'said to be the largest shipyard in the world; Belfast Harbour built the largest dry dock '... it had Sirroco Works, the world's largest tea-drying machinery maker, Belfast Ropeworks largest maker of rope, and the greatest maker of linen. Edgerton, D.L. (2018). The Rise and Fall of the British Nation: a twentieth-century History. London: Penguin Books, Pg 132.

3 The Granville Hotel Company at 17, Sackville St (Mrs. H. M. Smith, manageress). One of its waiters found a pocketbook and passed it to Joseph Plunkett, according to Grace Plunkett's witness statement, Page 6. bmh.militaryarchives WS0257

4 "there's a great gap between a gallous story and a dirty deed " (Act 3, line 573) The Playboy of the Western World, by J.M. Synge. Gallous: 1.

n., alt. gallows; 2. adj., deserving to be hanged; 3. daring, wicked, mischievous; 4. type of humour

5 Irish Crown Jewels, current value about £20 million, were stolen from Dublin Castle in 1907 and have never been recovered. The police found evidence of wild parties, orgies, and homosexual affairs. King Edward VII closed down the enquiry. A suspect was the brother of explorer Ernest Shackleton who was later jailed for fraud.

Chapter 2 A Chip Off The Old Block
6 Dáil loans: bonds first issued June 1919 by the Dáil (parliament) of the Irish Republic to fund government functions in opposition to the British administration. People bought bonds in huge numbers in Ireland and the USA. The money in the USA was the source of considerable dispute over the years.

7 "Willy Reilly and his Colleen Bawn": 1920 silent film based on William Carleton's 1855 novel. Set in Cavan it concerns religious tolerance. Premiered at Manchester's Free Trade Hall on 5 January 1920.

8 'Dáil Bonds Film' is a 1919 short propaganda film to promote the sale of Dáil Loan bonds. Copies of the film are in the Irish Film Archive, in RTÉ, and accessible online Player, A. (2016). Republican Loan Film. IFI Archive Player. https://ifiarchiveplayer.ie/historical-material-republican-loans/ [Accessed 24 Oct. 2024].
Socialist candidate James Connolly(q.v.), standing for Wood Quay ward, was the only candidate to distribute his election leaflets in Yiddish in 1902. Archive.org. (2024)

9 Black and Tans: unemployed former British soldiers from England who had fought in the First World War. Some were Irish-born. Notorious for

brutality. Often confused with the Auxiliaries, a unit of the Irish Constabulary, made up of former British officers; well-paid but poorly trained for police duties. 10,000 used by end of 1920. After service in Ireland some went to assist policing in Palestine.

10 Little Jerusalem: Name for area of Dublin. Donore Avenue in the West to Camden Street in the East, synonymous with Dublin's Jews. In 1888 they opened a Synagogue on St. Kevins Parade. Some pertinent names: Estella Francis Solomons (member of Cumann na mBan), Michael Noyk (Arthur Griffith's personal solicitor) and Robert Briscoe who worked directly for Michael Collins. Murray, R. (2018). » Little Jerusalem and a History of the Jewish Community in Dublin. Www.frg.ie. https://www.frg.ie/local-history/little-jerusalem-and-a-history-of-the-jewish-community-in-dublin/ [Accessed 20 Oct. 2024]. Socialist candidate James Connolly(q.v.), standing for Wood Quay ward, was the only candidate to distribute his election leaflets in Yiddish in 1902.

11 Stuart Rosenblatt, genealogist, described the incident in his book Moments to remember in Jewish Ireland. "Those who attended the Dublin Hebrew Congregation, then at Adelaide Road Synagogue passed down the tale orally and Rosenblatt first heard of it from the late Julie Lapedus, a participant. He has also heard 'secondhand' accounts, including one from the late Sybil Fishman, whose father was also a witness. Kumar, A. (2022)

Chapter 3 Time's Up, Mr.Bell
12 Eamon Broy's Witness Statement (WS1280,Page 135)-Arthur Cope (q.v.) has 'the British agent, Jameson, had been able to get in contact with him without Mick knowing that Jameson was an intelligence officer. Mick replied that he knew all along what Jameson really was,

but played with him for his own purposes and then had Jameson "plugged".

13 Phoenix Park murders: 1882, Lord Frederick Cavendish, Chief Secretary for Ireland and Thomas Burke, the Permanent Under-Secretary, were killed by militant republicans. Parnell condemned the murders but The Times printed letters where he apparently sympathised with the killers. Richard Pigott, a journalist, had forged the letters – he lost a court case and went to Spain where he shot himself.

14 Evictions: Bad weather caused low crop prices in 1874 and farmers struggled to pay rents; some landlords refused to reduce rents. MP Charles Parnell campaigned to lower them but evictions occurred. The Ashbourne Act of 1885 helped by allowing tenant farmers buy their freeholds; this was greatly extended by the 1903 Wyndham Land Purchase Act. Augustine Birrell's Act of 1909 allowed for compulsory purchase, and the purchase and division of untenanted land. www.lurganancestry.com. (n.d.). Lurgan Ancestry ~ The Irish Land War. https://www.lurganancestry.com/landwar.htm [Accessed 10 Nov. 2024].

15 Resident Magistrate Alan Bell set up what was basically a 'Star Chamber' where he demanded answers from Bank Managers. under oath, private with no legal representation. They could be committed to prison for refusing to answer. Fox, S. (2023). Chronology of Irish History 1919 – 1923. Irishhistory1919-1923chronology.ie.

16 Aintree, Liverpool, Grand National, 26 March 1920 (When Alan Bell was killed), won by Irish horse Troytown. Poethlyn started favourite but fell at the first fence, ridden by Ernest Piggott (grandfather of Lester), and had won the race the two previous years. The King attended.

Chapter 4 James Connolly, The Early Years

17 In 1900, Connolly wrote an article, "The coming generation", published in The Workers' Republic quoting a poem by socialist poet Fred Henderson with these lines. The Connolly Archive. (2022). The Coming Generation. https://eirigi.org/latestnews/2022/7/20/the-connolly-archive-the-coming-generation 'Worker's Republic' July 15th 1900. The Irish Citizen Army's Constitution stated that "The ownership of Ireland, moral and material, is vested of right in the people of Ireland." The Citizen Army provided 250 men and women combatants in the Easter Uprising, almost a third of the total. Higgins, M. (2016). Speech at a Reception to Mark the 102nd Anniversary of the Irish Citizen Army. media-library. https://www.president.ie/en/media-library/speeches/speech-by-president-higgins-at-a-reception-to-mark-the-102nd-anniversary-of [Accessed 3 Nov. 2024]. Also Burtenshaw, R. (2018). Connolly at 150. Jacobin.com.

18 1870 Education Act in England, and later Scotland, established a system to build and manage schools in areas where they were needed. Education was not compulsory until 1876.

19 There is no certainty as to which regiment Connolly joined nor what name he used when enlisting. Possibilities are: 2nd Battalion of the Royal Scots Regiment or 1st Battalion, King's Liverpool Regiment, or Royal Irish Fusiliers. His brother, John, enlisted in the Border Regiment in 1878 as James Reid. There is a possibility that James Connolly was 'John Henry' who deserted in 1889 from the Royal Scots. Ó Néill, J. (2018). Where, oh where, is our James Connolly: #Connolly150. The Treason Felony Blog.

Chapter 5 – A civilized people

20 A Royal Welsh Regiment was established in 2006 from the Royal Welch Fusiliers (23rd Foot) and the Royal Regiment of Wales (24th/41st Foot).

Chapter 6 – A high-minded and courteous man

21 The character 'Kurtz' in Joseph Conrad's novel *Heart of Darkness* is thought to have been based upon Barttelot. Wikipedia Contributors (2024a). Edmund Musgrave Barttelot.

22 Herbert Ward described Casement: "Imagine a tall and handsome man, of fine bearing; thin, mere muscle and bone, a sun-tanned face, blue eyes and curly black hair. A pure Irishman he is, with a captivating voice and a singular charm of manner. A man of distinction and great refinement, high-minded and courteous, impulsive and poetical. Quixotic perhaps some would say, and with a certain truth, for few men have shown themselves so regardless of personal advancement.' Ward, H. (1910). A Voice from the Congo. CHARLES SCRIBNER'S SONS, p.233. Also: Costigan, G. (1955). The Treason of Sir Roger Casement. The American Historical Review, 60(2), page 286.

23 Force Publique was established in 1886 by Captain Léon Roger on the instructions of Leopold II of Belgium. It was a mixture of Belgian regular soldiers and foreign mercenaries but later mainly native Congolese soldiers (19,000 in 1900). They enforced the rubber quotas for workers using slave labour, flogging and raping.

24 In a letter to a friend Casement wrote "In those lonely Congo forests where I found Leopold, I found also myself, the incorrigible Irishman."

Roger Casement to Alice Stopford Green, 20 April 1907, MS 10,464(3), Alice Stopford Green Papers, National Library of Ireland.

25 'Stokes' character as a gun runner even deadened much of the pain that might have otherwise been felt by the British journalists over the « cruel death of one of their fellow subjects." Louis, W.R. (1965). The Stokes Affair and the Origins of the Anti-Congo Campaign, 1895-1896. Revue belge de Philologie et d'Histoire, 43(2), pp.572–584. Page 581 refers. doi:https://doi.org/10.3406/rbph.1965.

26 "In 1903 the British Congo Consul Roger Casement provided the direct documentary evidence to substantiate the rumors of the 1890's and thereby gave the Foreign Office a basis on which to act if pressed to do so by public opinion. The publication of Casement's report in February 1904 proved to most Englishmen that reform of the Congo administration was imperative. "Page 582, Louis, W.R. (1965). The Stokes Affair and the Origins of the Anti-Congo Campaign, 1895-1896. Revue belge de Philologie et d'Histoire, 43(2), pp.572–584. doi:https://doi.org/10.3406/rbph.1965.2576.

27 "Through the high public profile of the campaigns around the Congo and the Putumayo, Casement not merely had access to a cohort of Liberal intellectuals and a press profile but had relations with senior figures within the Foreign Office, in particular one of its most senior members". O'Callaghan, M. (2016). Ireland, Empire and British Foreign Policy: Roger Casement and the First World War. Breac: A Digital Journal of Irish Studies. https://breac.nd.edu/articles/ireland-empire-and-british-foreign-policy-roger-casement-and-the-first-world-war/#_edn28.

Chapter 7 A Good Life

28 James Connolly aged 43 and family: Nationalarchives.ie. (2024). National Archives: Census of Ireland 1911. Pembroke_West/Lotts_Road__South/10339/ [Accessed 12 Nov. 2024]. Residents of a house 70 in Lotts Road, South (Pembroke West, Dublin).

Chapter 8 British Justice

29 'I trust he will conduct his cross-examination with all the added bitterness of an old friend' was said to Sir Edward George Clarke, Wilde's lawyer. Clarke had tried to dissuade Wilde from bringing the libel action against the Marquess of Queensberry; when he lost, he was charged with gross indecency and jailed. Alberge, D. (2021). Sworn enemies: the real story of Old Bailey clash that ruined Oscar Wilde. the Guardian. 2021/jan/24/oscar-wilde-old-bailey-libel-trial-grandson-bbc-edward-carson-and-the-fall.

30 The then Prime Minister Earl of Rosebery was suspected of having had a homosexual affair, when he was Foreign Minister, with Francis Douglas, another one of Queensberry's sons who died (possibly suicide) shortly before Queensberry's pursuit of Wilde. Linder, Professor, D. (1995). The Trials of Oscar Wilde: An Account. The Trials of Oscar Wilde: An Account. https://www.famous-trials.com/wilde/327-home UMKC School of Law

31 Bandon is four miles from Innishannon (Claire Sheridan's home) and nine miles from Béal na Bláth where Collins was shot. It was once solely Protestant, having a bye-law that no Roman Catholic be permitted to reside in the town.

Chapter 9 – Anything's legal if you're a Protestant

33 Winchester College: Considered one of the most prestigious schools in the world; independent boarding school in Hampshire, England, for pupils aged 13-18. About 600 pupils in 1900. The following people were educated at Winchester (some of them being contemporaries of 'Jack' White):-

- Raymond Asquith (born 1878), son of Prime Minister. At Winchester 1892-1897
- Sir Norman Fenwick Warren Fisher (born 1879): British civil servant. Permanent Secretary to the Treasury and Head of the Home Civil Service. At Winchester 1892-1898
- Edward Grigg (born 1879), private secretary to Prime Minister David Lloyd George. At Winchester 1893-1898 (N.B. He would have known Fisher very well.)
- Jack White (born 1879) helped create Irish Citizen Army. At Winchester 1892-1896
- Robert William Seton-Watson (born 1879) a British political activist and historian who was involved in border decisions at Versailles after WW1. Worked in the Intelligence Bureau of the War Cabinet in the Enemy Propaganda Department 1917-1918. Friend of Thomas Masaryk. At Winchester 1893-1898
- Sir Maurice Bonham-Carter (born 1880) – he was Prime Minister Asquith's Principal Private Secretary 1910 to 1916 and went with him to Ireland after the Uprising. Married the Prime Minister's daughter, Violet Asquith (at one point she was thought to be engaged to Churchill). At Winchester 1893-1899
- Wilfred Spender (born 1876) He signed the Ulster Covenant even though he was an officer in the Army. Close friend of Edward Carson, he helped organise the UVF. At Winchester 1891-1896

34 Robert Seton-Watson arranged for Masaryk to brief Sir Edward Grey on Independence for Bohemia (Czechoslovakia) and to give lectures at King's College. McNamara, K.J. (2016). Dreams of a Great Small Nation. PublicAffairs.

35 16-year-old "Jack" White spoke on a motion (" That a statue should be erected to Oliver Cromwell in the House of Commons.") at Winchester College in Oct. 2, 1895. The 'School News' in College Magazine states "J. R. White, in the best speech he has made as yet, advocated the cause of Cromwell, whom he looked upon as honest if unloveable, and eminently suited for the needs of the time" Winchestercollegearchives.org. (1895). Winchestercollegearchives.org. (1895).
https://winchestercollegearchives.org/PDFViewer/web/viewer.html?file=%2fFilename.ashx%3ftableName%3dta_wykehamist%26columnName%3dfilename%26recordId%3d370%23page%3d5&searchText=cromwell [Accessed 4 Nov. 2024]. Page 141 No. 316—OCT. 1895.

Chapter 10 – Three of a Kind

36 Crucial to Connolly's position was his belief that an accommodation could be reached between the socialist movement and the Church. While he countered clerical attacks on the Left with often grim ferocity, he nevertheless rejected anti-clericalism as outmoded.' Newsinger, J. and Newsinger, J. (1986). 'As Catholic As The Pope': James Connolly and the Roman Catholic Church in Ireland.Saothar,11,pp.7–18. https://www.jstor.org/stable/23195983.

37 Magdalen Laundries: The first, 1765, was for Protestants only. Catholic versions sprang up providing a cost-free labour source. Supposedly to care for "fallen women", an estimated 30,000 were

confined in them behind locked gates. Increasingly violent and abusive, most of the day was spent working in silence. The government awarded lucrative contracts to the laundries without any insistence on protection and fair treatment. without any insistence on protection and fair treatment. The last closed in 1996. McAleese, M., Senator (2013). Report of the Inter-Departmental Committee to establish the facts of State involvement with the Magdalen Laundries. Gov.ie. Dublin: Department of Justice. https://www.gov.ie/en/collection/a69a14-report-of-the-inter-departmental-committee-to-establish-the-facts-of/?referrer=https://www.justice.ie/en/JELR/Pages/MagdalenRpt2013 . The films The Magdalen Sisters (2002) and Philomena (2013) and "Small Things Like These" (2024) refer to the Laundries. Some Catholics reject the criticisms.

38 William Murphy came into an inheritance when he was 18, married, and acquired a very influential father-in-law. A Catholic, he was active in the St Vincent de Paul Society. Apparently, he was involved in many 'private' acts of assistance to the less well-off; although if 'private', then it's difficult to understand how they became so well known – perhaps by articles in his own newspapers. Friends described him as the typical sweet little old Irishman: softly spoken, with a humorous twinkle in his eye, and proudly Gaelic when overseas.
Maume, P. (2009). Murphy, William Martin. Dictionary of Irish Biography. doi:https://doi.org/10.3318/dib.006106.v1.
39 "By late September some 20,000 men and women in Dublin city and County were either on strike or locked out." John_Dorney (2013). Today in Irish History – August 31, 1913 – Labour's Bloody Sunday – The Irish Story. Theirishstory.com.

Keogh, D. (2013). William Martin Murphy and the Origins of the 1913 Lockout. Saothar, pp.28–30. Yeates, P. (2001). The Dublin 1913 Lockout. History Ireland. https://historyireland.com/the-dublin-1913-lockout/.

40 Alice Brady 1911 Census Nationalarchives.ie. (2024b). National Archives: Census of Ireland 1911. Alice Brady family.

41 Murphy, F. (1984). Dublin slums in the 1930s. [Read to the Old Dublin Society] https://www.jstor.org/stable/30100635 [Accessed 29 Oct. 2024]. Page 106 refers to Asylum Yard

42 Sheey-Skeffington was a vice-chairman of the Irish Citizen Army and 'approved of it as long as its sole purpose was to defend the workers against the police; when it became an armed military organisation, he left.' McHugh, R. (1956). Thomas Kettle and Francis Sheehy-Skeffington. University Review, 1(9), pp.6–18.

Chapter 11 – Self Respect for Ireland

43 The third Home Rule Bill was always an exercise in hypocrisy. Asquith's government never intended that it should be enacted in the form in which it was introduced; political expediency demanded that Birrell conceal his convictions.' Fanning, R. (2014). Ronan Fanning: Why commemorating the Home Rule Bill would be unwise. IrishTimes.com. irishtimes.com/news/politics/ronan-fanning-why-commemorating-the-home-rule-bill-would-be-unwise-1.1898370 [Accessed 22 Oct. 2024].

44 Birrell writes of Ireland, 'Her nationality has thus been checked and mutilated, but that it exists in spirit and in fact can hardly be questioned by any impartial traveller.' And, 'The attitude of some Englishmen

towards Scotch and Irish national feelings requires correction. ... The Scotsman's feelings are laughed at. The Irishman's insulted. So far as the laughter is concerned, it must be admitted that it is good-humoured. ... it must be admitted that Scotsmen are not conciliatory. They do not meet people half-way. I do not think the laughter does much harm. Insults are different.... "

Birrell, A. (2011). The Project Gutenberg eBook of Res Judicat, by Augustine Birrell. Gutenberg.org. 'Nationality'

Chapter 13 Mutiny? No, no

45 'A cigarette is the perfect type of a perfect pleasure. It is exquisite, and it leaves one unsatisfied. What more can one want?' The Picture of Dorian Gray (1891) ch. 6

46 Gordon Shephard wrote, "Why cannot they give home rule to Ireland now that the six Ulster counties are excluded? I cannot see on what grounds the Unionist base their objections. I like Mr Redmond's speech. It is time the Coalition realised that they should at least make a show of keeping to agreements." 23rd June 1916. Adams, D.T. (2020). Who was Gordon Shephard – the man who never was? The Dragon's Voice. wwfa.org.uk/index.php/newsletters/2020/july [Accessed 4 Nov. 2024].

47 According to David Edgerton, colonial policing protocols stipulated that arms be used early and decisively. Not used as warning shots, but rather fired at 'ringleaders' in the crowd. Edgerton, D.L. (2018). The Rise and Fall of the British Nation: A Twentieth-Century History. London: Penguin Books. Page 57.

[48] Connolly was a determined socialist, with his own ideas, who believed that Irish liberation and Irish socialism could only happen as a result of the efforts of the working class. Unfortunately many of these workers

were in Ulster and supported the Unionist cause. The threat of Partition meant that Irish liberation became Connolly's priority. For a discussion of the evolution of Connolly's beliefs and political ideas see Newsinger, J. (1983). James Connolly and the Easter Rising. Science & Society, 47(2), pp.152–177. https://www.jstor.org/stable/40401707 [Accessed 25 May 2019].

Chapter 15 – Three Little Maids from School

49 MacNeill, leader of the Irish Volunteers Executive, wrote to Carson discussing co-operation between the Irish Volunteers and the Ulster Volunteers. Catalogue.nli.ie. (1914). Collection: Bulmer Hobson Papers, 1905-1968.

50 Ms. Sydney Gifford describes going to St. Enda's "McDonagh came running down to welcome her and she introduced us, saying "I want you to fall in love with one of these girls and marry her". bmh.militaryarchives.BMH.WS0909.pdf.

[51] 'His education was bound to be patchy at best, given the erratic, eccentric and sadistic regime imposed by his unbalanced mother'. Vivid Faces, the Revolutionary Generation in Ireland 1890-1923, RF Foster, Penguin Random House, UK, 2014

Chapter 16 – A Little Help From Some Friends

52 (Casement) 'was fanatically opposed to everything English and was prepared to consider every means to obtain Ireland's independence. He considered that the most direct method would be through a German victory and I recommended him to go to Berlin and discuss there the measures best calculated to ensure a British defeat.' Franz Von Papen

(1952). Franz von Papen: memoirs. Translated by B. Connell. London: Deutsch, p.35.

[53] "The war was only a few months old when he sent a telegram to Sir Hedworth Meux" Dovkants, Keith (2015). Churchill's World – Twentieth-Century Fighting Sail. International Churchill Society.

Chapter 18 – I need a job

54 Michael Collins worked in London 1906-1915. He studied at King's College, Strand, but left probably 1909 or 1910. This may have been due to the civil service classes in the basement, 'Strand School', being relocated to Brixton Hill in South London. The Life and Times of Michael Collins. (2021). London Years.
Collins, M. (1906). King's College London arithmetic examination papers and answer papers completed by Michael Collins. UCD Digital Library. https://digital.ucd.ie/view/ivrla:10965 [Accessed 8 Nov. 2024].
Wikipedia Contributors (2024). Strand School. Wikipedia. https://archives.kingscollections.org/index.php/strand-school-london-1897-1979 King's College London Archives.

[55] Jeremiah O'Donovan Rossa (aka 'Dynamite'). In 1865 he was jailed for life but in 1870 exiled to the US. He organised a dynamite campaign targeting both government and civilian targets in Britain. When he died Tom Clarke told John Devoy, "Send his body home at once".

[56] Joseph Plunkett wrote to Grace on Dec 2 1915 asking her to marry him. The letter has a PS "By the way, I am actually a beggar. I have no income and am earning nothing. Moreover there are other things more desperate, practically speaking to prevent anyone marrying me.' Plunkett, J. (1915).
Plunkett, G. G. Letter (how happy he is and how much he loves her). https://catalogue.nli.ie/Record/vtls000652679.

Chapter 19 – D'yer Want a Rebellion or Not?

57 Connolly: "Ireland without her people is nothing to me, and the man who is bubbling over with love and enthusiasm for "Ireland," and can yet pass unmoved through our streets and witness all the wrong and the suffering, the shame and the degradation wrought upon the people of Ireland, aye, wrought by Irishmen upon Irishmen and women, without burning to end it, is, in my opinion, a fraud and a liar in his heart, no matter how much he loves that combination of chemical elements which he is pleased to call "Ireland." The Connolly Archive. (2022). The Coming Generation. https://eirigi.org/latestnews/2022/7/20/the-connolly-archive-the-coming-generation 'Worker's Republic' July 15th 1900.

Chapter 20 – Powerful Friends

58 Rerum Novarum responded to communist theories; it opposed class struggle but asserted that workers had rights. He said that private property should stay private; capitalism must protect both the worker and the capitalist, so that wages were sufficient to support a worker and his family; state socialism, based in the sin of envy, is unjust, inhumane, and likely to hurt the "working man" more than the wealthy. POPE LEO XIII (1891). RERUM NOVARUM. [Encyclical].

[59] Of the cases in which we may put men to death without incurring the guilt of murder. Aurelius Augustine (n.d.). The city of God. REV. MARCUS DODS, M.A. ed. Edinburgh: T. & T. CLARK, p.32. https://www.gutenberg.org/files/45304/45304-h/45304-h.htm.
[60] "None of these 'volunteers' knew anything about code breaking, but were chosen for their knowledge of the German language and the

feeling they were the sort of 'chaps' who could keep a secret!" South, A. (2018). Room 40: Cryptanalysis during World War I. Navy General Board. https://www.navygeneralboard.com/room-40-cryptanalysis-during-world-war-i/.

Chapter 22 – 'Throttling and Neck Breaking, Sir?'

61 "1876 "Thomas aged 13 and Roger aged 11 on a charge of book stealing from a newsvendor in York Road, Lambeth ... Their father, described as a captain in the militia residing in South Lambeth, was ordered to enter into recognisances for their future conduct." Dudgeon, J. (2016). Roger Casement: a campaigner, not a conspirator or even an Ulster Protestant. The Irish Times. https://www.irishtimes.com/culture/books/roger-casement-a-campaigner-not-a-conspirator-or-even-an-ulster-protestant-1.2680244 [Accessed 9 Nov. 2024].

[62] 'The most important British informant on Casement's activities in the early months of the war was his bisexual Norwegian-American manservant and lover, Adler Christensen'. Andrew, C.M. (2012). The Defence of the Realm. Penguin Group

[63] At Larkfield, "Collins had a conversation with Con Keating and myself about the possibility of getting a wireless receiving and transmitting set" https://bmh.militaryarchives.ie/reels/bmh/BMH.WS0110.pdf Denis Daly was one of the drivers and provides a credible (albeit 30 years after the event) to the Bureau of Military History.

[64] Monsignor Henry Athanasius **Brann** was rector of St. Agnes Church (1890-1921) in New York. Brann was a close associate of members of Clan-na-Gael, John Devoy and Joseph McGarrity. A baptismal

certificate for De Valera was located at St Agnes when he was listed for execution.

[65] 'Casement begged to be allowed to communicate with the leaders to try and stop the rising but he was not allowed.' Andrew, C.M. (2012). The Defence of the Realm. Penguin Group

[66] It is generally accepted that the Diaries are genuine. However, it is conceivable that parts could have been 'sexed up'. Thomson's own accounts have several versions as to when and how he obtained the diaries. Toibin, C. (1997) A Whale of a Time. London Review of Books, 19(21), 30 Oct. https://www.lrb.co.uk/the-paper/v19/n19/colm-toibin/a-whale-of-a-time.

[67] 22 March 1916 'Secret' report from British Intelligence concerning information from an apparently reliable source: extreme Irish-American 'Party' contemplates an armed rising in Ireland and is seeking German assistance'. It has 'local leaders' who want action urgently and the rising should be timed for the 22nd April; arms to be delivered from Germany to Limerick. Intelligence report about an armed rising in Ireland. (1916). Éamon De Valera Papers: British documents relating to 1916. Dublin:UCD Library, University College.

[68] "Although the British authorities in Dublin appear to have been taken by surprise, the Royal Navy was fully prepared for the uprising. " Page 187 Beesly, P. (1984). Room 40: British naval intelligence 1914-1918. Harcourt Brace Jovanovich, p.188. ca.archive.org/0/items/room40/Room%2040%20%3B.pdf.

[69] Uprising: For a discussion on 'warning' and 'response' and possible reasons for failure to act on the warning, see: Sloan, G. (2013). The

British State and the Irish Rebellion of 1916: An Intelligence Failure or a Failure of Response? Intelligence and National Security, 6(3), pp.328–357.

Chapter 23 – Getting Things Together

70 The 'Castle Document': Grace Plunkett's witness statement (below) gives one version of how the Castle Document was obtained from Eugene Smyth and decoded. This does not fully relate to Eugene Smyth's own statement nor to the details in Patrick Little's 'A 1916 DOCUMENT THE MYSTERY OF THE DUBLIN CASTLE CYPHER'. Smyth, E. (1950). Index of /reels/bmh. Militaryarchives.ie.

[71] Plunkett, G. (1949). Index of /reels/bmh. Militaryarchives.ie. WS0257.pdf [Accessed 23 Oct. 2024].
[72] Little, P. (1941). A 1916 DOCUMENT THE MYSTERY OF THE DUBLIN CASTLE CYPHER. The Capuchin Annual, Dublin: Irish Capuchin Franciscans, pp.454–462.

[73] "Hall, probably fearful of compromising Room 40, failed to give advance information to the Irish government in Dublin Castle." Simkin, J. (1997). Reginald Hall. Spartacus Educational. https://spartacus-educational.com/SShallW.htm [Accessed 2 Nov. 2024].
[74] Joseph Plunkett's location on the Saturday and Sunday before the Uprising seems to change hour by hour. The 2:45pm Saturday note from Joe has 26 Upper Fitzwilliam Street at the top. Grace Plunkett Papers, NLI MS 21, 590/28 https://catalogue.nli.ie/Record/vtls000652817 But Grace's BMH Witness Statement 257 says she went to see him the Hotel Metropole at 6pm on Easter Saturday. Perhaps Collins told her verbally that Joe would be there. Grace Plunkett Papers, NLI MS 21,590/29 is a note marked Larkfield from him dated Easter Sunday saying that he will

be sleeping at the Nursing Home overnight. https://catalogue.nli.ie/Record/vtls000652820

[75] There are no documented reasons by the Military Council for occupying some buildings but not others; nothing about how much was known of British troop strengths; no details about possible British responses; nothing about how to deal with troops arriving at the docks, or which roads were to be blocked. Nobody knows why trenches were dug on St. Stephen's Green.

Plunkett may have been a telecommunications enthusiast as far as wireless was concerned, but it seems that cutting telephone cables was of second order importance; the Telephone Exchange in Crown Alley, close to the GPO, was not disabled. Troops from Royal Irish Rifles (3 RIR), stationed in Portobello Barracks, rushed to both the Castle and the Exchange. Throughout the Uprising, Dublin Castle was able to communicate with London and other military posts in Ireland. Strategic planning seems to have been no better than that of the British and German High commands in Europe.

Chapter 24 – 'Yes-No-Yes!'

76 Due to the Uprising all transport had been commandeered by the Military, as a result All Sorts had to be walked back to his stables in Co Westmeath, more than 100 kilometres away.

[77] The O'Rahilly was one of the main organisers of the Howth acquisition of rifles in 1914. John Dorney (2015). 'Glorious Madness' – The Life and Death of Michael O'Rahilly – The Irish Story. Theirishstory.com. 2015/04/09 [Accessed 24 Oct. 2024].

Chapter 25 – Charge!

78 The Dublin Castle action/inaction was typical of the Uprising for many reasons. In coming years, there'd be a range of memories about happened. Some thought several Irish rebels had passed through the gates, entered the guard house and captured soldiers. Others recalled that the gates had been closed before any entry was made. Some thought the attack was planned; others on the spot were surprised when the constable had been killed. In 1803 it was Robert Emmet's primary objective; the great edifice had been the symbol of British oppression for centuries. In 1916 it may have been a last-minute decision. Once taken, it's walls would have more resilient to shelling and incendiaries; one estimate of the number of troops inside was 25 but nobody amongst the rebels had bothered to find out. If the Castle had been an objective, then a larger rebel force would have surely been sent with a more senior officer.

[79] Helena Moloney's witness statement has 'On the flash, the gates were closed. The sentry went into his box, and began firing... Seán Connolly veered round his gun, and said, "Get into the City Hall'. According to witness statement W1686 by Captain Henderson (based on information from others and completed in 1957) Sean Connolly led a force of 45 out of Liberty Hall and 6 of these entered the Castle guard room. However, the statement (Page 68) identifies locations for 45 Volunteers – omitting the six who supposedly occupied the Castle guardroom. William Oman (Statement WS421) describes decisions to occupy the Castle and decisions 'not' to **occupy**. He was with Sean Connolly and his lengthy and confusing description of the action does nothing to confirm or deny whether part of the Castle was occupied by rebels.

[80] "the intention of the Military Council was that the proposed force for this area should also seize the main Telephone Exchange in Crown Alley, or, to demolish all wires emanating from it, as well as the wires passing from the Castle through the manhole (X) in Dame Street in front of the Lower Castle Yard. At the last moment this work of Demolition was, it seems entrusted to a supplementary squad the objective, for some reason not now clear, was not effected." Witness W1686 statement by Capt. Henderson, Page 10.

[81] "En route we. passed the Telephone Exchange and I never could understand why it was not taken as it only had a small guard of British soldiers. The British afterwards paid tribute to the assistance this was to them in quashing the Rebellion." John Scollan Witness Statement W318, Page 7.

[82] "It was against our rules to use any church, Protestant or Catholic, in our defense, no matter what advantage that might give us. But this church, close at hand, had been occupied by the British and was cutting us off from another command" Pg 144 Skinnider, M. (2016). DOING MY BIT FOR IRELAND. US: Gutenberg.

Chapter 26 – A Republic at Last

83 A messenger, Christine Caffrey, 'had been almost prevented from reaching headquarters by a crowd of poor women gathered about the post-office for their usual weekly "separation allowance." Their husbands were all fighting in France or Flanders for the British. They would not get their allowance this week, and were terror-stricken, crowding about the post-office and crying and shouting hysterically'. Pg 166 Skinnider, M. (2016). DOING MY BIT FOR IRELAND. US: Gutenberg.

https://www.gutenberg.org/cache/epub/52740/pg52740-images.html.

Chapter 27 – Lions and Donkeys

84 Hughes, B., Campbell, B. and Schreibman, S. (2017). Contested Memories: Revisiting the Battle of Mount Street Bridge, 1916. British Journal for Military History, 4(1).

Chapter 28 – Cup'la Murders

85 "The earnestness with which he maintained that nobody could force you to do anything against your will impressed his son, Owen, even at the age of five, and he remembers saying to his father: " But then they might kill you," and his father's earnest reply: " Yes, but they could not make you do it" McHugh, R. (1956).

[86] Thomas (married to Anna) Haslam thought that Women's Suffrage would be introduced. 'Mr Asquith, in the judgement of those who personally know him, is an honorable man. His promises, therefore, can be relied upon.' Haslam, T. (1916). Some Last Words on Women's Suffrage. https://catalogue.nla.gov.au/catalog/1943612 Ormond Printing Co., Ltd. (Dublin).

[87] Sheehy-Skeffington wrote to Thomas MacDonagh, 'Are not the bulk of the Irish Volunteers animated by the old bad tradition that war is a glorious thing, that there is something 'manly' about going out to kill your fellow man, something cowardly about the desire to see one's end accomplished without bloodshed?' And, 'I want to see the manhood of Ireland no longer hypnotized by the glamour of the 'glory of arms' ... no longer blind to the horrors of organised murder.'

Sheehy-Skeffington, F. (1915). Against Militarism. Published in the 'Irish Citizen']

[88] Mid-day on Easter Monday, British Captain Pinfield was shot and lay in the street bleeding to death; due to the cross-fire no one dared to go to his aid. Sheehy-Skeffington persuaded a chemist to accompany him. They crossed the square under a hail of bullets but British troops had dragged Pinfield away. Sheehy-Skeffington, H. (1916). British Militarism as I Have Known It. [1916-1917 — Speech delivered at numerous fundraising events across the United States] https://speakingwhilefemale.co/war-sheehy-skeffington/. (The location for the shooting varies according to source. Some say near Saint Patrick's cathedral; some imply near the Castle.)

[89] 'Hordes of Dubliners, mainly women and children, raided the shops on and around Sackville Street ... toy shops, haberdashers, shoe shops, grocers, no shops resisted the frenzied attacks of a mob driven by sapping hunger, survival, but also a desire for fun and mischief.' arrow.tudublin.ie/ Deleuze, M. (2016). 1916: Dublin Youths' Sweet Revolution. In: 2016 – Food and Revolution. Dublin: Dublin Gastronomy Symposium, Page 3.

"One could see some bizarre sights from the windows during that week: corner-boys wearing silk hats, ladies from the slums sporting fur coats, a cycling corps of barefooted young urchins riding brand new bicycles stolen from some of the shops, and members of the underworld carrying umbrellas. One citizen was carrying a large flitch of bacon on his back, with another walking behind cutting off a piece at bacon with a large knife." Page 51 Colonel Broy Witness Statement https://bmh.militaryarchives.ie/reels/bmh/BMH.WS1280.pdf#page=48

90 "He was involved in an August 1912 incident, when he delivered a pro-suffragist speech in the Phoenix Park some distance from an official

suffragette meeting and experienced anti-Semitic taunts from members of the crowd, suggesting a certain emotional instability" ... He was accused of collaborating with Councillor J. J. Kelly in relation to the scandal sheet, The Eye-Opener. He was also accused of giving false information to the authorities about the use of Kelly's premises by rebels, leading to the arrest of two men, Dickson and McIntyre. Maume, P. (2009b). Edelstein, (Eli) Joseph. In: Dictionary of Irish Biography. Dublin: Royal Irish Academy. https://www.dib.ie/biography/edelstein-eli-joseph-a2878.

[91] For a version of Bowen-Colthurst's activities see Kildea's article. This involves an unnamed Australian soldier. Kildea, J. (2003). Called to arms: Australian soldiers in the Easter Rising 1916. Journal of the Australian War Memorial, (39).

[92] 'Vane is the only officer concerned who made a genuine effort to see justice done. He went to Dublin Castle, finding that the Portobello officers would do nothing. He saw Colonel Kinnard and General Friend, as well as Major Price (head of the Intelligence Dept.). All deprecated the "fuss" and refused to act. Major Price said, "Some of us think it was a good thing Sheehy-Skeffington was put out of the way, anyhow." Sheehy-Skeffington, H. (1916). British Militarism as I Have Known It. [1916-1917 — delivered at numerous fundraising events across the United States] https://speakingwhilefemale.co/war-sheehy-skeffington/.

Chapter 29 – The End of the Beginning

93 The doctor who later treated Connolly describes the injury as being to his leg. However, some Witness Statements refer to his ankle. Some to the left leg, some say the right.

Page 3 Witness Statement 1431 BMH.WS1431.pdf. "suffering a serious injury to his ankle" rte.ie/centuryireland/articles/james-connolly Dr Ridgway: 'He had sustained a bullet wound on the right leg causing a compound fracture of the two long bones (Tibia and Fibula) in their middle third.' This is contrary to Rough sketch of "Jim" Connolly's wounded left leg by Lt. D.J. Steele RAMC (SR) Dublin Castle Red Cross Hospital, https://catalogue.nli.ie/Record/vtls000654049
Also: A. de Burca: "wounded in the lower part of the left leg; the bone was broken and the flesh very much lacerated." Witness Statement 359. https://bmh.militaryarchives.ie/reels/bmh/BMH.WS0359.pdf

Chapter 30 – Surrender? God Save Ireland!

[94] Bureau of Military History 1913-21, Statement by Witness 290 Sean McLaughlin. Pages 22-23

95 God Save Ireland, song about the Manchester Martyrs, three Fenians executed in 1867. One of the five, Edward O'Meagher Condon, concluded his speech from the dock with the words "God Save Ireland". 1867. Lyrics by Timothy Daniel Sullivan. https://www.youtube.com/watch?v=J_KEcfmHeN0

96 Company Quartermaster Sergeant Robert Flood's small group of Royal Dublin Fusiliers captured and killed Lieutenant Algernon Lucas and William John Rice, a night clerk, and also Lieutenant Basil Worsley-Worswick and Cecil Dockeray, clerk. Apparently, Flood's group was too small to hold them securely and they were all assumed to be Sinn Fein; but they were not and the officers spoke with very English accents. Sergeant Robert Flood was later acquitted at a court-martial.

[97] 'The rifles of the firing party were waving like a field of corn.' McGarry, F. (2016). Essay, The courts-martial of the 1916 leaders. https://courtmartial.nationalarchives.ie/court-martial-of-the-1916-leaders.html Essays on the Court Martials.

Chapter 31 – "Tears fall from the Skies"

[98] Anzacs and the Easter Rising 1916: Australia's role in Ireland's past. The Sydney Morning Herald. Towell, N. (2016). https://www.smh.com.au/national/anzacs-easter-rising-and-the-20160317-gnl5oo.html [Accessed 24 Oct. 2024]. Kildea, J. (2003). https://www.awm.gov.au/articles/journal/j39/kildea. Called to arms: Australian soldiers in the Easter Rising 1916. Journal of the Australian War Memorial, (39).

[99] 'I See His Blood Upon The Rose ' poem by Joseph Plunkett.

[100] Song, *'Grace'* Anthony Kearns available on Youtube. Song available on Youtube by various artists, Jim McCann, Dubliners, Rod Stewart. https://www.youtube.com/watch?v=j7NcTCfnJAY [Accessed 4 Nov. 2024]. And mise me fein (2016). Grace – Jim McCann. https://www.youtube.com/watch?v=A8LVlJ1I5pQ [Accessed 4 Nov. 2024]. Written in 1985 by Frank O'Meara (melody) and Seán O'Meara (lyrics). O'Connor, Rachael (4 March 2021). "Who was Grace Gifford Plunkett? The heartbreaking true story behind the song 'Grace'". The Irish Post. Retrieved 4 November 2024.

Chapter 32 – 'Well, that's something!'

[101] "Lieutenant William Evelyn Wylie, a Dublin barrister. Wylie left a record of his own in the form of a memoir written for his daughter. It is

an account of his increasing disillusionment with the courts-martial process." Also, "Blackader's involvement was, to say the least, of dubious legality. Even under the more permissive Field General Court Martial process, the rules of procedure excluded presiding officers who had a potential conflict of interest; as commander of 176 Brigade, which included the Sherwood Foresters and which incurred most of the 1916 military casualties, Blackader should have stood down." Dungan, M. (n.d.). The 1916 Courts-martial and the Dublin Executions. Essays on the Court Martials. https://courtmartial.nationalarchives.ie/1916-court-martial-and-the-dublin-executions.html.

[102] Sean Murray writes that an attorney in Philadelphia named Michael Francis Doyle was formerly employed by the US State Department and had a direct line to President Wilson. 'There was in fact no birth certificate available.' With De Valera in danger of being executed, Clan-na-Gael leader Joseph McGarrity started a massive search: a baptismal record was suddenly found. Then an original birth certificate 'appears' despite Doyle's claim that one didn't exist.
Murray, Sean Patrick. "The Case for Eamon de Valera's Birth and Baptismal Records Being Forgeries." *Iarmhí: Journal of the Westmeath Archaeological and History Society*, vol. 1, no. 4, 2025, debanked.com/pdfs/deValeraBirthRecordForgeries.pdf.

Chapter 33 – A Reprieve? Yes, No

103 A note (1916 May 4) concerning Asquith by John Redmond has 'He sd. that he had written and wired General Sir Maxwell to stop executions.' https://catalogue.nli.ie/Record/vtls000845818
Asquith appears to have mislead Redmond with regard to his instructions to Maxwell. National Library of Ireland website also seems to have been misled. It states that he sent a telegram which included:

'except under special and exceptional circumstances.'
https://www.nli.ie/1916/exhibition/en/content/aftermath/
The actual telegram (dated 10th May) states "Prime Minister directs that no more executions are to take place' Www.cso.ie. (2017)

[104] 'I casually opened it and this is what I read: "Officer Commanding Dublin Castle. The execution of James Connolly is postponed. Asquith". Dr Ridgway Witness Statement BMH.WS1431.pdf This conflicts with Www.cso.ie. (2017). Census and People of the 1916 Rising Life in 1916 Ireland: Stories from statistics – Central Statistics Office. https://www.cso.ie/en/releasesandpublications/ep/p-1916/1916irl/cpr/cmp/imp/ [Accessed 18 Jan. 2025]. It is difficult to understand why the telegram was given to a doctor and barely credible that he would be so casual with regard to reading it.

[105] "When the wallet was taken, they found the photograph; and they were looking for that son. We never got that photograph back." Nora O'Brien (Connolly) Witness Statement 286. Page 55, July 1949https://bmh.militaryarchives.ie/reels/bmh/BMH.WS0286.pdf

Chapter 34 – Let's Eat Grandma! Let's Eat, Grandma!

106 The Battle of the Somme resulted in 125,000 British deaths. On September 15, 1916, 32 Mark I tanks were used in an attack at Flers-Courcelette. At 3 miles an hour they were too slow, too difficult to manoeuvre over cratered, muddy, ground and too vulnerable to grenades . Only 136 of the 720 soldiers in the Accrington Pals battalion went through the first 30 minutes unharmed – 584 were either killed or maimed. 21-year-old Captain Wilfred Nevill blew a whistle, kicked a soccer ball forward and called on his East Surrey men to chase it into the

German trenches. The battalion had less than 800 men and of these 147 were killed and 279 wounded; Nevill was shot in the head.

[107] McNamara, K.J. (2016). Dreams of a Great Small Nation. PublicAffairs, Page 92.

[108] The British Government gave strong support to Tomas Masaryk (q.v.)

[109] "My 'leader' [Alexander Martin Sullivan] played me a sad trick at the appeal in dropping so important a part of my appeal without a word of notice ... I wish I'd stuck to my two Welshmen" [John H. Morgan and Artemus Jones]. Letter from Sir Roger Casement, Pentonville Prison, to "Dick" [Richard Morten], about his lawyers at the trial, 1916 July 28.
https://catalogue.nli.ie/Collection/vtls000531148?recordID=vtls000531153 accessed 10/11/2024

Casement argued, as GB Shaw did, that he could not be disloyal to England because he was Irish, not English. The British government was portraying the Czeck Masaryk as a hero for doing much the same as Casement. Masaryk was born in the Austria-Hungarian empire but campaigned for Czechoslovakia's independence and encouraged POWs (from the Austria-Hungarian army) in Russia to fight in a special brigade for the Allies. 19 October 1915, Masaryk spoke at the School of Slavonic Studies at King's College London on "The Problem of Small Nations in the European Crisis", arguing that the UK should support the independence efforts of "small" nations such as the Czechs. (See Biographical Note on Seton-Watson). Masaryk gave a lecture at King's College expecting Lloyd George to 'be in the chair' but he backed out. Taylor, A.J.P. (1987). The First world war: an illustrated history. Harmondsworth: Penguin Books, p.146.

[110] Ruppel acknowledges the lack of specific evidence, but identifies much that is circumstantial, concerning Conrad's possible bisexuality. Ruppel, R. (2008) Homosexuality in the Life and Work of Joseph Conrad: Love Between the Lines. See Review by Harrington, Ellen Burton. 2010.

[111] F.E. Smith (Lord Birkenhead) suggested to the Defence that they read the Diaries and use them for a plea of insanity. This may have been a ploy to enable them to be made known publicly (for which Smith and the Prosecution didn't want responsibility). Toibin, C. (1997).

[112] After being found guilty, Casement gave one of the world's greatest speeches. He covered issues that should have been used by his barrister. "Self-government is our right, a thing born in us at birth; a thing no more to be doled out to us or withheld from us by another people than the right to life itself—than the right to feel the sun or smell the flowers or to love our kind." Casement, R. (1916). Speech of Roger Casement from the dock. https://doi.org/10.48495/pn89d807q.

Chapter 36 – Outlived the failure of all her hopes

[113] Margaret Keogh: A nurse since 1897 at the South Dublin Union, a 50-acre facility with thousands of destitute, infirm and insane, she was shot wearing her uniform when she went to the aid of a dying man. The hospital was thought by the rebels to be an ideal position to stop troops entering the City but it was much too large for the 100 rebels to defend. Fallon, D. (2016). Nurse Margaret Keogh, the first civilian fatality of the Rising. independent.ie. https://www.independent.ie/irish-news/nurse-margaret-keogh-the-first-civilian-fatality-of-the-rising/34510459.html [Accessed 28 Oct. 2024].

Chapter 37 – Autumn 1917

[114] Josephine Bernadette McAliskey (née Devlin) aged 21 was elected to Parliament in 1969 for mid-Ulster. She advocated for a 32-county socialist Irish republic. And said "I will take my seat and fight for your rights" – signalling her rejection of the traditional Irish republican principle of abstentionism. On 22 April 1969, the day before her 22nd birthday, she swore the Oath of Allegiance and made her maiden speech within an hour. Convicted of incitement to riot in December 1969, she served six months imprisonment. Re-elected. After the 1972 Bloody Sunday she was denied the right to speak in the House of Commons despite her having witnessed the shootings – so she slapped the Conservative Home Secretary across the face when he said the troops acted in self-defence.

115 Eamon O'Duibhir (in jail with Ashe),
Witness Statement "I certainly did not like this pipe being passed down through my throat and I began to have a horror of it." https://bmh.militaryarchives.ie/reels/bmh/BMH.WS1474.pdf#page=95 Page 15

[116] For a detailed discussion of force-feeding and description of Thomas Ashe Inquest, see Miller, I. (2016). 'The Instrument of Death': Prison Doctors and Medical Ethics in Revolutionary-Period Ireland, c.1917. In: A History of Force Feeding. Palgrave Macmillan, Cham. https://doi.org/10.1007/978-3-319-31113-5_3

[117] Redmond withdrew from the Convention and "Not a single vote was taken in the Convention until the 12th of March, 1918, when it had been sitting for nearly seven months, and two days later the question which it had been summoned to consider, namely, the relation of Ulster to the

rest of Ireland, was touched for the first time. ... Thus, on the only issue that really mattered, there was no such "substantial agreement" as the Government had postulated as essential before legislation could be undertaken; and on the 5th of April the Convention came to an end without having achieved any useful result, except that it gave the Government a breathing space from the Irish question to get on with the war." McNeill, R. (2004). Ulster's Stand For Union. Cambridge University Press. https://www.gutenberg.org/files/14326/14326-h/14326-h.htm.CHAPTER_XXII

[118] Étaples was a notoriously unpleasant base camp where officers and NCOs, that had never been to the Front, trained recruits in the harshest way. In August 1916 an Australian private was insubordinate and there was a mutiny. Next year there was another, involving more than 300 soldiers. Many were punished, one was executed.

[119] Khalidi, R. (2020). Hundred Years' War on Palestine: a History of Settler Colonial Conquest and resistance, 1917-2017. S.L.: Picador. Page 25

[120] The Balfour Declaration has 'nothing shall be done which may prejudice the civil and religious rights of the non-Jewish communities' but makes no mention of political rights. (ibid., 24)

Chapter 38 – A German "Plot"

121 In 1927 De Valera's followers took the oath of allegiance so that they could be electoral candidates. Archbishop Mannix said They no more told a falsehood than I would if I sent down word to an Importunate visitor that I was not at home,' Hahessy, E. (2022)

Chapter 39 – St Enda's: The Sequel

122 https://www.youtube.com/watch?v=5CfrkvE7_hs "The Republican Loan film, 1919"

[123] Boland took the jewels to his mother's house in Marino Crescent, Fairview, and hid them behind a wall. They apparently stayed there until, eventually, handed to President De Valera and then returned to Russia in exchange for $20,000. In 1948 Christie's valued them at £1,600. Thomas, C. (2019). 'Take them to hell': The curious tale of the hidden Russian jewels and Dev's deal with the Bolsheviks. TheJournal.ie. https://www.thejournal.ie/russian-jewels-state-papers-4942636-Dec2019/ [Accessed 21 Nov. 2024]

O'Keeffe, H. (2020). How Russian crown jewels went from the Romanovs to Harry Boland. RTE.ie. doi:urn:epic:1115356.

Chapter 40 Just Stop

124 'Alcohol is a very necessary article... It makes life bearable to millions of people who could not endure their existence if they were quite sober. It enables Parliament to do things at eleven at night that no sane person would do at eleven in the morning.' Major Barbara, Act II, 1905.

125 Mrs Ellen Quinn shot: Hansard. Parliament.uk. (1920). https://hansard.parliament.uk/Commons/1920-11-04/debates/66fa768a-8505-47b5-aee1-5ccccf230286/GalwayFatality?highlight=lawn#contribution-f9463a02-d9be-4a4c-aff7-106723e7656d [Accessed 28 Oct. 2024]. Galway Fatality Hansard UK Parliament.

Chapter 41 – Three Events in November 1920

126 Witness statements give varying details. Seamus Kavanagh (WS 0493) describes the location of Irish Volunteers, but these differ somewhat from Sean O'Neill WS1154. Both statements are dated 30 years after the event. Both say there were about 20 British troops. O'Neill says, 'three of us got to lorry and when I got to the corner of same I drew my gun and gave the order to the troops: "Hands up, drop your rifles." Everyone of' them obeyed both orders and kept their hands up for about 10 seconds but when they found only one man covering them they, being fully trained, grabbed their rifles and then the battle started." But Kavanagh says, 'One of the Volunteers ... ran out in front shouting "Hands up" and fired; I gave the order to fire, at the same time opening up myself. We drew our guns and charged, shooting as we ran forward. Some of the troops put their hands up, others returning the fire.'

Researcher Ainsworth quoting from a British report writes that there were only 4 unarmed men and 6 armed soldiers. Ainsworth, J. (2002). Kevin Barry, the Incident at Monk's Bakery and the Making of an Irish Republican Legend. The Historical Association, 87(287), Jul., pp.372–387. https://eprints.qut.edu.au/247/1/Ainsworth_Kevin.PDF.

[127] Amritsar, India 1919: A crowd of at least 10,000 men, women, and children gathered in a large park, enclosed by walls with only one exit and sealed by soldiers. Without warning, they opened fire on the crowd, shooting until they ran out of ammunition. An estimated 379 people were killed, and about 1,200 wounded. Pletcher, K. (2019). Jallianwala Bagh Massacre | Causes, History, Death Toll, Importance, & Facts. In: https://www.britannica.com/event/Jallianwala-Bagh-Massacre.

[128] https://bmh.militaryarchives.ie/reels/bmh/BMH.WS0767.pdf#page=88 May 30, 1921, Cope met with Patrick Moylett (associate of Griffith) and he said that 'although he was only an ordinary civil servant he was here to make peace'. Cope said Britain wanted access to ports (Moylett did not agree to that) but regarding administration: 'We are willing to withdraw our whole establishment from the lowest policeman to the highest judge".

[129] Fisher wrote to Bonar Law, 'for centuries we exploited the country &, when we didn't do that, we prevented her development lest it shd. damage our own undertakings... They have in the past been desperately wronged – their minds dwell on that, the results remind them of it- they are revengeful and suspicious.' Page 921 O'Halpin, E. (1981).

[130] Fisher went with Cope to assess Dublin Castle administration in 1920 resulting in a detailed report to Fisher outlining the more important deficiencies they had encountered. Fisher passed this on to Cabinet but it was ignored. Fisher wrote to Bonar Law, 'for centuries we exploited the country &, when we didn't do that, we prevented her development lest it shd. damage our own undertakings... They have in the past been desperately wronged – their minds dwell on that, the results remind them of it- they are revengeful and suspicious.' doi:https://doi.org/10.1017/s0018246x00008268. Page 921 O'Halpin, E. (1981). Sir Warren Fisher and the Coalition, 1919–1922. The Historical Journal, 24(4), pp.907–927. In 1921 Fisher was responsible for forcing the resignation of Basil Thompson (British Special Branch). (page 922).

Chapter 42 – You Go and Talk to Them

131 New York Times July 23 1921 published details of an interview, later denied, where King George V said to Lloyd George, "Are you going to

shoot all the people in Ireland? ... This thing cannot go on. I cannot have my people killed in this manner."

Chapter 43 – Get Together In London

132 'The drunken results of a drunken "Treaty" drunkenly arrived at'. Boland, H. (1922), placing 'on record the events that have led up to this British manufactured war on the Republic'. Letter from Boland, two weeks before he was killed, to Joseph McGarrity in USA.

[133] The main group including Griffith stayed at 22 Hans Place. Collins, Eamon Broy and Emmet Dalton stayed at 15, Cadogan Gardens.

[134] "Notes by Robert Barton of two sub-conferences held on December 5/6, 1921 at 10 Downing St." Documents on Irish Foreign Policy (DIFP) https://www.difp.ie/volume-1/1921/notes-by-robert-barton-of-two-sub-conferences-held-on-december-5-6-1921-at-10-downing-st/213/#section-documentpage

[135] Crown Forces in Ireland were costing £10,800,000 a year. Morrison, G. and Tim Pat Coogan (1999). The Irish Civil War -its Origins and Courwerese. London: Weidenfield and Nicholson . In 1922 Britain gave Egyptians their Independence after they had been 'suppressed with great difficulty by the colonial power' 'Khalidi, R. (2020). Hundred Years' War on Palestine: a History of Settler Colonialism and resistance, 1917-2017. S.L.: Picador. Page 33.

Chapter 44 – Well, I'm Happy

[136] Frank Thornton (IRA intelligence staff officer) Bureau of Military History Witness Statement 0615 (page 6) claims 'Collins rarely took anything and when he did it was a small sherry.' This lacks some credibility because he then says, "Drinking was naturally discouraged

everywhere those days because of the necessity of keeping a cool head under the very strenuous circumstances."
[137] 'In many senses, the Northern government never got over the traumatic experience of its birth and for the rest of its fifty-year existence would remain in a virtual state of emergency.' Lynch, R. (2022). Ireland's Other Civil War: Ulster January-June 1922. www.rte.ie. https://www.rte.ie/history/ira-convention/2022/0209/1278754-irelands-other-civil-war-ulster-january-june-1922/.

Chapter 45 – The Split

138 Claire Sheridan was Churchill's cousin; Lord Birkenhead (F.E.Smith) and she were lovers. Henry James, Rudyard Kipling, and H.G. Wells wrote to her. Mussolini tried to rape her. She was a famous sculptress, having watched Epstein at work. She sculpted Gandhi. Possibly had an affair with Lev Kamenev and may have had sex with Trotsky. Lenin sat for four hours as she sculpted his bust – he said he knew that Churchill was her cousin; she responded that she couldn't do much about that but, anyway, she had a cousin who was a Sinn Feiner; Lenin laughed and said it must be a cheerful time when the three of them got together.

Apart from sculpting, she was a very good journalist. She later recalled being interviewed and asked by a reporter from a women's publication for her "opinions regarding women's beauty" – annoyed, women's beauty not being her main focus at that time, she responded, "Beautiful women are the women with dead babies at their breasts, the women with terror and pain in their eyes, the women who starve themselves to give to their children, the women who are widowed in the fight for independence". After recalling those words, in 1923, she added, "Maybe before this book of mine is printed, Europe will be plunged headlong into another war. And one cannot help wondering if the United States will be able to preserve her aloofness." Sheridan, C. (1923). In Many Places. London: Jonathan Cape, Chapter 3 Rory

O'Connor. Pages 29-33 Michael Collins. And Sheridan, C. (2018). Russian Portraits. The Project Gutenberg, p.109. www.gutenberg.org/cache/epub/58009/pg58009-images.html [Accessed 18 Nov. 2024]. Simkin, J. (1997a). Clare Sheridan. Spartacus Educational. https://spartacus-educational.com/Clare_Sheridan.htm [Accessed 18 Nov. 2024].
Stafford,D(2020).https://winstonchurchill.hillsdale.edu/clare-sheridan/ Clare Sheridan: 'The nearest thing to a sister that Winston ever had.' 23 Mar. Adapted from David Stafford's book Oblivion or Glory: The Making of Winston Churchill 1921. Virtual Treasury (2022). Clare Consuelo Sheridan. https://www.youtube.com/watch?v=7VOQ0y0GYEM [Accessed 24 Nov. 2024]. Actor Shona Gibson reads from Clare Sheridan's Diary as part of 'Inside the Railings: A Portrait of Life within the Public Record Office of Ireland'.

Chapter 46 – We Did the Right Thing

139 The 1921 Treaty gave Britain access to Irish ports – but in 1938 all such rights to Queenstown and Berehaven ports and Lough Swilly base were renounced. Churchill was appalled, 'I remain convinced that the gratuitous surrender of our right to use the Irish ports in times of war was a major injury to British national life and safety.' Churchill, W. (1960). The Second World War; [part I]: The Gathering Storm. London: Penguin Books. Page 249

[140] 'By 1919, Mannix had firmly nailed his colours to the political mast in favour of the Sinn Fein cause'. Mannix, P. (2011). The Belligerent Prelate. Cambridge Scholars Publishing.

[141] Joseph McGarrity (in USA) handwritten note has surnames Pepard, McGuire, O'Connell, McCallister. BMH Witness Statement 1399 Thomas Peppard refers to IRA men named "Bok" McGuire, Bernard McCallister,

James O'Connell. Men with these names were in Dublin Battalions. McGarrity, J. (1923). Context: Note in Joseph McGarrity's handwritting listing the names 'of those who murdered brave Harry Boland in his hotel at Skerries, Ireland',. Catalogue.nli.ie. https://catalogue.nli.ie/Record/vtls000588256 [Accessed 22 Dec. 2024].

Chapter 47 – Trip Back Home

142 Poem by Brendan Behan:-
"T'was on an August morning, all in the dawning hours,
I went to take the warming air, all in the Mouth of Flowers,
And there I saw a maiden, and mournful was her cry,
'Ah what will mend my broken heart, I've lost my Laughing Boy.
So strong, so wild, and brave he was, I'll mourn his loss too sore,
When thinking that I'll hear the laugh or springing step no more.
Ah, curse the times and sad the loss my heart to crucify,
That an Irish son with a rebel gun shot down my Laughing Boy.
Oh had he died by Pearse's side or in the GPO,
Killed by an English bullet from the rifle of the foe,
Or forcibly fed with Ashe lay dead in the dungeons of Mountjoy,
I'd have cried with pride for the way he died, my own dear Laughing Boy.
My princely love, can ageless love do more than tell to you,
Go raibh mile maith agat for all you tried to do,
For all you did, and would have done, my enemies to destroy,
I'll mourn your name and praise your fame, forever, my Laughing Boy."
Baker, M. (2019).https://poetscorner.blog/2019/03/20/the-laughing-boy/ The Laughing Boy. poetscorner.blog. [Accessed 28 Oct. 2024].

[143] Details of Collins death are wrapped in opinions and unsubstantiated comments; some of them are contradictory or conflicting. Official

documents have been destroyed. There are suggestions that Dalton killed him. Egan, D. (2022). Solving the Murder of Michael Collins The Conclusive Evidence. https://www.irishpeople.ie/solving-the-murder-of-michael-collins-the-conclusive-evidence/ [Accessed 7 Nov. 2024]. It is difficult to envisage how Dalton could have been the killer. Collins' body was found around a bend of the road. Dalton would surely have been seen following him. There are assertions that Collins was shot from someone very close by, but others would almost certainly have seen the act. A distance of 200 yards would be within the capability of an average trained rifleman. One anti-Treaty suspect (O'Neill) had a disabled arm but must have been capable (else why was he there?). https://www.youtube.com/watch?v=SLrGnImYCwU&list=PLCVN7OI0v nzzaSm4zxk_tveVWLzocx7CH [Accessed 8 Nov. 2024] Chris Dalton (2017). Emmet Dalton remembers: The Irish Civil War, Michael Collins, Beal na Blah, Ardmore Films.

There have been suggestions that MI5 was involved. Brennan-Whitmore, W. (1968). 'Collins murdered by a British Secret Agent'. Orwellianireland.com. http://www.orwellianireland.com/collins.jpg [Accessed 7 Nov. 2024].

A summary of Collins' assassination and discussion of the possible killer is in https://sarasmichaelcollinssite.com/a_grisly_business [Accessed 7 Nov. 2024] Sara's Michael Collins Site – A Grisly Business. Sarasmichaelcollinssite.com.

[144] *A Shropshire Lad, XL by* A. E. Housman 1859 –1936

Into my heart an air that kills
From yon far country blows;
What are those blue remembered hills,
What spires, what farms are those?

That is the land of lost content,
I see it shining plain,
The happy highways where I went
And cannot come again.

[145] Collins worked in London 1906-1915. He studied at King's College, Strand, but left in 1909 or 1910. This may have been due to the civil service classes in the basement, 'Strand School', being relocated to Brixton, South London. The Life and Times of Michael Collins. (2021).

[146] Collins lodged with his elder sister Hannah in London. She wrote that he read English Literature copiously, including Byron Shelley and Keats. Collins, J. (1923). 'Short account of Michael's life in London' to Piaras Beaslai. [Letter].

[147] O'Connell's Christian Brothers School, in Drumcondra Dublin, past pupils include John Devoy (Fenian, journalist in USA), James Joyce, Luke Kelly (Dubliners), Brendan Bracken (Churchill's friend), Emmet Dalton (he was with Collins when he died), Ernie O'Malley (anti-Treaty rebel), Frank Flood (one of those in the ambush during which young Kevin Barry had been arrested and was later hanged), Tom Kettle, Sean Lemass. About 1300 Irish Volunteers took part in the Dublin Easter Uprising; 134 had attended this school, including Eamonn Ceannt, Con Colbert, and Sean Heuston (all 3 were executed May 1916).

[148] Ireland "owes more than it probably will ever realise to the Christian Brothers," said Eamon De Valera. 'The impact of the Brothers on the minds that formed the state cannot be overstated.' Fintan O'Toole (2021). We Don't Know Ourselves: A Personal History of Modern Ireland. London: Head of Zeus, pp.116–117. For a critical assessment of the Brothers see The Brothers grim. The Guardian. Barkham, P. (2009).

https://www.theguardian.com/world/2009/nov/28/christian-brothers-ireland-child-abuse [Accessed 28 May 2020].

[149] There is no evidence that Collins, although a senior military officer, had been trained in the military skills of Field Craft. He had been at the GPO in 1916 as an aide-de-camp but the extent of his involvement in any fire-fights or shooting before August 1922 is not known.

[150] Collins, M. (1906). *King's College London arithmetic examination papers and answer papers completed by Michael Collins.* UCD Digital Library. https://digital.ucd.ie/view/ivrla:10965 [Accessed 8 Nov. 2024].

[151] Collins, P. (1915). *Letter from Patrick Collins (brother) to Michael Collins concerning the possibility of Michael going to Chicago.* UCD Digital Library. https://digital.ucd.ie/view/ivrla:11519 [Accessed 8 Nov. 2024].

9 780646 718248

Printed by Libri Plureos GmbH in Hamburg, Germany